# BLACK GARDEN

THOMAS DE WAAL

# BLACK GARDEN

*Armenia and Azerbaijan through Peace and War*

**New York University Press** • *New York and London*

**NEW YORK UNIVERSITY PRESS**
New York and London
www.nyupress.org

© 2003 by New York University

First published in paperback in 2004.

Library of Congress Cataloging-in-Publication Data
De Waal, Thomas.
Black garden : Armenia and Azerbaijan through peace and war /
Thomas de Waal.
p.  cm.
Includes bibliographical references and index.
ISBN 0-8147-1944-9 (cloth : alk. paper)
ISBN 0-8147-1945-7 (pbk : alk. paper)
1. Nagorno-Karabakh Conflict, 1988–1994. 2. Armenia (Republic)—
Relations—Azerbaijan. 3. Azerbaijan—Relations—Armenia (Republic)
I. Title.
DK699.N34 D4 2003
947.54085'4—dc21                    2002153482

New York University Press books are printed on acid-free paper,
and their binding materials are chosen for strength and durability.

Manufactured in the United States of America

c  10  9  8  7  6  5  4  3
p  10  9  8  7  6  5

War is kindled by the death of one man, or at most, a few;
but it leads to the death of tremendous numbers.
—Elias Canetti, *Crowds and Power*


Mercy on the old master building a bridge,
The passer-by may lay a stone to his foundation.
I have sacrificed my soul, worn out my life, for the nation.
A brother may arrange a rock upon my grave.
—Sayat-Nova

# Contents

All illustrations appear as a group following p. 110.

# Author's Note

The research done for this book is based on around 120 original interviews done in 2000–2001, supplemented by eyewitness reporting and secondary sources. Personal testimony is of course subjective, so I have tried to balance my reconstruction of events from as many sources as possible. The problem is that the written record on the subject is also frequently unreliable, partisan, and incomplete. It will take many years for a full picture of what happened in Armenia and Azerbaijan after 1988 to be assembled. This is intended as a beginning in a field that has very few accounts interested in both sides. Many Armenians and Azerbaijanis will take an interest in what is written here, and I would make a plea for them not to quote some of the information here selectively, to suit their own political agendas. The book stands or falls as an entire whole.

The use of names is problematic. Written Azeri has two alphabets, Armenian has a Western and Eastern version, and most of the written material I have drawn on is in Russian anyway. I have tried to be as consistent as possible. One of the more disputed things about the disputed province in the middle is what to call it. I have chosen not to use the Russianized form, which has become prevalent in most of the outside world, but to use the more grammatically correct Nagorny (rather than Nagorno) Karabakh. Where a town has two names, one Armenian and one Azerbaijani, I use the one that was in currency when the dispute started in 1988. So I say Shusha, rather than Shushi, and Stepanakert, rather than Khankendi. In an ideal world there would be an agreed linguistic distinction between the ethnic group of Azerbaijanis and the citizens of the state of Azerbaijan; because there is not an ideal world, I have forgone using the word "Azeri" (apart from when referring to the language) and stuck to the word "Azerbaijani" throughout.

Dozens of people helped me in the research and writing of this book. Some of them knew they would not like all the things I say, which makes me appreciate their generosity all the more.

The book was made possible because of a generous one-year research grant from the United States Institute of Peace in Washington. In London, I received valuable administrative and moral support from Juliet Williams and above all Jonathan Cohen of Conciliation Resources (CR). CR also helped me make my trip across the front line in May 2001. I am deeply grateful to both organizations. I did not set out on this project with an agenda focused on "peace," but I finished it with a deep conviction that compromise from both sides is the only fair and feasible way out of this impasse.

In Azerbaijan, my special thanks go to Zaur Aliev, who fixed up the majority of the interviews in Baku; to Azad Isazade for his practical help, detailed knowledge, and humanity; and to Arif Yunusov, whose in-depth knowledge, objectivity, and fair judgment on the Karabakh issue are unrivaled in the Caucasus. I would also like to thank Arzu Abdullayeva; Vugar Abdusalimov and Ulvi Ismail of the United Nations High Commissioner for Refugees; Fuad Akhundov; Sabina Alieva; Halid Askerov and Oleg Litvin for their photographs; the staff of the BBC office in Baku; Craig Dicker; Rauf Husseinov; Tahir Jafarov; Kerim Kerimli; Vahid Mustafiev and the staff of ANS Television; Shahin Rzayev; Hikmet Sabioglu; Rauf Talyshinsky; Roger Thomas; Anne Thompson; Peter Van Praagh; and Leila Yunusova.

In Armenia, Tigran Kzmalian and family were the warmest of hosts and friends; Alyosha Manvelian and Karen Topchyan of the BBC were always exceptionally helpful, and Suzanna Pogosian was a brilliant organizer and researcher. My thanks go also to Larisa Alaverdian; Michael Bagratuni; Alla Bakunts for much help and advice; Mark Grigorian for sharing thoughts and old newspapers; Tim Jones; Onnik and Gohar Krikorian for friendship, contacts, and photographs; Eduard Kzmalian; Leonid Mirzoyan for good company on many long trips to Karabakh; Asya Mirzoyan; Grigory Mosesov; and David Petrosian.

In Karabakh, I would like to thank Iosif Adamian and family; Armine Alexanian; Ani Azizian and family; Ashot Gulian; and Simon Porter.

Elsewhere, my thanks go to Behrouz Afagh, Famil Ismailov, Stephen Mulvey, and Jenny Norton of the BBC; everyone in the BBC office in Moscow; Jonathan Rowell of CARIS at the BBC World Service; Terry Adams; Kenan Aliev; Jonathan Aves; Robin Bhatty for supplying large amounts of useful material and comments; Tony Borden and the Institute for War and Peace Reporting (IWPR); Bruce Clark; Alan Cooperman and Martina Vandenburg; Felix Corley; Sasha Deryabin; Madalena Fricova and Lawrence Sheets; Thomas Goltz; Edmund Herzig; Robert Hewsen; Lee Hockstader; Scott Horton; Alik Iskandarian; Nev Jefferies; Jon Jones; Jan Koehler; Brady Kiesling; Edward Kline; Marina Kurkchian; Laura Le Cornu; Steve Levine; Gerard Libaridian; Anatol Lieven; Dov Lynch; Andrew Martin and Dennis Sammut of LINKS; Wayne Merry; David Michelmore; Boris Nefyodov; Michael Ochs; Craig Oliphant; Arkady Ostrovsky; Paul Quinn-Judge; Razmik Panosian; Philip Remler; Peter Rosenblatt; Laurent Ruseckas; Leonora Soroka of the Hoover Archives; Nina Sovich; Ronald Suny; Len Taylor; Hratch Tchilingirian; Valery Tishkov; Effie Voutira; Christopher Walker; and Edward W. Walker.

My agent, David Miller, was helpful from first to last; at NYU Press Niko Pfund commissioned the book and Stephen Magro saw it through to publication; Brenda Shaffer gave exceptionally useful comments and insights on several chapters; my mother, Esther de Waal, was hugely supportive for several crucial weeks of writing; it would not have been half so much fun without the company and hospitality of my Caucasian kindred spirits Wendell Steavenson and David Stern. Finally, the love, humor, patience, fine editing skills, and constant support of my wife, Georgina Wilson, have been beyond measure and it is to her this book is dedicated.

# Preface to the Paperback Edition

Some conflicts demand urgent attention. Others are hidden away, apparently quiet but unresolved and the world risks waking up to them only when it is too late, when the threat of violence is again imminent. The Armenian-Azerbaijani conflict over Nagorny Karabakh belongs to this category. More unstable than Cyprus, far less noticed than Israel and Palestine, it still lurks as a potential danger to the world in the hills of the Caucasus.

Writing these lines in early 2005, five years after I began the research for *Black Garden*, it seems that the peace process to resolve the Karabakh issue is more stuck than ever, while the baleful consequences of the war still blight both societies in different ways. To adapt Leo Tolstoy's famous formula in *Anna Karenina*, "All peaceful countries are alike, but every country in conflict is unhappy in its own way." Azerbaijan continues to bear the heavier burden in the form of numbers of refugees and destroyed towns and villages; but the Armenians also continue to suffer from closed borders, a damaged economy, and displaced people.

This is not a conflict where both sides can slowly heal their wounds and return to some kind of normal life. Hundreds of thousands of people remain hostages to its non-resolution. The Azerbaijani refugees in the seven occupied regions outside Karabakh are prisoners of the lack of a settlement, as, in a different way, are the Karabakh Armenians living in a suspended unrecognized condition between Armenia and Azerbaijan.

In the past three years a lot has changed in and around Armenia and Azerbaijan. In the summer of 2003, President Heidar Aliev, the political colossus who had dominated Azerbaijan for more than thirty years and whose presence also dominates this book, fell terminally ill. He died in 2003, having barely managed to allow his son, Ilham, to succeed him as president in a bitterly disputed election. With little preparation the younger Aliev inherited a country that is set to become extremely wealthy from the three-billion-dollar Baku-Tbilisi-Ceyhan pipeline, which will carry Caspian Sea oil to Western markets, but that is also riven by political feuding and ever-widening social tensions.

Armenia has also been turbulent, with President Robert Kocharian's controversial reelection for a second presidential term in 2003 being accompanied by opposition protests and international criticism. In Karabakh itself the year 2003 saw an upsurge of shooting incidents across the front-line. And in February 2004 the murder in Budapest of an Armenian officer by an Azerbaijani studying on the same NATO language course, and the aggressive rhetoric that succeeded it in both countries, was a painful reminder that passions about this conflict can still be lethal.

More than most conflicts, the Armenian-Azerbaijani dispute is "all in the mind." To listen to people on both sides talk about the conflict is often to hear a litany of views that have been learned almost unconsciously by the speaker. None of the opinions are fresh and they have been recycled so many times that they often bear little relation to reality—but no one challenges these assumptions about a neighbor who is geographically near but otherwise entirely remote.

In writing *Black Garden* I made it my business to learn these stories—these myths—and then to investigate the truth behind them. To take two small examples: in Armenia there is a general belief that no Azerbaijanis suffered violence when they were expelled from their country in 1988 to 1990. In Azerbaijan most people believe that Azerbaijanis were not responsible for the anti-Armenian violence in Sumgait and Baku. I do not blame ordinary people for repeating these pseudo-facts—but neither of them are true and their repetition feeds the dangerous belief on both sides that they are the victim, the other side is the aggressor and compromise amounts to surrender.

Working on the book I began to feel the psychological effects of the conflict inside myself. The research was an experience that can only be described as schizophrenic. In the year 2000 I did research and conducted interviews for approximately three months in Azerbaijan and for the same length of time in Armenia and Nagorny Karabakh, which can only be reached via Armenia. Separated by a ceasefire line and a long ribbon of minefields, the sides inhabit parallel worlds, next door to each other on the map, but having, for more than a decade, almost no contact with one another. Inevitably I found that after a few weeks in Azerbaijan the Azerbaijani argument on the tragedy of Karabakh would become familiar and persuasive to me: how the Azerbaijanis were the victims of the Armenians, who continued to occupy large parts of their land.

Then, travelling across the ceasefire line via Moscow or Georgia, I would cross to the Armenian side and slowly begin to see the dispute through their eyes and hear their argument that the Armenians had no choice but to fight for their identity and rights. Only at the third or fourth crossing of the line, did I begin to feel "inoculated" against these two partial versions of reality that were coexisting in my mind. I could understand perfectly how, if I lived permanently in Armenia or Azerbaijan and had no contact with the other side, I too would begin to see the situation in this way.

Gradually, however, I was able to form my own picture of two societies that were fated to come into conflict, but actually had much in common. And when I was asked—frequently—which side I found more sympathetic, I could answer—truthfully—that there were people on both sides whom I respected and liked, while being depressed by the situation I found.

Like many before me in the Caucasus I have loved it intensely and at other times come close to despair. I came to love the landscapes, especially the woods of Karabakh and the streets of Baku. I made many friends. And in government offices and refugee camps I saw appalling cynicism and wasted lives. Grisha Movsesov, an Armenian exile who sang songs around a Yerevan kitchen table about the city he had lost, tragically died in an accident on the funicular railway in April 2004, having suffered bad luck on an almost cosmic scale. Unfortunately there are too many like him.

It is frustrating for an outsider to see how much can be gained by peace and how far away agreement is. We are talking about two peoples who still have an enormous amount in common, who are much closer than, let us say, the Israelis and the Palestinians and are tied together by many threads of friendship, marriage, trade and culture.

The problem is that the patterns of mutual insecurity between the two sides mean that these ties cannot be used to make a political agreement work. It is all too convenient for Armenians and Azerbaijanis to blame the mediators from the Great Powers—chiefly Russia, the United States, and France in the "Minsk Group"—for failing to resolve the conflict. Perhaps they could have done more but the uncomfortable truth is that the biggest obstacles to peace lie within the societies themselves. It is actually not so hard to draw up a peace plan on paper for this conflict.

The problem is generating the kind of trust that would make this plan and its implementation possible. In a strange way it thus falls to outside mediators and experts to act in the role of storytellers reminding Armenians and Azerbaijanis of how much they have lost and how much they could stand to gain.

One of the aims of this book is to tell as much as I could these old stories of long shared coexistence between Armenians and Azerbaijanis. I have tried to give space to the sane reasonable voices of former friends and neighbors whose views are not heard so often. And I have tried to bring out the alternative history of the Armenians and Azerbaijanis in which these two cultures are compatible and complementary, not in conflict. The benign patron of *Black Garden* is the Armenian-born troubadour poet Sayat Nova, who lived at the court of the Georgian king and wrote most of his verse in the Azeri language. His poetic spirit is an example to the Caucasus today—still beautiful, still brimming with life, but frustratingly wracked by fear and division.

Thomas de Waal
London, February 2005

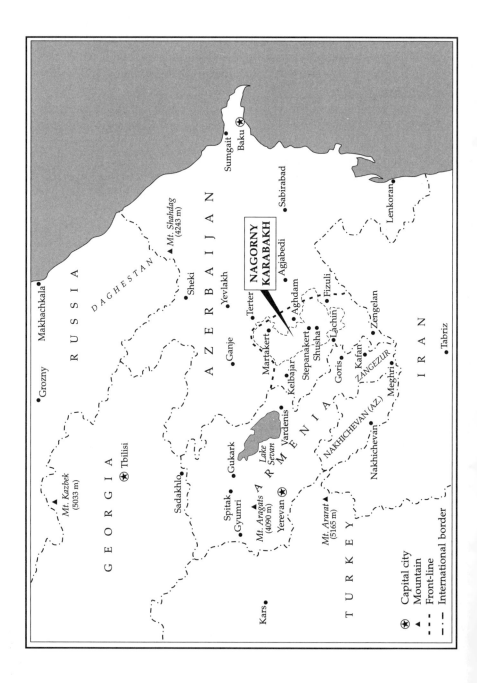

NAGORNY KARABAKH

RUSSIA
GEORGIA
DAGHESTAN
AZERBAIJAN
ARMENIA
TURKEY
IRAN
ZANGEZUR
NAKHICHEVAN (AZ)

Makhachkala
Grozny
Mt. Kazbek (5033 m)
Tbilisi
Sadakhlo
Spitak
Gyumri
Mt. Aragats (4090 m)
Yerevan
Gukark
Vardenis
Lake Sevan
Mt. Ararat (5165 m)
Kars

Sheki
Yevlakh
Ganje
Terter
Martakert
Kelbajar
Stepanakert
Shusha
Lachin
Goris
Kafan
Meghri
Nakhichevan

Mt. Shahdag (4243 m)
Sumgait
Baku
Sabirabad
Agjabedi
Aghdam
Fizuli
Zengelan
Tabriz
Lenkoran

*Capital city*
▲ Mountain
– · – · – Front-line
– · – International border

• Getashen

Shaumian

Talish

Gulistan

Mt. Gamish ▲
(3724 m)

Mt. Mrov
(3340 m)

† Yeghishe    Maragha
Arakyal

• Terter

River Terter

Martakert

Haterk •      Sarsang
Resevoir

• Kelbajar        Gandzasar      Srkhavend
                          †

A  Z  E  R  B  A  I  J  A  N

NAGORNY        • Aghdam        River Gargar

Askeran •
Nakhichevanik •
Khojali •

Stepanakert

Kosalar        Martuni •

Shusha •  KARABAKH

• Karintak

Amaras †

Lachin •        ▲ Mt. Kirs
                     (2725 m)

Tug •        Fizuli •

Hadrut •

Goris •

ARMENIA                                    Horadiz

• Jebrail

• Kubatly

River Araxes

†      Monastery
▲      Mountain
-----  Front-line
-·-·-  International border

0    km    10

# Introduction

*Crossing the Line*

## THE FRONT LINE: 19 MAY 2001

No border is more closed than this one. A few miles after the Azerbaijani city of Terter, the road stopped in a dusty field. Soldiers at a guard post blocked the way. Sheets of camouflage and dried grass covered the barbed wire.

From here Colonel Elkhan Aliev of the Azerbaijani army would escort us into no-man's-land. We were a party of Western and Russian diplomats and journalists. The mediators were hoping to build on progress made the month before at peace talks in Florida between the presidents of the two small post-Soviet Caucasian republics of Armenia and Azerbaijan.

By crossing the front line between the positions of the Azerbaijanis and of the Armenians of Nagorny Karabakh, who occupied the land on the opposite sides, the party of diplomats and journalists wanted to give the peace process a public boost. But by the time we reached the front line, a peace deal was slipping off the agenda again.

No one had crossed here since May 1994, when the cease-fire was signed that confirmed the Armenians' military victory in two and a half years' of full-blown warfare. From that point, the line where the fighting stopped began to turn into a two-hundred-mile barrier of sandbags and barbed wire dividing the southern Caucasus in two.

Colonel Husseinov, dressed in neat camouflage fatigues, was inscrutable behind his dark glasses. There had been a shooting incident across the line that morning, he said, but no one had been hurt. Some of the party put on flak jackets. Nikolai Gribkov, the Russian negotiator, was wearing a New York Yankees baseball cap and someone teased him that if there was an Armenian Mets fan on the other side of the line, he might get a bullet through the head.

The colonel led us around the wall of sandbags to a narrow strip of country road, which his men had de-mined that morning. We must have looked incongruous as we walked into no-man's-land to the chirrup of birdsong: some of us were carrying briefcases, others were trundling suitcases on wheels along the tired asphalt. On the edges of the road, the white and purple thistles in the dead zone were already neck-high.

After five minutes, we reached the "enemy": a group of Armenian soldiers waiting for us on the road. They were wearing almost the same khaki camouflage uniforms as Husseinov and his men, only their caps were square and the Azerbaijanis' were round, and the Armenians wore arm patches inscribed with the letters "NKR," designating the unrecognized "Nagorny Karabakh Republic." With them was a group of European cease-fire monitors from the Organization for Security and Cooperation in Europe (OSCE). They handed round a light lunch of bottles of Armenian beer and caviar sandwiches—a diplomatically devised culinary combination from the two enemy countries.

Vitaly Balasanian, the Armenian commander, was a tall man with graying sideburns. He exchanged a curt handshake with Husseinov and they did not meet each other's eyes. Had they ever met before we asked. "Maybe," replied Husseinov, implying that they might have done so on the battlefield. The two commanders do not even have telephone contact, although it would reduce casualties from snipers (about thirty men a year still die in cross-border shooting incidents). Would they consider setting up a phone link? Balasanian said it would be useful, but Husseinov said that was not his responsibility. Earlier, he had called the Karabakh Armenian forces "Armenian bandit formations."

Balasanian led us down the other half of the country road to the Armenian lines. In front of us were the blue wooded hills of Karabakh. It was a shock. Because of the inviolable cease-fire line, the only way into Nagorny Karabakh nowadays is via Armenia from the west. In my journeys back and forth between the two sides over the course of fourteen months in 2000–2001, I had been forced to travel hundreds of miles around, going by road through Georgia or flying via Moscow. Now, moving between one side and the other within a few minutes, I was hit by both the strangeness and the logic of it: the two areas on the map did join up after all.

■

This snatched handshake in no-man's-land was the only meeting of hands the Armenians and Azerbaijanis could make across a vast historical and political divide.

Two versions of history collided on this road. To hear the Armenians and Azerbaijanis tell it, this was the fault line between Christians and Muslims, Armenians and Turks, west and east. The trouble was neither side could decide where the boundary lay. For one side, the Armenian possession of Nagorny Karabakh, the beautiful range of wooded hills stretching up in front of us, was an enemy occupation; for the other, it was a fact of historical justice.

The cultural and symbolic meaning of Nagorny Karabakh for both peoples cannot be overstated. For Armenians, Karabakh is the last outpost of their Christian civilization and a historic haven of Armenian princes and bishops before the eastern Turkic world begins. Azerbaijanis talk of it as a cradle, nursery, or conservatoire, the birthplace of their musicians and poets. Historically, Armenia is diminished without this enclave and its monasteries and its mountain lords; geographically and economically, Azerbaijan is not fully viable without Nagorny Karabakh.

On this crumbly road in 2001, it had turned into something else: a big international mess, which the Americans, French, and Russians were trying to sort out.

For seven years the Armenians had had full possession of almost the entire disputed province of Nagorny Karabakh, as well as vast areas of Azerbaijan all around it—in all, almost 14 percent of the internationally recognized territory of Azerbaijan. They had expelled hundreds of thousands of Azerbaijanis from these lands.

In response to this massive loss of territory, Azerbaijan, in concert with Turkey, kept its borders with Armenia sealed, crippling Armenia's economic prospects.

The result was a kind of slow suicide pact in which each country hurt the other, while suffering itself, hoping to achieve a better position at the negotiating table.

In the last few years, most international observers have tended to ignore this frozen conflict. They do so at their peril. The nonresolution of the dispute has tied up the whole region between the Black and Caspian Seas. Communications between Turkey and Central Asia, Russia, and Iran are disrupted; oil pipeline routes have developed kinks; railway lines go nowhere. The two countries have built alliances and polarized international attitudes. Armenia counts Russia and Iran as its closest friends, and a Russian military base is due to remain in Armenia until 2020. Azerbaijan has used its Caspian Sea oil fields to make friends with the West. It has forged an alliance with Georgia and Turkey, and by 2005 the Baku-Tbilisi-Ceyhan pipeline is scheduled to link all three countries to Western energy markets.

The United States is also involved, whether it likes it or not. The one million or so Armenian Americans, who live mainly in California and Massachusetts, are one of the most vocal ethnic communities in the country and the Armenian lobby is one of the most powerful in Congress. But companies like ExxonMobil and Chevron are also investing heavily in Caspian Sea oil, and Azerbaijan's anti-Russian, pro-Western stance has attracted the sympathy of senior politicians from James Baker to Henry Kissinger.

All that means Westerners could still have cause to worry quite a lot about what happens in these mountains: the resumption of the Karabakh conflict on even the smallest scale would send out disturbing ripples across Europe, Russia, and the Middle East. The nightmare scenario is a new conflict in which Armenia asks its military ally Russia for help, while the Azerbaijani army calls on its alliance with NATO-member Turkey. Nor do the oil companies like the idea of a war breaking out next to an international pipeline route. "No one is happy about spending 13 billion dollars in a potential war zone," as one Western oil specialist put it.

Beginning in April 1999, the presidents of Azerbaijan and Armenia, Heidar Aliev and Robert Kocharian, had more than a dozen bilateral meetings, where they struck up a good working relationship and haggled over a settlement. This led eventually to the five-day meeting in Key West, Florida, in April 2001, when diplomats from the three "Great Powers," Russia, France, and the United States, broadened the format of the negotiations. By all accounts, the meeting went well and Aliev and Kocharian came closer than ever to resolving their differences. A framework peace agreement, with several gaps that needed filling, was on the table. The goal of this trip to the Caucasus was to close the gaps.

President Heidar Aliev was displeased. Seated at the middle of a long table, surrounded by his courtiers and facing a bank of television cameras, the president, a veteran of the Politburo and the KGB, was now playing the role of the aged and disappointed king.

We were in the Azerbaijani capital, Baku, at the beginning of the mediators' trip across the Caucasus. After the Florida peace talks, they had given the two presidents a breathing space to consult more widely at home. A further presidential meeting, in June, was planned for Switzerland, where, it was hoped, they might settle the remaining issues. One of the mediators told me that Aliev and Kocharian had got "80 or 90 percent" of the way there at Key West. The mediators had designed a high-profile tour across the region, which would underline how ordinary people continued to suffer from the nonresolution of the Armenia-Azerbaijan dispute. As well as political leaders, it would take in encounters with refugees in Azerbaijan and the poor and unemployed in Armenia.

Looking gaunt, Aliev smiled beneficently and began a verbal joust with the three foreign mediators, glancing occasionally at the television cameras. Evidently, the consultations had not gone well. As it later transpired, Aliev had been virtually ready to give up Karabakh to the Armenians in return for other concessions at the negotiating table, but this was anathema to the group of people whose advice he sought after Key West.

The Russian envoy Gribkov offered the Azerbaijani president belated congratulations on his seventy-eighth birthday. "Thank you for congratulations on my birthday but . . . ," Aliev paused. "The most real birthday will be when we sign peace, when our lands are liberated," he went on. "So for all the years that I have dealt with this question for me a celebration has not been a celebration and a birthday even more so. I forgot that it was my birthday because thoughts about this problem were always in my head." He looked grave, daring us to believe him.

The American envoy Carey Cavanaugh congratulated Aliev on his political courage in pursuing peace. But, he stated, foreign powers could offer only political, financial, and logistical support for a deal, they could not actually make one happen: that was up to Aliev and President Kocharian. Aliev batted back the hint, saying that the United States, France, and Russia had to do more to make a peace agreement possible. The public part of the meeting was declared over, but the omens were not looking good.

The next day we flew west from Baku across the waterless plains of central Azerbaijan. In the refugee camp outside the town of Agjebedi, a cracked mud road ran down through a biblical scene of mud-brick houses surrounded by cane fences. The camp had served as the home for about three thousand people from the city of Aghdam since they had been expelled by the Armenians eight years before.

The refugees waiting to see the foreign delegation were half weary, half angry. It seemed the recent talks in the United States had made little impression on them. I talked to Allahverdi Aliev, a portly man with silver hair and a row of gold teeth, who described himself as an agricultural economist. Aliev told me that the there was no work in the camp and the earth was too salty to grow vegetables. "How long can we go on living like this? It's like living in a railway station," he said, sweating from the May sun. I asked about the Armenians. "The Germans didn't behave as badly as they did," he replied. Did he have any message for them? "Tell them to leave our lands." Aliev told me I should look out on the other side of the line for his two-story house in Aghdam, five hundred meters west of the mosque and next to a restaurant.

A few hours later we crossed no-man's-land and the cease-fire line onto the Armenian side and soon afterward came to Aghdam. Or what is left of it. If a peace agreement is signed and Allahverdi Aliev were to come back here, he would find neither the restaurant nor his house. Both are sunk somewhere in a sea of rubble. The only standing structure is the plum-and-white-tiled mosque, its minarets rising above ruins.

Two months before, I had come here from the Armenian side and stood on top of one of the minarets. It was a lucid spring day and the view was clear all the way to the magnificent white peaks of the Caucasus, sixty miles to the north. But instead my eyes were drawn to what was a small Hiroshima lying below. Aghdam used to have fifty thousand inhabitants. Now it is completely empty. After the Armenians captured the town in 1993, they slowly stripped every street and house. Thistles and brambles swarmed over the wrecked houses. Looking out from the minaret onto the devastation, I puzzled again over the reasons for this apocalypse.

After the ruins of Aghdam, the road began to climb out of the empty arid plain into Armenian-inhabited lands and the mountainous and fertile "Black Garden" of Karabakh. The hills collected thick beech woods. It is a sudden juxtaposition: apart from anything else, this is a conflict between highlanders, the Karabakh Armenians, and lowlanders, the Azerbaijanis of the plains.

The roads of Nagorny Karabakh were quiet after Azerbaijan. That evening we came to Stepanakert, the local capital and a small modern town, pleasant and unremarkable, patchworked with gardens and or-chards. During the war, it was badly damaged by artillery and bombing but has now been completely rebuilt. This is where most of the fabric of Aghdam has gone, its bricks and window frames recycled for the re-construction of the Armenian town.

Stepanakert and Aghdam are only fifteen miles apart and well within artillery range of each other. The Karabakh Armenians say that it was a case of kill-or-be-killed, that their conquest of Aghdam was purely an act of self-defense. In a shop on the main street, Gamlet Jan-garian, a butcher with another row of gold teeth, turned his balding head sideways to show me a small scar. He said it was caused by a piece of shrapnel of a shell fired from Aghdam that had slammed into his block of flats.

In Gamlet, I found the same mixture of defiance, suspicion, weari-ness, and longing for an end to the suffering that we had met in Azer-baijan. "This all used to be ours," he told me, drawing his finger across the shop's counter. "Then they gradually came in and took everything bit by bit." He said he had no faith in the negotiations: "They won't give anything."

The final leg of our Caucasian odyssey took us west again out of the enchanted Eden of Karabakh into Armenia. From the air, it was obvious to the eye why this oasis of green hills lying in between two dry plains is so prized. We flew into the rocky impoverished landscape of Arme-nia and arrived at the town of Spitak, still half empty twelve years after it was destroyed by the devastating earthquake of 1988. Spitak's facto-ries did not work and a railway junction was deserted.

In Armenia's capital, Yerevan, President Kocharian received first the mediators and then us, the journalists. We pressed him as to why he was doing nothing to build on the momentum of the Key West talks and engage the Armenian public on the issue of peace and compromise with Azerbaijan. "I would not want to raise their expectations, without knowing for sure that the conflict will definitely be resolved," came his answer. In other words, he seemed to be saying that it was better for people to be kept in the dark about the negotiations. Little wonder that the peace deal caught no one's imagination. A vicious circle of inertia and distrust was undermining it.

Later, in the lobby of the Hotel Yerevan, even the normally ebullient Carey Cavanaugh seemed subdued and had nothing positive to report. His big push for a peace agreement was faltering. A few months later

Cavanaugh had stepped down and the Karabakh peace process was in full deadlock once again.

The Black Garden of Nagorny Karabakh has swallowed up many regimes, presidents, and mediators. It has also shaped the story of the past fourteen years in the southern Caucasus. Erupting in 1988, the dispute galvanized both Armenians' and Azerbaijanis' movement for decolonization from Moscow. It created two anti-Communist oppositions in both republics, which both then came to power with independence.

It has not always been a place of conflict. The name "Nagorny Karabakh" itself suggests the fruitful crossbreeding of cultures that has also occurred there. The word "Karabakh" is a Turkish-Persian fusion, most commonly translated as "Black Garden." Perhaps it refers to the fertility of the region—although the "Black" now seems more appropriate as a symbol of death and misery. The name dates back to the fourteenth century, when it began to replace the Armenian version "Artsakh." Geographically, "Karabakh" as a whole actually comprises a much larger amount of territory, which extends down into the plains of Azerbaijan. "Nagorny" is the Russian word for "mountainous," and it is the fertile highland part, with its large Armenian population, that is now the object of dispute.

For centuries, the region has had an allure. Karabakh has been famous for its mixed Christian-Muslim population; for the independence of its rulers, whether Christian or Muslim; for being fought over by rival empires; for its forests and monasteries; for producing warriors and poets; for its grapes, mulberries, silk, and corn. In 1820, the English aristocrat Sir Robert Ker Porter found many of these elements when he came here a few years after the Treaty of Gulistan joined it to Russia:

> Kara Bagh was reduced almost to desolation by the late war between the great Northern power and the Shah but peace appearing now to be firmly established, and the province absolutely becomes a part of the conqueror's empire, the fugitive natives are rapidly returning to their abandoned homes, and the country again puts on its usual face of fertility. The soil is rich, producing considerable quantities of corn, rice and excellent pasturage, both in summer and winter. Raw silk is also another of its abundant productions. Shiska [Shusha], its capital city, occupies the summit of a singularly situated and curiously formed mountain, six miles in circumference, and perfectly inaccessible on the

eastern side. All these provinces, whether under the sway of one empire or another, have their own native chiefs: and Russia has left the internal government of Kara Bagh to one of these hereditary princes, who pays to the imperial exchequer an annual tribute of 10,000 ducats; and engages, when called upon, to furnish a body of 3000 men mounted and on foot.[1]

Since 1988, the number of meanings imposed on the region has multiplied. In the West, people first perceived it through the distorting prism of Mikhail Gorbachev's *perestroika* as being a remote nationalist dispute that threatened to derail Gorbachev's reforms. That was true of course. The Armenia-Azerbaijan quarrel of February 1988 was the first stone in the avalanche of ethnoterritorial disputes that swept away the Soviet empire. But, like Gorbachev's other headache, Afghanistan, it has carried on, long after all the commissars have hung up their uniforms and become entrepreneurs.

After 1991, when the Soviet Union ended, the words "Nagorny Karabakh" were a shorthand for intractable conflict fought by exotic and implacable people. Many Western observers sought to define the conflict in terms of ethnicity and religion: it was a convulsion of "ancient hatreds" that had been deep frozen by the Soviet system but had thawed back into violent life as soon as Gorbachev allowed it to. That too was a simplification. After all, relations between the two communities were good in the Soviet period and the quarrel was not over religion.

Now, the heat has gone out of the Armenia-Azerbaijan conflict and it is frozen and inactive, like Cyprus. But it cannot be ignored. It is the tiny knot at the center of a big international security tangle. The story of how the knot was closed takes in the coming to independence of both Armenia and Azerbaijan, and the rediscovery of the Caucasus by the outside world. It is a tragic story that helps explain how conflicts begin and how the Soviet Union ended. In retrospect, it should perhaps have been obvious that the suppressed problems lurking in this corner of the Soviet Union would be dangerous if they ever came to the surface. Yet, when it all began in 1988, almost everyone was taken by surprise.

# I

# February 1988

## An Armenian Revolt

### A SOVIET REBELS

The crisis began in February 1988 in the depths of the Soviet Union. The central square of Stepanakert, a small but beautifully situated town in the mountains of the southern Caucasus, was a large open space, perfectly suited for public meetings. A large statue of Lenin (now removed) dominated the square with the neoclassical Regional Soviet building and a steep hill raking up behind it. A long flight of steps fell down to the plain of Azerbaijan below.

On 20 February 1988, the local Soviet of the Nagorny Karabakh Autonomous Region of Azerbaijan—essentially a small regional parliament—sitting inside a concrete-and-glass building on the square, resolved as follows:

> Welcoming the wishes of the workers of the Nagorny Karabakh Autonomous Region to request the Supreme Soviets of the Azerbaijani SSR and the Armenian SSR to display a feeling of deep understanding of the aspirations of the Armenian population of Nagorny Karabakh and to resolve the question of transferring the Nagorny Karabakh Autonomous Region from the Azerbaijani SSR to the Armenian SSR, at the same time to intercede with the Supreme Soviet of the USSR to reach a positive resolution on the issue of transferring the region from the Azerbaijani SSR to the Armenian SSR.[1]

The dreary language of the resolution hid something truly revolutionary. Since 1921, Nagorny Karabakh had been an island of territory dominated by Armenians inside the Soviet Republic of Azerbaijan. Essentially, the local Armenian parliamentary deputies wanted the map of the Soviet Union redrawn and to see their region leave Soviet Azerbaijan and join Soviet Armenia. The USSR was already in the third year of rule by Mikhail Gorbachev, but it was still a frigid and orderly state. Gorbachev had proclaimed the doctrines of *glasnost* and *perestroika*, but they were still policies that the Communist Party regulated from above. The resolution by the Soviet in Nagorny Karabakh altered all this. By calling on Moscow to change the country's internal borders, the Karabakh Armenians were, in effect, making politics from below for the first time in the Soviet Union since the 1920s.

A week before the Regional Soviet's resolution, on Saturday, 13 February, a group of Karabakh Armenians had staged another unprecedented event in Lenin Square: an unsanctioned political rally. Several hundred people gathered and made speeches calling for the unification of Karabakh with Armenia. Two or three rows of policemen surrounded the demonstrators, but they were local Armenians who had been tipped off in advance and allowed the protest to go ahead. The rally was timed to coincide with the return of a delegation of Karabakh Armenian artists and writers who had taken a petition to Moscow. The head of the returning delegation, the local Armenian actress Zhanna Galstian, made the first speech to the assembled crowd. She spoke very briefly, saying that she felt happy "because by coming out here, the Karabakhi has killed the slave in himself."[2] The crowd chanted back the Armenian word "Miatsum!" or "Unity!" the one-word slogan that came to symbolize their campaign.

The organizers of the rally had every reason to be afraid. No one had organized political demonstrations in the Soviet Union in living memory. At least two of the activists later admitted that they had fully expected to be arrested.[3] To ward off arrest, they had devised slogans that proclaimed that they were Soviet loyal citizens acting within the spirit of *glasnost*. Banners carried the slogan "Lenin, Party, Gorbachev!"

In the course of these days in February 1988, many Soviet officials found that the ground under their feet was not as firm as they had believed. Members of the Communist Party hierarchy were openly disagreeing with one another, and the leadership in Moscow quickly concluded that it could not simply crush the dissenters by force. Practicing Gorbachev's new spirit of tolerance, the Politburo told the Azerbaijani Party leaders that they should use only "Party methods"—persuasion, rather than force—to resolve the dispute. Gorbachev also decided that neither local Karabakh Armenian nor republican Azerbaijani security forces could be relied on to keep order and had a motorized battalion of

160 Soviet Interior Ministry troops dispatched from the neighboring republic of Georgia to Karabakh. As it turned out, Interior Ministry soldiers were to stay there for almost four years.[4]

The demonstrators in Stepanakert became more vocal. Within a week there were several thousand people in Lenin Square. Zhanna Galstian remembers an almost religious exaltation as people began to shake off the fear inbred in all Soviet citizens. "There was the highest discipline, people stood as though they were in church," she commented. The Armenian political scientist Alik Iskandarian, who went to Stepanakert to investigate, says he found "a force of nature": "I saw something elemental, I saw a surge of energy, energy that could have been directed in another direction. Actually, the conflict began very benignly at the very beginning . . . it was an astonishing thing. I had never seen anything like it in the Soviet Union—or anywhere."[5]

Yet Nagorny Karabakh was not only an Armenian region. Roughly a quarter of the population—some forty thousand people—were Azerbaijanis with the strongest ties to Azerbaijan. This sudden upsurge of protest in the mainly Armenian town of Stepanakert, however peaceful its outer form, could not but antagonize them. You had only to tilt your head in Stepanakert to see the neighboring town of Shusha—90 percent of whose inhabitants were Azerbaijani—high on the cliff top above. The Azerbaijanis there were angry and began to organize counterprotests.

Events moved with speed. Eighty-seven Armenian deputies from the Regional Soviet exercised their right to call an emergency session of the assembly for Saturday, 20 February. Two top officials—the local Armenian Party leader, Boris Kevorkov, who was still fully loyal to Azerbaijan, and the first secretary of the Communist Party of Azerbaijan, Kamran Bagirov, tried and failed to stop the session's taking place. The emergency session finally began at about 8 P.M., four or so hours behind schedule and in an explosive atmosphere. Late in the evening, 110 Armenian deputies voted unanimously for the resolution, calling for Nagorny Karabakh to join Soviet Armenia. The Azerbaijani deputies refused to vote. In a scene of high farce, Kevorkov tried to swipe the stamp needed to confirm the resolution.[6]

Journalists at the local newspaper, *Sovetsky Karabakh*, doubled the impact of the resolution by working late into the night on a special edition. Next morning, amid the usual dull TASS bulletins and reprints of *Pravda*, the paper published two columns on the right side of the front page announcing the local Soviet's intention to leave Azerbaijan.

## "SOMETHING COMPLETELY NEW"

On 21 February 1988, the Politburo met in the Kremlin to hold the first of many sessions devoted to the crisis. Heeding a keen instinct of self-preservation, members began by rejecting out of hand the Regional Soviet's demand. Gorbachev said later that there were nineteen potential territorial conflicts in the Soviet Union and he did not want to set a precedent by making concessions on any of them. The Communist Party's Central Committee passed the text of a resolution blackening the disloyal Karabakhis as "extremists":

> Having examined the information about developments in the Nagorny Karabakh Autonomous Region, the CPSU Central Committee holds that the actions and demands directed at revising the existing national and territorial structure contradict the interests of the working people in Soviet Azerbaijan and Armenia and damage interethnic relations.[7]

Other than taking this rhetorical step, it was far less obvious to the Politburo what it should do next. It ruled out the option of mass arrests but lacked any experience of dealing with mass political dissent. As the Politburo's adviser on nationalities, Vyacheslav Mikhailov, admitted, "This was something completely new for us." After all, the revolt came from a Soviet institution, and the Karabakh Armenians were prepared to make the argument that all they were doing was shaking the dust off Lenin's moribund slogan "All power to the Soviets."

Gorbachev tried dialogue. He dispatched two large delegations to the Caucasus, one of which traveled to Baku and then on to Nagorny Karabakh. In Stepanakert, the Moscow emissaries called a local Party plenum, which voted to remove Kevorkov, who had been the local leader in Nagorny Karabakh since 1974, the middle of the Brezhnev era. Kevorkov's more popular deputy, Genrikh Pogosian, was appointed in his place. However, this created new problems for Moscow when, a few months later, Pogosian, who enjoyed much greater respect with the Karabakh Armenians, began to support the campaign for unification with Armenia.

One of the junior officials in the Politburo delegation was Grigory Kharchenko, a Central Committee official who spent most of 1988 and 1989 in the Caucasus. Kharchenko was no doubt picked for the job because of his big physical stature and open character, but he declares that he found it impossible to hold a coherent conversation with the demonstrators:

> We went to one of the rallies . . . I would begin to say, "We have met with representatives of the intelligentsia, all these questions need to be resolved. You are on strike, what's the point of that? We know that you are being paid for this, but all the same this question will not be resolved at a rally. The general secretary is working on it, there will be a session of the presidium of the Supreme Soviet, the issue will be studied, of course all legal complaints have to be dealt with." But no! "Miatsum, Miatsum, Miatsum!"[8]

The slow descent into armed conflict began on the first day. The first tremors of violence were already stirring the two communities. The writer Sabir Rustamkhanli says he was one of several Azerbaijani intellectuals who traveled to Nagorny Karabakh wanting to begin a dialogue, but he was too late:

> In the Shusha region everyone was on their feet, they were ready to go down [to Stepanakert], there would have been bloodshed. And in [the Azerbaijani town of] Aghdam, too. We didn't want that and at the same time we did propaganda work, saying that if the Armenians carried on like this, we would be ready to respond to them. We organized the defense of Shusha. It was night, there was no fighting. The Armenians wanted to poison the water. We organized a watch. We were in the Regional Committee. I was the chief editor of the [Azerbaijani] publishing house and I had published their books in Armenian. The writers were all there. Ohanjenian was there. Gurgen Gabrielian, the children's writer and poet who had always called me a brother. And this time, when they were standing on the square, they behaved as though they didn't know me. There was already a different atmosphere.[9]

How much violence occurred during those days will probably never be known because the authorities pursued a concerted policy to cover up any incidents. But, in one example, something nasty, if not fully explained, did happen among the trainee student teachers of the Pedagogical Institute in Stepanakert. In the Azerbaijani capital Baku during the second week of the protest, the historian Arif Yunusov and a col-league, both of whom were already collecting information on events, were called to the city's Republican Hospital. Apparently, two Azerbai-jani girls from Stepanakert had been raped. At the hospital, the head doctor denied the two academics access to the girls. The hospital nurses, however, confirmed that "these girls had come from the Peda-gogic Institute in Stepanakert, that there had been a fight or an attack on their hostel. The girls were raped. They were in a bad way."[10]

Two days after the local Soviet's resolution, angry protests took place in the Azerbaijani town of Aghdam. Aghdam is a large town twenty-five kilometers east of Stepanakert, down in the plain of Azer-baijan. On 22 February, a crowd of angry young men set out from Agh-dam toward Stepanakert. When they reached the Armenian village of Askeran, they were met by a cordon of policemen and a group of Ar-menian villagers, some of whom carried hunting rifles. The two sides fought, and people on both sides were wounded. Two of the Azerbai-janis were killed. A local policeman very probably killed one of the dead men, twenty-three-year-old Ali Hajiev, either by accident or as a result of a quarrel. The other, sixteen-year-old Bakhtiar Uliev, appears to have been the victim of an Armenian hunting rifle. If so, Uliev was the first victim of intercommunal violence in the Armenian-Azerbai-jani conflict.[11]

News of the death of the two men sparked Aghdam into fury. An angry crowd collected trucks full of stones, crossbows, and staves and began to move on Stepanakert. A local woman, Khuraman Abasova, the head of a collective farm, famously climbed onto the roof of a car and threw her head scarf in front of the crowd. According to Azerbaijani custom, when a woman does this, men must go no further. The gesture of peace apparently restrained the crowd, and Abasova later persuaded her fellow citizens not to march on Stepanakert at a public rally. This in-tervention probably averted far more bloodshed.[12]

## ORIGINS OF A CAMPAIGN

The events of February 1988 in Nagorny Karabakh occurred as if out of the blue and quickly acquired their own momentum. But the initial phase of the Armenian campaign had been carefully planned well in advance. Many Azerbaijanis, caught unawares by the revolt, believed that it had been officially sanctioned in Moscow. This was not the case, although the Karabakh movement did use the influence of well-placed Armenian sympathizers in the Soviet establishment.

An underground movement for unification with Armenia had existed inside Karabakh for decades. Whenever there was a political thaw or major political shift in the USSR—in 1945, 1965, and 1977, for example—Armenians sent letters and petitions to Moscow, asking for Nagorny Karabakh to be made part of Soviet Armenia. (It was an indication of the way the Armenians thought and the Soviet Union worked that they never raised the issue in their regional capital, Baku). With the advent of *glasnost* and *perestroika* under Gorbachev, they begin to mobilize again. On 3 March 1988, Gorbachev told the Politburo that it had been remiss in failing to spot warning signals: "We must not simplify anything here and we should look at ourselves too. The Central Committee received five hundred letters in the last three years on the question of Nagorny Karabakh. Who paid any attention to this? We gave a routine response."[13]

The latest Karabakh Armenian campaign was different from its predecessors in one important respect: previous campaigns had been run from inside Nagorny Karabakh itself, but the main organizers of the new movement were Karabakhis living outside the province. In the postwar years, many Karabakh Armenians had settled in Moscow, Yerevan, or Tashkent, and they now formed a large informal network across the Soviet Union.

The man in the middle was Igor Muradian, an Armenian from a Karabakhi family who was only thirty years old. Muradian had grown up in Baku and now worked in the Armenian capital, Yerevan. At first glance, he did not look the part of leader of such a big movement. Large and shambling, he speaks with a stammer and, like many Baku Armenians, is more comfortable speaking Russian than Armenian. But Muradian was both a formidable political operator and utterly uncompromising in his hard-line Armenian nationalist views. Muradian says that he was convinced that the Azerbaijani authorities were trying to settle Azerbaijanis in Nagorny Karabakh and force out Armenians, such that within a generation the province would lose its Armenian majority. He therefore argued that Armenians must seize the historical moment afforded them by Gorbachev's reforms.

Muradian was a Soviet insider. He worked as an economist in the state planning agency Gosplan in Yerevan and had good connections among Party cadres. He learned the lesson early on that if a petition were presented in the right way, with the appropriate expressions of loyalty to the Soviet system, many influential Soviet Armenians could be persuaded to support it. For a 1983 petition on Nagorny Karabakh to then General Secretary Yury Andropov, he had secured the signatures of "veterans of the Party, people who had known Lenin, Stalin, and Beria. There was a lot of blood on their hands."[14]

The scope of the Gorbachev-era campaign was much more ambitious. "The aim was set for the first time in the Soviet Union to legitimize this movement, not to make it anti-Soviet, but to make it completely loyal," said Muradian. It is not clear whether Muradian actually believed the Soviet system would deliver Karabakh into the arms of Armenia—if so he was making a big miscalculation—or whether he was merely seeking the maximum political protection for a risky campaign.

In February 1986, Muradian traveled to Moscow with a draft letter that he persuaded nine respected Soviet Armenian Communist Party members and scientists to sign. The most prized signature was that of Abel Aganbekian, an academician who was advising Gorbachev on economic reforms: "When [Aganbekian] went into this house where he signed the letter he didn't know where he was going and why they were taking him there, and before he signed he spent four hours there. During those four hours he drank approximately two liters of vodka."

The Karabakh activists even received the tacit support of the local Armenian Party leader, Karen Demirchian, for one of their schemes: a campaign to discredit the senior Azerbaijani politician, Heidar Aliev, whom they had identified as the man most likely to obstruct their campaign. Aliev, the former Party leader of Azerbaijan, had been a full member of the Politburo since 1982. One of Muradian's more outrageous ideas was that he and a fellow Armenian activist should open a prosecution case against Aliev, based on Article 67 of Azerbaijan's criminal code "Discrimination against National Dignity." The case failed, but it may have played a small part in Aliev's downfall from the Politburo. Aliev stopped work in the summer of 1987 on grounds of health and formally stepped down from the Politburo in October of that year. Armenian Party boss Demirchian was reportedly delighted at the political demise of his rival. Muradian says that in 1990 he got a message from Demirchian, through a mutual friend: "The main thing we did was to remove Aliev before the beginning of the [Karabakh] movement. That was very important."

Muradian's work with Party figures was only the outer layer of his activities. At the same time he was also working on another far more subversive track. He made contact with members of the banned radical nationalist Dashnaktsutiun Party (known as the Dashnaks) in their underground cells in Yerevan and abroad. And he even procured weapons. Muradian said that the activists received a first consignment of small arms from abroad in the summer of 1986 with the help of the Dashnaks. More then came in at regular intervals, among which "for some reason there were a lot of Czech weapons." Most of these weapons went straight on to Nagorny Karabakh: "All the organizations in Karabakh were armed. The whole of the Komsomol [the Communist youth organization] was under arms." This extraordinary admission confirms that one Armenian activist at least fully expected that the dispute could turn into an armed conflict.

## INTERCOMMUNAL TENSIONS

The beginnings of the modern "Karabakh dispute" between Armenia and Azerbaijan are usually dated to February 1988. But the first violence, little recorded even in the region itself, occurred several months before that and elsewhere in Armenia and Azerbaijan. In the mid-1980s, there were roughly 350,000 Armenians in Azerbaijan (not including Nagorny Karabakh) and 200,000 or so Azerbaijanis in Armenia. In the fall of 1987, intercommunal relations in both republics took a marked turn for the worse, as if both sides were picking up a high-frequency radio signal.

In October 1987, a dispute broke out in the village of Chardakhlu, in the North of Azerbaijan, between the local Azerbaijani authorities and Armenian villagers. The Armenians objected to the appointment of a new collective-farm director. They were beaten up by the police and in protest sent a delegation to Moscow. Chardakhlu was a famous village to the Armenians because it was the birthplace of two marshals of the Soviet Union, Ivan Bagramian and Hamazasp Babajanian. A small protest demonstration about the Chardakhlu events was held in Yerevan on 18 October.

Soon after, trouble broke out in the southern Armenian regions of Meghri and Kafan, which had many Azerbaijani villages. In November

1987, two freight cars arrived at the Baku train station containing Azerbaijanis who had just fled Kafan as a result of interethnic violence. Very little is known about the incident, and it was not reported at all in the media, but there are witnesses to what happened. Sveta Pashayeva, an Armenian widow from Baku, told the story of how she saw the refugees arrive in Baku and brought them clothes and food:

> People came and said that two carriages had come from Kafan with naked unclothed children, and we went there to look. . . . They were Azerbaijanis from Kafan. I was at the station. There were two freight cars. The doors were open and there were two long planks, like floorboards, nailed over them so that people wouldn't fall out. And they said that people should bring what they could to help. And I—not just me, lots of people—collected together old children's dresses, things like that. I saw it myself. There were men, dirty country people, with long hair and beards, old people, children.[15]

Around 25 January 1988, the historian Arif Yunusov was going to work in the Academy of Sciences in Baku when he saw more evidence of Azerbaijanis having fled Kafan. Four red Icarus buses were standing outside the government headquarters on the top of the hill: "They were in a terrible state. On the whole it was women, children and old people. There were few young people. Many of them had been beaten. They were shouting."

The full story of these early refugee flows has not been told, largely because the Azerbaijani authorities did their best to suppress information about them. In Armenia, Aramais Babayan, who was second secretary of Kafan's Party committee at the time, says that he did not recollect any Azerbaijanis leaving the region before February. He did, however, confirm that on one night in February 1988, two thousand Azerbaijanis had left the Kafan region—an episode he blamed on rumors and "provocations." Babayan declares that on one occasion he crossed into Azerbaijan to try to persuade the Azerbaijanis who had left to come back to Kafan: "Earlier we had traveled freely. My vehicle was stopped in the next village. In the next village, Razdan, youths with blood on their faces were picking up stones. Anything was possible." Babayan turned back and none of the Kafan Azerbaijanis ever came back to Armenia.[16]

## PETITIONS AND DELEGATIONS

In 1987 the latent Karabakh Armenian movement gradually smoldered into life. Activists toured farms and factories in Nagorny Karabakh collecting signatures for what they called a "referendum" on unification with Armenia. The work was completed by the summer of 1987, and in August a vast petition in ten volumes with more than seventy-five thousand signatures from Karabakh and Armenia was sent to officials in Moscow.[17] The Karabakh Armenians then organized two delegations that went to Moscow to press their case with the Central Committee.

Senior Armenians were lobbying abroad. The historian Sergei Mikoyan, son of the famous Communist Anastas Mikoyan and the writer and journalist Zori Balayan, openly backed the idea of Nagorny Karabakh's joining Armenia in interviews to Armenian Diaspora newspapers in the United States. Then, in November 1987, Abel Aganbekian —clearly not regretting the two liters of vodka he had drunk with Muradian the year before—spoke up. On 16 November, Aganbekian, who was one of Gorbachev's main economic advisers, met with French Armenians in the Hotel Intercontinental in Paris and offered his view: "I would like to hear that Karabakh has been returned to Armenia. As an economist, I think there are greater links with Armenia than with Azerbaijan. I have made a proposal along these lines, and I hope that the proposals will be solved in the context of *perestroika* and democracy."[18] Aganbekian's views were reported in the French Communist newspaper *L'Humanité*, which was available in the Soviet Union. It was with his intervention that Azerbaijanis first became aware of an Armenian campaign against them.

By February 1988, the mechanism was primed and ready to go off. A third Karabakhi delegation, consisting of writers and artists and led by Zhanna Galstian, traveled to Moscow.[19] Ten thousand leaflets were printed and flown into Nagorny Karabakh. Everything had been coordinated to begin with the homecoming of the delegation. Muradian says:

> On the night of the 12–13 February absolutely all the post-boxes of Stepanakert received these leaflets. . . . There were already no big problems. Already on that day, the twelfth, we felt that the town was in our hands because the police, law enforcement organs, Party officials, all came up to us and said "You can rely on us." They gave us

information about what the KGB was up to, who was coming from Baku, who was coming from Moscow. It was full information, there were no secrets.

Muradian's account of how he planned and organized the modern Karabakh movement suggests a formidably organized campaign that drew tacit support from senior Party figures and succeeded in mobilizing large numbers of people. But his tale reveals the terrifying blind spot in his thinking—and that of many Armenians. In telling his story, Muradian made absolutely no reference to the position of Azerbaijan or what would be the reaction of the forty thousand Azerbaijanis of Karabakh. He even used the phrase "all the population of Karabakh" when talking about the referendum. So what about the Azerbaijanis? Did he make no effort to consult with them or ask their opinions? Muradian's gaze hardened at this question. "Do you want to know the truth?" he replied. "I will tell you the truth. We weren't interested in the fate of those people. Those people were the instruments of power, instruments of violence over us for many decades, many centuries even. We weren't interested in their fate and we're not interested now."

A lack of interest in the views of your neighbors was inherent in the rigidly vertical structure of the Soviet system, where Union Republics like Armenia and Azerbaijan never talked to each other directly, only through Moscow. When Aganbekian spoke out in Paris, many Azerbaijanis noted that he was not just any Armenian but an adviser to Gorbachev—albeit on economic matters—and therefore concluded that Gorbachev was backing the Armenian cause. In fact, it was soon clear that Aganbekian did not have Gorbachev's support—and in the end all the efforts of the Armenian lobby in Moscow could not sway the Politburo. Yet the mixed messages coming out of Moscow made Azerbaijanis deeply suspicious of Gorbachev's intentions; many are still are persuaded of a conspiracy in Moscow against them, which no evidence to the contrary can dispel.

The Armenian activists, inhabiting their own Soviet bubble, made, if anything, an even bigger miscalculation. Many of them were encouraged to think that they were pushing at an open door and that the Soviet leadership would eventually agree to transfer Nagorny Karabakh to Armenia. They therefore persisted in ignoring Azerbaijan's point of view. When the Politburo refused to support them, the Armenians were left without a "Plan B," which might have left them able to negotiate with Azerbaijan.

## ARMENIA RISES UP

After the protests in Karabakh, Soviet Armenia rose up in a series of vast street demonstrations. Armenia was one of the most homogeneous and self-confident republics in the USSR, yet no one, including the leaders of the demonstrations themselves, anticipated what energy they would release. It seemed that the Nagorny Karabakh issue had the capacity to touch a deep nerve inside Armenians. Explaining how Karabakh could suddenly bring hundreds of thousands of people onto the streets, the political scientist Alik Iskandarian uses the term "frozen potential." "The Karabakh factor was frozen, but it needed absolutely nothing to bring it to the surface," he says. Even those who knew almost nothing about the sociopolitical situation in Karabakh itself felt that they could identify with the cause of Armenians encircled by "Turks" (a word that in the Armenian vernacular applies equally to Turks and Azerbaijanis).

On 15 February 1988, at a meeting of the Armenian Writers Union, one of the more outspoken groups in society, the poet Silva Kaputikian spoke up in support of the Karabakh Armenians. Three days later, in Yerevan, protests about the environment attracted few people. The environment was the safest and most "nonpolitical" subject for protest—and therefore the first focus for public rallies in many other parts of the Soviet Union. The demonstrators complained about the condition of Lake Sevan, the Metsamor nuclear power station, the Nairit chemicals plant, and air pollution in Yerevan. But the organizers were being disingenuous. According to the leading activist Zori Balayan:

> We gathered on Theater Square with purely ecological slogans. . . . But among them was, let's say, one slogan saying "Karabakh is the historic territory of Armenia." No one paid any attention to it. At the next rally there were a few of those slogans. Igor Muradian, when he was bringing people there, also brought portraits of Gorbachev. "Lenin, Party, Gorbachev" was his slogan. He thought it up. Three weeks later he thought up another one: "Stalin, Beria, Ligachev." In this way people got used to the idea that they could talk about the national question as

well as Nairit and Sevan. A month later, Nairit and Sevan would get mentioned only for five minutes.[20]

The rallies were held in Theater Square, a large arena in the center of Yerevan, in front of the city's Opera House. On 20 February, shortly before the Regional Soviet met in Stepanakert, 30,000 demonstrators rallied there. Every day, the number redoubled. On 22 February, it was above 100,000 people—a phenomenal number in any country, but especially in the Soviet Union of 1988. The next day an estimated 300,000 gathered, and a transport strike was declared in Yerevan. The mass meetings were not reported in the Soviet media, but news of them got back to Moscow and reached Western reporters. Russian human rights activists, including the best-known dissident in the Soviet Union, Andrei Sakharov, expressed a rather simplistic support for the Armenian protestors.

On Thursday, 25 February, there were perhaps close to a million people on the streets of Yerevan, or more than a quarter of the population of Armenia. Film footage of the demonstrations shows an endless sea of caps, trilbies, raincoats, and overcoats, as people stand packed together in the sunshine. The faces of the demonstrators are eager and expectant. Every now and again a three-syllable chant surges out of the throng: "Gha-ra-bagh!"[21] Attending these rallies became almost an end in itself, a collective ritual of self-assertion. People walked for hours to get to Theater Square. Ashot Manucharian, a schoolteacher who later became one of the leaders of the Karabakh Committee, joined the rallies on the second or third day. He describes Theater Square as a "magnetic field" that drew everyone:

Atmosphere is a very attractive thing. Really, people began to feel something new, that it was possible to speak, it was possible to gather, talk about the fate of Karabakh. . . . So an atmosphere was created, which became fantastic. When I say a situation is fantastic, I mean it's like when the Pope speaks on St Peter's Square to the faithful, the true believers gather, and then the situation after the Pope's sermon. It was a state very close to that. Everyone loves everyone else. An atmosphere of total warmth. If something happens to someone else, the whole square starts to help that person. Doctors rush in, strong men come and form a stretcher. Someone gives medicine, someone else water.[22]

Zoya Shugarian, a Karabakhi Armenian who had lived in Yerevan for many years, declares that she could not believe her eyes when she saw what was happening. At first, few Yerevan residents knew much about Nagorny Karabakh, but rallies and pamphlets were soon giving everyone a crash course in the Armenian version of the dispute. "All those years I'd fought with Armenians, who didn't know where Karabakh was on the map," said Shugarian. "On 21 February I went out on to the street and the whole of Armenia was shouting 'Gha-ra-bagh!' For the first few days I did nothing but weep."[23] Shugarian went on to remark, however, that she has second thoughts about those early rallies, which she now believes were being used for unscrupulous political ends: "I regret the stupid euphoria, when we were pleased with everybody."

The Yerevan rallies were peaceful, but they also had a terrifying momentum. No one was able to apply the brakes. Even the new "leaders" of the movement had little idea where their movement was going. Rafael Gazarian was the eldest member of the newly formed Karabakh Committee:

> You know, the whole people rose up. It isn't that we lifted them up, the people lifted *us* on its wave. We were simply on the crest of a wave. Those who were a bit more desperate, more decisive, who didn't stop to think about the consequences, ended up on the crest of the wave. Those who were a bit more cautious did not. But the whole people rose up, both in Karabakh and here. If people walked thirty or forty kilometers on foot to come to a rally and hundreds of thousands of people collected—it was something incredible. On one day, a terrifying number of people gathered around the opera, several hundred thousand—it seems to me it was difficult to suppress this with any arguments. All the more so because we were convinced that Gorbachev would resolve it within a week. God forbid that he should drag it out for a month! I felt that my heart would not withstand it if it lasted a whole month![24]

The official message coming from the Party leadership in Moscow was very clear: there would be no change in Nagorny Karabakh's status. So why did Gazarian and others believe for several weeks that Gorbachev would agree to their demands? Perhaps the very fact that Politburo members came to Yerevan and talked to the demonstrators was perceived as a concession by Moscow; or they believed that their "people power" was so overwhelming that it would force the Politburo to change its mind.

The local Armenian Communist leaders found themselves on perilous ground, caught between the demands of Moscow and the crowd. It was not that the leaders opposed the idea of the unification of Karabakh and Armenia in principle, merely that the crisis threatened their hold on power. A former high-ranking Party official, Grant Voskanian, says that the leadership in Yerevan had been warned to expect a campaign in Stepanakert, but were unable to keep pace with developments:

> We knew that this question existed, but we had agreed with [the Party leadership in Stepanakert] that they would let us know in advance when they passed their resolution about leaving Azerbaijan. But, as it turned out they caught us by surprise when they passed the resolution. I called Genrikh Pogosian and said, "Listen, if you had to do this, why didn't you let us know?" He apologized and said that "it took place so spontaneously, that we didn't have time [to warn you]."[25]

On 22 February, local Party boss Demirchian announced on Armenian television that the demands for unification could not be met and that "the friendship of nations is our priceless wealth—the guarantee of the future developments of the Armenian people in the family of Soviet brotherly nations."[26] When he was finally compelled to talk to Theater Square, Demirchian sounded rattled, asking the crowd rhetorically whether they thought he had Karabakh "in his pocket."

The task of the two envoys from the Politburo sent to Yerevan, Anatoly Lukyanov and Vladimir Dolgikh, was equally difficult. They were to deliver a tough message that Soviet borders were inviolable, but, in line with the "new thinking," they also were supposed to engage in a dialogue. No one was interested in their message. When Dolgikh wanted to speak to the crowd on Theater Square, he needed the cooperation of the poet Silva Kaputikian to get a hearing; she asked the gathering to listen respectfully to what the man from Moscow had to say. It was a vivid illustration of how Soviet power was vanishing in Armenia.

## GORBACHEV AND THE WRITERS

Mikhail Gorbachev and his colleagues were caught entirely unawares by the Armenian rebellion. This much is obvious from the transcripts of two Politburo meetings from this period, 29 February and 21 March 1988, which were released, along with thousands of other Kremlin files, in 1992. They allow us to read verbatim the Politburo members' struggle to deal with the first phase of the crisis.

In his opening remarks to the 29 February Politburo session, Gorbachev sounds equivocal. He tells his colleagues that the Armenians' demands are unacceptable, but also that he is pleased to note that the demonstrations are peaceful: "I should say that even when there were half a million people on the streets of Yerevan, the discipline of the Armenians was high, there was nothing anti-Soviet." The Soviet leader's summation of the cause of the dispute shows sympathy with the Armenians' sense of historic grievance. "For my part I see two causes: on the one hand, many mistakes committed in Karabakh itself plus the emotional foundation, which sits in the [Armenian] people. Everything that has happened to this people in history remains and so everything that worries them, provokes a reaction like this."[27] The Soviet leader may have felt that the well-educated Armenians were his most natural allies outside Russia for his political reforms. While resolving to keep Nagorny Karabakh within Azerbaijan, he therefore sought to appease the Armenians by promising political, economic, and cultural improvements for the province.

This message failed to make an impact in either Armenia or Azerbaijan. Possibly, it might have met with more success if Gorbachev had deployed some of the personal charm that made him so popular in the West. Instead, he kept the lofty distance customary of most Soviet leaders: he did not travel to the region, made no public comments on the dispute, gave no interviews. Then on 26 February, Gorbachev issued his "Appeal to the workers of Armenia and Azerbaijan," which was read out in the two republics by visiting Politburo members. The appeal rested on a grand but empty call to respect Soviet friendship: "Not a single mother would agree to see her children threatened by national factionalism in exchange for the firm ties of friendship, equality, mutual help—which are truly the great achievement of socialism."

On the day of his appeal, Gorbachev received the Armenian writers Zori Balayan and Silva Kaputikian in the Kremlin. Gorbachev's Ar-

menian aide Georgy Shakhnazarov sat in. Shakhnazarov was himself
descended from a Karabakh Armenian noble family, a fact that naturally aroused suspicions in Azerbaijan. However, judging by his memoirs, it seems that he came from an internationalist Soviet Armenian tradition, forged in Baku and Moscow. He writes that he was against
Nagorny Karabakh's leaving Azerbaijan and favored giving it the en-
hanced status of Autonomous Republic. The meeting with the writers
was difficult. Shakhnazarov's account of how it began:

> Right from the start the conversation was direct, sometimes even
> harsh, although it was conducted in a friendly tone. "What is happen-
> ing around Karabakh is a stab in the back for us," said Mikhail Ser-
> geyevich [Gorbachev]. "It is hard to restrain the Azerbaijanis and the
> main thing is that it is creating a dangerous precedent. We have sev-
> eral dozen potential sources of conflict on ethnic grounds in the coun-
> try and the example of Karabakh can push those people, who have not
> so far risked resorting to violence, into impulsive action."[28]

Both Armenian writers combined loyal Party membership with Armenian nationalism but were very different in nature. Zori Balayan, a
writer and journalist with the Soviet newspaper *Literaturnaya Gazeta*,
was the chief ideologist of the Karabakh movement. His hard black eyes
speak of an uncompromising character. For him, the whole Karabakh
issue is part of a larger theme, the dangers posed by a "Great Turan" of
Turkic powers to Armenia and the "civilized world." In an interview in
2000, he enthusiastically weaved together evidence of the pan-Turkic
threat from such diverse elements as the 1915 Genocide, Communist
veteran President Aliev of Azerbaijan, and the recent stabbing to death
of two British soccer fans by rival Turkish supporters in Istanbul. This
is part of Balayan's version of the meeting with Gorbachev:

> He listened to us for more than an hour. We spoke about everything.
> Silva got out a map published in Turkey, a map of the Soviet Union. On
> this map all the territory of the Soviet Union, I mean Transcaucasia, the
> Volga region, the Northern Caucasus, Central Asia, Yakutia, many of
> the autonomous republics were all painted in green. Turkey was teach-
> ing this map in school that all these territories were Turkish, including
> Armenia. We showed this to Gorbachev, laid it out on the table. Gor-
> bachev looked it and pushed it aside, very quickly pushed it back at

us. . . . And he said "This is some kind of madness." I said "Mikhail Sergeyevich, mad ideas sometimes become realities."

Silva Kaputikian has a more calm and regal demeanor. With a flat nose, green eyes, and an elegant white bouffant hairdo, she looks like a *grande dame* from the court of Louis XV. Kaputikian is Armenia's most famous living poet and, as it emerged from the meeting, counted Raisa Gorbacheva as one of her fans. Despite her nationalist views, she has spoken up frequently for conciliation and dialogue with Azerbaijan. Kaputikian recalls begging the general secretary for some concession to take home to the crowds in Yerevan:

> Gorbachev said, "Now we have to put out the fire." "Good, but what with? Give us water. Some kind of promise, some kind of hope. I will go [to the crowds] but what will I tell them?" Shakhnazarov spoke up for the first and only time and said, "Tell them there will be a conference devoted to the nationality question. That's where a decision will be taken." And so he gave me a few buckets to put out this huge fire![29]

At the end of the meeting, Gorbachev again rejected the transfer of Nagorny Karabakh to Armenia but promised cultural and economic improvements for the region. He wanted to see, he said, a "little renaissance" in Karabakh.[30] He took note of twenty specific complaints raised by the two writers and later allocated 400 million rubles for the region— an enormous sum for that period. For their part, Balayan and Kaputikian agreed to tell the Yerevan crowds to call off their demonstrations for a month.

The pair traveled back to Armenia to relay Gorbachev's message. Balayan spoke to the crowds in Theater Square; Kaputikian preferred to appear on television. She says that Balayan spoke very exultantly, but she spoke "in very despondent tones," referring to difficult moments in Armenian history but promising that they would "turn this defeat into a victory." There was a brief pause in the unfolding events, as the Armenian organizers agreed to suspend their rallies for a month. But the very next day, everything was turned upside down, as news began to emerge of horrific mob violence in the Azerbaijani city of Sumgait.

# 2

# February 1988: Azerbaijan

*Puzzlement and Pogroms*

THE EXTRAORDINARY EVENTS in Nagorny Karabakh in February 1988 caught Azerbaijan by surprise and revealed its hidden insecurities.

Azerbaijan had a far more diverse population than Armenia. With double the number of inhabitants—more than seven million in 1988—it had a far greater ethnic mix, with substantial minorities of Russians and Armenians, as well as smaller Caucasian nationalities, such as Talysh and Lezgins. Its population centers ranged from the cosmopolitan capital Baku to some of the most deprived towns and villages of the Caucasus.

Superficially, as soon as the Politburo upheld Azerbaijan's claim to Nagorny Karabakh, the local Party leadership was in a secure position; indeed, in contrast to the Armenian Communist Party, the Azerbaijani Communist Party was able to hold on to power until 1992. Yet local Party boss Kamran Bagirov, a protégé of the former Azerbaijani Party leader Heidar Aliev, was out of favor and sick.[1] Gorbachev showed his distrust of the local Azerbaijani leadership by taking direct handling of the Karabakh crisis out of its hands.

Azerbaijan's first political protest took place on 19 February 1988, the seventh day of the Armenian rallies. A group of students, workers, and intellectuals marched from the Academy of Sciences on the top of the hill in Baku down to the building of the republican parliament, the Supreme Soviet, carrying placards that proclaimed that Nagorny Karabakh belonged to Azerbaijan. They had almost no organizational backup, however. Many intellectuals in Baku say that they had never taken an interest in the Karabakh issue before 1988; unaware that it was a potent theme for Armenians, they had simply taken for granted that Karabakh would always be theirs. So the eruption of protests in Karabakh represented something both vaguer and more universal. Azerbaijanis felt that Armenians were trying to break up their republic and threaten Azerbaijan's national identity.

The first to react was a group of Azerbaijani historians who had been engaged in an aggressive politicized debate with their Armenian counterparts since the 1960s. The poet Bakhtiar Vahabzade and the historian Suleiman Aliarov published an "Open Letter" in the journal *Azerbaijan* in which they declared that Karabakh was historical Azerbaijani territory, that the Karabakh Armenian campaign came out of a dangerous irredentist tradition, and that "the Azerbaijani people, in the new era of international competition, have been among the first victims."[2] The "Open Letter" also mentioned the hitherto taboo subject of "southern Azerbaijan" across the border in Iran. But this rare counterblast to the Armenians was published only in Baku, not Moscow, where the Armenian argument was receiving a much more favorable hearing.

## BAKU IN FERMENT

Baku had always stood apart from the rest of Azerbaijan. It was the largest city in the Caucasus and home to dozens of nationalities. Russian was the preferred *lingua franca* and intermarriage was common. At the same time, the city's rich ethnic mix also made it vulnerable; intercommunal tensions simmered below the surface.

The vote by the Nagorny Karabakh Soviet on 20 February to leave Azerbaijan immediately raised the temperature in the city. The situation worsened with the influx of Azerbaijanis fleeing the Kafan district of southern Armenia, many of whom descended on relatives in Baku. Although there were no reports of deaths, many of the refugees were bandaged from beatings and fights. In the fevered atmosphere, many Azerbaijanis perceived that they had a fifth column in their midst in the Armenian quarter known as Armenikend. A Soviet official sent to Baku at that time was given one example of the growing hatred: a leaf of checked paper from a school exercise book that had been pushed into an Armenian's mailbox. Written on it in red capital letters were the Russian words "POGOSIANSHCHIKI VON IZ BAKU POKA ZHIVY" (meaning: "Pogosian supporters [i.e., supporters of the new Armenian leader of Nagorny Karabakh Genrikh Pogosian] get out of Baku while you are still alive!")[3]

Baku's local Party boss was a bluff and energetic former soccer player and construction engineer named Fuad Musayev. His abrasive approach to problem solving was controversial but possibly what was needed in this situation. On 20 Feburary, Musayev was called back to Baku from a vacation in the Russian spa town of Kislovodsk and found the city tense: "Someone was provoking them, propaganda work was going on."[4] That night Musayev and his Party Committee decided to restrict outsiders' access into Baku. People's volunteer groups were formed and patrolled the streets with wooden staves, keeping a careful watch on the Armenian quarter.

The trouble died down in Baku, and timely action by the city authorities may have averted at least two other attempts at pogroms there later that year.[5] Yet, arguably, Musayev had only moved the trouble on to the town of Sumgait, twenty miles away. As one of his precautionary measures, he restricted the access of the thousands of workers who traveled from Sumgait to work in Baku every day, and he sent the Azerbaijani refugees from Armenia on to two villages, Fatmai and Sarai, on the edge of Sumgait. So, as Baku became calmer, Sumgait seethed.

## A MODEL SOVIET TOWN

There was something darkly appropriate about the way Sumgait produced the first-ever mass violence of the late Soviet era. It was a purely Soviet town, built to fulfill the dream of creating a modern internationalist workers' community. Instead, it created a large class of poorly housed and disaffected *lumpenproletariat*.

The patch of Caspian Sea shoreline north of Baku, where Sumgait now stands, was empty until World War II. It is a pleasant sandy spot, sprouting palm trees and other tropical greenery, where in the late 1940s, a town began to grow. Its population was filled by the lowest ranks of Soviet society: *zeks* (political prisoners) let out of Stalin's camps; Azerbaijanis who had left Armenia to make way for Diaspora Armenian immigrants; and poor Armenian migrant workers from the hills of Karabakh. In 1960, the new city already had a population of sixty-five thousand.

By the 1980s, this internationalist dream had turned into a nightmare. The population had rocketed to a quarter of a million and there were acute housing shortages. Factory workers lived in crowded hostels. The city's chemical factories gave it one of the worst pollution records in the Soviet Union. The infant mortality rate was so high that Sumgait had a cemetery set aside especially for children. The average age of its residents was twenty-five, and one inhabitant in five had a criminal record. Between 1981 and 1988, more than two thousand released prisoners called it home.[6]

In 1963, serious trouble had broken out in Sumgait when Nikita Khrushchev was leader of the Soviet Union and dismantling the cult of Stalin. On 7 November, the day of celebrations of the October Revolution, an unruly crowd from the Pipe-Rolling Factory broke away from the festive march through the central square of the city. The workers stormed the podium, where the local Party leaders were standing, and ripped down a vast portrait of Khrushchev that covered the façade of the Palace of Culture. The police battered the rioters with truncheons, but disturbances continued for several hours. According to one version of these events, the protestors had economic grievances and were protesting against bread queues and rising prices. Another version has it that the riots had a distinct anti-Armenian streak and were in reprisal for an incident in which an Azerbaijani had been killed in Stepanakert. According to another story, the organizers planned a repeat performance of the trouble on the tenth anniversary of the riots in 1973 but were foiled by the KGB.[7]

## A POGROM BEGINS

In February 1988, while Fuad Musayev was forcibly suppressing any signs of trouble in Baku, Sumgait was ignored. In the crucial days of the Armenian protests in Nagorny Karabakh, many local leaders, including the Party boss, Jehangir Muslimzade, were away. On 26 February, according to eyewitnesses, a small demonstration of perhaps forty or fifty people formed on Lenin Square in front of the Town Committee building and protested about the situation in Karabakh.[8] The raw material for the demonstrations was the same group of Azerbaijanis who had recently fled Armenia. A man with a long face, beard, and narrow moustache, whom some of the Armenians later dubbed the "Leader," an Azerbaijani from Kafan, told the crowd how he had been expelled by the Armenians, who had killed several of his relatives.[9]

On Saturday, 27 February, the number of demonstrators had swelled to several hundred. The speakers used a megaphone, which could be heard several streets away. Armenians remember hearing the word "Karabakh" repeated endlessly into the night. The second secretary— or number-two official—in the local Party committee, a woman with the surname Bairamova, also reportedly addressed the crowd and demanded that Armenians leave Azerbaijan. The Leader's tales had become yet more blood curdling. He said members of his wife's family had been killed and women had had their breasts cut off.[10]

That evening, the first incidents of violence, in a cinema and the market, were reported. Another factor, which seems to have been a necessary condition for ethnic violence to begin, came into play: the local police did nothing. It later transpired that the local police force was overwhelmingly composed of Azerbaijanis and had only one professional Armenian officer.[11]

That same evening, the military prosecutor of the USSR, Alexander Katusev, who was in Azerbaijan, spoke on national television and on Baku Radio. Questioned about the events in Karabakh, he confirmed that two young men had been killed in Askeran five days before and gave their obviously Azerbaijani names.[12] Katusev was putting a match to a tinderbox. According to one Sumgait Armenian, "[W]hen he said that . . . you know how bees sound, have you heard how they buzz? It was like the buzzing of millions of bees . . . and with this buzzing, they flew into our courtyard, howling and shouting."[13]

The next day, Sunday, 28 February, an angry crowd filled the entire central square of Sumgait. The local Party boss, Jehangir Muslimzade, had finally returned from Moscow. According to one Georgian witness, he reassured the crowd that Karabakh would never be given to the Armenians—but this was no longer enough to satisfy them. Then he said: "Brothers, we need to let the Armenians leave the city freely; once this kind of feud has started, once national issues have been opened up, force awakened, we need to let the Armenians leave."[14] Muslimzade was unable to quell the crowd.

The details of what happened next are not entirely clear, but at around 6:30 P.M. Muslimzade descended into the crowd. An Azerbaijani flag was planted in his hand, and he marched at the head of the demonstrators. The Party boss led them two blocks west, then south along Ulitsa Druzhby (Friendship Street), then east again toward the sea. Muslimzade later said that his intention had been to lead the crowd out of the city center, down toward the sea, and out of trouble. Instead, he helped unleash a mob in the center of the city. The tail of the crowd broke up into small groups that began to swarm about the center of town seeking out Armenians.

The peacetime Soviet Union had never before experienced what happened next. Gangs, ranging in size from about a dozen to more than fifty, roamed around, smashing windows, burning cars, but above all looking for Armenians to attack. Several blocks of Sumgait turned into a war zone. Its epicenter was the area around the city's bus station, which, in a piece of unintended Soviet black irony, was situated on the corner of Friendship and Peace Streets. Ordinary inhabitants were terrified. Natevan Tagieva, a doctor's wife, related how she had come back to the city from her *dacha* to find the mob in complete control of the streets: "When I saw the crowd I realized that the syndrome of the crowd really does exist. You look at their eyes and you see that they are absolutely switched off from everything, like zombies."[15]

The horrors of what the Armenian residents of these streets suffered have been meticulously documented. A book of the accounts of forty-four survivors was compiled later in Armenia and provides an extremely powerful and detailed anatomy of the pogrom. The roving gangs committed acts of horrific savagery. Several victims were so badly mutilated by axes that their bodies could not be identified. Women were stripped naked and set on fire. Several were raped repeatedly.[16]

Almost thirteen years after the events, a group of Sumgait Armenians could be found in the village of Kasakh, north of the Armenian capital Yerevan. They had been given neat cottages to live in, but few of them had permanent jobs and they were still obviously metropolitan folk, conversing with one another in Russian and not entirely at home with the wood-burning stoves in their front rooms. They all had perfect recall of the three days of terror that had destroyed their lives in Sumgait. And, although they had experienced it as an eruption of elemental evil, they also identified a certain pattern in what had happened.

The attackers came in separate waves, said Rafik Khacharian, an elderly man with an elegant plume of gray hair. "One group shouted, made a noise, smashed things and left," he said. "A second group came to take good things and then left again. The third did the torturing and killing. They had three groups. The first were just boys of fifteen, sixteen, seventeen, they were vandals; the second were looters." The *pogromshchiki* were easy to identify, he declared. They were either rural folk, often with beards—refugees from Armenia—or workers from the overcrowded hostels on the edge of Sumgait. They were all young, ranging in age from fourteen to their early thirties.

Khacharian and his family had fled their apartment. When they returned, they found all their possessions overturned and smashed such that "there wasn't a single glass left in the morning to drink water out of." Otherwise they were unscathed. Maria Movseyan, an old lady wearing a turquoise blouse, wept as she recalled a worse trauma. One of the men who invaded her apartment pursued her daughter, who ran in terror, jumped off their first-story balcony into a tree, and broke her leg in the fall. The next thing Maria knew, her daughter was being carried away in a blanket in the street below.

Most of the attackers were not well armed but relied on sheer force of numbers. Some Armenians resisted the attacks and fought back, which may account for some of the six Azerbaijanis included in the final death toll.[17] Many of the rioters, however, were carrying improvised weapons—sharpened pieces of metal casing and pipes from the factories—which would have taken time to prepare. This is one of many details that suggest that the violence was planned in at least a rudimentary fashion. Several survivors remembered other details: the invaders carefully avoided smashing their television sets; they also did not touch children.[18]

Some of the rioters had also gotten the idea that they would be housed in the apartments of the Armenians they were attacking. One of the Armenian victims, Lyudmila M, lay in a bloody heap on the floor, after being raped and left for dead, and overheard the conversation of a group of men in her apartment:

> There were six people in the room. They talked among themselves and smoked. One talked about his daughter, saying there was no children's footwear in our apartment that he could take for his daughter. Another said that he liked the apartment—recently we had done a really good job fixing everything up—and that he would live there after everything was all over. They started to argue. A third one says "How come you get it? I have four children and there are three rooms here, that's just what I need. All these years I've been living in god-awful places." Another one says "Neither of you gets it. We'll set fire to it and leave."[19]

Although the police did nothing, several Azerbaijanis tried to organize help independently for their Armenian neighbors. Members of the local young Communist organization, the Komsomol, went out in small teams and ferried Armenians to the safety of the Palace of Culture in the central square.[20] A Mrs. Ismailova was briefly made into a hero by the Soviet media for protecting several families in her apartment. The doctor's wife, Natevan Tagieva, remarked, "We lived in a fourteen-story building with lots of Armenians in it. There were Armenians on the fourteenth floor and we hid them, none of them spent the night at home. In the hospital, people formed vigilante groups, every patient was guarded."

The violence had one darkly surreal aspect: it was often very difficult for the killers and looters to know who the enemy was. Soviet Armenians and Azerbaijanis can look very alike, in Sumgait they tended to converse in an indistinguishable Russian, and many of the Armenians also spoke good Azeri. Several Armenians managed to escape by successfully pretending to be Azerbaijani or Russian—unwittingly exposing the absurd premise underlying ethnic violence, as well as saving their own lives. In the hunt for Armenians, angry young men stopped buses and cars and demanded to know if there were Armenians on board. To smoke out an Armenian, they would force the passenger to say the word *fundukh* ("hazelnut" in Azeri). Armenians had a reputation for not being able to pronounce the initial "f" and turning it into a "p" sound. In one courtyard, the rioters came upon a dinner being held for someone who had died forty days before, a wake known as a *karasunk*. The only way they could identify that the people at the table were worthy of attack was that they were eating bread—a custom that is apparently forbidden for Azerbaijanis at a *karasunk*.

These fine distinctions are an instance of what Michael Ignatieff, borrowing the term from Freud, has called the "narcissism of minor difference." Analyzing the Serbo-Croat conflict, he writes:

> Freud once argued that the smaller the difference between two peoples the larger it was bound to loom in their imagination. He called this effect the narcissism of minor difference. Its corollary must be that enemies need each other to remind themselves of who they really are. A Croat, thus, is someone who is not a Serb. A Serb is someone who is not a Croat. Without hatred of the other, there would be no clearly defined national self to worship and adore.[21]

In this sense the Sumgait pogroms could be said to have caused the first violent fission of a "Soviet" identity.


## THE CENTER REACTS—SLOWLY

The authorities were painfully slow in reacting to events. Baku was only half an hour's drive away, but no one responded for several hours. According to one of the Moscow officials in Azerbaijan at the time, Grigory Kharchenko: "Gorbachev is absolutely incorrect when he says that we were three hours late. Nothing of the sort. We were late by a day. Because we waited a whole day for the decision to be taken to send the troops in there."[22]

Kharchenko, together with Filip Bobkov, the deputy head of the Soviet KGB, was the first Soviet official to travel from Baku to Sumgait on the evening of 28 February 1988. For a Communist official, used to the dreary order of Soviet life, it was something extraordinary. Shop windows had been smashed, the streets were full of burned trolleybuses and cars. Angry crowds were still roaming at will. He says:

> It was impossible to control the situation because the whole town was in panic. Crowds of Azerbaijanis walking around, screaming came from the courtyards, "Help! Help!" We had an escort, we were led to one place . . . I don't want to show you the photographs. I simply destroyed them. But with my own eyes I saw dismembered corpses, a body mutilated with an axe, legs, arms, practically no body left. They took the remains of dry leaves off the ground, scattered them over corpses, took petrol from the nearest car and set fire to them. Terrible corpses.

Bobkov and Kharchenko immediately decided that the military must be called in to restore order, but this was easier said than done. It was several hours before a regiment of Soviet Interior Ministry troops and cadets from the military academy in Baku arrived, only to be confronted by a furious mob. Kharchenko remembers that they were "bands that were ready for anything, they had already tasted blood, they realized that they had no way back." The young soldiers were under instruction from Moscow to fire blanks rather than live rounds. The rioters threw Molotov cocktails and lunged with their sharpened metal casings at the soldiers, stabbing them in the legs. A hundred or so soldiers were wounded.

On Monday, 29 February, the Politburo met in the Kremlin to discuss the crisis in the Caucasus. Strangely, the Politburo members spend a long time discussing the situation in Armenia before they come around to debate the situation in Sumgait. Worries are expressed that the violence is spreading to other towns in both Azerbaijan and Armenia. The document shows the leaders of the Soviet Union struggling to deal with an unprecedented situation:

[DMITRY] YAZOV [DEFENSE MINISTER]: But Mikhail Sergeyevich [Gorbachev], in Sumgait we have to bring in, if you want— it may not be the word—but martial law.

GORBACHEV: A curfew.

YAZOV: We have to pursue this line firmly, Mikhail Sergeyevich, to stop it getting out of hand. We have to send in troops and restore order. After all, this is an isolated place and not Armenia with millions of people. Besides, that will surely have a sobering effect on others.

GORBACHEV: Alexander Vladimirovich [Yakovlev] and Dmitry Timofeyevich [Yazov], you mean the possible situation in Baku, in Leninakan [in Armenia] and in that town, where there is an Armenian area . . .

[VIKTOR] VLASOV [INTERIOR MINISTER]: Kirovabad [Azerbaijan's second city, now Ganje].

GORBACHEV: Kirovabad.

VLASOV: They smashed windows and that was all.

GORBACHEV: We have to bear in mind that they did not yet know what happened in Sumgait, but that this is growing like a snowball.

[EDUARD] SHEVARDNADZE: It is like a connecting vein. If they find out about the casualties in Armenia, then it could cause trouble there.

[ALEXANDER] YAKOVLEV: We must announce quickly that criminal cases have been opened in Sumgait and criminals have been arrested. We need that in order to cool passions. In Sumgait itself, the city newspaper should say this firmly and quickly.

GORBACHEV: The main thing now is we need to send the working class, people, people's volunteers into the fight with the criminals. That, I can tell you, will stop any hooligans and extremists. As happened in Alma-Ata. It's very important. Soldiers provoke hostility.[23]

Gorbachev was very reluctant to deploy the security forces but was finally persuaded of the need for a limited military presence and a curfew in Sumgait. This deliberate restraint caused bitter recriminations later from Armenians.[24] Judging from this transcript, the leaders were sincere in their efforts to defuse the crisis but also completely out of their depth. Gorbachev still talked about mobilizing "the working class," although it was the working class in Sumgait that was out on the street, burning and killing. And he spent much of the session talking about the need for a big Party "plenum on the nationalities question," which could redefine Soviet nationalities policy, while ordinary Armenians and Azerbaijanis were already making a bonfire of Soviet internationalism.

In Sumgait itself on 29 February, the situation was far less under control than the Politburo believed. Attacks continued throughout the day in the "41st Quarter," west of the city's bus station. Five members of the same family—a husband and wife, their two sons and daughter —were all murdered. Finally, a company of well-armed marines from the Caspian Sea flotilla and a parachute regiment arrived. A General Krayev took charge in the evening as martial law was formally established. Over loudspeakers he announced a curfew, which would take effect at 11:00 P.M.—another unprecedented step in the peacetime Soviet Union. Four hours before the deadline several thousand angry young men were still collected on the square by the bus station. Krayev ordered the paratroopers to take the station by storm. Several Azerbaijanis died in the assault. By the end of Monday, the official death toll was thirty-two and more than four hundred men had been arrested.

Five thousand Armenians had taken shelter in the vast Palace of Culture on Lenin Square, protected by a cordon of marines. Kharchenko went to check on them. As he was hearing their hysterical complaints, he was struck on the back of the head and taken hostage. A group of desperate Armenians were demanding an airplane to fly out of the city; only when they had been persuaded that Moscow had plans to evacuate them, did they let him go. One detail strongly impressed Kharchenko: all the Sumgait Armenians wanted to go to Russia, not Armenia: "No one that we spoke to then expressed a desire to fly to Armenia. They all asked for Krasnodar, Stavropol, and Rostov regions. Why? They said, 'No one in Armenia needs us, they don't think of us as real Armenians, we are not real Armenians.'"

## THE AFTERMATH

The Sumgait killings were a watershed for the Soviet Union. It goes without saying that they were a catastrophe for the Armenians. Between 26 and 29 Sumgait Armenians lost their lives and hundreds more were injured. Almost all the 14,000 Armenians of Sumgait left the city. Outside Sumgait, the violence shocked the community of around 350,000 Armenians throughout Azerbaijan, thousands of whom left the republic. Sumgait was also a catastrophe for Azerbaijan, which, as it struggled to react to the unexpected events in Karabakh, had produced the most savage intercommunal violence in the Soviet Union in living memory. The brutality was a painful contrast to the more peaceful demonstrations in Armenia, and ordinary Azerbaijanis were horrified and confused.

The Soviet authorities' first instinct was to suppress information about the events. The lack of coverage by official Soviet media illustrated that Gorbachev's *glasnost* stopped a long way short of full press freedom. All week Soviet news broadcasts ran reports of riots in Israel, South Africa, and Panama but gave no inkling of what was going on in Azerbaijan. On the evening of Sunday, 28 February, when violence was exploding in Sumgait, the main Soviet evening news program, *Vremya*, merely reported that Armenian workers had pledged to work extra days to make up for production lost during their strike the previous week.[25] When it was over, the Soviet leadership decided to play down the anti-Armenian nature of the pogroms, calling them "acts of hooliganism" instead.

This distorted coverage aggrieved the Armenians and the failure to print a list of casualties convinced them that a far higher death toll had been suppressed. People who visited the Baku morgue after the pogroms were over counted 32 bodies—26 Armenians and 6 Azerbaijanis. The first book on the pogroms to come out in Armenia the following year added only 3 more Armenian names to the list—evidently victims who had died later or not been kept in the morgue. And yet Armenians

continued to believe that there had been a massacre of far greater proportions, followed by a cover-up. The Armenian writer Sero Khanza-
dian asserted that 450 Armenians had died in the pogroms. In 1991, the
French Armenian writer Claude Mutafian could still say that "[t]he official death toll of 32 was a derisory understatement."[26]

Nor did the trials of the perpetrators satisfy anyone. Some of the
more sensitive trials were transferred to Russian courts, to remove them
from the politically charged atmosphere of Azerbaijan and allow Armenians to testify more freely. They were given little press coverage. In
Sumgait itself, the trials that did take place there were closed to the public. In the end, around eighty men were convicted of crimes, far fewer
than that had taken a part in the riots. One man, Akhmed Akhmedov,
was executed. The atmosphere in the republic had changed so radically
by the end of 1988, the time of the trials, that some extremist demonstrators in Baku carried placards praising the "Heroes of Sumgait."[27]

## PLOTS AND CONSPIRACIES

Perhaps the biggest failing of the Soviet leadership over Sumgait was
that it did not allow an official investigation into the violence, something that both Armenians and Azerbaijanis called for. This only increased suspicion that the organizers of the pogroms had escaped justice. The lack of full information on the issue encouraged conspiracy
theorists—who need no encouragement in the Caucasus anyway—to
crank up their rumor mills.

There are reams of conspiracy theories about the pogroms. Many
people have pointed a finger at the central KGB, alleging that it organized the violence. One version has it that the KGB organized the violence to "frighten the Armenians" and make them back away from their
protests; another, that it was done in order to sow ethnic discord and
maintain Moscow's iron grip on both Azerbaijan and Armenia. A third
version was that the KGB staged Sumgait in order to discredit Gorbachev and *perestroika*.[28]

The KGB certainly had the means and the lack of scruple to provoke
violence, but no anecdotal or archival evidence has emerged in support
of the theory. To believe that the KGB planned and carried out the pogroms, one has to believe that in 1988 it was already acting independently of Gorbachev and had a radical long-term political agenda (which

backfired). One also has to cast the then chairman of the agency, Viktor Chebrikov—a dour man who in all his recorded comments on the Karabakh issue called for restraint—in the role of master manipulator, a Soviet Iago. This does not really add up. Judging by its activities in this period, the KGB was no less impotent and confused than the other Soviet agencies in the Caucasus.

On the Azerbaijani side even wilder conspiracy theories emerged, which tried to exonerate Azerbaijanis of the crimes. One persistent story was that outside conspirators had put cameras in place waiting for the pogroms to begin and that the footage they shot was immediately distributed round the world—yet no one has ever set eyes on this film.

In May 1989, the historian Ziya Buniatov, who was then president of the Academy of Sciences and Azerbaijan's foremost Armenophobe, came up with the most complete work of denial yet. In an article entitled "Why Sumgait?" he concluded that the Sumgait pogroms had been planned by the Armenians themselves in order to discredit Azerbaijan and boost the Armenian nationalist cause. "The Sumgait tragedy was carefully prepared by the Armenian nationalists," Buniatov wrote. "Several hours before it began, Armenian photographers and TV journalists secretly entered the city where they waited in readiness. The first crime was committed by a certain Grigorian who pretended to be Azerbaijani and who killed five Armenians in Sumgait."[29]

By the early 1990s, when all the Armenians of Azerbaijan had left and war with Armenia had completely poisoned relations between the two nations, the filmmaker Davud Imanov built an even more elaborate construction on this. His rambling trilogy of films entitled *Echo of Sumgait* is a cry of despair that accuses simultaneously the Armenians, the Russians, and the Americans of plotting against Azerbaijan. Imanov finally presents the whole Karabakh phenomenon as a plot by the CIA to destroy the Soviet Union.[30]

Buniatov and Imanov stitch their theories together from the same scraps of evidence. One was that before the events, Sumgait Armenians had withdrawn more than a million rubles from their saving accounts. If true, this is hardly surprising, given that trouble between Armenians and Azerbaijanis had been rumbling for some time.

Their other item of evidence is the participation in the violence by an Armenian called Eduard Grigorian. Grigorian, a Sumgait factory worker, took part in several of the mass attacks and gang rapes (although it would be misleading to suggest, as Buniatov did, that he personally "killed five Armenians"). He was subsequently sentenced to twelve years in prison. In Azerbaijan, a whole mythology has grown up about "the Armenian" who supposedly stood behind the Sumgait pogroms. Yet he was in fact just one of eighty-four men arrested for taking part in the violence, of whom eighty-two were Azerbaijani and one other was Russian.[31] Grigorian was a very lowly figure. A native of Sumgait, he was brought up by his Russian mother after his Armenian father died. He had three criminal convictions. According to one version, he egged others on during the riots; according to another, he was persuaded to join the violence by his Azerbaijani workmates. In sum, Grigorian bears the profile of a *pogromshchik*, a thuggish young man, of indeterminate nationality with a criminal past, seeking violence for its own sake. It is very hard to make a political conspirator out of him, let alone a key player in a sinister Armenian plot.

If the violence was planned, it may have been done so inside the city itself. After the pogroms were over, several local officials were sacked and the local Party boss, Muslimzade, was expelled from the Party.[32] Several of the Armenian survivors said they saw Party officials taking part in the rallies on Lenin Square and calling on Armenians to leave the town; some of the Armenian survivors said that there were even town officials among the *pogromshchiki*. Many of the killers and rioters had been made promises, given names and addresses of Armenians, and armed with homemade weapons.[33] Perhaps some of the local officials deliberately manipulated the crowd, hoping they could force Armenians to leave Sumgait and thus solve the town's most pressing social problem—the housing shortage. Whoever were targeting the Armenians, what they planned almost certainly got out of control.

In one sense, the conspiracy theorists are posing the wrong question. The violence did not happen in a vacuum and even if provocateurs were at work in Sumgait, they still needed willing material to provoke. The writer and journalist Anatol Lieven has described watching Soviet military cadets masquerading as Russian civilians trying to start a riot with the Latvian police—unsuccessfully, because the phlegmatic Baltic policemen did not overreact. Unfortunately, a crowd in the Caucasus contains more flammable material.[34]

It might be more useful to ask how violence could have been *avoided* in Sumgait, a deprived city, filling up with refugees in a volatile situation. Anti-Armenian pogroms were barely averted during these days in Azerbaijan's other big cities, Baku and Kirovabad, but in Sumgait the combination of elements was too combustible. The violence erupted so quickly that it is surprising that more Armenians were not killed. That they were not, when the police did nothing and the military arrived a day late, suggests that some Soviet civic values were acting as a brake on intercommunal bloodletting. Horrible as the pogroms were, the death toll in Sumgait was far smaller than that of the massacres in Baku in 1905 and 1918.

Azerbaijanis, who have a rather easygoing image of themselves, might find it easier to come to terms with the pogroms, if they realized that this kind of violence is not so uncommon. "One important reason for the rapid growth of the baiting crowd is that there is no risk involved," writes Elias Canetti in his seminal study of crowd psychology, *Crowds and Power.* "A murder shared with many others, which is not only safe and permitted, but indeed recommended, is irresistible to the great majority of men."[35] Savage pogroms took place not long afterward in Soviet Central Asia, in Osh and Dushanbe. Another country that has a peaceful self-image, Great Britain, was the scene of little-remembered ethnic pogroms in the East End of London in 1915. After the sinking of the British ship *Lusitania* by a German submarine, gangs took to the streets, smashing German shops and beating German shopkeepers.[36] More than two hundred people were hurt. The depiction of Sumgait would also have been less black-and-white, if it had been more widely known that Azerbaijanis were expelled violently from Armenia. The violence, which happened in rural areas, was less dramatic than the Sumgait pogroms, but in the course of 1988, hundreds of Azerbaijanis suffered at the hands of Armenians.

As it was, in the Soviet Union and the wider world, Sumgait came to stand as a symbol of ethnically motivated violence, with the Armenians portrayed as its sole victims. In Armenia, the killings caused a great upsurge of grief and anger. The comparison was immediately felt and expressed with the massacres of 1915, the "Genocide." Memorials were set up to the Sumgait victims. In Yerevan, demonstrators carried placards bearing the twin dates, 1915 and 1988. Many Armenians now believed that they had to fight against a coming wave of aggression. Arkady Gukasian, now elected leader of Nagorny Karabakh, says that Sumgait made eventual conflict with Azerbaijan "inevitable." "After Sumgait we began to think about where all this was leading, but the wheel had already started turning. Sumgait was an attempt to frighten us, to say, 'Look the same thing will happen to you.'"[37]

# 3

# Shusha

## The Neighbors' Tale

DRINKING TEA IN their garden, surrounded by nodding flowers and looking out at their old ruined school, Albert and Larisa Khachaturian seemed like the survivors of an earthquake.[1]

The Khachaturians' house in the upper part of Shusha is one of the few in the town that is still intact. As I walked up through the flagged streets of this formerly prosperous city, in the shade of oak and apple trees, I passed the black empty shells of old balconied mansion houses. Shusha (called Shushi by the Armenians), situated high above a gorge in the central hills of Nagorny Karabakh, was once one of the great cities of the Caucasus, famous for its theaters, mosques, and churches. Now its ruins support only a tiny populace, the streets are empty and lined with devastated buildings. Yet this comprehensive ruination was the result of a man-made disaster, not an earthquake.

The Khachaturians are some of only a few original natives who still live in Shusha. They come from what was a small Armenian minority in a majority-Azerbaijani town. In February 1988, when the Karabakh Armenians began their protests, the Azerbaijanis of Shusha were afraid. "No one slept," said Zahid Abasov, a local town official. The Shusha Armenians, people like Larisa and Albert Khachaturian, were doubly afraid. They were teachers who had done well under the Soviet system, and they had dozens of Azerbaijani friends and colleagues. But in 1988, they were suddenly members of an especially vulnerable social group: they, to be precise, were Armenians living in an Azerbaijani town inside an Armenian province inside Azerbaijan. Who would protect them now? Their story—the story of Shusha as a whole—is one of how Soviet neighbors came to fear and then fight one another.

Shusha did not have the socioeconomic problems of Sumgait, and at first the two communities in the town did not fight. But the Sumgait pogroms in February 1988 immediately created tensions, which

45

increased, when refugees—first Armenians from Sumgait, then Azerbaijanis from Armenia—began to arrive in Nagorny Karabakh. The fuse took longer to burn down in Shusha—a tribute perhaps to relationships of trust forged over many years. But it did ignite in September 1988, when, within a few days, all the Armenians were expelled from Shusha and all the Azerbaijanis were driven from Stepanakert. Albert recalled for me the day he came home to find a crowd trampling his garden and breaking his possessions:

> We thought it would be solved peacefully. It was very hard because Shusha is not a big town. We all knew each other, we were friends, we went to each other's weddings and funerals. I came in and saw Hussein the tailor smashing up my veranda. I said "Hussein, what are you doing?" I had managed to get his son-in-law into the Communist Party. He went away.

From late 1988 to early 1992, after the Armenians had left, Shusha was a defiant Azerbaijani outpost in the middle of Armenian-controlled Nagorny Karabakh. When full-scale war broke out after the collapse of the Soviet Union in 1992, Armenian fighters eventually captured Shusha. Shusha Armenians, like the Khachaturians, came back to a town that was now their home again—and was also utterly destroyed.

When the couple drink tea in their garden, they look across at their ruined former place of employment. The neoclassical *Realschule* is one of the saddest wrecks in the town. The three-story school, which was built in 1906, once had four hundred pupils and educated all the children of the bourgeoisie. Its graduates went to universities in Moscow and Saint Petersburg. Today, the school's grand façade has three rows of black windows, like an empty packet of pills in which the holes have been punched out. As we walked in, an inscription on the marble floor at the entrance still welcomed us in Latin: *Salve*. But a winding staircase of pink marble led up only to more rubble and corridors of grass growing between the stone floor tiles.

Re-creating the story of Shusha required traveling back and forth between the town itself in Karabakh, controlled by the Armenians, and Shusha-in-exile, the community that carries on in Azerbaijan. The two halves of the town have been wrenched apart, first by fighting and now by the cease-fire line.

I began on Azerbaijan's Caspian Sea coast at a sanatorium, where the name "SHUSHA" had been painted in thick white capitals on the steps. Long webs of washing, suspended on wires, stretched from the windows and crisscrossed one another. In 1992, thousands of Shusha Azerbaijanis were washed up in this old seaside resort north of Baku. It is a dry and sandy place, with only a few spindly pine trees to remind them of the forests of Karabakh.

The Jafarov family lived in a dark room, piled high with cushions and blankets. They told me that their son Chengiz was killed on 8 May 1992 by the Armenians as Shusha was falling. Yet when I asked about Soviet times, they gave the sort of reply that I was to hear dozens of times from both sides: "We lived normally with the Armenians." As far as they were concerned, the destructive germ of hatred had come from outside, not from within.

Chengiz's best friend, Zaur, a gentle man with a thick moustache and the outsize stature of a rugby player, hobbled into the Jafarovs' room with a stick. In the spring of 1992, he said, he had been a policeman and one of the Azerbaijani defenders of the town. Six weeks before the final Armenian assault, a "Grad" missile landed near him and its shrapnel crashed into his legs. Zaur had had his left leg amputated and had needed twenty-two operations to get back on his feet. He said he does not have a full-time job and spends most of his time in the stuffy sanatorium. "The summer is beginning here and in three or four months time we will be dying of the heat. We are mountain people, we are not used to this heat and that's when our longing begins."

Zaur had had two close Armenian friends. They had grown up together on the street that runs down from the upper mosque, played volleyball and soccer, helped one another buy things on the black market. When Zaur went into the army, one of them came to the barber and paid for his haircut as a good-luck gesture. "During the war I was always afraid that I would suddenly see Vigen or Surik through the sights of my gun," he recalled. "I had nightmares about that."

Zaur gave me an entrée into a circle of Shusha Azerbaijanis in exile. They were excited that I was actually planning to travel to their home city. Yusif was a lawyer. He was in his late thirties or early forties and had a rather Chekhovian sadness about him with his soft voice, thin black moustache, and unhappy eyes. He was more introspective and more bitter than Zaur and told me he had only recently broken his vow not to get married until his town was liberated from the Armenians.

Yusif wanted to know what had happened to his house. He drew a little map on a scrap of paper, giving me precise instructions on how to find it in the town.

In the spring of 2000, fewer than three thousand people were living in semiruined Shusha—perhaps a tenth of its former population. Most of them were poor Armenian refugees from Azerbaijan. In a queue of people holding buckets to collect water from a water-jet in a marble facing, I found only two original inhabitants who knew the town. It was quite likely that Zaur's friends had left. Eventually however, I was led to a four-story apartment block next to the church and a stocky man with a thick moustache and big black eyes. It was Zaur's friend, Vigen. As I explained my business, Vigen's wife brought us coffee.

Vigen was puzzled at first, then overjoyed to hear the message from Zaur, whom he had last seen more than ten years before. "How is his family?" Vigen asked. "His father died, didn't he?" The war vanished for a moment, as he wanted to catch up on old Shusha news and gossip—which I was unable to supply. He already knew that his friend had lost a leg. "I was fighting in the Martakert region," Vigen explained. "I heard an acquaintance from Shusha on the radio. I tuned in and we caught up with the news. He told me that Zaur had been hit." The Shusha street telegraph carried on across the front line and some "enemies" still remained friends.

I told him what Zaur had recalled about fearing the appearance of a friend in the sights of his gun. "I had the same fear!" he said with a smile. But Vigen's assessment of the future was much more sober. After all, he too had fought in the war and was now working for the government of the separatist statelet of Nagorny Karabakh. Would it be possible for the Shusha Azerbaijanis to return? "I think that his generation will grow up before that can happen," Vigen answered, pointing to his six-year-old son.

My other errand seemed less promising: in this shattered city there seemed little hope of finding anything left of Yusif's house. All the same, a few days later two journalist friends and I went looking for it. We found one of Yusif's former neighbors who recognized the name and led us to his four-story apartment-block. Almost all the apartments had been burned out, but half a dozen or so were inhabited. No. 28, Yusif's home, seemed to be one of them and there, leaning over the first-floor balcony of what should have been his home, was a dark-haired Armenian woman whose name was Anoush.

Anoush called us up. We explained ourselves, rather apologetically. She was agitated—not surprisingly—by this sudden visitation but invited us in. She was a teacher about the same age as Yusif, in early middle age, with thick blue eye shadow surrounding her big black eyes. Her daughter made more coffee while we sat on the sofa and heard Anoush's story of how she had ended up here. Hers was another account of a life wrecked by war. Shusha was still burning, she said, when she first arrived here on 10 May 1992, less than two days after Yusif and his father had left. The Karabakh Armenian authorities were encouraging people who had lost their homes to move up to Shusha and they wanted to act fast, because they were worried that the whole town would be burned to the ground by looters. Anoush was a perfect candidate for a new home: three months before she had lost her apartment in Stepanakert to a "Grad" missile fired from Shusha and before that, her house in her native village had also been burned in an Azerbaijani assault. So she moved into Apartment No. 28, which was now her only home. "The door was open, everything was gone," she said. We hastened to say that we had not come to assert the rights of its previous owner or to query hers, but the difficult—and unanswerable—question "Whom does this house belong to?" still hung in the air.

On one wall of Anoush's sitting room was a floor-to-ceiling photographic reproduction of a Russian autumnal scene. It was the kind of picture that hung on the walls of a million Soviet homes: a group of silver birch trees turning to orange and gold in a northern forest. Anoush pointed out an eight-inch piece of the picture on one side, which had been torn away, and how they had repainted the missing section of tree. She and her daughter had done the repair job with such care that it was not obvious at first glance. She smiled nervously as if to say that here was a token of her attachment to her home.

It was the birch tree photograph that confirmed that I had found Yusif's apartment. Back in Azerbaijan, I sought him out in his noisy lawyer's office in central Baku, taking with me a few photographic snaps of Shusha. When we had shuffled through to a picture of the birch trees on the wall, he drew in a breath and said, "Yes, that's my house." We got up, went out into the traffic noise, and carried on talking in a café on

Baku's Fountain Square serving kebabs, but Yusif's conversation became more disjointed as he became sunk in thought. Perhaps I had been
wrong to act as I did. It was one thing for him to say in rather abstract
terms that he had lived at Apartment No. 28; quite another to be confronted with the reality that it still existed, inhabited by the enemy.

Then Yusif became transfixed by another photograph, of his garden. At the back of the apartment block in Shusha a water pipe
stretched out into a small square of green. Within a few yards, there
were tiled paths, fruit trees, and currant bushes: a tiny oasis of verdancy.
"We guessed it must belong to the apartment, when we saw where the
pipe comes from," Anoush had told me. She grew her own vegetables
there. In Baku, Yusif told me how this garden had been his father's
pride and joy. "I don't know if my father could bear to see this," he said,
intently studying my photograph of his garden at its glorious-May
greenest.

In Baku, I spent time with the exiled *Shushalilar*. Apart from Zaur,
the wounded policeman, and Yusif the lawyer, there were Kerim and
Hikmet, journalists, and Arif an artist. The fact that I had visited their
hometown, now out of reach, gave me a strange talismanic status
among them. My photographs reawakened the pain of the loss of
Shusha but also opened a door into a lost world of memories, on which
they feasted. My photos were studied and restudied and no detail was
too small. "What street is he standing on?" one of them asked of a picture of a little boy on a street corner. Or "If you look past the mosque on
the left you can see a corner of Hussein's house."

One windy June afternoon the *Shushalilar* took me to lunch in a café
on the edge of Baku overlooking a lake. Over our four hours of conversation one subject kept recurring: their friend-enemies, the Armenians.
Kerim, who edited the Shusha newspaper, had the sharpest wit and
turned a few heated moments into irony. Zaur, dressed in a navy blue
blazer and looking like a professional rugby player on an evening out,
was the most moderate. He volunteered stories about his friends and
talked without hatred about Armenians, yet he did not believe any
progress would be made by peace negotiations.

The others were more aggressive. When I said that France and Germany had made peace after generations of conflict, for example, one of
them said, "Yes, and Armenian fascism must be defeated like German
fascism." Arif, who had a ragged pepper-and-salt beard and a pinched
gloomy face, was the group's hard-liner. He wanted to fight another

war to "liberate" Shusha and was pinning his hopes on the next Azerbaijani leader after President Heidar Aliev. "After Aliev, we'll have a
democratically elected president and he'll fight to make sure there isn't
a single Armenian left in Karabakh," he declared. Arif was also the most
artistic of the group. He was a trained craftsman in stained glass, an old
Azerbaijani tradition that had all but died out. His expulsion from
Shusha had sent him on a downward spiral, and in Baku he was struggling to make a living. As the meal was ending, Arif revealed another
seam of his bitterness toward the Armenians. For eight months he had
been married to an Armenian girl, he admitted, but their marriage had
fallen apart.

I continually noticed how my new friends blamed Russia for everything that had gone wrong. In their telling of it, the 1991–1994 war had
been fought just as much with Russians as with Armenians—although,
when pressed for details, they had very little actual supporting evidence. At table, one would say: "It wasn't the Armenians who took
Shusha, it was the Russians" or "I don't blame the Armenians, the Russians are using them" or "The Russians settled Armenians in Karabakh
in the nineteenth century to drive a wedge between us and Turkey."
There is evidence of Russia's having supported the Armenians during
the war, but this went far beyond that. To hear my friends talk, it was almost as if the Armenians had not fought in the war at all. Was this a ra-
tionalization of Azerbaijan's painful defeat by blaming it on big Russia?
Or are they exempting their former Armenian neighbors from blame by
attributing the conflict to Russia? In this matter, I noticed, no one ever
had any personal enemies; it was always mysterious outside forces who
were to blame.

Shusha is a good subject for a study of the conundrum of how neighbors can stop being friends and start fighting one another. The town
was burned to the ground three times in the past century, in 1905,
1920, and 1992, once by both sides, once by the Azerbaijanis, and once
by the Armenians. Even by the fratricidal standards of the Caucasus,
this must be a record. Yet in the intervals between these infernos, it
was a thriving town and there was widespread intermarriage between
the communities.

Two bonds that tied the two communities together were commerce
and Russian power, the first quite naturally, the second more artificially.
The devastating sack of 1920 came after the Russians had left and at the

end of another period of economic disruption and civil war. On that occasion an Azerbaijani army rampaged through the Armenian upper town, burning whole streets and killing hundreds of Armenians. When the Russians returned, wearing Bolshevik uniforms, Stepanakert was made the new capital of Nagorny Karabakh. The ruins of the Armenian quarter of Shusha stood, ghostly and untouched, for more than forty years. In 1930, the poet Osip Mandelstam visited the town and was terrified by its silent and empty streets. In a poem he shuddered at Shusha's "forty thousand dead windows."

Finally, in 1961, the Communist authorities in Baku gave the order for the ruins to be demolished, even though many of the old buildings could have been restored. Sergei Shugarian, who was an Armenian Party official in Shusha at the time, told me that he refused the demand to head a special commission to oversee the demolition operation. Now an old man in Yerevan, his voice still trembled as he spoke about the razing of the old Armenian quarter. "Those ruins were still standing," Shugarian said. "All the houses could have been restored, all that was needed were the wooden sections and doors. For years I had scrambled all over those ruins. I saw wells, bones. In my heart I felt hatred toward the people who had set fire to the town."[2]

The main cause of war, it has been said, is war, and perhaps that should include the memory of war one or two generations back. In Karabakh, the sense of historical grievance was sharpest among the Armenian townsfolk, many of whom remembered the old pre-1920 Shusha. The actress Zhanna Galstian, one of the founders of the Armenian nationalist movement in Karabakh, told me that as a child the conversations she overheard at home about the prerevolutionary period made a deep impression on her. Her grandmother's family had been deported from a village named Alguli and fled to Khankendi, the village that later became Stepanakert. Alguli was then completely settled by Azerbaijanis:

> We had just one small bed and Grandmother and I slept on this bed. And every night, my grandmother's relatives from Alguli came, these beaten, deported people, who had gone on foot to Khankendi and settled here. Those old people were still alive then, and I was small, and they talked about it all in whispers. It wasn't allowed, it was the years of Stalinism. You know what a child's brain is like, it records everything like a tape recorder.[3]

In a dingy windowless office in a back street of Baku, I met another Shusha patriot. Zahid Abasov, a chubby man, is now the official in charge of culture of the Shusha administration in exile in Azerbaijan, a more or less meaningless position, which gives him plenty of time to reflect on what might have been. In the 1980s, he ran the local young Communist or Komsomol organization in Shusha. Working in a predominantly Armenian province, he worked mostly with Armenians, and remembered them all well. When I mentioned the Khachaturians, he exclaimed, "What a pleasant couple!" "How she's aged," he commented of Larisa Khachaturian as he studied a photograph of her in her garden. Of Zhanna Galstian, he remarked ironically, "Zhanna once gave me a crystal vase as a present. I left it behind in Shusha. She's very welcome to it, if she wants it."[4]

Then Abasov pulled from his desk drawer a stack of old black-and-white photographs. One of them, bleached with sunlight, showed six smiling tanned young men sitting at a café table on a terrace. The third man along, grinning broadly, in wide sunglasses, was Abasov. If the man on the right of the picture, in a white short-sleeved shirt, his watch glinting in the sun, looked familiar, that was because he is now president of Armenia. It was a younger Robert Kocharian. The group of friends from Nagorny Karabakh had gone on vacation to the Gurzuf sanatorium in Yalta in the Crimea in the summer of 1986.

Fate decreed that while Abasov lost pretty much everything and was driven into exile, several of his old Komsomol friends have become the leaders of independent Armenia. Abasov's closest colleagues were the first secretary of the Stepanakert Komsomol, Serzh Sarkisian, now minister of defense in Armenia; his deputy Robert Kocharian, the Armenian president; and Nelli Movsesian, Armenia's minister of education.

Abasov used to come down from Shusha to work every day in Stepanakert and, rather than have him head back up the mountain, his colleagues took turns inviting him home to lunch. When had he first noticed Armenian nationalist feelings, I asked. "Toward the end I started to feel something with Serzhik [Sarkisian]," Abasov responded. "He became rather quiet. But with Robik [Kocharian], right up to the end I felt nothing." Even, it seemed, during soccer matches, the moment when nationalist feelings traditionally rose to the surface: "There were workers in the Regional Committee who supported the Ararat soccer team, but Robik didn't even do that." Abasov added that he kept up with his friends even after 1988, but political conflict made their meetings fleeting and furtive, as national cause made friendship with the other community undesirable. Abasov hunched over his desk, more gloomy now. He still didn't want to believe what had happened. "How much longer can this go on?" he asked me, as if the conflict were only a terrible misunderstanding that could be set right by a few friendly conversations.

In Yerevan, the Armenian minister of defense Serzh Sarkisian laughed when I passed on the greetings of his former friend and colleague. Yes, he remembered him well, Sarkisian said, and he was a good man. Sarkisian told me that he himself spoke good Azeri and had a lot of Azerbaijani friends—but pointed out that he had also studied in Armenia, a side of him that Abasov had evidently never seen. The Armenian cause mattered more than personal friendships, Sarkisian seemed to be saying. "The problem was inherent in the Soviet system. But as for Zahid or Rohangiz, the first secretary of the Shusha Komsomol, she was a pleasant normal woman."[5]

The further I went to the top looking for answers, for the personal roots of all the killing, the more frustrated I became. No one felt that they personally were to blame. In an interview, Robert Kocharian offered only general thoughts on personal friendship and ethnic conflict. "Of course I do have [Azerbaijani] friends. The situation, the path of life meant that I did not have a wide circle of friends. But I do remember those friends that I did have, I have no complaints about them, we had normal friendly relations. But usually when ethnic conflicts begin, it always retreats into the background."[6] The president of Armenia had been one of the leaders of the Karabakh Armenian national movement "Krunk" from the very beginning, in 1988. In 1992, he had taken part in the operation to capture Shusha. Yet he talked almost as if he had played no role in starting the conflict, as if it had come out of the blue. Again the language was passive, as though simply "ethnic conflicts begin," like natural phenomena. The president had no explanation.

# 4

# 1988–1989

## An Armenian Crisis

### THE KARABAKH COMMITTEE

In May 1988, hostility between Armenians and Azerbaijanis, spreading like an infection through Nagorny Karabakh, reached the village of Tug. It was a fateful moment. Tug, in the South of Karabakh, was the only village in the region with a mixed population. Both nationalities lived side by side, with only a small brook separating them; if intercommunal harmony could not be maintained there, it could not survive anywhere. Yet on 3 May, Interior Ministry units were called out to Tug to prevent fighting between hundreds of villagers. The Moscow official Grigory Kharchenko had visited the village in February 1988, and came back seven months later. He saw how enmity had taken hold in the intervening months:

> It was an old village. All the Armenians and Azerbaijanis had intermarried. . . . They divided everything, resolved these national issues among themselves. I remember their words when they told me, "This won't affect us, this is a landslide from out of nowhere, which won't make us quarrel." Then in September I went there with a company of soldiers and billeted them in the school. By that time they had already divided the square and drawn a border. One half of the village had gone to the Armenians, the other to the Azerbaijanis. An Azerbaijani husband had even stayed in one half with three children and the Armenian wife had gone over to the other half with three children.[1]

The cause of unification with Armenia now had almost all the Karabakh Armenians in its grip. The only disagreement was over tactics. Communist Party officials still wanted to work with Moscow; the radicals were already planning more confrontational tactics. In March 1988, the radicals formed a new grouping called Krunk, the Armenians' word for the bird crane, a symbol of yearning for the "motherland," Armenia.[2] Robert Kocharian, the head of the Party organization in the Stepanakert Silk Factory, was put in charge of Krunk's "Ideological Section." Krunk was the first organization in Gorbachev's Soviet Union to use the strike as a political weapon.

Armenia in 1988 was the stage for the growth of the first big mass opposition movement in Gorbachev's Soviet Union. Its leaders, the eleven-man "Karabakh Committee," had all but eclipsed the Communist Party by the end of the year. The committee—mostly composed of Yerevan intellectuals—edged aside the two original leaders, Igor Muradian and Zori Balayan, both Karabakh Armenians and Party members, in May and formed a permanent committee with no single leader. Seven of the committee members were academics, and four were to become the leaders of post-Communist Armenia.[3]

Although the new leaders still called themselves the Karabakh Committee, their agenda was broader than just Karabakh. They were all part of a generation whose defining moment had been the nationalist demonstrations in Yerevan in 1965–1967. As a result of those protests, an open-air memorial with a constantly burning flame was opened in the city to commemorate the 1915 Genocide, and 24 April was made Armenia's Genocide Day. They were pursuing the "Armenian cause," or *Hai Dat*: the old goal of uniting Armenians across the world, from Beirut to Los Angeles, around common nationalist aims.

Two years later the committee and its successor, the Armenian National Movement, were the first non-Communist group to come to power in a Soviet republic. To a large degree, they owed this new success to the organizing skills of its two main leaders, Vazgen Manukian and Levon Ter-Petrosian. Much later, they quarreled and violently disputed the results of the 1996 presidential elections, but in the preindependence period, they made a strong tandem.

Manukian was a mathematician with an owlish look and an impulsive streak. He was also the organizer and fixer for the group, and collected the new-style Karabakh Committee in his apartment. Manukian says he deliberately picked people who were "not offended by fate," or who, in other words, were not joining the movement merely out of a personal grudge against the authorities. He argues that the Karabakh issue was a means of waking Armenians from their Soviet-era slumber and that other political goals, such as democracy, were secondary: "In Armenia the dominant issue for people was the national question. . . . The idea of democracy could not in itself create such a wave. In Armenia, that wave was created by the question of Karabakh. In the Baltic republics, it was the issue of independence."[4]

Levon Ter-Petrosian was the committee's chief strategist. His father had been a founding member of the Syrian Communist Party and had brought his family to Armenia in the 1940s. Ter-Petrosian was a scholar of ancient Semitic languages and this purely academic background shaped his political outlook. He has a quiet power to him and intense hooded eyes that seem to suck the energy from you. Throughout an interview, he took long puffs from cigarettes planted in a long holder and considered every question as if it were a text for exegesis. He batted away questions about "public opinion" almost wearily, as though they were secondary to the real stuff of politics. Ter-Petrosian conceded that the unification of Nagorny Karabakh and Armenia was the "catalyst" of the 1988 movement but not necessarily its central goal:

> The first Karabakh Committee—Igor Muradian, Zori Balayan, Silva Kaputikian, and others—thought only about Karabakh. For them, issues like democracy or the independence of Armenia simply did not exist. And this was the ground where the split occurred. When they felt that we were already becoming dangerous for the Soviet system, they left. A natural change took place. They thought that the Karabakh question had to be solved, by using the Soviet system. And we understood that this system would never solve the Karabakh issue and that the reverse was true: you had to change the system to resolve this problem.[5]

## THE POLITBURO PERPLEXED

In early 1988, the leadership in Moscow was already worried about the implications of the crisis in Armenia and Azerbaijan. "A cardinal question is being decided," Gorbachev told the Politburo on 21 March. "We are talking about the fate of our multi-national state, about the fate of our nationalities policy, laid down by Lenin."[6] It seems as if the leaders half-anticipated the slow descent into conflict—even though they failed to halt it.

On one point, a refusal to countenance any changes in Soviet borders, the Politburo was absolutely inflexible. According to Andrei Girenko, who was serving as an official in the new Sub-Department on Nationalities Policy at the time: "Proposals came from Tajikistan for them to receive several mountain pastures as a concession from Kirgizia [Kyrgyzstan]. I personally swept them aside because if you try to transfer something, then what had happened in Nagorny Karabakh would start there."[7]

On 21 March, the Politburo spent most of its session debating how to shore up the Party's crumbling authority in Armenia. The moratorium on protests, agreed upon by Gorbachev and the Armenian writers, was due to expire in five days' time, and Politburo members feared that the new opposition might simply try to take power. The discussion reveals the contradictions at the heart of Gorbachev's reform policies. On the one hand, he opposed the use of force to crush the Armenian opposition movement. On the other, he outlined a series of autocratic measures to undermine the Karabakh Committee. These included tightly controlling the local media, cutting telephone lines between Armenia and abroad, barring foreign correspondents from visiting the region, and keeping under review a possible arrest of the Karabakh Committee activists. Yet Gorbachev also spoke about the need to mobilize "healthy forces" and engage people in debate. These contrary impulses show up in the constricted language the Soviet leader used to the Politburo. In one sentence he talked about openness and isolation in the same breath, saying: "It seems that in the press we need to speak more openly and to isolate [the Karabakh Committee], but do it in such a way so as not to make heroes out of them."

The Moscow leaders' efforts to maintain control were severely hampered by the fact that their principal agents on the ground, the Communist leaders of Armenia and Azerbaijan, were no longer fully obedient, but were, instead, tacking between the demands of Moscow and their own societies. At the 29 February Politburo session, Gorbachev complained: "We need information and it's hard to obtain it—both sides are hiding it. Everyone is involved. Comrades from the Central Committee of the Communist Party in Azerbaijan and the Communist Party in Armenia, do nothing, they are involved—both this comrade and that one."[8]

Gorbachev decided to sack the two republican Party leaders, Kamran Bagirov and Karen Demirchian, and to draft two replacements, Abdurahman Vezirov and Suren Harutiunian, who were both working outside the region and thought to be untainted by local clan politics. Vezirov was the Soviet ambassador to Pakistan; Harutiunian worked for the Party apparatus in Moscow. Two Politburo members were delegated to go to Baku and Yerevan to introduce the new first secretaries at special Party meetings. Here Gorbachev made a serious mistake. He sent his liberal right-hand man, Alexander Yakovlev, to Armenia, and the leading Politburo conservative, Yegor Ligachev, to Azerbaijan. As a result, Yakovlev, a firm believer in the need for more reform, showed sympathy for the Armenians' grievances and even spoke at a public rally in Yerevan. In Baku, Ligachev stuck firmly to the message, gratefully received by the Azerbaijanis, that Nagorny Karabakh would never be allowed to leave Azerbaijan.

Yakovlev now says that he had persuaded the Armenian Communist Party to suspend its call for the unification of Nagorny Karabakh and Armenia in return for a statement in Baku renouncing its claim on Karabakh. He says that he telephoned Gorbachev, who promised to call Ligachev in Baku with this proposal:

> But in the night I was woken by a telephone call that said "You deceived us, you are a deceiver, we don't believe you." It was the [Armenian] members of the meeting I had attended. What did they mean? Ligachev had just said that Karabakh would always be inside Azerbaijan and we would never take another position. After that, I refused to have anything to do with the Karabakh issue.[9]

The Karabakh issue had opened cracks in the Politburo consensus and, says the nationalities specialist Vyacheslav Mikhailov, the Party elites in both republics took advantage of this:

> As there wasn't a single position in the Politburo on this matter, of course the [republican] elites felt that you had just to press the Politburo a bit harder, put pressure on a certain Politburo member and a decision would be taken at the highest level. And this is what happened. It stemmed from a certain ambiguity in the Politburo's position, which did not come out in documents—on paper everyone was very correct —but in personal contacts, personal relations, which inspired hope. And it was true of every member of the Politburo. Ligachev flies to Baku and says that territorial integrity is the highest principle and

there is no problem; Alexander Yakovlev lets it be known to applause that the Armenians have the correct position on this issue.[10]

According to Gorbachev's aide Georgy Shakhnazarov, rows began to break out in the Politburo:

> The obvious loss of control caused ever-greater alarm in our ruling elite. This broke to the surface ever more frequently in angry comments during discussion of the Karabakh problem, and this issue was touched upon at almost every Politburo session. At one of these sessions, on 4 July, the *leitmotif* of the interventions by Ligachev, Vorotnikov, Solomentsev, and other members of the leadership was "That's enough concessions, we need to impose order!" No one demanded the use of armed force, however; yet these were intelligent people and they were certainly aware that you cannot solve anything by words alone. The paralysis of will, which now people ascribe to Gorbachev alone, was in reality also an attribute of his colleagues.[11]

## A WAR OF LAWS

In May 1988, perhaps the last serious effort at compromise between Armenia and Azerbaijan failed. The proposal was to leave Nagorny Karabakh within Azerbaijan but upgrade its status to that of Autonomous Republic. Doing so would have given the province new privileges, such as its own local parliament, constitution, and government. Genrikh Pogosian, the local Armenian leader in Karabakh, was apparently on the verge of accepting the plan. "He had a constitution of an Autonomous Republic in his pocket, with very wide powers, practically equal to a Union Republic, and which included the building of the Lachin road, which would have removed all the problems, including the fear of Azerbaijanification," says Vyacheslav Mikhailov. However, at the last moment Pogosian bowed to his own local radical constituency and decided to reject the plan.

The installation of new leaders in Armenia and Azerbaijan did nothing to halt the crisis. The new Armenian leader Suren Harutiunian quickly decided to run before the prevailing nationalist wind. A week after he took office, on 28 May 1988, Harutiunian allowed the outlawed flag of the First Armenian Republic, the red-blue-and-orange tricolor, to be unfurled for the first time in almost seventy years in Yerevan. On 15 June, the local parliament, the Supreme Soviet of Armenia, adopted a resolution in which it formally gave its approval to the idea of Nagorny Karabakh's joining Armenia. The resolution was the opening shot in what came to be called "the war of laws." Regional Party organs, ditching the old Soviet principle of "democratic centralism," passed legislation that openly antagonized one another. On 17 June, the Azerbaijani Supreme Soviet passed a counterresolution, reaffirming that Nagorny Karabakh was part of Azerbaijan. Then on 12 July, the Regional Soviet in Stepanakert passed an even more implacable resolution than it had in February: it voted to secede unilaterally from Azerbaijan and rename Nagorny Karabakh "the Artsakh Armenian Autonomous Region."

Armenia, formerly one of the most loyal of republics, turned into the leading rebel in the Soviet Union. The Politburo hard-liner Anatoly Lukyanov reportedly threatened the Karabakh Committee, telling its members, "You don't frighten me with your demonstrations, I saw Czechoslovakia [in 1968]."[12] On 5 July, a contingent of troops was sent in to remove demonstrators by force from Yerevan's Zvartnots Airport. Shots were fired and truncheons were wielded, and one student protestor died. A new wave of demonstrations with a more markedly anti-Soviet flavor followed.

The 18 July session of the full Soviet parliament, the USSR Supreme Soviet, in Moscow was invited to give a definitive verdict on the dispute. The atmosphere was stormy, as an often-angry Gorbachev clashed with several of the Armenian delegates. The session reconfirmed that Nagorny Karabakh was staying within Azerbaijan. In his closing remarks, Gorbachev declared: "I will tell you that today's Presidium meeting saw more self-criticism on the part of the Azerbaijanis and less on the part of Armenia's representatives." He went on to accuse the Armenians of an "unacceptable" campaign that undermined *perestroika*.[13] But the general secretary also took a step that was unpopular in Azerbaijan, deciding to appoint a "special representative" for Nagorny Karabakh, who would have the power to overrule the Party leaders in Baku.

## RESISTANCE AND DEPORTATIONS

The implacable resolution by the Supreme Soviet in July 1988 forced a change of tactics on the Armenian opposition. The Karabakh Committee made plans for a longer-term struggle and began to form a broad-based organization, which it named the Armenian National Movement.[14] Its program called for wholesale reform of Armenia but stopped short of advocating independence. In response, the Moscow leadership sent Interior Ministry troops to Yerevan and imposed a curfew.

Autumn of 1988 saw the Armenians turn against their Azerbaijani minority and expel them from Armenia. There is a misconception that the Azerbaijani population of Armenia did not suffer in the dispute. Many of them did leave peacefully, and there was little or no intercommunal violence in Yerevan, but Yerevan had only a tiny Azerbaijani population and it was not hard for the security forces there to keep order. In rural areas, there was widespread violence. Armenian gangs raided Azerbaijani villages; many of their residents were beaten, shot, had their homes burned, or were forced to flee on foot. By the end of the year, the Armenian countryside had dozens of deserted villages that had been depopulated of most of Armenia's more than 200,000 Azerbaijanis and Muslim Kurds.[15]

By 1989, all of the remaining Azerbaijanis of Armenia were being deported, although most of the worst violence had ended. A system of exchanges was set up, such that many resident Azerbaijanis were able to trade their houses for those of Armenians fleeing Azerbaijan. Seiran Stepanian, the former deputy head of the town administration in the Armenian resort town of Jermuk, described how he made contact with his Communist Party counterparts across the border in Azerbaijan. In the latter half of 1989, they arranged for one thousand Azerbaijanis to leave Jermuk by bus and train. In return, seven hundred Armenians from Mingechaur and Baku were housed in Jermuk's hotels and sanatoria.[16] These ethnically motivated exchanges were pursued to almost ridiculous levels until both Armenia and Azerbaijan had been almost entirely purged of the other ethnic group. According to one story, in 1989 a group of patients from each of two psychiatric hospitals were exchanged at the Armenia-Azerbaijan border. It took hours to persuade the patients, who were showing more political sanity than their rulers, to leave their nurses and cross the border.[17]

Armenia in 1988 had been far more chaotic and violent, and dozens of Azerbaijanis had died in a savage few weeks at the end of November and the beginning of December. In painstaking research carried out over two years with Azerbaijani refugees, Arif Yunusov compiled lists of the dead and injured. The overwhelming majority of the casualties were from 1988. Yunusov concluded that 127 Azerbaijanis had been murdered by Armenians in this time, generally beaten, burned, or killed. In the most horrific incident—which has still to be fully researched—twelve Azerbaijanis from the village of Vartan in northeastern Armenia were burned to death in November 1988. Yunusov's total Azerbaijani death toll is 216; among that number he includes those who froze to death as they walked into Azerbaijan, committed suicide, died subsequently in Azerbaijani hospitals, or were still missing three years later.

The Soviet interior minister Vadim Bakatin traveled to both Armenia and Azerbaijan at the end of 1988 to try to halt the deportations. He recounts in his memoirs how he met frightened Azerbaijanis outside the town of Spitak in Armenia and equally frightened Armenians across the border in the Azerbaijani town of Kirovabad. All of them asked for protection he was unable to provide. Bakatin charged the local Interior Ministry officials in both republics to make sure the vulnerable minorities came to no harm, but he felt from the policemen's mechanical responses that he could not rely on them: "The local leadership disputed all [the allegations], promised to sort things out, but I no longer believed that they would do anything. And there were few people here that I as a minister could depend on. You can't sack everybody."[18]

Yunusov's research shows that many Armenian Party officials and Karabakh Committee supporters were actively involved in deporting Azerbaijanis. On 27 November 1988, for example, a KGB official, a police chief, and a local Party boss went to two villages in the Spitak region in the North of Armenia called Saral and Gurasly and told the Azerbaijani population to get out within two weeks. When the Azerbaijanis refused to go, armed gangs attacked the villages. The officials came back and repeated their menacing demands. Carrying only a few possessions, the villagers left on buses, but the column of buses was fired on, resulting in three deaths.[19]

It was a very black irony indeed that the violent expulsion of these Azerbaijanis from the area around Spitak actually saved them from comprehensive destruction in the Armenian earthquake only a few days later. The Azerbaijani death toll from the earthquake on 7 December was thirty-three. Had most of them not been deported over the preceding weeks, their losses would have been much greater.[20]

## THE ARMENIAN EARTHQUAKE

The earthquake struck at 11:41 A.M. on 7 December 1988 near the town of Spitak. Poorly built Soviet apartment buildings crumpled, trapping thousands. Spitak was almost leveled and nearby Leninakan (now Gyumri) suffered appalling damage. The earthquake is estimated to have destroyed 1,500 villages and 35,000 private dwellings. The official death toll for these few seconds of catastrophe was 24,817, almost certainly more than died in the six years of the Nagorny Karabakh conflict.[21]

The earthquake brought out the best and worst in the people of the region. Thousands of Armenians helped dig through the rubble with their hands looking for survivors and came to the aid of the earthquake victims—but there were also allegations later of looting and that much of the reconstruction money was stolen. In Azerbaijan, thousands of people forgot their political differences and scrambled to send aid to the victims. And there were also reports of some gleeful Azerbaijanis setting off fireworks to celebrate the "punishment" of Armenia.[22]

The catastrophe did not, as many had hoped, curtail the Armenian-Azerbaijani dispute. The Moscow journalist Viktor Loshak was sent to the earthquake zone and remembers a terrible state of "psychosis" among the survivors in which the natural disaster and nationalist feeling were intertwined.

> What did these people speak about to me, a journalist, and to each other? Not about death, not about their loved ones, not about forecasts for a new earthquake. They spoke about how the Azerbaijanis had sent them a consignment of medicine—they had sent a few wagons of medicines because they were very near and the Central Committee had helped them to do so—the Azerbaijanis had sent them medicine and they believed of course that the Azerbaijanis wanted to poison them. It was already on the level of an absolute psychosis.[23]

The disaster altered the political as well as the physical landscape of Armenia. For the first time, the Soviet government allowed the Armenian Diaspora to get directly involved in Soviet Armenia as they were providing aid. The members of the Karabakh Committee set up an emergency relief headquarters in the Union of Writers building in Yerevan. "Immediately after the earthquake, imperceptibly to ourselves, we discovered that we were in charge of the people and even in charge of the rescue work, aid to the victims and so on," recalls Rafael Gazarian. "It was unexpected. The levers of power went from the government to us."[24]

On 7 December, Mikhail Gorbachev was at the United Nations in New York. He hurried back to Moscow and then flew down to Armenia on what was his only trip to the Caucasus during his entire tenure as Soviet leader, and it turned into a public relations disaster. Gorbachev visited the earthquake zone and then drove back into Yerevan. As was his custom, he got out at one of the city squares and talked to a crowd of people. The chairman of the Armenian Supreme Soviet, Grant Voskanian, was with him and remembers what happened. "[Gorbachev] said, 'We won't leave you alone in your troubles, we will help you.' And someone shouted out, 'And Karabakh?' Well, Gorbachev was furious and said, 'Listen, I thought that you would not raise this Karabakh question again at such an hour of national calamity. I think that many people won't understand that.'"

Shakhnazarov, Gorbachev's Armenian aide, was also with him and observed the reaction of the crowd to this incident:

> Mikhail Sergeyevich [Gorbachev] was not so much making the bearded man see reason as appealing to the people around him. And some women really did react and threw reproaches at the young man in Armenian. But the rest of them kept silent. Standing next to them, I looked in their faces and saw that the mention of Karabakh did not upset them. Obviously, the thought of it had been driven into the head of each of them like a nail; it did not give them rest and even the earthquake could not distract them from it.[25]

Before he returned to Moscow, Gorbachev gave an interview to Armenian television in which he said that Karabakh issue was being exploited by "unscrupulous people, demagogues, adventurers, corrupt people, black shirts" who were "hungry for power."[26] This was his signal for the arrest of the Karabakh Committee. Troops surrounded the Union of Writers building and detained nine of the committee members. The two others were arrested a few days later. The eleven were sent to prisons in Moscow for pretrial investigations but were released six months later before going to trial.[27]

## RUSSIAN REACTIONS

Another celebrated visitor to Armenia after the earthquake was Russia's most famous dissident and voice of conscience, Andrei Sakharov. He was completing a tour of Azerbaijan, Nagorny Karabakh, and Armenia with his wife, Yelena Bonner. In Armenia, they visited the earthquake zone and made contact with opposition figures.

Sakharov's stand on the Karabakh issue was controversial. Early on, he took a straightforwardly pro-Armenian stand, declaring that Stalin had unjustly awarded Nagorny Karabakh to Azerbaijan in 1921 and calling the issue "a touchstone for perestroika and its capacity to overcome resistance and the weight of the past." Sakharov's pro-Armenian stance was shaped by his Armenian wife. Yelena Bonner's parents—whose surname was Alikhanian—were Armenians from Shusha who had been driven from the town in 1920. This family memory obviously made a deep impression, yet as Sakharov and Bonner heard both sides of the issue, they amended their positions somewhat. As a solution, Sakharov had proposed that there be a referendum in which each village in the province would be allowed to decide to join Armenia or Azerbaijan. Touring Nagorny Karabakh and seeing for himself its complex geography, he realized the idea was unworkable. Bonner now admits that the plan "was not an ideal solution" but defends it as at least an example of creative thinking when the debate on Karabakh was full only of polemic. "We wanted to move to conversation from fight and the road to war."[28]

The early stance taken by Sakharov reflected a general pro-Armenian attitude among the Russian intelligentsia. Armenian and Russian intellectuals had had a traditionally close relationship, and after the Sumgait pogroms most of the Moscow intellectual elite supported the Armenian cause without reserve. Today, the Russian journalist Viktor Loshak agrees that this pro-Armenian consensus was harmful:

> It seemed to us that the return of Karabakh to Armenia was part of the process of democratization of the Soviet Union. It seemed to us simply that justice was being restored. We were right in our thoughts. But we were wrong from the point of view that we completely ignored the feelings of the other side. We did not think what would be the reaction of those who had lived with the fact that Nagorny Karabakh was part of their country.

The emerging Azerbaijani opposition resented this attitude. In February 1989, the Azerbaijani scholar and opposition activist Zardusht Alizade attended a meeting of the "Moscow Tribune," a dissidents' forum, in the House of Scholars in Moscow. Sakharov was the presiding genius. The participants voted to call for the release of the Armenian Karabakh Committee, detained two months before. Alizade says that he told the meeting that the Karabakh Committee had caused suffering for Azerbaijanis. According to Alizade's account, one former dissident angrily told him that he had no right to make such a statement. Alizade quoted Dostoyevsky to the effect that no cause was worth the single tear of a child. His opponent countered, "What right do you Azerbaijanis have, after Sumgait to talk about the tear of a child?" and Alizade replied, "Do you really think that the whole people carried out the Sumgait pogroms?"[29]

## A SPECIAL REPRESENTATIVE

In July 1988, with the crisis unabated, Gorbachev decided that he had no choice but to institute direct administrative control of Nagorny Karabakh by Moscow. On 24 July, he invited industrialist Arkady Volsky, who had visited the province three months before, to the Kremlin. Within a few minutes, Volsky found himself agreeing to be the Politburo's representative in Karabakh for "six months." In the event, he was to stay for almost eighteen months.[30]

Volsky's official title was "Representative of the Central Committee and the Supreme Soviet," but in fact he became a kind of governor-general, responsible, in his own words, for "everything from inseminating cows to military issues." He was, it is generally recognized, a good candidate for the job. A man of great personal charisma, he had—at least at first—the respect of both sides and was able to dampen tensions. He displayed the same qualities again as a Russian mediator in Chechnya in 1995, when he struck a good working relationship with the Chechen rebel delegation.

Volsky's main strategy was socioeconomic. In the first half of 1988, strikes had brought Nagorny Karabakh's factories to a halt and were beginning to send ripples down the rigidly connected links of the Soviet command economy. As Boris Nefyodov, Volsky's chief aide, put it, "A strike in the condenser factory [in Stepanakert] caused problems in 65 television and radio factories of the Soviet Union." For their part, the Karabakh Armenians complained that they were getting no profit from delivering their raw materials, such as raw silk and grape juice, to Azerbaijan. Volsky's proposed solution was to look for new economic partners for the Karabakh factories in Russia—a move that of course proved unpopular in Azerbaijan. Despite Volsky's efforts, the economic battle was eventually lost. In November 1989, Moscow's representative estimated that the Karabakh dispute had cost the Soviet economy one billion rubles, far in excess of the four hundred million rubles of investment Gorbachev had pledged the year before.[31]

On a daily basis, Volsky and his team became firefighters, trying to defuse quarrels between the two communities. The Karabakh-born Russian journalist Vadim Byrkin worked as Volsky's press secretary:

> Disputes began between Armenian and Azerbaijanis on an everyday level. "Who will use the well?" The Azerbaijanis would not allow the Armenians to, as happened in the village of Kerkijahan, on the edge of Stepanakert, up in the hills. Or "Who can go along this road and who can't?" These things became more acute. Once Volsky sent me [to Kerkijahan] to investigate. . . . I went with a camera to see whether people could use [the well] or not. The Azerbaijanis attacked me, took away the camera and exposed the film.[32]

Throughout 1988 and 1989, the two communities of Nagorny Karabakh began to use whatever weapons they could against each other. The Armenians, three-quarters of the population, exploited their greater force of numbers against the Azerbaijanis. Armenian youths stoned buses and trucks taking goods to the Azerbaijani town of Shusha, high in the hills of Karabakh. Azerbaijani workers were sacked from their jobs in Stepanakert's factories. The Armenian villagers of Vank even blocked Azerbaijani shepherds trying to bring half a million sheep down from their summer pastures, causing Volsky to protest crossly, "Sheep have no national ambitions."

Azerbaijan's main weapon was economic pressure against an enclave entirely inside its territory. The Azerbaijanis were able to block the supply of goods to Karabakh by road and rail. Oleg Yesayan, an Armenian who served as head of Volsky's Socioeconomic Department, complained that Azerbaijanis would unload railway cars before they reached Stepanakert and take the goods themselves. The Azerbaijanis also had full control over Karabakh's tiny airport outside the village of Khojali.[33] When the war ended five years later in 1994, this battle of demography against geography had reached its ultimate conclusion: the Armenians had used their greater numbers to drive out all the Karabakh Azerbaijanis; the Azerbaijanis had used their economic superiority to put Karabakh in an economic stranglehold.

On 18 September 1988, violence erupted on a scale hitherto unseen. A crowd of Azerbaijanis near the village of Khojali attacked a convoy of Soviet soldiers and Armenian civilians bringing supplies to Stepanakert. Several hundred Armenians, armed with axes and hunting rifles, set out for the village to wreak revenge. Interior Ministry soldiers prevented most of the Armenians from getting through, but some entered Khojali and fought a pitched battle with Azerbaijani villagers. At least two dozen people were hurt, and two of the soldiers later died. The violence heralded disaster for the minority communities of Karabakh's two main towns, as all the Armenians were driven from Shusha and the Azerbaijanis were expelled from Stepanakert.[34]

Volsky was away, and two of his team, Grigory Kharchenko and Boris Nefyodov, had been left in charge. Kharchenko spoke by telephone to Gorbachev and was struck by how out of touch the general secretary was:

> Volsky was on leave. Boris Nefyodov and I were there on our own. Gorbachev was in Krasnoyarsk [in Siberia] and he rang me from Krasnoyarsk. Fires had broken out, people were burning buildings, there was shooting and people were wounded. He rang and said, "You call in Pogosian, members of the Party Committee! Tell them that if they don't stop this, we will expel them from the Party!" I said, "Mikhail Sergeyevich, they've all already trampled on their Party cards. The members of the committee are all the organizers of these demonstrations! What are you talking about? . . . What Party methods are you talking about? They've been collecting passports in sacks and rejecting their Soviet citizenship."

Volsky hurried back to Karabakh. He remembers being called out to a burning house in Stepanakert and having to help forty Azerbaijani children climb out of a smoldering basement. He decided they needed to impose martial law but says that Gorbachev was reluctant to agree to it:

It was 2:00 A.M. They had woken [Gorbachev] up. At first the guards had not wanted to wake him up. I then got into a rage—he remembers this—and at 9:00 A.M. the next morning I went on television, without any agreement with Moscow. I omitted the word "military" and said we are introducing [a] "special regime" for a time. For a time the work of parties and movements was to be postponed, constitutional guarantees would be postponed. . . . I say to you frankly it was the only correct step.

## 1989: A DESCENT INTO VIOLENCE

The year 1989 saw an upsurge of protest throughout the rest of the Soviet Union. As other serious nationality disputes broke out in Georgia, the Baltic republics, and Central Asia, the continuing crisis in Nagorny Karabakh slipped down the agenda in Moscow. At the same time, by far the most serious political challenge began to emerge to Gorbachev's rule from inside Russia. The Soviet Union's first freely elected parliament, the Congress of People's Deputies, which met in the spring of 1989, became a focus for all the new opposition movements. Zori Balayan was one of the deputies elected to the Congress from Nagorny Karabakh and used his parliamentary status to organize more concerted opposition.

In January 1989, Moscow gave Arkady Volsky's "special regime" a more permanent status. Volsky was made head of an eight-member "Committee of Special Administration for Nagorny Karabakh," which also contained four other Russians, two Armenians, and one Azerbaijani. Local Party organs were disbanded, and political rallies and gatherings were forbidden. The new Special Committee had four thousand Interior Ministry troops at its disposal to try to keep order.

Even this proved insufficient as the Karabakh Armenians stepped up their insubordination. In July, the Armenians of the Shaumian region of Azerbaijan, north of Nagorny Karabakh (geographically in the plains of lower Karabakh), entered the struggle. The local Party committees of Shaumian region resolved unilaterally that they were joining Nagorny Karabakh, a decision that, of course, was rejected in Azerbaijan. On 16 August, meeting in the theater in Stepanakert, the Karabakh Armenians elected a seventy-nine-member National Council, which declared that it was now in charge of Karabakh and that it would cooperate with Volsky's committee only on terms of its own choosing.

Nagorny Karabakh was breaking up. There were now four sources of power in the region: Volsky's Special Committee and two Armenian and one Azerbaijani groupings. Until this point, casualty figures had been low, with perhaps as few as a dozen deaths in the disputed province overall. As Karabakhis got hold of small arms to replace their hunting rifles and crossbows, casualties began to increase steadily. "The second half of 1989 began with the handing out of weapons," said Volsky. "That is really a fact." Bridges were blown up, roads were blockaded, and the first hostages were taken. A group of Azerbaijanis even took the local commander of Interior Ministry troops, Yury Shatalin, hostage in Shusha, and Volsky had to send an armored car to free him. A new escalation began in the autumn of 1989, when the Azerbaijani opposition declared a railway blockade on Karabakh and tried to stop deliveries of fuel and food to the Armenians.

In a document from the archives dated 4 September 1989, the Politburo approved new draconian security measures recommended by two of its members. The two urged that "nationalist and extremist armed groups" should be "exposed" and "disarmed" and warned of the possibility of "massed armed clashes" in Karabakh. They proposed that army units replace Interior Ministry troops. The Politburo resolved, among other things, to confiscate automatic and sniper weapons from police officers; to impose guards on warehouses holding explosive materials, public buildings, and airports; and to order the Defense Ministry to take over heavy weapons in the territory of Azerbaijan and Armenia.[35]

Yet nothing seems to have changed on the ground. The political climate was shifting, and Volsky was falling out of favor in Moscow. In the fall of 1989, the Soviet leadership had begun to switch the focus of anxieties from Armenia to Azerbaijan. Support for the Azerbaijani Popular Front was growing, and both the opposition and the Party leadership demanded that Volsky's committee be disbanded and Karabakh returned to direct rule by Baku. On 28 November, the Supreme Soviet in Moscow formally dissolved the Special Committee and decreed that it would be replaced by a new "Organizational Committee," run from Baku. For a while everything remained the same, and Volsky and his committee stayed on in Karabakh, exercising the same powers. He and his team left Karabakh only after the "Black January" events in Baku.

The threat to return to direct rule from Baku, however, triggered the most extreme response yet from the Armenians who now proclaimed the full unification of Nagorny Karabakh and Armenia. On 1 December, the Armenian Supreme Soviet and the Karabakhi National Council passed a joint resolution whose third point states simply: "The Supreme Soviet of the Armenian SSR and the National Council of Nagorny Karabakh announce the reunification of the Armenian SSR and Nagorny Karabakh. The population of Nagorny Karabakh is granted rights of citizenship of the Armenian SSR."

Earlier in the year, in May 1989, the members of the Karabakh Committee had been released from prison after the Moscow authorities had decided they could not pin charges on them. When they returned to Yerevan, they were heroes or, in Ashot Manucharian's words, "something in between Saint Francis of Assisi and the Pope."[36] They now resumed their opposition activities with vastly increased authority.

In public, the newly released opposition leaders still rejected the idea of Armenia's leaving the Soviet Union. In July 1989, Levon Ter-Petrosian told the French newspaper *Le Figaro*: "We are talking about building a federation of the peoples of the USSR and achieving the democratization of the country."[37] Yet discussion of independence was no longer a taboo, and Armenians were reminded that they had briefly been a separate state, two generations before, in the years 1918–1920. Ter-Petrosian says that he seriously began to ponder the idea that summer.

> I was a skeptic while all this was happening in the Baltic republics, in Armenia, in Ukraine, Moldova; I said that we could not yet think about independence. Until the same thing began in Russia, there wouldn't be any independence. I myself came to the conclusion that the Soviet Union was ending and we would achieve independence only after the miners' strikes in Russia in the summer of 1989, when those million-strong strikes took place and were immediately politicized by Sakharov and others. . . . That was something mighty. After that I said, "That's it, we have to fight for independence." Because it would have been very dangerous if the Soviet Union had collapsed and we had not been ready.[38]

# 5

# Yerevan

*Mysteries of the East*

IN 1905, A journalist named Luigi Villari was captivated by a small city in the Caucasus with twenty-eight thousand inhabitants and an abundance of Eastern charm:

[T]he vaulted passages themselves, redolent of all the mysteries of the East, with their dark curtained shops, the crowds of Tartars clad in long blue tunics, and the green turbans of the *mullahs* passing up and down, are very attractive. In one small open room I came upon a teacher imparting religious instruction to about a dozen little boys; he was droning out his lesson in a sing-song, monotonous voice, swaying to and fro. In another den a barber was shaving a victim to his last hair. At every turn were coffee and tea stalls, but those strange and delicious sweetmeats of the East which I had tasted at Constantinople and Sarajevo were not to be found. In queer galleries and tiny courts huge ungainly camels were reposing. Then through the foul-smelling bazar you come out suddenly on the great mosque called the Gok Djami.[1]

The city was Yerevan. At the time it had a mixed Armenian and Muslim population, a Russian governor, and a thoroughly Middle Eastern atmosphere. For several centuries, Yerevan had been an outpost of the Persian empire, and when Villari visited it had been under Russian administration for less then eighty years. The city became the Armenians' capital almost by default. "Many Armenians regard Van as their capital city," wrote another traveler, William Eleroy Curtis, who came to Yerevan five years after Villari, in 1910.[2] He was referring to the city in Turkish Armenia to the south, but he might have added the Georgian capital Tiflis to the north, which had a large and wealthy Armenian population.

With its straight roads and square buildings in deep red granite and tufa, modern Yerevan feels like a Soviet town. It has turned into a fully Armenian city, but its more-than-human scale and tidiness seem at odds with the quirkier side of the Armenian character. Only in summer, when people invade its parks to sit in cafés, drink coffee, and hold animated conversation, is the city more domesticated. All the wide avenues lead to the circular neoclassical Opera House. It was here in 1988 in Theater Square, dotted with the statues of composers, that the Armenians turned the monumental scale of the city to their advantage, using the square as the stage for their million-strong rallies—and appropriately the Armenian word for *glasnost*, *hraparakainutiun*, comes from the word for "square," *hraparak*. Since 1988, however, Yerevan has been hit by an energy crisis, war, and the drain of emigration. Its residents complain that a once lively city has become dull and spiritless.

One day I stepped out of the mayhem of Yerevan's Mashtots Avenue into a quiet courtyard to seek out a remnant of old Yerevan, the building Villari called "the great mosque called the Gok Djami." It was still opposite the main bazaar, now a closed hangar in front of which country folk were sitting and selling flat discs of unleavened bread, tomatoes, and sheaves of tarragon. In the courtyard, at the far end of a serene rectangular pool overhung with mulberry trees, glimmered a sheet of tiles: the outer wall of the eighteenth-century mosque.

The architect Grigor Nalbandian led me on a tour of the site. Apart from a couple of moustachioed Iranian workers chipping away with chisels at blocks of stone, we were the only people around. Nalbandian has been supervising the restoration of the mosque complex in a joint venture of Armenia and Iran, two countries that, despite religious differences, are political allies. The mosque walls had been restored with Armenian red brick and faced with Persian turquoise tiles. We took off our shoes to go into the echoing interior, whose floor had just been relaid with Isfahan marble. It was entirely empty; the only regular worshippers here are the dozen or so diplomats from the Iranian Embassy. This strange quiet oasis in the middle of Yerevan is all that remains of the city's Persian period.

Yerevan has ancient archaeological remains at the old city of Erebuni, suggesting that Armenians have lived there for centuries. But between the sixteenth and nineteenth centuries Armenian cultural and religious life was centered on Echmiadzin, the seat of the head of the church, the *Catholicos*, ten miles to the west. Yerevan, the capital of a khanate, was basically a Muslim city that contained no large churches but had six mosques. When the Russians conquered Eastern Armenia in 1827, there were only twenty-five thousand Armenians living in the Yerevan region, outnumbered by a much larger Muslim population.[3] The nineteenth-century city acquired a more Armenian character as the Russians settled thousands of new Armenian immigrants from Turkey and Persia there, but even in the 1870s, Yerevan had only around twelve thousand inhabitants. It was far smaller than Shusha, and Armenian migrant workers were far more likely to seek their fortunes in Baku.[4]

What made Yerevan the city that it now is, was another, far bigger wave of migrants. In 1915–1918, perhaps a quarter of the Armenian population of Turkish Anatolia fled north to eastern Armenia, escaping the massacres and deportations by Turks and Kurds. Perhaps one million Armenians died in the massacres, which are incomparably the greatest tragedy of Armenian history. Armenians call them the *mets eghern*, the "great slaughter"; in English, they are customarily called the Armenian Genocide.[5] From 1918 to 1920, Yerevan was the capital of the briefly independent first republic of Armenia and the main refuge for hundreds of thousands Armenians fleeing Anatolia. In 1920, it became the capital of Soviet Armenia. When the writer Arthur Koestler visited Yerevan in 1932, as a Jew, he was reminded of the new Jewish settlements in Palestine:

> The enthusiasm, the muddle, the errors and bad taste which accompanied the fever of construction were all touching and familiar reminders. Here, too, drab, cheap, ugly utilitarian buildings were superseding the charming, colourful and filthy Orient. Erivan, too, was an informal and chaotic pioneer-town, the unfinished streets, between half-finished buildings, a labyrinth of pipes and cables. There were as yet so few telephones that calls were made by asking the exchange for the name, and not the number of the subscriber. Familiar, above all, was the Babel of languages, for a sizeable part of the population were refugees and immigrants from Turkey, Armenia, Europe and America. It often happened that, when I asked my way from a passer-by in halting Russian, the answer was given in fluent German or French. The town had a lively and well-informed intelligentsia whose political orientation, in contrast to Tiflis, was very friendly towards Russia and the Soviet regime.[6]

Modern Armenia grew in the shadow of the great catastrophe of 1915. To make a simplification, if twentieth-century Azerbaijan's most urgent task was to construct a "nation," Armenia had a quite different challenge: it had an identifiable nation that was scattered across the world but no state. The Soviet Republic of Armenia was built to fit this role and become a new Armenian homeland. With its Opera House, National Gallery, museum of ancient manuscripts known as the Matenadaran, Yerevan thus became a repository of Armenian myths and hopes. Koestler called it "a kind of Tel Aviv, where the survivors of another martyred nation gathered to construct a new home."[7]

On the early afternoon of 24 April 2000, I joined the crowds walking up to the Genocide Memorial of Tsitsernakaberd on the western side of Yerevan. We moved in a slow, thirty-people-wide torrent up the broad paved path, as the anguished brass-laded music of the composer Komitas played over loudspeakers. Since 1967, Armenians have marked Genocide Day on the anniversary of the day in 1915 when Armenian intellectuals were arrested and then murdered in Istanbul.

It was a family occasion. The crowds climbing the hill were unsolemn, chatting and taking photographs. They carried spikes of tulip and florid bunches of lilac, their tips pointing downward. There was no sign of the dignitaries who had laid their wreaths earlier in the day. Our progress up the hill was slow, yet my friends were struck only by how modest the turnout was. In the late 1980s and early 1990s, literally the whole of the city had taken part in this ceremony. "Ten years ago this was a big thing for all of us," said Tigran. "You moved ten yards or so and then stopped and waited. And then moved on. It took four or five hours"

We reached the top of the hill. On our left was a long gray wall engraved with the names of the cities whose Armenian communities had been wiped out: Kars, Erzerum, Trebizond, Van, and so on. Ahead stood the memorial: twelve vast shields of gray basalt, each standing for a *vilayat*, or Turkish province, lean inward toward a central bowl, sunk in the ground, inside of which a fire was burning. We laid our flowers on a waist-high bank of red and white petals that was rising from the rim of the bowl. Then we came out on to another broad flight of steps that descended into the city. Before us, the great white cone of Mount Ararat was spread over the entire horizon, and it seemed as though the designers of the memorial had deliberately planned this view and this descent. The sight of Ararat has come to be another symbol of loss for Armenians, for it now lies out of bounds in Turkey.

Something was different in the air in Yerevan for the rest of Genocide Day, but it took a while for me to realize that it was the background musical hum of the city. For this day only the radio stations, turned up full blast in every taxi and café, had forgone their diet of tinny Russian pop music and were playing Armenian tunes. The wail of the *duduk*, the Armenian pipe, sounded out. Armenia shed its Soviet identity for a day and assumed a much more alluring Middle Eastern garb.

The lack of big official ceremonies or public meetings on 24 April made the commemorations more dignified, but this perhaps also reflected the priority the modern population of Armenia put on the Genocide. So many other issues—from Karabakh to economic survival—had intervened in people's lives that it seemed that the events of 1915 had ceased to be a collective defining principle for modern Armenians. My friend Tigran offered another thought: Victory over Azerbaijan, he said, had altered the previous fixed self-image of Armenians as "the noble victim." This time, after all, they had won, and others had lost. How can you remain "the weeping nation" when you have inflicted a defeat on your neighbor?

Yet for the wider Armenian world, the 1915 Genocide still largely defines what it means to be Armenian. This is not so surprising, given that the Armenian Diaspora, especially in the United States and France, comprises mainly the descendants of people who fled Eastern Anatolia after 1915. Since the 1950s, Diaspora groups have focused huge energies and spent millions of dollars trying to make Turkey admit that it committed genocide against the Armenians and other countries, to recognize the massacres as such.

To the surprise of many, Armenia's first president, Levon Ter-Petrosian, deliberately chose not to make 1915 a political issue. The closure of the Armenian-Turkish border in 1993 and the lack of diplomatic relations were a result of the Karabakh dispute, rather than the quarrel over 1915. Ter-Petrosian's successor, Robert Kocharian, also sidestepped the "genocide" issue at first. Then, in 2000, he began lobbying around the world for the recognition of the massacres as "genocide." The European Parliament and the French Senate passed resolutions calling the 1915 massacres "genocide." The U.S. Congress was about to follow their example when a telephone call from President Bill Clinton, worried about the Turkish reaction, persuaded Congress to suspend the motion.

The parliamentary resolutions in Europe enraged Turkey, which canceled several French commercial contracts. Turkey's version of events is that the 1915 massacres were far smaller in scale than the Armenians allege and occurred during a civil war at the end of the Ottoman Empire, in which both Turks and Armenians died. In Turkish national ideology, the events thus have a very different resonance: the Armenians are perceived as the fifth column of the Great Powers, who were seeking to destroy the new Turkish state in its infancy.

Amid the mutual recriminations, a few brave attempts have been made to start a Turkish-Armenian dialogue about what really happened. A Turkish-Armenian Reconciliation Committee was formed in 2001 but was much criticized in both countries. In 2000, Turkish and Armenian historians met and corresponded. They were not helped by the fact that access to both the Ottoman archives from the period relating to the massacres and the archives of the Armenian Dashnak government of 1918–1920 are restricted to a small handful of favored scholars.

In this cacophonous atmosphere, I was impressed by the argument of the Armenian historian Gerard Libaridian, who was also President Ter-Petrosian's chief foreign policy adviser, that to politicize the "genocide issue" was to demean it. Once the issue became political, he said, it became an imperative for both sides to stick to intransigent positions, rather than engage in intelligent debate. "It seems that in the battle for and against recognition, both sides appear to be repeating the logic of the past in order to justify it," Libaridian wrote. "The tail ends of the two rejectionist positions—comprehensive rejection of the other—seem to be feeding off each other."[8]

Much of the discussion of the issue was less about history than a visceral assertion of victimhood vis-à-vis one's neighbors. Armenians' perception that they had been destroyed in 1915 had a strong resonance in 1988, when the Nagorny Karabakh dispute began. "Fear of being destroyed, and destroyed not as a person, not individually, but destroyed as a nation, fear of genocide, is in every Armenian," Lyudmila Harutiunian, a well-known Armenian sociologist told me. "It is impossible to remove it."[9] Harutiunian made the point that in colloquial speech, most Armenians call both Turks and Azerbaijanis "Turks" and make no distinction between them. In 1988, the "Turkish threat" of 1915 was therefore transposed onto the Azerbaijanis and a memorial to the victims of the Sumgait pogroms was put up on Tsitsernakaberd hill near the Genocide memorial. But when Armenians committed acts of violence against Azerbaijanis, Harutiunian said, many in Armenia refused to believe they had happened. "Armenians responded with approximately the same methods [as the Azerbaijanis], but the Armenians' historical memory does not have a basis for that."

War changed the nature of the debate. In 2000, with the Nagorny Karabakh dispute unresolved, it was inevitable that Azerbaijan would get involved in the Genocide controversy. In October 2000, President Aliev declared: "In history there was never such a thing as the 'Armenian genocide,' and even if there had been, it would be wrong to raise the matter after 85 years."[10] After its defeat and suffering at the hands of the Armenians, Aliev wanted to assert Azerbaijan's right to victimhood too.

Yerevan has many secrets. One of them, I believed, lay among a jumble of garages, outhouses, and vegetable plots behind a tall apartment block at No. 22 Vardanants Street, not far from the city center. At the top of a narrow flight of steps was a small open space, surrounded by rusty green garages and piled with bricks and sand. Here, I was pretty sure, had been a mosque, used by Yerevan's Azerbaijanis, that had had the misfortune not to be classified as "Persian" and was demolished.

The space was so miserable and empty that I wondered if I was in the right spot. At the foot of the steps, an old woman in a floral dress, sitting on a camp stool with a cloth laid on the ground before her, was selling grapes, beans, and onions. She had a swarthy face and drop earrings; it looked as though she came in from the countryside every day to sell fruit and vegetables. "Was there ever a mosque up there?" I asked her, pointing up the steps. Yes, she answered, there had been.

"What happened to it?"

"We didn't touch it till the last day, after they destroyed the Armenian church in Baku." She seemed to mean the beginning of 1990.

"But why did they knock it down?"

"Why leave it?" she shrugged. "We are Christians, they are Muslims. When there were problems with Azerbaijan, our Armenians came and destroyed it in three days. They brought a special machine, I don't know what it's called, which goes like this . . ." She made a flat rolling motion with the palm of her hand, miming the path of a bulldozer.

I said, tentatively, that a building shouldn't be made to suffer for the actions of people.

"Yes, walls aren't to blame," the woman agreed. "But they fight against everything. What's left for the people? What kind of life is that?" Her words didn't make sense, but I guessed that the "they" she was talking about had nothing to do with the mosque.[11]

That the Armenians could erase an Azerbaijani mosque inside their capital city was made easier by a linguistic sleight of hand: the Azerbaijanis of Armenia can be more easily written out of history because the name "Azeri" or "Azerbaijani" was not in common usage before the twentieth century. In the premodern era, these people were generally referred to as "Tartars," "Turks," or simply "Muslims." Yet they were neither Persians nor Turks; they were Turkic-speaking Shiite subjects of the Safavid Dynasty of the Iranian Empire—in other words, the ancestors of people whom we would now call "Azerbaijanis." So when the Armenians refer to the "Persian mosque" in Yerevan, that name obscures the fact that most of the worshippers there, when it was built in the 1760s, would have been, in effect, Azerbaijanis.

In modern-day Armenia these basic facts are simply not known. But that Armenia was home to many Turkic-speaking Muslims would have seemed only natural to one Armenian national hero, the great eighteenth-century troubadour Sayat-Nova, after whom one of Yerevan's big avenues is named. Born in Armenia, he trained as a monk in the monastery of Sanahin but became a poet at the court of the Georgian king Irakli II in Tiflis. Sayat-Nova composed verse in Armenian, Azeri, Georgian, and Persian (one of his most famous poems moves between all four). The majority of his surviving ballads are in Azeri, which was the *lingua franca* of the Caucasus at that time.

Yet by the twentieth century the Azerbaijanis people, who had lived in eastern Armenia for centuries, had become its silent guests, marginalized and discriminated against. The Armenians asserted their right to their homeland at the expense of these people. In 1918–1920, tens of thousands of Azerbaijanis were expelled from Zangezur. In the 1940s, tens of thousands more were deported to Azerbaijan to make way for incoming Armenian immigrants from the Diaspora. The last cleansing, in 1988–1989, got rid of the rest.

If modern Armenians remember their former Azerbaijani neighbors, it is generally as farmers. They say you could always rely on them to sell the best quality fruit and vegetables in the markets. Yet many were also well-to-do townsfolk whose descendants form a powerful political community in exile in Azerbaijan. They are known as the *Yeraz*, or

"Yerevan Azerbaijanis." A prominent *Yeraz*, the former presidential adviser Eldar Namazov, told me that his grandfather had been a merchant who owned large parts of what is now the city's National Park. His family was forced to leave Armenia in 1947. "In our family there were always many tales of what the Armenians did to the Azerbaijanis in the city of Yerevan," Namazov reminisced. "I had many relatives who died at the beginning of the century during the slaughter of Azerbaijanis in the city of Yerevan and very many of our relatives died during the deportations."[12]

Officially, there are now around eight thousand Azerbaijanis in Armenia. In reality, the figure must be much lower; there are perhaps only a few hundred left, mostly pensioners. And yet Yerevan has many Azerbaijanis in it every day, driving their trucks into the city, buying fruit and vegetables and selling cheap consumer goods or washing powder in the markets. How so? They are actually Iranian Azerbaijanis, for whom Armenia is a profitable market. Their gaudily colored trucks, with bright snub-nosed orange cabs and green and blue tarpaulins, crawl along Armenia's roads to virtually captive buyers in the landlocked republic. Perception is everything. Iran is a friendly neighbor, and the drivers, although Azerbaijani by language and ethnicity, are Iranian citizens—the living equivalent, you might say, of the "Persian mosque." They are easily tolerated by Armenians, who do good business with them.

The Iranian Azerbaijanis are not numerous. It would need Armenia's borders with Turkey and Azerbaijan to reopen for Yerevan to recover its former dynamism—the kind of business and bustle that Villari found so attractive in 1905. But in the year 2000 that seemed a remote prospect. The tortuous postwar geography of the Caucasus, with all its closed borders and front lines, made Moscow or Los Angeles closer to Yerevan than Erzerum or Baku. The Eastern bazaar was still closed.

# 6

# 1988–1990

## An Azerbaijani Tragedy

ON THE AFTERNOON of 23 July 1988, five Azerbaijani academics stood disconsolately on the pavement in front of the main Communist Party headquarters in Baku. They had just come out of a two-and-a-half-hour meeting with the new Party leader of Azerbaijan, Abdurahman Vezirov, and they were depressed. One of the group, Leila Yunusova, confessed that Vezirov had been even more conservative and blinkered than she had expected. Another, the physicist Tofik Qasimov, remarked that the best course of action he could think of was going home and finishing the repair work on his apartment. A third, the Arabist scholar Zardusht Alizade, says that he declared that the only way forward was to set up a rival political movement to the Communist Party, a Popular Front of Azerbaijan. Some of the others were skeptical, but Alizade recalls, "We went to Leila's house, bought a cake on the way, had the cake and some tea. And from the next day I began to work on creating a Popular Front."[1]

By September, the intellectuals had formulated the first draft program for "The Popular Front of Azerbaijan in Support of Perestroika." As the name implies, it was a pro-Gorbachev reformist organization. Many of its policy ideas were adapted from a copy of the Estonian Popular Front program, which they had obtained by chance. More important than the program was the fact for the first time Azerbaijan had an alternative political banner around which activists could gather.

From very tentative beginnings, the Azerbaijani nationalist opposition traveled a long road to power. It finally ousted the Communist Party and its successors only in 1992 and after a formidable struggle. In 1988, Azerbaijan was still one of the most conservative republics in the Soviet Union, and almost no political dissent was tolerated. In Armenia, large sections of the Party hierarchy proved willing to work with the new nationalist movement, and it took power relatively smoothly; in

Azerbaijan, there was no basis for the authorities and opposition to strike a deal and no consensus about what the future held. Another constant source of tension was the gulf between the cosmopolitan and generally Russian-speaking intellectuals of Baku and the rest of the republic. Several of the members of the "Club of Scholars" were Party members and were despised by the more radical activists, who spoke a language of undiluted nationalism and had no interest in Gorbachev's *perestroika*. The two most prominent radicals, the historian Etibar Mamedov and the trade unionist Neimet Panakhov, both came from *Yeraz* families that had left Armenia in the 1940s.

The failure to agree on the "rules of the game" both between the ruling authorities and a divided opposition made for a continuing power struggle. Eventually, it helped precipitate the bloody confrontation between Moscow and the Popular Front in Baku in January 1990, when for the first time the Soviet leadership sent the army into one of its own cities, killing more than a hundred people. This tragedy accelerated Azerbaijan's journey toward independence and arguably began the death agony of the Soviet Union.

In 1988, as in Armenia, so in Azerbaijan, only one issue, Nagorny Karabakh, was able to raise passions and bring large numbers of people out on to the streets. "I had hundreds of conversations," said the Moscow official Vyacheslav Mikhailov, who traveled between the two republics. "I didn't meet a single Armenian or a single Azerbaijani who held a compromise position on this question, from shepherds to academicians."[2] In Baku, the spark for mass protests was the exodus of tens of thousands of Azerbaijanis from Armenia in November 1988. Vast crowds filled Lenin Square—subsequently renamed Freedom Square— the great space near the waterfront between the city's two biggest hotels. From 17 November, the rallies carried on without a break and demonstrators camped overnight in the square. At night, there were estimated to be roughly twenty thousand protestors; by day, as many as half a million.[3] Panakhov and Mamedov were among the most popular and powerful speakers and stirred up anti-Armenian feelings. They stoked indignation with assertions that the Armenians were planning to build a guest house for workers from a Yerevan aluminum factory in a beautiful Karabakh "grove" named Topkhana.[4] On the eighteenth day of the protest, 5 December, the Soviet police moved in and cleared the square by force. Panakhov was one of those arrested, and a curfew was imposed that lasted ten months.

The crackdown in December 1988 drove the burgeoning movement back in on itself, and it was wracked by intrigue and suspicions of treachery. All the new Soviet opposition movements had to contend with the danger that they were being infiltrated by *agents provocateurs* and government agents. It was later revealed that in the Baltic republics, several of the original activists had links with the KGB—not that this made any difference in the long run. A declassified KGB report on the Karabakh Committee mentioned that one of its Moscow members was working for the agency, although it named no names.[5] In the feuding clan politics of Azerbaijan, these fears of infiltration were especially acute. One of the founders of the Club of Scholars, Eldar Namazov—who did not take part in the mass rallies—says that in 1988 the Communist authorities made an unsuccessful attempt to co-opt him. He was invited to enter the Government House on Lenin Square by the back door and go up to the podium, where the speakers addressed the crowd and delivered a message of their liking:

> They told me the names of the public figures, whom they were sending there. I said, "No thank you, I don't take part in these things." I went to the rally and was among the crowd. And those people who were on the list really did go through the back courtyard, go up onto the podium and speak, and many of them have entered history as leaders of the Popular Front . . . I won't name their names.[6]

It is the nature of allegations such as Namazov's, of course, that they cannot be verified. The only source that could confirm or deny them, the KGB archives of Azerbaijan, were never opened to the public, even by the post-Communist government of Abulfaz Elchibey. Yet even KGB archives would have only limited usefulness; the problem for Azerbaijan was that even the KGB was splintering into political factions involved in a bitter internal power struggle.

In May 1988, Azerbaijan had a new Party boss in Vezirov, but it was still dominated by former clients of Heidar Aliev, who was now officially in retirement in Moscow. Even as a pensioner, Aliev still cast a long shadow over Azerbaijan. He had dominated the republic, in senior positions in either Baku or Moscow, for thirty years. Aliev was born in the exclave of Nakhichevan in 1923, the third of eight children in an Azerbaijani family that had just moved there from across the border in

Armenia.[7] He made his career in the Stalinist secret police; an NKVD lieutenant at the age of eighteen, he rose to become the head of Azerbaijan's KGB in 1960 and the republic's first party secretary nine years later. Aliev's preferred political method was and is total control. He built up a powerful network of Nakhichevanis who filled posts at every level and who resented the arrival of Vezirov in 1988. Ayaz Mutalibov, who was head of the Council of Ministers at the time, says of this period: "In essence it was a fight between two clans, Aliev's and Vezirov's. They couldn't agree."[8]

Several of Azerbaijan's new opposition activists feared that some of their comrades-in-arms were in fact merely pawns in this struggle. These suppositions became more plausible in 1990, after Aliev returned from Moscow to his home province of Nakhichevan and several leading Popular Front activists, including the right-hand man of Abulfaz Elchibey, Bejan Farzaliev, began to work with him. There is also compelling evidence that the radical tribune of the people himself, Neimet Panakhov, had contacts with Aliev. Panakhov is a forbidding figure with a gaunt face, trim beard, and piercing eyes. In an interview he constantly clicked his fingers or ran them through rosary beads, emitting the same intense energy that had once mesmerized whole crowds. Panakhov's family comes from Armenia and he grew up in Nakhichevan. When the Karabakh events started, he was twenty-five and working as a lathe operator in the Lieutenant Schmidt Factory.

Yet Panakhov confirmed that even as a twenty-five-year-old factory hand in 1988, he had frequently visited the office of the head of the one of Baku's districts, Rafael Allahverdiev, an old ally of Aliev's. Panakhov says that "Rafael Allahverdiev tried to convince me that Heidar Aliev was a good man, that he knew about [the protests] and so on. Our meeting didn't take place."[9] However, subsequent events suggest that Panakhov was actually playing a double game. On his return from exile in Turkey to Azerbaijan in 1991, he began to work for Aliev. And in 1993, when Aliev became president of Azerbaijan, he gave Panakhov a job in his presidential administration—and also made Allahverdiev mayor of Baku. At the very least, there is something fishy about the way this simple worker was able to attain these heights. How much damage these power games did to Azerbaijan became obvious only in retrospect.

## A POPULAR FRONT

The year 1989 began quietly in Azerbaijan before accelerating to a terrifying climax. On 16 July, the Popular Front began its second phase of activity by holding its first congress and electing as its new chairman Abulfaz Elchibey, the man who would later become Azerbaijani president in 1992. Elchibey was a former dissident and scholar of the Middle East who, even his critics conceded, had great personal honesty and moral authority. He saw Azerbaijan's future in the closest possible ties with Turkey, and he consistently emphasized that Azerbaijanis were "Turks." He was hostile to Iran and Russia and pointedly refused to speak Russian in public, using an interpreter even when he traveled to Moscow.

In the new Popular Front, there was broad agreement that Azerbaijan must win autonomy from Moscow. Its members wanted a higher status for the Azeri language and more contact with their ethnic cousins in Iran—and there was also consensus that they wanted a secular, not an overtly Islamic, movement. Historians published articles questioning the official account of the Bolshevik takeover of Azerbaijan in 1920, and hence the whole legitimacy of Soviet rule. People shed their Russified surnames.

There was much less agreement about political methods and goals. One wing was composed of moderates who had set their sights only on winning Azerbaijan's parliamentary elections, due to be held in the spring of 1990. At the other extreme were the radicals such as Panakhov, who had been released from prison in the summer of 1989 and begun to advocate Azerbaijan's independence from the Soviet Union. Elchibey and his advisers tacked between the different factions but increasingly inclined toward the radicals. One of the moderates and founders of the Popular Front, Leila Yunusova, complained that in the fall of 1989 the movement was being taken over by "Bolsheviks," who were beginning to use intimidation and violence against their opponents. She wrote later: "Having condemned the Communist Party of the Soviet Union for its totalitarianism, some of the leaders of the Popular Front of Azerbaijan had already managed to borrow the very worst from Bolshevism."[10]

In the late summer of 1989, a new wave of protests began, again inspired by the Karabakh cause and supported by hundreds of thousands of Azerbaijanis. Mamedov and Panakhov organized mass rallies and galvanized the popular support for their most devastating tactic yet: a total rail blockade against Armenia. Eighty-five percent of Armenia's rail traffic came from Azerbaijan, and the embargo caused shortages of petrol and food in Armenia. Soviet Interior Ministry troops were drafted in to keep the railway line open but met with limited success.[11] The blockade began an economic rupture between Armenia and Azerbaijan that continues to this day. It also cut off Azerbaijan's exclave of Nakhichevan, whose only link to the rest of the Soviet Union was through Armenia.

The blockade also proved to be an effective lever against the Azerbaijani leadership. On 25 September, under pressure from the Popular Front, the Azerbaijani Supreme Soviet passed a law on sovereignty that accepted the jurisdiction of Soviet laws only "when they do not violate the sovereign rights of the Azerbaijani SSR." Although not an independence declaration, it was a big step away from the center—and was duly declared invalid by the Supreme Soviet in Moscow.[12] On 4 October, the authorities made another concession and registered the Popular Front as a legal organization. In return, the Popular Front agreed to lift the railway blockade; even so, transport communications between Azerbaijan and Armenia never fully recovered.

## A SLIDE INTO CHAOS

The Azerbaijani capital entered the last month of 1989 in an increasingly menacing atmosphere. The remaining Armenians in Baku felt intimidated. In the mid-1980s, there had been two hundred thousand Armenians in Baku, one-tenth of the population, but all but a few had left. Those who stayed behind were mostly women and pensioners. Baku Armenians say that from December 1989 they rarely ventured out of doors. Bella Saakova, a widow who had managed to hang on to her job in Baku's Tea-Packing Factory, said that a colleague drove her to work every day because she was too afraid to go by bus: "Even to go out and wait for a bus at a bus stop was very dangerous, because young men came along and it was as if they were sniffing you like dogs. The tension was such that, whether you liked it or not, you would give yourself away as an Armenian."[13]

Nominal Party leader Vezirov had lost all authority—the crowds on Lenin Square mockingly Armenianized his name by calling him

"Vezirian" and carried his effigy in a woman's dress through the streets. Instead, Azerbaijan's Russian second secretary, Viktor Polyanichko, was now in charge. Physically large and fearless, Polyanichko had come to Baku from Afghanistan, where he had been the Soviet Union's main commissar, running the country from behind the scenes. He brought with him a taste for political manipulation. On one occasion, for example, Polyanichko invited two Popular Front moderates, Tofik Qasimov and Zardusht Alizade, to his office and apparently tried to persuade them to inject radical Islam into their program. "He had a Koran in his office, and he went over to it and said, 'The Koran is a good book,'" *New York Times* reporter Bill Keller quoted Qasimov: "He said, 'In Baku, this European thinking may be fine, but out in the country-side, the Muslim faith is very strong. So you should take the Islamic factor into account.'"[14] It was strange and suspicious advice from a Communist apparatchik.

By December 1989, the "radicals" were fully in charge of the Popular Front and Polyanichko had switched his attention to them. A select group was frequently given airtime on Azerbaijani television. In the last week of the year—just as Nicolae Ceausescu was being swept from power in Romania—the Azerbaijani leadership began to fear the worst. Ayaz Mutalibov, who was the chairman of the republic's Council of Ministers—its prime minister, in effect—recalls how Vezirov made a panicky telephone call to him around 25 December:

> He told me a catastrophic situation was developing, we absolutely had to ask for help from Moscow . . . we didn't have our own Interior Ministry forces with helmets and truncheons. . . . They were subordinate only to Moscow. We had to ask the Interior Ministry and the Council of Ministers to send us people, otherwise there could be very big trouble.[15]

Trouble did break out. On 29 December, Popular Front activists, including Neimet Panakhov, seized local Party offices in the southern town of Jalilabad, wounding dozens of people. The attack led to the suspension of a debate in the Baku Soviet designed to fix a date for elections.

Nakhichevan was the setting for the next drama. Panakhov arrived in the exclave and led crowds in physically dismantling the frontier fences with Iran and burning watchtowers. Thousands raced across the border, and there were ecstatic scenes as Azerbaijanis met their ethnic cousins from Iran for the first time in years. The Soviet leadership reacted angrily. It denounced this unprecedented action and hostile media reports claimed that the Azerbaijanis were rushing into the embrace of Islamic fundamentalism.

## BLACK JANUARY PART I

Azerbaijan's "Black January" of 1990 was ushered in with all the disturbing portents of mass violence already visible: a defenseless Armenian population, whom none of the security structures seemed ready to defend; a Popular Front, where radical elements had squeezed out the moderates; a local Party leadership losing power and looking for ways of hanging on to it; and the Soviet leadership in Moscow, which was prepared to take any steps it thought necessary to prevent Azerbaijan's breaking away from the Union.

News from Karabakh exacerbated the situation. On 9 January, the Armenian parliament voted to include Nagorny Karabakh within its budget, a step that enraged Azerbaijanis. Fighting then broke out between Armenians and Azerbaijanis in the villages of the Khanlar and Shaumian regions in northern Azerbaijan. Hostages were taken and four Russian Interior Ministry soldiers were killed.[16]

In Baku on 6–7 January, the Popular Front split apart. A small group of moderate intellectuals led by Leila Yunusova and Zardusht Alizade left to form the Social Democratic Party. The remainder of the Front, already in two distinct camps, held mass rallies on Lenin Square. Moscow sent in thousands more Interior Ministry troops and soldiers.

On 11 January, a group of Popular Front radicals stormed Party buildings and effectively took power in the southern town of Lenkoran. Two days later, a journalist from the *Bakinsky Rabochy* newspaper went to investigate and found that Soviet power had been overthrown:

> I had agreed to meet the First Secretary of the Town Committee Ya. Rzayev and went to the Regional Committee building. But there were armed young men standing in the doorway. They did not let me in and one of them came up and said: "The Regional Committee does not exist any more. No one works here. You can't come in."[17]

On 12 January, Polyanichko came up with another confounding plan. He held talks with the Popular Front that ended with the announcement that Azerbaijan was forming a new "National Defense Council," which would defend its frontiers against Armenian incursions. Four of the council's five leaders were Popular Front radicals, who, by any other reckoning, were the sworn enemies of the republic's Party leadership.[18] Two of these men, Panakhov and Rahim Gaziev, were shown on local television. Panakhov told the television audience that Baku was full of homeless refugees and that thousands of Armenians were still living in comfort—in effect, inciting the viewers to anti-Armenian violence.

The next day, 13 January, murderous anti-Armenian violence overwhelmed Baku. A vast crowd filled Lenin Square for a rally, and by early evening men had broken away from it to attack Armenians. As in Sumgait, the savagery was appalling and the center of the city around the Armenian quarter became a killing ground. People were thrown to their deaths from the balconies of upper-story apartments. Crowds set upon and beat Armenians to death. Thousands of terrified Armenians took shelter in police stations or in the vast Shafag Cinema, under the protection of troops. From there they were taken to the cold and windy quayside, put on ferries, and transported across the Caspian Sea. Over the next few days, the port of Krasnovodsk in Turkmenistan received thousands of beaten and frightened refugees. Airplanes were on hand to fly them to Yerevan. With this terrible flourish, Armenia and Azerbaijan completed their ethnic cleansing of each other's populations.

Around ninety Armenians died in the Baku pogroms. It is hard to verify the death toll because yet more chaos was to descend on Baku within days and no official investigation was ever launched. Also, the Baku Armenians were scattered to Armenia, Russia, and Turkmenistan, and some of the elderly victims died on the Caspian Sea ferries or in Yerevan hospitals.[19] Certainly, the casualties would have been much higher if the authorities had not staged an operation to evacuate the Armenians.

There are troubling questions as to why both sides in the power struggle did not manage to avert the bloodshed of the Baku pogroms. Moscow had sent thousands of Soviet Interior Ministry troops into Baku who did nothing to intervene. Arzu Abdullayeva, the human rights activist, remembers appealing to a policeman to go to the aid of a desperate Armenian being set upon by a mob and being told, "We have orders not to intervene."[20] One story has it that the writer Yusif Same-doglu telephoned the Central Committee building and begged them to intervene. He got the reply "Let them slaughter."[21]

The strange collaboration between Viktor Polyanichko and the na-tionalist radicals in forming the National Defense Council is especially fertile territory for conspiracy theorists. One of the radicals, Etibar Mamedov, offers the explanation that they could not turn down the op-portunity to take up arms legally; Panakhov says that "[w]e ourselves asked to be invited on television so as to end the tension amongst the population, to take measures"—although of course tension increased, rather than diminished, after his appearance. There are more cynical in-terpretations: perhaps the Party leadership was desperately trying to shore up its authority by co-opting the Popular Front and channeling its energies in a "patriotic" direction; or perhaps Polyanichko was plan-ning an out-and-out "provocation," which would provoke the Front to violence, discredit it, and serve as the pretext for a crackdown.

There are contradictory accounts about the role of the Popular Front in the violence. In their stories of Black January, Armenian refugees from Baku unanimously blame "Popular Front people," young male ac-tivists with beards, for the pogroms. Popular Front activists counter this by saying that they helped to save Armenian lives. In fact, both versions are probably true, for by then the Front had a vast and amorphous membership. The Popular Front breakaways, Alizade and Yunusova, make a more precise accusation against the radical leaders, blaming them for failing to do anything to halt the coming violence. Alizade says that several days before the pogroms began, lists of Armenian ad-dresses were hung up outside the Popular Front headquarters on Rashid Beibutov Street. When they were taken down, someone put them up again. He continues:

> After the session of the ruling council finished, they went to a rally attended by the whole city. At the rally there were constant anti-Ar-menian calls and the last call was "Long live Baku without Armeni-ans!" It was at a Popular Front rally. During the rally anti-Armenian pogroms began in Baku. Do the leaders of the Popular Front bear re-sponsibility for this? I think that they do.

## BLACK JANUARY PART II

With the Armenians violently expelled from Baku, the stage was set for a showdown between Moscow and the Popular Front. Even as the pogroms were going on, on 14 January, a Politburo delegation led by Gorbachev's close political ally Yevgeny Primakov arrived in Baku to try to take charge. Soviet defense minister Dmitry Yazov flew down to take charge of the thousands of troops, still in barracks on the edge of the city. The decision was made to impose a state of emergency in Nagorny Karabakh, the border areas between Azerbaijan and Armenia, and the city of Ganje—but, inexplicably, not Baku.

Nationalist activists ruled the streets of Baku. They put up barricades of trucks and concrete blocks on the roads leading to the barracks on the edge of the city. On 17 January, they began a nonstop rally in front of the Central Committee building, blocking access to it. They erected a gallows in front of the building—whether as a threatening symbol or as an actual instrument of execution never became clear. The Moscow emissaries and the Popular Front leadership played a game of bluff. According to Andrei Girenko, one of the Politburo delegation:

> We met Elchibey and other leaders of the Popular Front. Primakov and I received them, talked to them. Then it was already clear to me that Vezirov had completely lost control. I met one of the [Popular Front] activists literally on the eve of the events that happened that night. I knew that troops could not stay blockaded forever in that position. I begged him to take down the barricades that were blocking the roads, the airfields, to rescue people from a dangerous confrontation with the troops.[22]

The stakes were high. According to Etibar Mamedov, Primakov was warning them he would not tolerate Azerbaijan's seceding from the Soviet Union and implicitly threatening to use force. "Primakov told me, 'You are one step away from independence,'" Mamedov recalled.[23] Yet the decision to bring in the army had still not been made, and Primakov also reportedly tried to persuade Gorbachev in a telephone conversation not to authorize a military intervention.[24]

Gorbachev and his security ministers finally decided to send the army into Baku on the night of 19–20 January. A State of Emergency was declared, to begin at midnight. Yet the residents of the city were unaware of what was happening because television broadcasts had gone off the air at 7:30 in the evening, after an explosion at the television station, almost certainly carried out by the security forces. As a result, most Bakuvians learned about the State of Emergency at 5:30 the next morning from the radio and leaflets dropped from helicopters.[25] By then it was too late.

Shortly after midnight, troops had come out of their barracks and tanks had started rumbling toward the city. Most of the troops who approached from the south were from local garrisons and did not fight their way into the city, but the troops who approached form the north entered Baku as if it were a city under enemy occupation. Tanks rolled over barricades, crushing cars and even ambulances. Witnesses spoke of soldiers firing at people who fled and of soldiers stabbing and shooting the wounded. A bus full of civilians was hit by a volley of bullets and many of its passengers, including a fourteen-year-old girl, were killed.

Some one hundred thirty citizens of Baku were killed and several hundred were wounded on the night of 19–20 January. An independent military investigation group known as "Shield" ("Shchit," in Russian) later concluded that the Soviet army had waged war on one of its own cities and called for criminal proceedings against Defense Minister Dmitry Yazov, who had personally commanded the operation. At least twenty-one soldiers also died. How they did so is disputed; this death toll implies there was armed resistance from protestors, although some of the soldiers may also have been victims of bullets fired by their own side in the dark city's general mêlée.

## AFTERMATH

The intervention in Baku, with the Soviet army for the first time taking one of its own cities by force, was a tragedy for Azerbaijan and the Soviet Union. The army took full control of Baku within a few hours and reestablished rule by Moscow. But on 20 January 1990 Moscow essentially lost Azerbaijan. Almost the whole population of Baku turned out for mass funerals of the victims. The victims were the first "martyrs" to be buried in the Alley of Martyrs on the top of the hill in the city. Thousands of Communist Party members publicly burned their Party cards and even the chairwoman of the Supreme Soviet, Elmira Kafarova, denounced the actions of "army criminals."

The profound effects of "Black January" went far beyond Baku. The intervention had exposed the center's increasing inability to cope with the problems beginning to overwhelm the Soviet Union. The failure to declare a State of Emergency to halt the Armenian pogroms, only to do so when all the Armenians had left, suggested deep cynicism or incompetence, or both. The confused and then brutal response to the Popular Front's challenge revealed that the Soviet Union had several different centers of power, each with its own priorities, and that Gorbachev wavered between them.

In the short term, the Communist Party was back in control. Dozens of Popular Front activists—including many members of the National Defense Council, formed with official consent only days before—were detained. Etibar Mamedov was arrested when he traveled to Moscow to hold a press conference, and Neimet Panakhov fled—or was allowed to flee—across the border to Iran. Resistance flickered for a few days in Nakhichevan, which became the first part of the Soviet Union ever to declare unilateral independence, before Popular Front resistance was crushed there as well. First Party Secretary Vezirov had decamped and was in Moscow, suffering from nervous exhaustion, and Ayaz Mutalibov was made his successor in a free vote of Party officials. Polyanichko remained the second secretary and the power behind the throne.

On 4 February, Mutalibov flew to Moscow to see Gorbachev. The same day a prominent article in *Pravda* vigorously denounced Heidar Aliev as a corrupt relic of the Brezhnev era; it had evidently been timed to coincide with Mutalibov's visit. Yet Mutalibov says that he went on to see Aliev and they talked until three o'clock in the morning.

That the new Party boss chose to visit the disgraced Aliev suggests that Aliev remained a powerful behind-the-scenes figure in Azerbaijani life. His connection, or lack of it, to the January events is an intriguing subplot to the main story, which has never been properly explained. Aliev himself has said that at the height of the demonstrations, Gorbachev telephoned him outside Moscow and asked him to "remove his people from the streets" of Baku and make a public statement—to which he responded by saying that he was in Moscow and had nothing to do with what was going on in Baku. Gorbachev's call suggests that he, for one, believed that Aliev was still pulling strings in Baku. Whatever his role before the bloodshed, Aliev used the aftermath of Black

January to begin his long climb back to power. After 20 January, he called a press conference in Azerbaijan's representative's office in Moscow and condemned the intervention in Baku.[26]

Azerbaijan entered a dull period of shock and reflection. As the opposition took stock of the bloody defeat it had suffered, the standing of the middle-of-the-road group in the Popular Front—men like Isa Gambar, Hikmet Hajizade, and Sabit Bagirov—climbed. Hajizade says: "The radicals, the schizophrenics, understood that it wasn't so simple, that you couldn't simply just take power through a revolution. It was a heavy blow for them. They were forced to make peace with the liberals, with the liberal leadership, who, in the end, came to power."[27]

# 7

# Baku

## An Eventful History

ON A CHILLY spring day in 2000, a crowd of Azerbaijanis, all dressed in long black coats, was standing under a canopy of pine trees on a hill high above the curving Bay of Baku. Everyone was holding carnations and chatting to friends—and waiting for something to begin. We were standing at the entrance to the Alley of Martyrs, or *Shehidler Khiyabani*, formerly the Kirov Park, which had been dug up in 1990 to make way for the graves of the one hundred thirty victims of the 20 January bloodshed. Every year on that day tens of thousands of people walk along the alley of tombs and remember the victims of the Soviet army intervention.

The twentieth of January would have been the day to witness a popular ceremony of grief and remembrance. But it was the thirty-first of March, and the crowd at the Alley of Martyrs had been specially invited to mark Genocide Day, a recently instituted commemoration of the sufferings of the people of Azerbaijan.

Azerbaijan's story of itself is of a nation formed in adversity. In the eighteenth century, a series of semi-independent *khanates* stretched from the southern Caucasus into northern Iran. Their rulers were Turkic-speaking but were part of the Persian, not the Ottoman, Empire. Their legacy is a strong tradition of regionalism—the Azeri word is *yerlibazliq*—in which local allegiances take precedence over national ones. The khanates were abolished by the Russians, who drew a new frontier along the River Araxes, under the Treaty of Turkmenchai in 1828, dividing the Azerbaijanis in two. After 1917, Russian rule briefly gave way to the short-lived first Azerbaijani republic but was brutally reimposed by the Bolsheviks in 1920.

Even the simplest elements of Azerbaijan's national identity are confusing. The Azerbaijanis are Turkic but mainly Shiite by religion, are of Persian lineage but with a heavy Soviet overlay. Nothing can be taken for granted. In the course of the twentieth century, for example, the Azeri language was written successively in Arabic, Latin, and Cyrillic letters. It is now making a painful return to the Latin script. Azerbaijanis still feel their independence is vulnerable, and the Armenians' campaign to take over Nagorny Karabakh was perceived as an attempt to break up their fragile state.

Many Azerbaijanis also feel, with some justification, that the outside world knows nothing of their sufferings. Neither the Soviet nor the international press gave much coverage to the often violent expulsion of roughly two hundred thousand Azerbaijanis from Armenia in 1988–1989. Few people know that roughly fifty thousand Azerbaijanis were deported from Armenia in the 1940s. Before that, thousands of Azerbaijanis died in the bloody conflicts of 1918–1920. In 1998, President Aliev stitched these disparate events together in order to proclaim Azerbaijan's Genocide Day. The thirty-first of March, the day the massacres of Muslims began in Baku in 1918, was chosen as the date of commemoration.

The choice of the word "Genocide" to link the events suggested, however, that the commemoration was less about the past than about present-day politics. The message was, if Armenia could have a Genocide Day, then why should Azerbaijan not have one too? By using the term, Aliev had initiated a duel of the martyred nations.

At a press briefing on 30 March 2000, Aliev's adviser on ethnic issues, Hidayat Orujev, declared the duel open. According to the Turan news agency report, Orujev came up with an astonishing figure that outtrumped the Armenians: about two and a half million Azerbaijanis had been the victims of "the genocide that Armenians committed against Azerbaijanis in the 20th century." Turan went on: "The state adviser said that without the Russian empire's patronage Armenians could not have committed these mass killings of Azerbaijanis. He said that by falsifying history, the Armenians were trying to conceal the truth from the world and to portray themselves as innocent victims."[1] In the public language of the Armenian-Azerbaijani conflict there is no moral shading.

In the Alley of the Martyrs the ceremony was about to begin. Limousines eased up at the curb and deposited the foreign diplomatic corps. The U.S. ambassador stepped out of his Chevrolet; the Russian *chargé d'affaires*, wearing an olive raincoat, got out of a black Volga. We were all waiting for someone, and we all knew who it was. Finally, in a long cavalcade of cars came President Heidar Aliev. Tall and gaunt, he emerged from his car and moved down the line of ambassadors, shaking hands. Wherever he stepped, a small reverential space opened up around him, which somehow emphasized his loneliness. Preceded by soldiers carrying an enormous red wreath, Aliev walked down the long alley toward the eternal flame at its far end. The brass band struck up martial music.

The crowd was allowed to follow and was funneled slowly down the alley. We walked past the tombs of the victims of 20 January 1990, the Karabakh war. Portraits of the dead are carved on the tombs. In the main, they are young boys in camouflage fatigues or in open-necked shirts and striped blue-and-white sailor's shirts. People stopped to lay their carnations.

The ceremony felt empty of emotion until one moment. A woman wearing a head scarf suddenly veered away from the crowd and banged her palms against the memorial of a man, pressed her body flat against the tomb, and started keening with grief. The lamentation was almost a song, "Ai-ai-ai," coming from a deep well of pain. Was this the tomb of her husband? The date of birth shown was 1933, and she seemed about the same age. A woman in her forties in a white raincoat —her daughter, I imagined—came up behind the widow and silently held her by the shoulders to contain this paroxysm of emotion. The woman's private grief had broken through the public façade of the ceremony. People moved on more slowly, exchanging sympathetic glances and muttering softly to one another.

Baku, a city of a million people, is the capital of Azerbaijan and its seat of power, but only recently has it become an identifiably Azerbaijani city. For most of the past hundred years to be from Baku is to have a distinctive nationality of one's own. Garry Kasparov, the world chess champion, born here of a Jewish father and an Armenian mother, when asked his nationality, used the Russian word *Bakinets* or Baku-vian. The city's *lingua franca* is still just as much Russian as Azeri, spoken with a gentle southern lilt that rises in intonation at the end of a sentence.

The city's cosmopolitan outlook and style sprang from a late-nineteenth-century oil boom. At its peak, Baku was producing half the world's petroleum output and drew immigrants of dozens of nationalities to service the new industry. The city's most famous rags-to-riches tale is that of Zeinal Abdin Tagiev. After a "gusher" of oil was found on his land, this illiterate Muslim farmer grew fabulously rich and went on to become the town's most famous patron and philanthropist, funding the performance of the "first opera in the Muslim world," *Leila and Majnun*.

Powered by this mercantile spirit, Baku became, in 1918, the capital of the short-lived "first Muslim democratic republic in the world," which legalized votes for women before the United Kingdom did. Here it was possible to be both Muslim and modern—although sometimes the transition required some agility. The classic Baku Muslim is Ali Khan, the hero of the novel *Ali and Nino*. He is proud of his Persian ancestry but also revels in the technology and progressive politics of Baku and marries his Georgian childhood sweetheart. Though he is a twentieth-century man, Ali still feels pain when his Christian Georgian wife, Nino, moves all the carpets out of his house in the Old Town to make way for European furniture.

Baku's rich blend of peoples and politics flowed into its architecture. From the narrow Middle Eastern alleys of the Old Town, one steps into a small Prague, built at the turn of the last century. The main street running through the center of the city, now called Istiqlalyat or "Independence" after a flurry of name changes, is a confection of different façades: a mock Venetian palace is followed by the grand Gothic porch of the City Hall. And style is still important in this city. It is hard to believe that people's standard of living has plummeted since independence as they perform the *passegiata* along the boulevard by the Caspian Sea every evening, arm-in-arm, well made up, and dressed in Italian suits and Benetton tops.

Yet the dynamism carries a cost: Baku is also famous as the city of ethnic strife and violent massacres. The worst outbreaks of bloodletting occurred when the Russian Empire was at its weakest and the Armenian and Azerbaijani communities each identified the other as a threat. If Armenians feared Azerbaijanis as the vanguard of the Turkish army, then Azerbaijanis suspected the Armenians were a potential Russian "fifth column." In February 1905, the so-called Tatar-Armenian War claimed hundreds of lives. The British writer J. D. Henry, describing the city a few months later, found that "the people of Baku lived on a hidden volcano of race plots, labour tyranny, political conspiracy and revolutionary propaganda."[2] In the title of Henry's book, they were fated to have an "eventful history."

Following the October Revolution, another inferno of violence en-
gulfed the city. "When one speaks of the streets of a town running with
blood," said one British political officer, "one is generally employing a
figure of speech. But if one is referring to Baku between 1917 and 1919,
one is being starkly literal."[3] A group of mainly Armenian commissars
took over the city and formed the Baku Commune, a small Bolshevik
bridgehead in an otherwise anti-Bolshevik Caucasus. When in March
1918 Azerbaijanis revolted against the Baku Commune, Armenian
Dashnaks and Bolshevik troops poured into the Azerbaijani quarters of
the city and slaughtered thousands. In September, just after a British
protection force withdrew and before the Ottoman army marched in, a
revenge match was played out. This time the Azerbaijanis went on the
rampage and thousands of Armenians were put to the sword. The total
death toll of the intercommunal fighting on both sides in 1918 ran close
to twenty thousand.

In the Soviet epoch, ethnic violence was in abeyance and intercommunal relations were good, but the tension did not entirely disappear.
Armenians knew not to venture out when the Yerevan soccer team
Ararat was playing in town—and especially if it won. In the Caucasus
an ethnic, rather than a civic, understanding of belonging prevails, and
the roles of "guest" and "host" are very well defined. In Armenia, the
Azerbaijanis were very definitely made to feel that they were "guests";
so, in a less overt way, were the Armenians of Baku. The British writer
Susan Richards picked up on this when she stayed with an Armenian
mother and daughter in Baku in 1989. Tatyana, the daughter, had almost exclusively Azerbaijani friends. Richards writes:

> The ascendancy of the Turkic Azeris had been confirmed in the repub-
> lic by Soviet power. As long as this was not threatened, the Azeris had
> little reason to be anything but easygoing. But there were terms. The
> appearance of Azeri ascendancy had to be maintained. . . . Tatyana's
> own attitude illustrated the delicate balance between Azeri tolerance
> and ascendancy. Her pale-skinned beauty marked her as an Armen-
> ian, but she had put herself under the protection of the Azeris. "The
> other day," she remarked to me, "my boss, who was introducing me to
> someone, said: 'This is Tatyana. She's Azeri.' It's quite obvious that I'm
> not, of course. But it was his way of saying 'She's one of us.' It's all a
> matter of attitude. Armenians who don't get on here have only them-
> selves to blame." That was all very well unless, as her mother feared,

she happened to come across an Azeri who did not happen to know that, despite her Armenian blood, she was "one of them."[4]

Black January 1990 destroyed all of these cultural negotiations. Even well-integrated Armenians like Tatyana and her mother were forced to leave Baku, and two currents of its history diverged.

"We live peacefully with them, peacefully and normally," said Bella Saakova. Bella, a Baku Armenian, was sitting in a small room in a hostel in a dusty suburb of Yerevan. By "them" she meant her neighbors, the Armenians of Armenia. She has lived in Armenia for the past ten years, since being deported from Baku in January 1990, yet still does not feel at home. Like most of her fellow Armenian refugees, Bella has not taken Armenian citizenship and her greatest sense of belonging is to her lost home city. If you were to x-ray Bella, you would find a Bakuvian all the way through.[5]

A good selection of Baku-in-exile was seated at Bella's table in Yerevan. All were Armenians, but they talked in Russian and had Russian first names. There was a softness about them, which I was not used to in Armenia, generally a dour straight-talking place, the Scotland of the Caucasus. These people had the unalloyed nostalgia and pedantry that goes with exile. Now they were arguing about Baku schools. "I went to School No 142, the best in Baku," maintained Grisha firmly. Alyosha began a song in Azeri about the wind blowing in from the sea to Baku. Grisha picked up one in Russian, "Baku, my own city . . ."

The conversation at Bella's table turned on two topics: their shared memories of Azerbaijan and the dark days in January 1990, when the last Armenians were expelled from Baku. All the guests at the table had different accounts of how it had ended, and it seemed that the manner of leaving had imprinted a defining idea of what Baku meant for them. Grisha told stories about those who had been beaten and were stripped and robbed in the Shafaq Cinema before being shipped on ferries across the Caspian Sea.

Bella's story of her last days in Baku reflected her forgiving character. She said she would remember forever the terror of standing on the cold, wind-battered quayside, waiting to board a ferry and leave the city, as a line of Soviet police protected a crowd of elderly and beaten Armenians. Yet her strongest memory was still of the kindness shown her by her Azerbaijani neighbors. She had left her possessions in the care of one neighbor, and still remembered another, who, in the minutes before she left her apartment to take refuge in the local police station, had packed a basket of food for her and her children for their terrible journey. In the basket were medicine, salami, cheese, and loaves of bread. "I can never forget that," Bella said. "Perhaps that's why I have a completely different attitude to Azerbaijanis. You know, when people say bad things about them—even when they deservedly say bad things—I remember my neighbor. I immediately remember her and I remember that bread."

Baku was still Bella's lost Eden. When I was setting off to visit her old city, she sighed, "I would give up ten years of my life to go back for *one hour*. No, really." Bella also had a very different view of Nagorny Karabakh from that of most Armenians: for her it wasn't the sacred Armenian cause but, rather, the bone of contention that had spoiled everything between Armenians and Azerbaijanis.

When I asked Bella if she had ever visited Karabakh, she replied that she had once, as a child. "To be honest, I would like to go there one more time, simply to see what I am being tormented for!" she told me with a laugh. "I've formed this idea of seeing with my own eyes the reason why I've been punished. I believe that I've been punished for something."

The gravel alleyways of Darnagül were well shaded by cedars and cypresses—and were also completely quiet. There was no one to ask for directions. I had come to visit the main resting place of Baku Armenians in the city's northern cemetery so that I could report back to Bella and her friends in Armenia on how the resting place of their parents and grandparents looked. I went through the gate of this forlorn place with some trepidation and soon ran into three cemetery wardens, who obviously did not like seeing a foreigner here at all. "You have to ask the proper authorities," one advised. I said that I wanted only to go for a stroll, shrugged them off, and set out at a brisk pace down a curving gravel path.

Turning a corner, I discovered why they had wanted to stop me. On either side of the path, the metal fences that surrounded the grave plots had been overturned and gravestones had been smashed or decapitated. In one plot the black marble headstone of Roza Markarova (1925–74), her earnest face etched into it, lay sideways on the ground. Fortunately, the destruction was only along the path. Further into the graveyard, the tombs were untouched and merely overgrown with weeds and nettles. The vandals had evidently made one sortie down the path, smashing everything they could find, and then left.

I wandered around for a few minutes, feeling the peculiar atmosphere of this utterly forlorn place. Coming back, I faced one of the cemetery wardens again. "So no one ever comes here now?" I asked. "Armenians and Azerbaijanis used to come in the old days," he told me. "That was before they dropped the bomb." "The bomb?" I wasn't sure I'd understood him correctly. "That was the *Yeraz*, who came in and destroyed everything, they exploded a bomb," he said. He was referring to the Azerbaijanis from Armenia and the hate-filled days of January 1990. I left the cemetery to its dead and its ghostly wardens.

The watershed of 1990 is not so long ago, but it already needs the patience of an archaeologist to uncover Armenian Baku. It is perhaps not as fully erased as Muslim Yerevan, but that would be much harder, because there were two hundred thousand Armenians here as recently as the mid-1980s. Still, Armenians have been removed from all the tourist literature and most of their monuments have simply vanished. In the center of Baku, only one visible remnant is left, the Armenian church of Gregory the Illuminator in Fountain Square, which dates to the 1860s. It remains a gutted shell eleven years after it was burned in December 1989; the cross has been removed from the belfry, now used as a pool hall. Where another smaller and older church, of the Virgin Mary, used to stand, in the shadow of the Maiden's Tower in the Old Town, there is now an empty space. A diplomat who served in Baku in 1992 at the height of the Karabakh war told me that he saw this eighteenth-century chapel being taken to pieces. The Armenian provenance of other buildings is now simply unknown to most people. For example, on the exuberant main street, Istiqlalyat, stands the Philharmonia, a pastiche of the casino in Monte Carlo, built in 1910 by the Armenian Gabriel Ter-Mikelov, who also designed the grand house opposite, a joyful creation in mock Arabian style, complete with a high faux-oriental balcony. Ter-Mikelov doubtless thought of himself as a Bakuvian first and an Armenian second; it is only the attempt to suppress his name that makes me stress his nationality.

A small Armenian Baku of sorts does live on. The Armenians there are spectral folk and not easy to spot. There are somewhere between five and twenty thousand of them in the city, almost all women married to Azerbaijani husbands. In this respect, Baku has preserved a little of its tolerant past—although these women do not readily advertise their nationality. There are still "terms."

I was introduced to several of the Armenian wives. Olga, with her black eyes and elegantly plucked eyebrows, looked as though she came out of an ancient Egyptian painting. She said that most of her Armenian relatives, including her brother, had fled and were in Russia or America, but she had stayed with her Azerbaijani husband and children. Hadn't she been afraid? I asked. She responded that when the Popular Front was in power and Azerbaijani nationalism was at its peak in 1992–1993, she had not stepped out of her house, but when the old Communist Heidar Aliev returned to power, she began to feel safe again. "Since Aliev came back, I've felt calm." "Nowadays I am only worried about earning enough to live," she insisted.

Other women in this city find life as Armenians very tough indeed. I met three Baku Armenians, all of whom had been scapegoated for their nationality. It seemed from their stories that it was all right to be an Armenian woman in Baku in the everyday course of things, but if you had a problem, you quickly discovered you had no rights.

Sofia was accompanied by her Azerbaijani husband of sixty years. She was an imposing woman, with a line of medals pinned on her jacket announcing that she had served in the war. She had spent years being refused a pension, and one official had said in her presence, "Send her documents to Yerevan." Sofia's two companions had both lost their apartments. Tanya had been dispossessed by Azerbaijani refugees; Yevgenia by her Azerbaijani daughter-in-law. Both had fought in vain in the courts to recover their legally owned property. Yevgenia, a little lady with a pinched face, looked terminally exhausted and close to tears. These women's problems were small personal tragedies in the larger scheme of things, but all of them had family in Baku and nowhere else to go.

I took the case of the three Armenian women to Hidayat Orujev, President Aliev's adviser and ideologue on nationality issues. Orujev is the spokesman both of Azerbaijan's tolerance and Azerbaijan's suffering at the hands of the Armenians. So in his office, high in the presidential building overlooking the Caspian Sea, he told me, "I haven't had a single complaint that was as a result of inter-ethnic relations." When I put the specific grievances of Sofia, Tanya, and Yevgenia to him, Orujev said he would investigate but suggested to me that I was naïve and being led astray: "There are people who falsify, who want to use the national question as a screen and solve their own problems, which simply don't have any basis in law."[6]

Orujev himself had lived in Armenia for eighteen years and was director of the Azerbaijani Dramatic Theater in Yerevan. He has enough experience to appreciate the complexity of Armenian-Azerbaijani relations, but he insisted that the guilt is all on the Armenian side. We began a rather surreal conversation. The presidential adviser told me in detail how Azerbaijan was the victim of sustained Armenian aggression and that tens of thousands of its citizens had died or been evicted from their homes. Yes, I prompted him and added that I had observed strong hostility to Armenians in Azerbaijan. "Not toward the Armenians but toward the *government* of Armenia," Orujev told me. Azerbaijanis had feelings of toleration toward Armenians, but hatred toward their leaders, he claimed.

Orujev's official role requires a schizophrenic switching of positions. One moment he must condemn Armenian "genocide" and aggression; the next he must insist that Azerbaijan's tradition of tolerance and harmony is alive and well and no Azerbaijani harbors any specific anti-Armenian feelings. I almost felt sorry for him—but his ersatz tolerance is almost as inauthentic as the concrete-and-glass building in which he sits. Coming out of the presidential apparatus into the sunshine, I turned into Istiqlalyat Street and immediately saw a far more noble but ignored example of Baku's synthesis of styles and traditions, Ter-Mikelov's wonderful art nouveau mansion.

The Samed Vurgun Park, just south of Baku's railway station, used to be a pleasant patch of green in the city center, frequented by lovers and people walking their dogs. When I came there, I saw a flotilla of white canvas tents ranged across the bald ground; in front of them were plastic tables, at which moustachioed men sat and played dominoes. This is yet another face of modern Baku.

After most of the Armenians left Baku in 1990, they were followed by tens of thousands of Jews and Russians. In their stead the city received the human flotsam of the conflict with the Armenians—first tens of thousands of Armenian Azerbaijanis and then an even bigger wave of refugees from the Karabakh conflict. This helped turn Baku into a completely Azerbaijani city for the first time in its history. The tents in Samed Vurgun Park were improvised teahouses, or *chaikhanas*, run by disabled war veterans. In January 2000, there were reports of a pitched battle here between the Baku police and a group of invalids. The police had attacked with batons and the invalids had defended themselves with crutches; six invalids and four policemen were reported hurt.[7]

Rufa, a war veteran turned cook, invited me into his teahouse tent. It was a tarpaulin structure with a sand floor; electricity wires sprouted out alarmingly from a hotplate with a kettle simmering on it, and a dusty white-and-gray kitten slept underneath. Rufa confirmed that there had been a fight but said the police had decided to leave them alone, after they resisted. Rufa's tent was run by two brothers from Aghdam; a third brother had died in the war. The veterans did not make much money—perhaps twenty or thirty dollars a month.

In the years 1999–2001, the battle of Samed Vurgun Park was just one of many fights between the war veterans and the government. The fight had a strong symbolic aspect: Who would lay claim to greater authority in Azerbaijan, the authorities or the men who had been wounded fighting for their country? The chairman of the Karabakh Invalids Association, Etimar Asadov, told me that the government had presented them with a $15,000 tax bill, even though they were a charitable organization and the meager benefits the veterans received were barely enough to live on.[8] A year later, when the veterans began political protests, the government arrested many of them and closed down the organization.

The president had his own political reasons for wanting to crush the veterans' movement. Aliev has always perceived the military as a threat, and many of Azerbaijan's leading commanders from the Karabakh war are now in jail. But it seemed to me that part of his spleen against them was that they were spoiling his vision of a new prosperous Baku. Crutch-dependent invalids filled up Baku's parks and demonstrated in front of government buildings reminding people of the other Azerbaijan, beyond its international oil boom.

Cosmopolitan Baku has made a comeback in the 1990s with the promise of new oil wealth. Over the past ten years, hundreds of Baku Azerbaijanis have studied abroad, found professional jobs in the oil industry, opened businesses. The city has begun to smarten up again and parts of it are almost flashy. Nowadays you can live in the Marriot Hotel, drink in Irish bars, eat sushi, and buy Gucci. Fountain Square is overlooked by the tinted glass of an instantly built skyscraper, the ISR Tower, which looks like a large American paperweight flung down from the sky. The Scots and Texans who work there are more sophisticated than the British soldiers in 1918, who apparently moaned about the caviar given them in their daily rations "until the reiterated complaint that 'this 'ere jam do taste of fish' got it removed."[9] The newcomers have made Baku into an international city once again.

But Azerbaijan's oil wealth has probably created more social problems than it has solved. Some people have become fabulously wealthy. The center of Baku is a bubble of prosperity. A few streets out from the center a grimier and more typical reality begins that stretches back into Azerbaijan. Because the non-oil economy has collapsed, most Azerbaijanis get by on a few dollars a month or the remittances of male family members who are guest workers in Turkey or Russia.

Down the street from Asadov's war veterans organization, I found a ten-story tower block that had formerly been a hostel for students at Baku's Pedagogical Institute but was now home to a group of refugees from the city of Aghdam. On the porch, a mosaic in gaudy colors harked back to more optimistic times: spacemen and rockets crowded around two earnest Soviet youths, who were staring at a test tube labeled $H_2O$.

Rovshan Abasov, a student, took me through the hostel. Alone in his family, he seemed to have found a purpose in life since they were washed up here in 1993. We went to visit his aunt, Zumrit Kulieva, and saw the miserable face of the new Baku. The room Zumrit lived in was stuffy and heated by an oil stove. Four people slept in the beds; the children slept on the floor. She said each refugee received fifty thousand manats a month, or about ten dollars, which was not enough for food. "We think that everyone has forgotten us," Zumrit said plainly. "We don't know what will happen to us."

Rovshan said that the water pump in the hostel had broken. The upper stories were no longer getting water through the taps, and the basement was filling up with water. Despite the refugees' complaints, no one had come to repair the water system and they were worried that one day the building might just collapse in on them. It was a disturbing metaphor for Baku. Everything was fine on the surface, but one day the roof might cave in—this time not under the weight of intercommunal tensions but because of the gap between rich and poor.

# 8

# 1990–1991

## A Soviet Civil War

### POLYANICHKO'S HOUR

In January 1990, as order broke down in Baku, the area around Nagorny Karabakh slid out of control. On 15 January, Moscow imposed a State of Emergency on the province and the border regions with Armenia. A delegation sent by the Politburo flew into Karabakh but was turned back at the airfield by Armenian villagers. There was fighting in the villages of the Khanlar region. Then, after the bloodshed of 20 January, Arkady Volsky and his team pulled out of the region, leaving it without any working administration.

This was Viktor Polyanichko's hour. After Black January, Azerbaijan's Russian second secretary had stayed in place as deputy to the new Party boss, Ayaz Mutalibov. When Volsky's team left Nagorny Karabakh, Polyanichko now took personal charge of the new Organizing Committee set up to run the province. A realignment was taking place in Soviet politics, which suited Polyanichko perfectly. In Moscow, Azerbaijan's continuing loyalty was deemed essential to the survival of the union, and he played the role of Moscow's de facto viceroy in the troubled outpost. He formed a strong relationship with the leaders of the security establishment—men like Dmitry Yazov, the defense minister, and Vladimir Kryuchkov, the head of the KGB—and apparently also won the trust of Mikhail Gorbachev.

On 26 January 1990, Polyanichko flew into Nagorny Karabakh, where he was met by the new enforcer of the State of Emergency, General Vladislav Safonov, and moved into the Regional Committee building in Lenin Square in Stepanakert to inaugurate the ten-member Organizing Committee that had been created on paper the previous November. The square itself was the staging area for Armenians who demonstrated against the presence of the Baku emissaries. Polyanichko's chief assistant Seiran Mirzoyev says that they were "completely besieged" for two months: "It was impossible to get out of the building, it was impossible to feed ourselves properly."[1]

Polyanichko and Safonov were the political and military prongs of Azerbaijan's new strategy for Karabakh. They wanted to put on a display of power that would force the Armenians to submit to rule by Baku. Safonov and several thousand extra Interior Ministry troops would impose order, and Polyanichko would wrench the region's political institutions back under Baku's control. According to witnesses who met Polyanichko during this period, he approached his role with gusto, in the manner of a Wagnerian *Heldentenor* taking on a heroic feat. He inspired fearful respect, but Scott Horton, an American lawyer and human rights activist who visited Karabakh in the summer of 1991, recalled an "extremely high level of distrust of Polyanichko." According to Horton, "He was viewed as almost an evil person. Over and over again people wouldn't speak directly about [Polyanichko]—they didn't want to be overheard. But they would speak about Arkady Volsky and they would say really positive things about Volsky—both Armenians and Azerbaijanis."[2]

The new administration showed its intent by arresting several dozen Armenian activists and holding them for up to thirty days. Over the following eighteen months, many were detained more than once, among them the journalist Arkady Gukasian, now the leader of Nagorny Karabakh, who was sent to prison in the Russian town Rostov-on-Don.[3]

Simultaneously, Polyanichko—doubtless using methods he had perfected in both Afghanistan and Azerbaijan—was trying to sow discord among the rebels. "We did everything to split the separatists," Seiran Mirzoyev remembers. "When we came to Nagorny Karabakh they were a single core. By the end of 1990 we had managed to split this core, or, to be more accurate, we had noticed the first cracks in this core." Mirzoyev declared that by spreading rumors and false allegations, they caused a public quarrel between conservative Party official Genrikh Pogosian and the young radical Arkady Manucharov.

A high priority for Azerbaijan was to reimpose economic control. In May 1990, Mutalibov returned from a trip to Moscow with news of the abolition of the separate "line" for Nagorny Karabakh in the budget of the Soviet planning agency Gosplan, which Gorbachev had announced in February 1988 and Volsky had tried to administer. Karabakh was formally a full part of the Azerbaijani economy once again.

At the same time the Baku authorities buttressed the Karabakh Azerbaijani population by resettling Azerbaijanis in Khojali, whereupon the village in the plains was officially upgraded to town status. Its newcomers were several hundred Azerbaijanis and a group of Meskhetian Turks, recently deported from Central Asia.

In the spring of 1990, Polyanichko deployed his most powerful weapon. Under new Soviet legislation, Union Republics had the right to form their own special police forces, which were in effect legalized paramilitaries. Armenia's force was called OMOR; Azerbaijani's force, like those of several other republics, was called OMON, and its members were often called "Black Berets" because of their distinctive headgear.[4]

The Azerbaijani OMON was deployed almost exclusively in and around Nagorny Karabakh. The ten thousand or so militiamen manned checkpoints, went on patrols, and made searches for weapons. They took over Karabakh's airport at Khojali, where they gained a fearsome reputation for shaking down passengers to whom they took a dislike and sexually harassing women. In July 1990, the members of an international human rights delegation complained vociferously that the OMON had abused them and detained five accompanying Armenians, and said that almost all the OMON men to whom they had spoken were Azerbaijanis who earlier had been deported from Armenia.[5]

A year after his arrival, Polyanichko reported that his tough tactics were working. His assistant Seiran Mirzoyev claims that by the spring of 1991 Armenian farm workers were sending their milk, meat, and wine to Azerbaijan and had accepted the inevitability of rule from Baku. "Political influence was restored, if not in the whole of Nagorny Karabakh, then in a significant part of it, the Nagorny Karabakh population clearly accepted the authority of the Republican Organizing Committee."

Others give a different view. Vadim Byrkin, who was correspondent for the Soviet news agency TASS in Nagorny Karabakh at the time, says that Polyanichko's authority was purely provisional:

> [Polyanichko] had no real mechanisms of administration because he had no power structures at his disposal. He had his Organizing Committee of ten people, which held meetings that the Armenians didn't

Rallying in Lenin Square, Baku, Azerbaijan, 1989. (Oleg Litvin)

Nationalist demonstration, Azerbaijan, 1989. (Oleg Litvin)

"Operation Ring." Azerbaijani fighters in village of Todan, 1991. (Oleg Litvin)

War breaks out. Coffin evacuated by helicopter to Armenia, winter of 1991–92. (Jon Jones)

Armenian fighters firing salute, winter of 1991–92. (Jon Jones)

Funeral of Armenian fighter, winter of 1991–92. (Jon Jones)

Maternity unit in the basement of parliament, Stepanakert, winter of 1991–92. (Jon Jones)

Armenian fighter overlooking Stepanakert, winter of 1991–92. (Jon Jones)

Karintak, the aftermath. Armenian fighter with Azerbaijani dead behind him, 1992. (Jon Jones)

In Aghdam, Azerbaijan, 1992. (Halid Askerov)

Azerbaijani refugees fleeing Kelbajar, 1993. (Halid Askerov)

On the way out. Azerbaijani president Abulfaz Elchibey (left) is being edged
out by his successor, Heidar Aliev (middle), 1992. (Halid Askerov)

But are they "Albanians?" Two medieval princes on the wall of the twelfth-century monastery of  Dadi Vank, Karabakh. (Thomas de Waal)

On the path to Yeghishe Arakyal monastery, Nagorny Karabakh. (Onnik Krikorian)

"Victory Day," 9 May 2000. Karabakh Armenian officers lay flowers at the tank outside Shusha. (Thomas de Waal)

In the ruins of Shusha. The view from the lower mosque, 2001. The rebuilt church of Gazanchetsots is in the background. (Onnik Krikorian)

"The Hiroshima of the Caucasus." Aghdam, the view from the mosque, 2001. (Onnik Krikorian)

At the Genocide Memorial, Yerevan, 24 April 2000. (Georgina Wilson)

Descending the hill from the Genocide Memorial, Yerevan, 24 April 2000. (Georgina Wilson)

The Children's Republic. A girls' dance class in Camp C-1, Sabirabad, Azerbaijan, 2000. (Thomas de Waal)

The Children's Republic, 2000. (Thomas de Waal)

Passing the days in S-3 refugee camp outside Saatly, Azerbaijan 2000. (Thomas de Waal)

"I left all my books behind." Gabil Akhmedov and his wife Agiyat, S-3 refugee camp, 2000. (Thomas de Waal)

attend. There were reports to Baku that everything was fine here, that the Armenians had begun to cooperate. In fact there was no cooperation. . . . There was only one Armenian, Valery Grigorian, who attended the committee meetings, but he was later killed. . . . The only mechanism they had was the Soviet army through the commandant, General Safonov.[6]

## ARMENIA: THE TAKING OF POWER

In the summer of 1990, the Armenian National Movement (ANM) completed its takeover of power. In the May 1990 elections to the new Supreme Soviet of Armenia, ANM members had won a majority of seats and they decided to use this as a bridgehead to make a bid for power.

Levon Ter-Petrosian was elected speaker of Armenia's Supreme Soviet on 4 August, a post that made him the de facto leader of the republic. On 23 August, the Supreme Soviet passed a declaration of sovereignty, which stated that Armenia was moving toward independence. Lenin's statue in the center of Yerevan was taken down. Another ANM leader, Vazgen Manukian, was made prime minister.

The leaders of the ANM were the first non-Communists to take power in a Soviet republic, and their first worry was that they be allowed to keep it. Manukian and Ashot Manucharian flew to Moscow and in a two-hour meeting with Politburo member Yevgeny Primakov tried to present themselves as pragmatists who posed no danger to the Soviet state. According to Manukian, the cautious Primakov had to weigh whether "the game was worth the candle"—whether Moscow should crush the new administration—and he decided against intervention.[7]

The Moscow leadership was most worried about Armenia's illegal armed paramilitaries. On 25 July 1990, Gorbachev signed "On the Prohibition of the Creation of Armed Formations," a decree aimed primarily at Armenia, where two small private militias had appeared in 1989. The Armenian Army of Independence (AAI) was founded by Leonid Azgaldian, who was killed in Karabakh three years later. The Armenian National Army (ANA) was founded by Razmik Vasilian and Vartan Vartanian. Together, the militias had perhaps two thousand men under arms, arms they had stolen or bought from Soviet bases. Several shootouts between paramilitary members and Soviet troops in Yerevan took place in 1990.

In August, three days of violence broke out between armed Armenian and Azerbaijanis on a section of the northern border between the two republics. Soviet Interior Ministry troops were called out but at least sixteen people were killed and fifty wounded on both sides. Ter-Petrosian used the fighting to try to bring the Armenian militias under his control, and his parliamentary administration formally dissolved one of the groups. "We were told we were next," remembered Levon Eiramjiants, one of the founders of the AAI. "When it became clear they would do the same to us as they had to the ANA, we decided to form a party to build a political roof for ourselves." The AAI made itself into a political party and, after the sovereignty declaration, formally laid down its arms. Its two thousand former fighters swore allegiance to the new Armenian Interior Ministry.[8]

The new Armenian administration did not want armed fighters in Armenia who would threaten its authority and provoke Moscow, but was happy to see them go to Karabakh, where after the Polyanichko administration had arrived, a low-intensity conflict had begun. "We understood that they would simply use the hands of the Soviet Interior Ministry forces to strangle us," says the Karabakh Armenian leader Arkady Gukasian. "And then partisan units began to form, which struck at the Soviet Interior Ministry Forces. We understood that war was inevitable." Inside Karabakh, weapons were either bought from soldiers or were homemade. One former fighter tells how Stepanakert's furniture factory was secretly producing homemade pistols and mine cases during this period. It was searched by the OMON several times, but its secret was never discovered.[9]

Increasing numbers of militiamen from Armenia now joined the struggle, infiltrating the hills of Karabakh and Armenian villages of Azerbaijan. The new rebel units adopted names that had been out of use since the Armenian partisan campaigns at the turn of the century. They formed *djogads*, or "hunter's groups." And they called themselves *fedayin*, a word taken from the Arabic, meaning sacrificial fighters willing to risk their lives for the cause. The Armenian writer and activist Zori Balayan tells of more than two hundred operations against the Polyanichko administration carried out by Armenian partisans. They blew up bridges and sections of railway track, fired on columns of vehicles, and took hostages, whom they exchanged for Armenian prisoners in the Shusha jail.[10] Polyanichko responded by sealing all roads between Nagorny Karabakh and Armenia.


## OPERATION RING: THE PLANNING

Armenia and Azerbaijan began the last year of the Soviet Union, 1991, heading down different political paths. Gorbachev was working on a new Union Treaty, which he hoped would preserve the Union, while delegating greater powers to the republics. Armenia, along with Georgia, Moldova, and the Baltic republics, had begun moving toward independence and refused to work with Gorbachev. Azerbaijan agreed to work on the treaty and stay in the Union, for a price.

The Azerbaijani Party boss Ayaz Mutalibov was becoming a pivotal figure in the bargaining process. In Black January, he had become leader of the republic almost by accident but was now hanging on tenaciously. Mutalibov was unusual for an Azerbaijani politician mainly in that he was from Baku, not Heidar Aliev's home region of Nakhichevan. He had had a conventional Party career, working for many years as head of a machine-building factory. Cultivated but rather vain, he lacked the natural authority of Aliev but proved adept enough at playing Moscow politics. He used his loyalty to extract maximum popular support from Moscow.

In January 1991, Mutalibov's written report to the Central Committee was full of alarming predictions about the prospects for Azerbaijan. An 11 January memo on the report by Vyacheslav Mikhailov, the Central Committee's nationalities expert, survives in the archives. He quoted Mutalibov as saying that the situation in Azerbaijan was deteriorating because of "the claims of the Republic of Armenia on Nagorny Karabakh. The telegram draws attention to how large quantities of weapons are piling up in the hands of armed formations, legalized by the Supreme Soviet of Armenia, and points out the possibility of an escalation of armed conflict."

From Mikhailov's summary, it appears that Mutalibov's letter was half warning, half threat:

> Further developments could lead to a wide-scale armed confrontation between Azerbaijan and Armenia, a serious destabilization of Azerbaijan and, in the final analysis, the seizure of power by extremist

circles of the Popular Front of Azerbaijan. It is entirely possible that in the case of a failure to adopt extreme measures, the Supreme Soviet of the Azerbaijani SSR will take the decision to create a national army, abolish the autonomy of the Nagorny Karabakh Autonomous Region and refuse to sign the new Union Treaty. The position of the Communist Party and its authority, won at elections to the Supreme Soviet of the republic, will be undermined in the most serious way.[11]

Mikhailov recommended that "the Minister of Defense, the Interior Ministry and the KGB of the USSR immediately carry out a special operation in the region together with the republican organs of Armenia and Azerbaijan to disarm illegal armed formations." On 17 January 1991, the Central Committee agreed to the recommendations.

The two documents show how closely the Nagorny Karabakh issue was tied to Moscow politics. Mutalibov was using the specter of domestic trouble in Azerbaijan to secure support for an even tougher crackdown on the Armenians. The Moscow establishment accepted the trade-off and gave strong backing to both Mutalibov and Polyanichko. In the short-term this played to the advantage of the Azerbaijani leadership as Soviet army and police units were deployed against the Karabakh Armenians. In the longer-term, however, it proved disastrous for Azerbaijan, as the republic lagged behind Armenia in building its own security forces.

On 17 March 1991, the Soviet leadership held a nationwide referendum on the future of the USSR. Azerbaijan took part and dutifully delivered a yes vote for preserving the Soviet Union in a new Union Treaty. Armenia, now ruled by the ANM, was one of six dissident republics that boycotted the referendum altogether. Instead, Armenia declared that it would hold its own referendum in September, on independence.

The Azerbaijani leadership's act of loyalty was a necessary condition for the next phase of its strong-arm tactics in and around Nagorny Karabakh: the implementation of the plan to "disarm illegal armed formations." The operation was referred to in Azerbaijan as a "passport-checking operation," but it became notorious by its code name, Operation Ring. The documents being "checked" were the internal passports carried by all Soviet citizens that stated their *propiska*, their official registration in a town or village. The declared intent of the Azerbaijani authorities was to check the internal passports of residents in a series of

Armenian-inhabited villages on the borders of Karabakh that were sheltering Armenian *fedayin*, expel the interlopers, and therby restore order.

Mutalibov now contends that the plans for what he called an operation for the "liquidation of terrorists" had existed on paper since 1989 and only needed implementing. He is candid about how he sold it in Moscow to the leadership as politically expedient: "I presented it in political terms, and I knew that you have to work here in Moscow."[12]

What followed was a small Soviet civil war, fought on very unequal terms. On one side were units of the Soviet 4th Army, based in Ganje, whose entire 23rd Division, complete with tanks and artillery, was made available for the operation. They were joined by units of the Azerbaijani OMON and groups of Azerbaijani villagers, who engaged in looting and intimidation. On the other were the Armenian *fedayin*. There were far fewer of them, perhaps a few hundred in all, but their morale was extremely high; they had not-so-secret backing from the new authorities in Armenia, logistical support from Armenian villagers, and even helicopters to fly them back and forth.

One of the ANM leaders, Ashot Manucharian, had become Armenia's interior minister in 1991. He helped the paramilitaries by giving them illicitly bought weapons and transport to Karabakh. Most of the arms, Manucharian admits, came from Soviet army bases. "We bought a lot of weapons in Georgian military units." They were mostly hand-held weapons, automatic weapons, and grenade launchers that could be taken either by helicopter or on foot across mountain paths into Karabakh.[13]

In the spring and summer of 1991, the violence escalated into a partisan-style conflict between villages; raids were made and hostages were taken. Six Azerbaijani villagers were killed in one attack by Armenian fighters on the village of Karadogly.[14] The Armenians started using a new weapon, the Alazan rocket, a device that had not been designed for warfare. It consisted of a thin shaft about two feet in length, capped by a small rocket head that the Soviet Meteorological Service fired into clouds in mountain regions to disperse gathering hailstorms. Alazans caused considerable damage and could kill if they hit a human directly. The Armenians first used them as a combat weapon in April, when they fired several into Shusha, hitting several houses and wounding three people.

A month later, on 10 May 1991, an Armenian partisan's rocket-propelled grenade struck Viktor Polyanichko's office. He survived the attempt on his life. (The military leader Safonov also escaped an Armenian assassination attempt, in April 1991, in Rostov-on-Don, which killed another Russian officer by mistake.) Polyanichko was eventually assassinated, long after he had left Karabakh. In July 1993, he was killed by Armenian assailants in the North Caucasian republic of North Ossetia.

## OPERATION RING: THE EXECUTION

In the spring of 1991, the main battleground in the Armenian-Azerbaijan partisan war was not Nagorny Karabakh itself but the wooded hills to the north of the Khanlar and Shaumian regions.[15] Both had mainly Armenian populations. *Fedayin* had infiltrated their Armenian villages, partly as the villages' self-appointed protectors against the Azerbaijani OMON, and partly to use them as a route into Karabakh. Several dozen fighters had established themselves in the villages of Getashen (known as Chaikend by the Azerbaijanis) and its near neighbor Martunashen (or Karabulakh) in the Khanlar region. They were led by Tatul Krpeyan, a Dashnak from Armenia who had been teaching in the village school.

On 10 April 1991, the decision was made to launch the operation against Getashen and Martunashen,[16] and in the last two weeks of the month the three thousand villagers were gradually sealed off from the outside world. A cordon of troops surrounded the villages, and its telephone lines and electricity supply were cut. The signal for the operation to start was the removal of the Interior Ministry post. Interior Ministry troops tended to be Russian and more likely to take the side of the Armenian villagers; the army units consisted mainly, and the OMON units wholly, of Azerbaijanis.[17]

The Moscow-based human rights group Memorial has reconstructed what happened. On 30 April, 4th Army soldiers and then the Azerbaijani OMON entered Getashen. Resistance was sporadic, but Krpeyan was killed and his men took several soldiers hostage. The OMON raided and looted houses and attacked many of the inhabitants; of the dozen or so killed, many were in their eighties and nineties. They took fifty hostages—half of whom were later exchanged for the soldiers and half were sent to the Ganje prison. The outnumbered *fedayin* slipped away. Within a week, the inhabitants of both villages had been deported, the majority ferried by helicopter to Stepanakert and from there to Armenia. Most had been forced to sign documents that they were leaving of their own free will. After they had gone, a hitherto un-advertised part of Operation Ring was enacted as Azerbaijani refugees, who had fled Armenia in 1988–1989, were brought into Getashen/ Chaikend and took over the recently abandoned Armenian houses as living quarters.

Successful in military terms, Azerbaijan's operation against the vil-lagers bore a heavy political cost. The new Russian parliament, whose speaker was Boris Yeltsin, had formed a close alliance with the ANM administration in Armenia; and they saw that they had a common enemy in the Soviet security establishment. Russian parliamentarians took up the cause of the beleaguered Armenian villagers. Later on they were to hold their first-ever parliamentary hearings on Operation Ring. It was the beginning of a new Armenian-Russian political relationship.

Another operation was planned for 6–7 May against the village of Voskepar on the northern section of the Armenia-Azerbaijan border. Voskepar was inside Armenia but had been involved in skirmishes with Azerbaijani settlements across the border. Azerbaijan's operation to "neutralize" the village shows how blurred the line between official and unofficial security forces had become. Outside Voskepar, a minibus car-rying about thirty Armenian policemen was ambushed by soldiers of the 23rd Division; eleven were killed and the others were taken captive. As far as the Azerbaijanis were concerned, they were Armenian para-military fighters; the Armenians could point out with equal justice that they were the uniformed policemen of a Soviet republic, killed on their own territory.

Four Russian parliamentary deputies arrived on the scene and one, Anatoly Shabad, stayed in the village. Shabad is half Armenian, but his main motive for getting involved seems to have been passionate oppo-sition to the Communist security apparatus. When full-scale war broke out, he distanced himself from the Karabakh Armenian movement, and later still become one of the leading critics of Russian military action in Chechnya.

Shabad recalls scenes of anxiety and confusion in Voskepar. He says he did not see armed fighters, who appear to have been on the edge of the village and acting on their own. Through a loudspeaker, a Soviet army commander gave the villagers a deadline to surrender their weap-ons. When no one reacted and the deadline had expired, an artillery bombardment opened up. Most of the shells were fired over or away from the village, but three villagers who had fled in fright were killed.

Shabad says that he later realized the bombardment was meant to in-timidate the civilians into submission rather than to hit the fighters. He saw exactly the same tactic used by the Russian army in Chechnya in 1995–1996:

> Armed men, who fight in wars, are not frightened by these things. They are only frightened when the firing is aimed at them. I under-stood later that if there is only noise all around you and the shells are flying in another direction, you can simply drink cognac and not react at all. All these things are designed to sow panic among the civilian population. Women begin to weep, dogs bark, cows moo, and a situa-tion is created.[18]

The presence of a Russian member of parliament evidently saved the villagers of Voskepar from becoming additional victims of Operation Ring. The division's troops did not enter the village, and Shabad man-aged subsequently to extract the surviving Armenian policemen from Azerbaijani custody by means of a large cash payment provided for him by the Armenian Interior Ministry. A week later, however, all of the inhabitants of seventeen smaller Armenian villages in the Hadrut and Shusha regions of Nagorny Karabakh were deported. Human rights ac-tivists estimated that during the first phase of the operation, five thou-sand Armenians were deported and between twenty and thirty were killed.

## AN ATTEMPT AT COMPROMISE

If Operation Ring had been planned as an act of intimidation against the Karabakh Armenians, it began to achieve results. After its first phase, with villagers from Getashen flooding into Stepanakert, the Karabakh Armenian movement showed its first serious cracks. On 19 June 1991, Party officials from the (still suspended) Regional Soviet passed a reso-lution expressing their intention to change "the course from a policy of confrontation to a policy of dialogue and negotiations." They appeared to be offering a political bargain: in return for the re-creation of Party or-gans and the "demilitarization" of Nagorny Karabakh, they would vote to suspend their secession from Azerbaijan. This looked to be a major concession. A delegation headed by the Party functionary Valery Grigorian went to Moscow to put these proposals. Mirzoyev of Azerbaijan's Organizational Committee says proudly: "The people understood that there was authority in Nagorny Karabakh and began to take account of that."[19]

Despite this, the violence between Azerbaijan and the Armenian villages continued. When operations began in the Shaumian region in July, a commander named "Colonel Felix" led a more professional defense of Armenian villages. Helicopters from Armenia, machine guns pointing out of their windows as they crossed Azerbaijani territory, landed at the nearby village of Gulistan, site of the famous Russo-Iranian peace treaty of 1813.[20]

The signal for the start of the operation in Shaumian was a decree, signed by Gorbachev, lifting the State of Emergency in the region on 4 July 1991 on the grounds that the situation was "normalizing." This was a cynical ploy, which forced the recall of Interior Ministry troops, who were either neutral or protecting the Armenian villages. As they moved out, the aggressive soldiers of the 23rd Division and the Azerbaijani OMON moved in and surrounded the villages of Erkech, Buzlukh, and Manashid.

The Bulgarian journalist Cvetana Paskaleva captured on film the drama of the final days of Erkech. In the footage, a helicopter buzzes over the village while a Russian officer from the 23rd Division warns over a loudspeaker that troops will come into the village to "check the passport regime." If the villagers do not cooperate, they will be subjected to the "most decisive measures." Frightened villagers show their children to Paskaleva's camera to prove that Erkech is not merely a nest of fighters. They complain that they have been under a blockade for six months, without proper food, water, and electricity. In another part of the village, we see the fighters: a group of bearded, swarthy men with ammunition belts twisted around their dirty olive uniforms. Resistance here is stronger than formerly. The men smoke, argue, and sing *fedayi* songs.[21] The artillery bombardment begins, and the villagers start to leave. The fighters make their way out in single file before the OMON moves in. A shell hits a lorry, killing two of the fleeing villagers.

Paskaleva returned to the village in September, when it was recaptured by Armenian fighters, and in her footage from that trip, we see what happened to Erkech after the Azerbaijanis moved in. It is now semidestroyed, and the names of the recent Azerbaijani tenants, already driven out, are written in white paint on the metal gates of the houses.

After the Shaumian operation, the Karabakh Armenian Party delegation traveled to Baku on 20 July for peace talks with Mutalibov. In a letter to the Azerbaijani leader, they declared that they were prepared to hold negotiations "on the basis of the constitution of the Soviet Union and the Republic of Azerbaijan and Union documents on Nagorny Karabakh" and wanted to discuss the timing of new local elections.[22] This was, in effect, an offer of capitulation in return for guarantees of self-government within Azerbaijan. It is interesting to speculate what might have happened had negotiations on this basis taken place in 1988 or if events had not canceled the peace initiative. By this point, however, it seems unlikely that the delegation had enough authority to deliver a compromise deal and it was heavily criticized on its return to Stepanakert.

Then on 10 August, Valery Grigorian, the man who had spearheaded the push for compromise, was shot and killed in the street in Stepanakert. It seems likely that he was assassinated by his fellow Armenians as a collaborator. The nationalist activist Zhanna Galstian told the Swedish scholar Erik Melander: "Anyone who signed such a document—a document that was invalid because neither we nor the people could have abided by it—we would have threatened his life; he would simply have been shot, even if this was a close friend of ours."[23] The attempt at compromise was over.

## THE RECKONING

Operation Ring marked the beginning of the open, armed phase of the Karabakh conflict. In that sense it is part of a process. It is also an important story in itself, in that it is arguably the first and last "Soviet civil war" in which units of the Soviet army were engaged in fighting on Soviet territory. The messy and brutal way in which this was done reveals much about the condition of the Soviet military and, by extension, of the Soviet state in 1991.

The official Azerbaijani version of the operation is that Azerbaijanis faced a genuine threat from the Armenian guerrillas who were infiltrating Karabakh. The Armenian *fedayin* were using the Khanlar and Shaumian regions as a route to Nagorny Karabakh and "terrorizing the Armenian population," says the former Azerbaijani president Mutalibov. Seiran Mirzoyev, Polyanichko's assistant, and by character a moderate man, was insistent that they had complaints from the Armenians villagers themselves about the fighters. For example, six old men from the Hadrut region had begged him to help them to leave; apparently they were unprotected in a village bereft of young men, and armed partisans from Armenia were coming and going at will.

There may be some truth in this. Fanatical fighters, wanting provisions and places to hide, can cause serious problems for ordinary folk who want a peaceful life. There were frequently scenes during the war in Chechnya in 1994–1996, when villagers would beg a group of fighters to leave in order to spare them an assault by Russian forces. Yet this does not mean the villagers wanted to leave their villages altogether, with no right of return—and it is wildly implausible that the people of Hadrut or Getashen wanted to see the Azerbaijani OMON enter their villages instead. If these villagers had a problem with Armenian fighters, an armed assault on their villages followed by their own mass deportation was not the solution they were anticipating. And the rapid settlement of Azerbaijani refugees in the villages the Armenians had left shows that this was about more than just "unmasking terrorists."

Two human rights groups who interviewed refugees found evidence of systematic violence. One of them concluded:

> Officials of Azerbaijan, including the chairman of the Supreme Soviet of the republic Ayaz Mutalibov and the Second Secretary of the Central Committee of the Communist Party Viktor Polyanichko, continue to justify these deportations, representing them as voluntary resettlement by the residents of Nagorny Karabakh. However we possess irrefutable testimony that these actions were carried out with the use of physical force and weapons, leading to murders, maiming and loss of personal property.[24]

What, then, was the real agenda behind the operation? Clearly, there was a strategic motive. By emptying Armenian villages on the edges of Karabakh, the Azerbaijani authorities were trying to block the Armenian *fedayin*, cut off their supply routes, and create a new "ring" of Azerbaijani villages around Karabakh. However, politics seems to been even more important.

The Soviet authorities were trying to win Azerbaijani support by taking a tough line on Nagorny Karabakh. They were trying to suppress the Karabakh Armenian movement—and to a degree they were successful. Azerbaijan's pressure showed not only on local Karabakhis but on the new Armenian leader, Levon Ter-Petrosian. On 20 July 1991, he put in his one and only attendance at the talks on Gorbachev's Union Treaty at Novo-Ogarevo outside Moscow, suggesting that he was also ready to make concessions. At the same time, a row developed in Yerevan between the nationalist ANM administration and Communist Party officials. The then Party leader, Aram Sarkisian, has accused Ter-Petrosian of wanting to sell out the Shaumian region in return for a more favorable deal on the rest of Nagorny Karabakh.[25] All of this shows that in 1991 the Armenian nationalist movement was far less monolithic and more fragile than it seemed on the surface.

Yet while some were talking compromise, Armenian armed resistance continued. In Shaumian, it took several weeks for the numerically superior Soviet and Azerbaijani forces, even using the tanks and heavy artillery of the 4th Army, to force out Armenian irregulars. Three witnesses who saw the Armenian fighters at the time were struck, variously, by their "vitality," "esprit de corps," and the fact that they were "strongly superior in the moral-psychological sense." In Armenia, the operation spurred a big recruiting drive for the *fedayi* movement, thereby undermining one of its main objectives. Shabad commented:

> Evidently Mutalibov had persuaded Gorbachev that there was a powerful partisan army of *fedayin* there and that its actions would lead to the secession of Armenian populated territories from Azerbaijan, that they were bandits and that they had to be liquidated. And Gorbachev —it was a great stupidity on his part of course—agreed to this operation. He probably understands now that an operation of that sort was doomed, it was impossible. We see in Chechnya that a war against partisans is an empty undertaking.

In the fall of 1991, when events had suddenly turned in their favor, the Armenians managed to recapture most of the villages in Shaumian with relative ease. In purely military terms, then, the operation was flawed: its planners had underestimated the strength of the partisan movement they were facing.

Operation Ring was made possible by the increasingly desperate political situation in Moscow. It was supported by the security chiefs who were already plotting to overthrow Mikhail Gorbachev. Several of the confused motives they showed in staging their coup d'état—trying to preserve the Soviet Union, putting on a show of strength, meting out punishment—were also present in the operation. Gorbachev himself, consistent with the vacillations and uncertainties he was prey to during this period, seems to have supported the operation without fully understanding what was going on. It is possible that he was being misled by those around him. The then Armenian Party boss, Aram Sarkisian, recalls a heated incident with the Soviet president during an interval at a session of the Supreme Soviet in Moscow in July 1991. If nothing else, his story suggests the chaotic state of decision making at the top:

> During the interval, I suddenly noticed that Mutalibov, Yazov, and Kryuchkov were all standing with Gorbachev, and Yazov was informing Gorbachev of something. I realized that they were talking about [Operation Ring] and went up and stood behind Gorbachev, knowing that that was not quite the "done" thing. Yazov saw me and stopped talking. Gorbachev turned round, took me by the arm, and said, "Let's go." We moved to one side and he said to me, "What are your Armenians up to down there?" I said, "What's that?" "Causing explosions, killing, driving people out, and so forth." I said, "Excuse me, that is information from the Azerbaijani side, and do you have any information from the Armenian side?" He said, "What meaning does that have?" I said that in actual fact Armenians were being deported and small groups of Armenians, more or less organized, were trying to resist them. He told me, "There can't be any deportations because I did not give any orders. I said, "I beg you, there is Kryuchkov, chairman of the KGB, let's invite him over and let him say in front of me that no deportations are happening." [Gorbachev] understood that something was not right and said, "OK, I will sort it out myself."[26]

Polyanichko, a supporter of the coup plotters, exemplified this mix of Soviet patriotism and brute force. Scott Horton, one of the American members of the human rights delegation that visited Karabakh in July 1991, received the impression that Polyanichko had no real loyalty to Azerbaijan as such, but he believed that by sowing discord in the region, he was entrenching Soviet power. Horton sat next to Polyanichko on the short flight from Baku to Stepanakert and got into a conversation with him about his past:

He started talking about Afghanistan and told me how he had played an important role in the war in Afghanistan. He had been a scholar of Oriental affairs and he understood the tribal nature of the Afghanistanis and was responsible for formulating and implementing Russian strategy designed to get advantage from that or something like that. I asked, "What did that mean?" He said that, for instance, they would transport ethnic groups and move them around. They would take a group that had a very hostile relationship with one group and put it right in the middle so it was surrounded by the others, to cause discord and tension and so forth. And then I said, "That's very interesting because that seems so much like Operation Ring, exactly what's going on here, with the way groups were being transported." He didn't want to talk about that at all.

Another American member of that delegation, William Green Miller, who was head of the Committee on U.S.-Soviet Relations, drew another conclusion from the same trip:

> It was very clear that the complications of the end of the Soviet Union were evident there: the loyalties to the Soviet past, confusion about the future of the Soviet Union, the confusion about the use of force in the presence of foreigners, even as observers. All of that was very evident . . . I thought [Polyanichko] was in a kind of confusion that represented the Soviet Union itself at the time.[27]

The Soviet Union was in fact going through its very last days. Between 19 and 21 August, it received the terminal shock of the attempted putsch in Moscow and its collapse. Like all other Soviet citizens, the people of Armenia and Azerbaijan emerged from the chaos of the coup attempt into a different world.

# 9

# Divisions

## *A Twentieth-Century Story*

ON THE BORDER between Soviet Armenia and Azerbaijan, between the towns of Ijevan and Kazakh and just south of Georgia, there used to stand a monument of a tree. At its crest it blossomed into a flower, whose petals symbolized the friendship of the three Soviet republics of the South Caucasus.

In Soviet times probably no one paid much attention to this exotic tree-flower, but that was probably because for most people its message appeared self-evident. Most inhabitants of the Caucasus insist that right up until the late 1980s they lived in friendship with their neighbors of all nationalities and thought of themselves as loyal Soviet citizens. For seventy years there was almost no instance of mass violence between Armenians and Azerbaijanis. They lived side by side, traded with each other and intermarried.

Yet the dispute between Armenians and Azerbaijanis in 1988 was more than just a misunderstanding that got out of hand. It was a deep rupture that completely split them apart and played a leading role in breaking up the Soviet Union. Why and how did mass peaceful coexistence turn so suddenly into conflict?

A tentative answer to this all-important and troubling question should begin with the fact that although there was coexistence, trade, and intermarriage between Armenians and Azerbaijanis, there was also astonishingly little dialogue. To hear leaders on either side talk about the origins of the Armenia-Azerbaijan conflict is to hear two narratives, each hermetically sealed from the other. Many Azerbaijanis, for example, reject the idea that there is such a thing as a "Karabakh question" at all. They say that they were the victims of a dangerous Armenian idea, which had almost nothing to with Nagorny Karabakh as such. The Azerbaijani opposition politician Isa Gambar argues for instance that the events of February 1988 in Karabakh were an irredentist movement, imported from Armenia, and it could have been suppressed by prompt action from the Azerbaijani leadership in Baku:

> The initiative was on the Armenian side. They began to make territorial claims on Azerbaijan, and they stood behind the beginning of the separatist movement in Nagorny Karabakh. So there is no doubting the responsibility of the Armenian ultranationalists in this question. At the same time, we believe that the then leadership of Azerbaijan bears its share of responsibility in the sense that had they taken a more tough and decisive position, then the question could have been resolved within the first few days.[1]

The Armenian leader Robert Kocharian proposes a completely opposite argument, that conflict in Karabakh was historically inevitable:

> In 1917, the Revolution happened. When central Russian authority ceased to exist, this problem arose in its most acute form. There was a war for three years and then in effect Soviet troops joined Karabakh to Azerbaijan. So this problem was always there and it was completely obvious that when central authority weakened or ceased to exist, then we would get what we now have. To all Karabakh Armenians, that was completely obvious. There was no doubt about that—and it seems to me that it was obvious to the Azerbaijanis too.[2]

The mutually exclusive alternative views of recent history show how in the Soviet era, Armenia and Azerbaijan ran on separate political, economic, and cultural tracks, which rarely intersected and had built into them a strong contempt and fear of the other.

## A TWENTIETH-CENTURY DISPUTE

In untangling the roots of the Karabakh conflict, we should first of all dismiss the idea that this was an "ancient conflict." Both the form and the content of the Armenia-Azerbaijan dispute date back little more than one hundred years. The central bone of contention, Nagorny Karabakh, was fought over in 1905 and in 1918–1920, was allocated to Azerbaijan in 1921, and had its borders drawn in 1923. As two American scholars put it, "[O]ne might say, the origins of the current conflict are 'shrouded in the mists of the twentieth century.'"[3]

The ideological framework of the dispute is also quite modern. Nationalist ideology—the belief that an ethnic group is entitled to some kind of statehood within certain borders—was not a strong factor in the region until the end of the nineteenth century. So what follows is a twentieth-century history.

The roots of the dispute can be traced back to the period when the Ottoman and Russian Empires were in their dying phases and both Armenians and Azerbaijanis discovered the idea of national self-determination. The Armenians began to be inspired by the example of independence movements in the Balkans and eastern Europe. The major Armenian nationalist party, the Armenian Revolutionary Federation (better known as the Dashnaktsutiun or Dashnaks) was founded only in 1890. At the same time Azerbaijanis began to discover their "Turkic brothers," forged closer links with Turkey, and militated to secede from Russia.

The catastrophic events of 1915 transformed and accelerated the whole process. The collapse of the Ottoman Empire and the mass slaughter of its Armenian population ended centuries of Armenian life in Turkey and turned Russian Armenia into a land of refugees. Then, with the end of the Russian imperial regime in 1917, the main nationalities of the Caucasus had independence thrust upon them. In May 1918, the three principal nations of the Caucasus became separate states. Independence was most to the advantage of Georgia because neither the Armenians nor the Azerbaijanis were in full control of their states. On 28 May, the Azerbaijanis proclaimed an independent Azerbaijan whose temporary capital was Ganje, in that Baku was still controlled by the Bolshevik Commune. The Armenians declared independence on the same day and, with great reluctance, in the Georgian capital Tiflis. They had just staved off total conquest by the Turks at the Battle of Sardarabad and within days had to sign a humiliating peace treaty.

The two nationalist regimes that took over Armenia and Azerbaijan in 1918, led by the Dashnaktsutiun and Musavat parties, quarreled over where their common borders lay. They fought over three ethnically mixed provinces, lined up on the map from west to east, like dominoes leaning against one another: Nakhichevan, Zangezur, and Karabakh. In Nakhichevan, the westernmost, Azerbaijan consolidated control that year, with Turkish support, driving out thousands of Armenians. In

Zangezur, across the mountains to the east, the ferocious Armenian guerrilla commander known as Andranik swept through the region, burning Azerbaijani villages and expelling their inhabitants. In the mountains of Karabakh, the situation was more complex: the local assembly of Karabakh Armenians tried to declare independence but had almost no contact with the Republic of Armenia across the mountains.

When World War I ended that November, Turkey capitulated to the Allies and withdrew from Azerbaijan. Great Britain moved in, and independent Azerbaijan effectively spent its first year under a British mandate. Chiefly interested in Azerbaijan as a bulwark against the Bolsheviks and a source of oil, the British made only half-hearted attempts to resolve the border disputes. In December, a British mission established itself in Shusha and stayed for eight months. (Two British soldiers—a Lancashire rifleman and a Pathan from the North West Frontier—are buried somewhere outside Shusha's walls.) General William Thomson, who led the expedition, imposed a hated Azerbaijani governor, Dr. Khosrov-Bek Sultanov, on Karabakh and persuaded the guerrilla leader, Andranik, to go back to Armenia. Thomson said this was a temporary arrangement and all outstanding territorial questions would be settled at the upcoming Paris Peace Conference.[4]

But the Paris peace conference did not adjudicate the border disputes. The British pulled out of Azerbaijan in August 1919, leaving behind unfulfilled expectations and unresolved quarrels.[5] In Karabakh, the Armenian community was split between the age-old dilemma of cooperation or confrontation. There were those—primarily Dashnaks and villagers—who wanted unification with Armenia, and those—mainly Bolsheviks, merchants, and professionals—who, in the words of the Armenian historian Richard Hovannisian, "admitted that the district was economically with eastern Transcaucasia and sought accommodation with the Azerbaijani government as the only way to spare Mountainous Karabagh from ruin."[6] The latter group was mainly concentrated in Shusha, but both groups were killed or expelled when an Armenian rebellion was brutally put down in March 1920 with a toll of hundreds of Shusha Armenians.

In April 1920, the British journalist C. E. Bechhofer, traveling in Armenia, was depressed by the scenes of chaos, extremism, and violence:

> You cannot persuade a party of frenzied nationalists that two blacks do not make a white; consequently, no day went by without a cata-

logue of complaints from both sides, Armenian and Tartar, of unpro-
voked attacks, murders, village burnings and the like. Superficially,
the situation was a series of vicious circles. Tartar and Armenian attacked and retaliated for attacks. Fear drove on each side to fresh ex-
cesses. The Dashnaks remained in power because conditions were
such as they were; and conditions were such as they were to no small
extent because the Dashnaks in power.[7]

Bechhofer's proposed solution has a strange resonance eighty years
later: he was persuaded that the only way to "cut the knot" was for all
sides to agree on Armenia's borders and for there to be an exchange of
Armenian and Azerbaijani populations across the new frontiers—as
happened in 1988–1990. Shortly after Bechhofer's visit, however, the
old imperial power, Russia, returned, wearing a new army uniform.
The Bolsheviks took control of Baku and deposed the Musavat government. In May 1920, the 11th Red Army marched into Karabakh and six
months later took power in Armenia.

The Bolsheviks initially decided to award all the disputed territories to Armenia, apparently as a reward for its conversion to Bolshevism. In December 1920, the Azerbaijani Communist leader Nariman
Narimanov welcomed "the victory of the brotherly people" and announced that the three disputed provinces, Karabakh, Nakhichevan,
and Zangezur would from now on be part of Soviet Armenia. The declaration was obviously made under duress and was not acted upon. In
the spring of 1921, the balance of forces changed, and an anti-Bolshevik
uprising in Armenia soured relations between Yerevan and Moscow.
All previous agreements were declared void. By then the fate of Zangezur and Nakhichevan had been decided by force of arms. The Dashnak
leader known as Njdeh had taken possession of Zangezur, driving out
the last of its Azerbaijani population and effecting what one Armenian author euphemistically calls a "re-Armenianization" of the region.[8]
The Azerbaijanis were in full control of Nakhichevan, and this status
was confirmed by the Treaty of Moscow, signed with Turkey in March
1921. The same treaty gave Kars, formerly a mainly Armenian region,
to Turkey.

This left only the fate of the highlands of Karabakh up in the air. The
final decision on its status was to be made by the six members of the
"Kavburo," the Bolsheviks' committee on the Caucasus that was under
the watchful eye of Commissar on Nationalities Joseph Stalin. On 4 July

1921, the bureau voted to attach Karabakh to Soviet Armenia, but Narimanov objected strongly. A day later, it decided that "proceeding from the necessity for national peace between Muslims and Armenians and the economic ties between upper and lower Karabakh, its constant links with Azerbaijan, Nagorny Karabakh remains within the Azerbaijani SSR, having been awarded wide regional autonomy, with its administrative center in the town of Shusha."[9] The Soviet authorities created the Nagorny Karabakh Autonomous Region in July 1923 and drew its borders a month later. The Armenian village of Khankendi was made the regional capital and renamed Stepanakert after the Baku Bolshevik commissar Stepan Shaumian. The new border gave the region an overwhelmingly Armenian population—94 percent of the total—but did not link it to Armenia.

Gallons of ink have been expended in discussing why Nagorny Karabakh was made part of Soviet Azerbaijan in 1921. The arguments for and against the move go to the heart of the politics of the Karabakh question: the economics and geography of Azerbaijan on one side are ranged against Armenian claims of demography and historical continuity on the other. Put simply, a region populated overwhelmingly by Armenians and with a strong tradition of Armenian self-rule was situated on the eastern side of the watershed dividing Armenia and Azerbaijan and was economically well integrated within Azerbaijan.

In 1921, the Bolsheviks were partly swayed by short-term strategic considerations. A major priority was to make secure their conquest of Azerbaijan, whose oil fields alone made it of far greater importance than Armenia. Moreover, in 1921 Azerbaijan was still formally an independent Bolshevik state, closely allied to Turkey. It had its own Commissariat of Foreign Affairs, diplomatic representatives in Germany and Finland, and consulates in Kars, Trebizond, and Samsun. The new rulers in Moscow hoped that the new Muslim Soviet republic would be, in the words of the local Bolshevik Sultan Galiev, a "red beacon for Persia, Arabia, Turkey," spurring them to join the worldwide revolution. The Armenian Communist leader Alexander Miasnikian complained later of Narimanov's threat that "if Armenia demands Karabakh, we will not deliver kerosene."[10]

The creation of the Autonomous Region of Nagorny Karabakh inside Azerbaijan is often adduced as an example of the politics of "Divide and Rule" in which Moscow imposed its authority by setting one subject people against another. This is also simplistic. Of course, the

Bolsheviks were reestablishing an empire with all means at their disposal. Yet if they had wanted merely to "divide and rule," it would have been more logical to allocate the enclave of Nagorny Karabakh to Armenia, leaving an awkward island of sovereign Armenia inside Azerbaijan.

In fact, the longer-term considerations behind the Kavburo's decision were probably as much economic as colonial. Lenin and Stalin created Nagorny Karabakh as one piece in a new complex mosaic of autonomous regions and republics designed to replace the old tsarist system of standardized *gubernii*. The new regions were intended to be economically viable territories, with all other considerations taking second place. So in the North Caucasus, for example, people from the plains and the mountains, such as the Kabardins and the Balkars, were brought together in one region. They had no ethnic relationship, but it was planned that they would work together to build a new socialist economy and drag the mountain tribes out of their backward ways. Leaving Karabakh inside Azerbaijan followed the same kind of economic logic. It especially suited the thousands of Azerbaijani and Kurdish nomads who regularly drove their sheep to the high pastures of Karabakh in the summer and down to the plains of Azerbaijan for the winter.[11] In this sense, the creation of Nagorny Karabakh could more exactly be called the politics of "Combine and Rule." And the Soviet brand of combination was just as dangerous in its own way because it incited intense competition between new partners.

## LITTLE EMPIRES

An unforeseen by-product of Lenin's new territorial arrangements for the Soviet Union was that by maintaining a link between land and nationality, they conserved nationalism in a latent form inside the new system. The USSR was constructed as a federation of republics, designated by their nationality and ethnicity. Each of the "Union Republics" —four in 1922, fifteen after 1956—retained elements of sovereignty, including the formal right to secede. They had their own flags, crests, anthems, and political institutions.

Most of the features of sovereignty were merely decorative and counted for little within the restrictions of a one-party authoritarian state. Even so, they pointed up perceived differences in nationality, which were formalized in the system. The Soviet Union was not a melting pot. Aged sixteen, every Soviet had to state his own ethnicity, which was recorded in the infamous "ninth line" of his Soviet internal passport. This meant that everyone in the USSR had at least a dual affiliation, and that some minorities—an Azerbaijani or a Kurd in Armenia, for instance, or an Armenian, a Lezgin, or a Russian in Azerbaijan—had a triple affiliation: they belonged first to the nationality recorded in their internal Soviet passport (Kurds, Azerbaijanis, Armenians, or whatever); second to the Union Republic of Russia, Armenia, or Azerbaijan; and last to the Soviet Union and the "Soviet people" as a whole.

In the postwar years, the Soviet Union had already acquired its superficial look of gray uniformity. All of its citizens had only the one Party to belong to, three types of sausage to buy, and *Pravda*, *Izvestia*, and *Trud* to read. An Armenian or Azerbaijani would find much to recognize—the same design of apartment block, and the same bar of soap—in Tashkent or Tallinn, as well as in Baku or Yerevan. Still, under the surface there were important differences. After Stalin's death the balance of economic power had begun to shift outward, from Russia to the republics. Some Russians even complained that the burdens of empire were becoming costly. According to the Gorbachev-era reformer Alexander Yakovlev:

> [In the 1970s and 1980s] the Politburo no longer had the powers, which it had under Stalin. Second, the understanding had begun to grow that we had to give the republics a certain measure of freedom. In the end they should take some responsibility and not constantly beg "Give money, give money, build this, build that." The idea came up more than once of making the republics pay for themselves, so they worked, they earned their own money. You see the Soviet Empire was a strange empire. Russia was politically dominant, but suffered economically, everything was done against the economic interests of Russia.[12]

The three republics of the Caucasus were increasingly self-assertive, and some of their burgeoning attributes of ministatehood were confirmed by the new "Brezhnev Constitution" of 1977. In each republic the language of the titular nationality, Georgian, Azeri, or Armenian, became the official "republican language" (in the case of Georgia, Moscow acceded to this after mass street protests). Article 72 of the constitution reaffirmed, if only on paper, the right of the Union Republics to secede from the USSR, and Article 78 stated that "the territory of a Union Republic may not be altered without its consent"—Azerbaijan's constitutional trump card in the dispute over Karabakh.

The greater confidence of the dominant national group in the Union Republics—Armenian, Azerbaijani, Georgian—made minorities feel insecure. The situation, which famously led Andrei Sakharov to call the Union Republics "little empires," is reflected in the demographic statistics. In Armenia, the ethnic Armenian population rose by 23 percent between the censuses of 1970 and 1979; the number of Azerbaijanis of Armenia grew by just 8 percent. This showed that many of the Azerbaijanis, whose birth rate was just as high, were leaving. The Armenians now constituted more than 90 percent of the population of their republic, making it the most homogeneous republic of the Soviet Union.[13] In Azerbaijan in the same period, the ethnic Azerbaijani population rose by almost a quarter; the Armenian and Russian populations actually fell. By 1979, the Armenians of Nakhichevan had declined to a level of only 1 percent of the population, or three thousand people. The Karabakh Armenians used the example of the slow "de-Armenianization" of Nakhichevan in the course of the twentieth century as an example of what they feared would happen to them.

Smaller indigenous Caucasian nationalities, such as Kurds, also complained of assimilation. In the 1920s, Azerbaijan's Kurds had had their own region, known as Red Kurdistan, to the west of Nagorny Karabakh; in 1930, it was abolished and most Kurds were progressively recategorized as "Azerbaijani." A Kurdish leader estimates that there are currently as many as 200,000 Kurds in Azerbaijan, but official statistics record only about 12,000.[14] The Russian expert on the nationalities issue, Valery Tishkov, comments: "[The Union Republics] behaved much more harshly to minorities than Moscow did. When the breakup [of the Soviet Union] is discussed all the attention is on Moscow, but the biggest assimilators were Georgia, Azerbaijan, and Uzbekistan (Armenia less so only because it had fewer minorities.)"[15]

## FEUDAL FIRST SECRETARIES

In the 1960s and 1970s, a new generation of Communist Party first secretaries stamped their authority on the three Caucasian republics. Three of them, Eduard Shevardnadze in Georgia, Karen Demirchian in

Armenia, and Heidar Aliev in Azerbaijan, stayed in power for more than a decade and established extensive patron-client networks. Essentially, they were feudal lords who paid homage to the court in Moscow but ran their own fiefdoms at home. This legacy helped both Shevardnadze and Aliev to return to power as presidents of independent Georgia and Azerbaijan in 1992 and 1993; no one was especially surprised that they had formerly been loyal Party bosses under one system and were now nationalist leaders in another. In 1998, Demirchian came close to following their example in Armenia but was defeated in the (disputed) second round of the country's presidential election.

As first party secretary of Azerbaijan between 1969 and 1982, Heidar Aliev was perhaps the most successful republican leader in the Soviet Union. He raised the profile of a hitherto underprivileged Soviet republic, consistently promoted Azerbaijanis to senior posts for the first time, and proved himself a master at flattering Leonid Brezhnev. Brezhnev visited Azerbaijan three times and was treated to lavish gifts and receptions each time. On one occasion, Aliev gave him a diamond ring with one large stone in the middle—Brezhnev—surrounded by fifteen smaller ones—the Union Republics. The ring was reportedly worth the vast sum of 226,000 rubles.[16] The payback was considerable. In a 1995 interview, Aliev told the story of how he managed to persuade Brezhnev to grant Azerbaijan a new air-conditioner plant. It all happened because the Soviet leader was unable to sleep at a Party meeting in Tashkent:

> In the morning [Brezhnev] joked that some kind of tractor was working in his room all night and only toward morning did he understand that it was an air conditioner. Someone said that this air conditioner was made in Baku. And we really had set up air-conditioner production in one factory, but of course without any technology. It made a terrible noise and didn't make things very cool, but there was nothing else. And when Brezhnev was astonished how this country does not produce air conditioners, I proposed building a factory in Baku. He agreed. After that I began to push through, really to push through, the solution of this question. Then I began to extract the finances. And when the money was handed out, the minister of electrotechnical industry Antonov decided to build the factory in Zaporozhye [in Ukraine], because he had trained workers there, he could begin pro-

duction more easily. One could understand his logic, but I went to Brezhnev and he kept his word.[17]

The story tells us a lot: how miserably hot Soviet citizens in the Caucasus and Central Asia were each summer for no good reason; how the command economy failed to provide appropriate consumer goods; how out of touch the leaders were with the everyday problems of Soviet life; how vital it was to have Brezhnev's ear; how important decisions were made.

Aliev's story also illustrates how the Soviet system, while preaching harmony and brotherhood, institutionalized competition and rivalry. This was very true in the Caucasus, where there was surprisingly little regional economic cooperation and, because of the absurdities of central planning, a factory in Armenia was just as likely to be linked to one in Minsk or Omsk as in neighboring Azerbaijan. In the political sphere, Brezhnev's authoritarian regime gave local leaders limited powers but almost no responsibilities: instead of power sharing, there was a continuous bargaining process between the regions and Moscow, the dispenser of all favors. Politically subservient to the center, the leaders in Baku, Stepanakert, and Yerevan hoarded their local powers jealously and had almost no incentives for cooperation.

As a result, relations between the three Caucasian republican leaders were poor. Aliev and Shevardnadze were reported to be strong rivals—although the two men patched up their relationship in the 1990s, as heads of state of Azerbaijan and Georgia. But the most difficult relationship was probably that between Azerbaijan's Aliev and Armenia's Demirchian.

In the 1970s and 1980s, Aliev and Demirchian feuded over the allocation of central resources. Their most celebrated spat concerned plans for a road link across Armenia to the Azerbaijani exclave of Nakhichevan—an issue that resurfaced in a very different form in 1999. As Azerbaijani Party boss, Aliev, himself from Nakhichevan, lobbied hard for the construction of a federal highway across the Armenian province of Meghri to Nakhichevan. This was a prestige infrastructure project, running entirely across Soviet territory, which would nominally bring benefit to all sides, yet Demirchian aggressively opposed it and eventually managed to have the plan blocked. He evidently believed that what was good for Soviet Azerbaijan was bad for Soviet Armenia.

When the issue of the Meghri highway came up, Igor Muradian, who later became the pioneer of the Karabakh Armenian movement, was working in the state planning agency Gosplan. He says that he was asked to look for arguments against it. "We had to prove that the traffic flow to Nakhichevan was insignificant." As we have seen, Muradian, although a nationalist activist, also received the discreet support of Demirchian in his campaigns to discredit Aliev and undermine Azerbaijan. Asked why the Communist Party boss should have helped him, a dissident, Muradian explained with a laugh that he was a useful weapon in an internal power struggle. "My dear, the Soviet Union did not exist from the beginning of the 1970s!" he said. "Different republics existed. One republic fought with another and so on. They were not interested in humanitarian ideals."[18]

The three Party first secretaries went further in making their republics separate and sovereign. They actively promoted a revival of "national culture," which helped legitimize their power at home and project each republic outside its borders.

The Khrushchev thaw of the 1960s released an upsurge of intellectual and cultural life in all the national republics. Any expression of disloyalty to Russia or the Communist Party was still firmly off limits, but writers and historians could now tackle many aspects of their culture and past that had been hitherto taboo. It was a kind of low-alcohol decolonization, with the hard politics taken out of it. The reflections of two poets, one Azerbaijani and one Armenian, are strikingly similar. First, Sabir Rustamkhanli, the popular Azerbaijani poet:

> That period, the 1960s, '70s, and '80s, was the period of a small renaissance in the Soviet Union. In different republics a process of self-identification began, national consciousness began to rise. . . . Despite the fact that when we were students, they were always making us study literature connected with Stalinism and so on, our generation completely rejected this. In our verse, in our works there isn't a single word about Soviet ideology, brotherhood with Moscow.[19]

And here is the Armenian Silva Kaputikian:

> The leadership did not really suppress our national strivings. The sort of books were coming out, such that when I was in America in 1964, I gave one of my books that was completely devoted to Armenia, Ar-

menian questions, the Armenian tragedies, and so on to a Dashnak woman, and she was astonished by how it could have been published. My explanation was that our leadership was more or less liberal—in the good sense of the word.[20]

Armenia adapted happily to this low-grade nationalism. Russia and Armenia had so many ties of tradition and history that it was not hard to reconcile Armenian nationalism and loyalty to the Soviet state. In the 1960s, symbols of Armenian nationhood sprang up across Yerevan. When Stalin's statue—formerly the largest in the world—was taken down, it was replaced by one of Mother Armenia. Not only was a memorial to the Genocide constructed, but monuments were unveiled to the fifth-century Armenian warrior Vartan Mamikonian and even to the guerrilla commander Andranik.

In Azerbaijan, it was harder to fit local nationalism into a Soviet mold; yet Aliev also made Azerbaijan more self-assertive vis-à-vis its neighbors. The Azeri language was made universal in public life and the bureaucracy. The remains of the poet Hussein Javid, who had been killed by Stalin, were returned from Siberia and reburied in Azerbaijan. Aliev unveiled monuments to Azerbaijani poets such as Vagif and Nizami. These were some of the foundation stones in building a new Azerbaijani state identity.

## KARABAKH, THE SNAG

As both Armenians and Azerbaijanis became more assertive in the postwar era, increasingly Nagorny Karabakh became the snag in the middle, where their ambitions clashed. With its majority Armenian population, Nagorny Karabakh was the only instance in the Soviet federal system wherein members of an ethnic group, which had its own Union Republic, were in charge of an autonomous region inside another Union Republic. From the beginning the Party leaders in Karabakh used the rather weak institutions that their autonomous status gave them to maintain a certain level of "Armenianness" in the form of libraries, school instruction, and radio broadcasts and valued their links with Armenia.

There were tensions over Nagorny Karabakh even when Stalin was in power. In 1945, the head of the Armenian Communist Party, Grigory

Harutiunov, wrote to Stalin requesting that the province be attached to Armenia. The Azerbaijani leader Mir Jafar Bagirov gave an ironic negative response. After Stalin's death, the Karabakh Armenians continued to lobby Moscow (but never Baku). In 1965, a group of thirteen local Armenian Party officials and intellectuals wrote a joint letter to the Soviet leadership complaining about the way Nagorny Karabakh was being run from Baku. Many of them were sacked, and six moved to Armenia.

The climate changed after Aliev became Party boss in Azerbaijan in 1969 and clashed with the two local Armenians, Gurgen Melkumian and Musheg Ohanjenian, who had been running the region for the previous decade. Ohanjenian, who was head of Nagorny Karabakh's Regional Executive Committee—a kind of prime minister for Karabakh—in the 1960s, is still a member of the local parliament in Stepanakert. He admits to contradictory feelings about Aliev, with whom he later worked closely in Baku. On the one hand, this Karabakh Armenian praises the former Party boss for what he did for Azerbaijan. Ohanjenian says he traveled to Party meetings in Moscow in the 1970s with his head held high: "When Aliev came to power we said with pride that we were from Azerbaijan. Because under his regime, both in the economy, in politics and materially, it was much better than under the other [Azerbaijani party leaders]."[21] On the other hand, Ohanjenian says that Aliev instituted a "sharp change in policy" to impose greater control by Baku on Nagorny Karabakh itself.

In 1973, Baku and Stepanakert quarreled over an apparently trivial issue, the festivities to mark the fiftieth anniversary of the creation of the Nagorny Karabakh Autonomous Region. Ohanjenian says that he and Melkumian planned a celebration that would emphasize Nagorny Karabakh's distinctive history and record within the Soviet Union as a whole, rather than as a part of Azerbaijan. To that end, they invited fifty Karabakh Armenian academicians and generals from all over the USSR to attend. According to Ohanjenian, the Baku authorities were angry, when they saw a guest list replete with invitees from Moscow and Yerevan. They postponed the festival for several months and then disinvited most of the outside Armenians and Russians. The eventual look of the celebrations, dominated by people from inside Azerbaijan, was designed to emphasize Nagorny Karabakh's Azerbaijani identity.

Aliev gradually exerted more control. In 1973–1974 he cleared out the entire local Party leadership in Karabakh. Melkumian was sacked, and Ohanjenian was given a top Party job in Baku. The new local Party boss Boris Kevorkov was an Armenian from outside Karabakh, was married to an Azerbaijani, and was extremely loyal to Aliev. He reportedly never once visited Armenia during his fourteen years in the post.

Opinions differ as to the socioeconomic condition of Nagorny Karabakh during this period. Visitors in 1988 were struck by its air of neglect. "The roads were as if after a nuclear war," says the Moscow official Grigory Kharchenko, who was also appalled by the unsanitary water system. These impressions should not be taken in isolation, however. Azerbaijan was the poorest of the Caucasus republics, with an official average wage around 25 percent lower than the Soviet mean.[22] The official statistics (which should be treated with some caution) suggest that Nagorny Karabakh had more better-than-average economic indicators than did Azerbaijan. The substance of the Karabakh Armenians' economic grievances is not so much that they were worse off than the rest of Azerbaijan but that they could expect a higher standard of living if they joined Armenia.

The distribution of wealth in the shadow economy, although much harder to quantify, was probably a bigger factor. Andrei Sakharov was told that the total capital of the underground economy in 1988 in Azerbaijan was ten billion rubles and in Armenia it was fourteen billion.[23] Azerbaijan had a thriving black market in fuel, flowers, and caviar, to name just three desirable Soviet products. Azerbaijanis say that marijuana was grown in Nagorny Karabakh. Illegal transactions were an integral part of everyday life. Of Azerbaijan, Arkady Vaksberg, the chronicler of the "Soviet mafia" writes, "It is possible that in no other republic has the mafia succeeded in taking so many posts from top to bottom in the state and party apparatus, in trade, science, agriculture and culture."[24] So what may have deepened the anxieties of the Karabakh Armenians in the 1970s and 1980s was that they were losing out to more powerful Azerbaijani networks in the underground economy: as a minority, they were not strong enough to claim a large slice of the pie.

Yet it would be a mistake to reduce the Nagorny Karabakh dispute to socioeconomic components. The Karabakh Armenians concede that their socioeconomic conditions were not catastrophic. Interviewed in January 1994, the Armenian leader Robert Kocharian said that Karabakh was a deprived region, but that this was not the crucial point. "All the same I would not rest the question on whether we lived well or badly. I don't exclude the possibility that even if it had been good in Azerbaijan, then these problems would have arisen all the same. I believe that there is something more than good or bad life, that peoples understand and that pushes those peoples towards independence."[25]

What was at stake was something larger and less tangible. It might be called the politics of self-determination—in the broadest sense and on both sides. Armenians and Azerbaijanis had fundamentally different notions about the cultural and political identity of Nagorny Karabakh. In this respect, one rather more reliable set of figures, the Soviet demographic statistics, is revealing. They show that inside Nagorny Karabakh, the trend was working against the Armenians throughout the Soviet period. While the Azerbaijani population of Karabakh was growing sharply, the number of Armenians stayed roughly level. In 1926, there were 117,000 Armenians and 13,000 Azerbaijanis in Karabakh; in 1979, there were 123,000 and 37,000, respectively.

One reason for these population trends was a targeted policy on the part of authorities in Baku: to settle Azerbaijanis in the population centers of Khojali and Shusha. Another factor was that Karabakh Armenians—mainly educated ones—were leaving. This again fits with the wider trends in the Caucasus and the Soviet Union as a whole. For the ambitious, all career opportunities were in the regional capital, in this case Baku; but the Karabakh Armenians, a minority, had fewer contacts and patrons and hence less chance of climbing the republican Party ladder. As a result, many Karabakh Armenians looked to Yerevan or Moscow instead, and many parents chose to send their children to Stepanakert's Russian schools. (Modern Karabakh is still as much Russian-speaking as Armenian-speaking.) Communities of Karabakh exiles formed in such disparate places as Tashkent, Moscow, and Grozny.

For this Karabakh Diaspora and for the intelligentsia in both Karabakh and Armenia, this was a cultural dispute in the widest sense. The role they played turns on its head the assumption that the educated middle classes act as an enlightened brake on conflict. In Karabakh, the opposite was true: the Soviet middle classes were the first to break the bonds of friendship with their neighbors, while workers and farmers continued living in harmony. Asked what intercommunal relations were like in Soviet times, the former Karabakh Armenian Party official Sergei Shugarian replies: "At the upper levels [of society] there were never clashes [on ethnic grounds] because people were afraid of confrontation. In the middle there were constant tensions on national grounds. Down below they lived in friendship, there were no problems at all."[26]

The Armenian intelligentsia had a long list of cultural complaints. For example, there was no Armenian-language television in Nagorny Karabakh; the history of Armenia was not taught in Armenian-language schools; 24 April, Genocide Day, was not marked in Stepanakert; the director of the local museum, Shagen Mkrtchian, was sacked on orders from Baku. One strongly felt grievance was that the dozens of Armenian medieval churches in Karabakh were not only closed for worship but falling down for lack of upkeep. Karabakh Armenians contrasted their situation to that in Armenia, where national culture was undergoing its officially sanctioned revival. In other words, their complaint was that Azerbaijan was suppressing their demands to have Nagorny Karabakh as a distinctively Armenian region. To Azerbaijanis, this was insupportable, for they had their own notions of Karabakh as a distinctively Azerbaijani region, with long cultural and historical traditions.

There is another important twist to this tale: if the Karabakh Armenians felt culturally and politically disadvantaged within Azerbaijan, the Karabakh Azerbaijanis felt disadvantaged inside Nagorny Karabakh. They talk of discrimination by Armenians and tell stories about how they were made to feel uncomfortable in Stepanakert, an overwhelmingly Armenian town. "The Armenians lived 100 times better than us," said Elkhan Alekperov, a schoolmaster who served as head of Shusha's Culture Department in the 1980s. He cites as an example a tiny Armenian village in his region that had a House of Culture, while a far larger Azerbaijani village had no cultural facilities at all. "They kept us down," Alekperov says. "Once we went down to Stepanakert for a music competition. Our region was the strongest. But when we came out on stage, our number began and our group started performing, they switched off all the lights and the microphones."[27]

## FROM DIVISION TO BREAKUP

The Soviet Union could be compared to a vast mansion with dozens of dark rooms and self-contained apartments. When in the 1980s the tired and ailing mansion owner—the Communist Party leadership—began to renegotiate the lease it had signed with its tenants, all of them made some unpleasant discoveries: The mansion had dry rot, the lease was badly drafted and full of contradictions, the spirit of "brotherhood" in which their grandfathers had entered the mansion was a sham. The tenants began to take matters into their own hands and quarreled with one another and the landlord. Even after the owner died, they were embroiled in angry disputes over who was entitled to what space.

It was the Armenian and Azerbaijani tenants, quarreling over Nagorny Karabakh, who first exposed that the Soviet structure was a tottering wreck. It seems that in the late 1980s three hitherto overlooked factors precipitated the situation here, as distinct from other places, from division into conflict.

The first factor was that the Karabakh Armenians were able to mobilize themselves by exploiting their dusty autonomous institutions. They used the Regional Soviet to vote for secession in February 1988, and deployed a few semiofficial weapons—a regional bureaucracy, a newspaper, a radio station—to continue their campaign. In this regard, Nagorny Karabakh was the first of several breakaway regions, including Chechnya and Abkhazia, that used its Soviet-era autonomous status as a springboard for secession.

This factor was a necessary but not a sufficient factor to initiate conflict. After all, Crimea, which was transferred from Russia to Ukraine only in 1954, had strong local institutions, but the Crimean Russians stopped short of a violent movement to secede from Ukraine. A second, more crucial, factor in starting the conflict was the ease with which hatred of the other could side be disseminated among the population. The Turkish historian Halil Berktay calls these mass expressions of fear and prejudice "hate narratives." They were the dark side of the "renaissance" of the 1960s. And they were much harder to instigate, by way of contrast, between either republic and Georgia. Armenian and Azerbaijani academics had been denigrating the claims of rival scholars in the others' republic for twenty years. In 1988, all that was needed was an injection of politics—of full-strength "alcohol"—into the mixture. In a war of pamphlets, drawing on years of tendentious scholarship, sarcasm, innuendo, and selective quotation incited ordinary people into hatred.

Two of the most chauvinistic intellectual warriors shared the same initials, Z and B. Both Zori Balayan and Ziya Buniatov were Party members who had done well out of the Soviet system. Buniatov had been writing anti-Armenian historical articles since the 1960s. When he became head of the Academy of Sciences in Baku, he used that position to publish a stream of anti-Armenian material.

In 1990, Buniatov's academy reissued thirty thousand copies of a forgotten racist tract by the turn-of-the-century Russian polemicist Vasil Velichko. Velichko's *Caucasus* of 1904 had argued that the Armenians' short skulls, like those of the Jews, make them a politically unreliable race and praised the obedience of Azerbaijanis to the Tsarist regime: "Just as the Armenians and Jews, as a result of their racial instincts, are at core hostile to any statehood and especially to the idea of unrestricted monarchy, so the Azerbaijanis are naturally and organically in sympathy with it—even the rebels, even the robbers." Only Velichko's hatred of Armenians seemed to have recommended his book to Buniatov for republication.[28]

Zori Balayan, a prominent Soviet journalist and writer, had published *Ochag* (The hearth) in 1984, in which he related his travels around Armenian lands. Among Armenian landmarks he provocatively includes Azerbaijan's exclave of Nakhichevan and the River Araxes, which runs along Azerbaijan's southern border: "I met dawn on the bank of the Araxes. We conversed with the Armenian river in the Armenian language."[29] Although it is still the pre-Gorbachev era, Balayan calls the Turks—and by extension the Azerbaijanis—the "enemy" of both Russia and Armenia. The book caused a storm of protest in Azerbaijan—as no doubt he intended. It was almost as though both "ZBs" were picking up from where their fathers and grandfathers had left off in the 1920s.

Yet this hatred might never have been allowed to spread beyond a few low-circulation publications but for the third precondition for conflict: the Politburo's loss of control and the gradual collapse of Moscow's authority. In 1988, the center, without fully realizing it, began to give up its imperial mandate. It was beyond the Soviet Politburo to initiate an open dialogue, as a democratic leadership might have done, to reconcile the two sides. Its only powerful weapon was force, which it declined to use with any conviction. Gorbachev's reforms revealed with frightening speed that the central doctrines that underpinned the Soviet Union were essentially bogus. In the words of Yury Slezkine, "The country's leaders found it harder and harder to explain what the 'socialist content' stood for and, when Gorbachev finally discarded the worn-out Marxist verbiage, the only language that remained was the well honed and long practiced language of nationalism."[30]

The scholar of nationalism Ernest Gellner uses another metaphor, saying that nationalism rushed into a vacuum in which it had no competition: "Ethnic nationalism . . . is naturally engendered by the conditions prevalent after seven decades of Soviet Jacobinism, and by its partial relaxation. It is favored by a double vacuum: there is no serious rival ideology, and there are no serious rival institutions."[31]

As the double vacuum filled up, local leaders in Armenia and Azerbaijan discovered with alarm that the "decorative nationalism" they had encouraged had real destructive power—and it destroyed most of them. Ordinary people responded with a mixture of fear and enthusiasm as the system they inhabited began to disappear from beneath their feet.

To allow conflict to break out, the center needed only to do nothing. In the event, it did both more and less than that. In 1991, it gave a last poisoned chalice to the two sides: it handed over the Soviet army's weaponry. By doing so, it enabled the two sides to turn a dispute waged with hunting rifles and pamphlets into a full-blown war of tanks and artillery.

# 10

# Hurekavank

## The Unpredictable Past

SAMVEL KARAPETIAN UNROLLED a six-foot square of stiff paper on the floor of his office. From a distance it was a large white space sprinkled with colored dots that could have been an abstract painting by Jackson Pollock. But standing beside it, Samvel was a general, outlining his campaign plan.

Before us was a map of the Caucasus, based on the Russian imperial census of 1914. Samvel had ascertained the ethnic makeup of all the settlements, large and small, between the Black and Caspian Seas and given each nationality a coded color. Then he had colored in every village and town on the map, according to its ethnic allegiance. The resulting galaxies of color were his attempt at a kind of historical x-ray of the Caucasus. The plains were crowded with black spots, which designated the "Tartars," or the Azerbaijanis. A thick cluster of green spots in the high mountains of the Kelbajar and Lachin regions signified the Kurds. Occasional light blue circles represented the Russians. Then, in what is now Azerbaijan, Samvel pointed out to me two long bands of red, one running along the southern foothills of the Caucasus mountains, the other vertically down through Nagorny Karabakh. These were the Armenians—Samvel's message was that they were the true custodians of the foothills of Azerbaijan.

Samvel Karapetian is a leading combatant in one of the fiercest conflicts between Armenia and Azerbaijan, the one over the ancient past. His office, buzzing with life, on the sixth floor of the Institute of Art in the center of Yerevan, looks like the Armenian staff headquarters in this campaign. Filing cabinets stuffed with documents, thousands of photographs, and more than two hundred maps of Nagorny Karabakh line the walls. Posters and calendars depict the monasteries of Karabakh.

Nagorny Karabakh, the disputed province is the battleground for the fiercest fights between Armenian and Azerbaijani historians. Recent history is of little interest to them. Instead they are moved by the notion, unrecognized by international law, that whoever was there first, is the true tenant of the land—what the Romans called *prior tempore-fortior jure*. As a result, Karabakh has become a place, as someone once said of the Soviet Union, with an "unpredictable past."

The first feathery leaves were coming out on the trees in the graveyard of Hurekavank. They were beginning to give the gray vault of the medieval church a green headdress. Samvel had brought me to the church and graveyard as the first stop in our expedition through the North of Nagorny Karabakh. He likes to make an annual spring journey there in late March or early April, when the weather is mild and there are fewer leaves on the trees that can obscure the monuments he wants to photograph.

Samvel and his two women colleagues set to work with Prussian efficiency. First of all, Emma and Narine undraped a long tape measure and recorded the dimensions of the church. Then they used twigs and pencils to scrape dirt from the long, cold slabs of tombs inside so as to read the inscriptions. Samvel deciphered the Armenian letters and noted down who lay beneath the tombs. Samvel's physical appearance made him a compelling sight; he is tall and has watchful restless eyes, and his head is completely bald and shiny.

Underneath the tombs, Samvel explained, were the bishops and princes of the Beglarian family. The Beglarians were one of five families of *melik*s, or princes, who dominated Karabakh from the fifteenth to the nineteenth centuries. They were feudal lords, and because they kept invaders at bay and kept Armenian traditions alive in the mountain fastnesses of Karabakh, they have been credited with carrying Armenian statehood through the dark days of Persian rule. Yet, judging by their histories, their schemes and feuds, hatched in drafty castles, have more of *Macbeth* than *Henry V* about them. Brother killed brother to take the title, *melik* families plotted against one another. In 1824, shortly before their feudal titles were abolished, the Russian governor general of the Caucasus, Alexei Yermolov, wrote a despairing letter to the tsar, detailing how Beglarian family members were bickering over the family estates and the serfs who went with the estates.[1]

Samvel and the women moved through the dewy grass of the Beglarians' graveyard like a film crew checking out a location. Brambles and saplings were stripped away. Each tomb was measured and scrubbed of moss and dirt, and had its inscriptions noted down. Then, while Emma or Narine held an improvised measuring stick with three paper numbers above the tomb, like a movie clipboard, Samvel captured it on camera. All the photographs were later digitalized and stored on CD.

"There isn't a village in Karabakh where I don't have somewhere I can call home," said Samvel. It was evening and we were sitting at the table in Zarmen Dalakian's front room. A rusty woodstove served as central heating system, cooker, and toaster, and heated the milk from a brown cow called Maral. Dinner was bread, cheese, and herbs. Samvel had stayed in this house twenty-one years before, when he was nineteen. Since then, the village of Talish had been captured by the Azerbaijanis, burned, held for almost two years, and then recaptured. Most of Talish is still in ruins.

Samvel began delving into history in 1978 at the age of seventeen. Instead of going to college, he made a long walk across Nagorny Karabakh, taking photographs of all the Armenian monuments he came across with a Smena camera, the cheapest Soviet model. Two years later, the year he first came to Talish, he walked for a whole summer, seven hundred miles across Azerbaijan and Nagorny Karabakh, camping or staying in village houses like this one. A mission was born.

In Soviet Azerbaijan, Samvel aroused suspicions. "There isn't a regional center in Azerbaijan, where I wasn't in the police station or the KGB headquarters more than once," he said. And very soon he began to identify the reason: he said he had stumbled across a concerted campaign to "Azerbaijanify" the cultural history of the republic by erasing Armenian artifacts. As he came back each year, Samvel said, he discovered wrecked monuments that he had seen intact before, a ninth-century cross-domed church in the Getabek region in northwest Azerbaijan, for instance: "I came there for the second time in 1982—I'd been there first in 1980—and it was half-ruined. I saw a shovel and pickax lying on the ground, as if someone had left his tools there during a lunch break. The only thing I could do was throw the tools into a gorge."

By the time he was in his midtwenties, Samvel had become a walking encyclopedia. He kept an archive on hundreds of churches, inscriptions, and tombstones in boxes in his apartment in Yerevan. All his spare time and money went to the research: "If I had a choice between buying a camera film and something to eat, I would choose the film."

But it would take more than one lifetime to complete the goal he had set himself: to record all the Armenian monuments outside the borders of the Republic of Armenia.

Our host Zarmen poured each of us a glass of *tutovka*, the viciously potent Karabakh mulberry vodka. The next day peace talks were due to begin in Key West, Florida, on the future of Nagorny Karabakh. I wanted to hear Samvel's opinion on the talks, although I guessed what his answer would be. Samvel said he opposed any attempt at diplomacy with Azerbaijan, which traded in ancient Armenian lands. "I don't even want to think about it. I hope there won't be a settlement." Still, he asked my opinion on what a peace deal would mean for the Armenian side. I said that it would mean giving up at least six of the occupied regions around Nagorny Karabakh and allowing the hundreds of thousands of Azerbaijanis, who had been expelled from there, to return. "Even Kelbajar?" Samvel queried. I nodded. "That's impossible," he answered. He had not fought in the war, but as soon as the Kelbajar region had been "liberated" in 1993, he had gone to the region, now emptied of its inhabitants, and found hundreds of Armenian tombs, churches, and fragments. It was a historic treasury of Armenian art, he asserted, that must remain in Armenian hands.

What claims does history have on the present? In what sense can Kelbajar be called "Armenian," when no Armenian had lived there for almost a hundred years? I said that I could not accept that Kelbajar was "liberated" territory, when all of its fifty thousand or so Azerbaijani or Kurdish inhabitants had been expelled. Surely, I argued, these people had the right to live in the homes in which they were born. But for Samvel, the past eclipsed the present: those people were "Turks" and interlopers. When he used to travel on buses in Azerbaijan, he would always end up losing his seat: "Every Turk or Azerbaijani asks you for a little land and says, 'Just give me a little land to live in!' But in a few years you end up with a tiny piece of land and he gets the lot."

The recorded history of Karabakh is agreeably untidy. The earliest known European visitor to the region, the German Johann Schiltberger, who served with the Mongol armies, spent the winter of 1420 in the lower plain of Karabakh and found both Christians and Muslims there. "The Infidels call the plain, in the Infidel tongue, Karawag," he wrote. "The Infidels possess it all, and yet it stands in Ermenia. There are also Armenians in the villages, but they must pay tribute to the Infidels."[2]

Schiltberger's account of an intermingled territory is consistent with a history of rule by both Muslim khans and Armenian *meliks*, often separately, sometimes together. Karabakh's population has shifted dramatically over the centuries, affected by invasions, famines and emigration. An additional complication is that a large sector of the Azerbaijani population was nomadic. Baron von Haxthausen, a European aristocrat, who traveled through the region in 1843 writes:

> The Tatars and Armenians of Karabagh form a motley and mixed population, the former mostly leading a nomadic life and roving about in the summer after they have cultivated their fields sufficiently to yield the bare necessary produce. They wander in the mountains, which are rich in wood and pasture, and during the hot months journey as far as the confines of the snowy regions, among the dwellings of the predatory Koordish Tatars. In the autumn they return for the harvest to the plains, which in the rainy season yield excellent pasture for their flocks. They are a wealthy and hospitable race: single Tatars possess thousands of horses of the finest breeds.[3]

The fact of this great seasonal migration suggests we should beware of most nineteenth-century population statistics. It seems quite likely that the mountainous part of Karabakh had an Azerbaijani majority in summer and an Armenian one in the winter.

Despite all this, historians on both sides have managed the feat of writing histories of the region that stretch back hundreds or even thousands of years and suggest an unbroken Armenian or Azerbaijani presence. And, of course, not content with championing their own claims, they denigrate those of the enemy. It is common to hear in both Armenia and Azerbaijan that the other nationality is really "gypsies," roaming people who never enjoyed proper statehood.

The Armenian version is of an unbroken lineage of Armenian dominion in Karabakh, going back to the ancient kingdom of Artsakh two thousand years ago. More recently, the *meliks* are portrayed as powerful princes, and the role of their Muslim overlords is played down. Armenians point out that at the end of the seventeenth century, the Karabakh *meliks* wrote joint letters to the pope, the Elector Palatine, and Peter the Great, appealing for protection against their Islamic neighbors. When the Ottoman Turks overran Armenia, the Karabakh *meliks* held out. It was to Karabakh that Yefrem, the *Catholicos* of Echmiadzin, fled in 1822, when he wanted to escape capture by the Ottoman Turks.

Armenian patriotic historians have the advantage of the great treasure house of monuments and inscriptions in stone that Samvel is recording: these are brought forth as the mute witnesses, as it were, to the Armenian past. Yet this story omits telling of the many alliances and friendships that characterized the two communities in the region. In 1724, for example, the Karabakh Armenians and Azerbaijanis of Ganje signed a common treaty to defend themselves against the Ottoman Turks.[4] If the Muslims left less behind in stone, it is not because they were not there but merely that they were less inclined to stay in one place. They did build caravanserais or bridges, but their enduring cultural achievements are less solid artifacts such as songs or carpets.

The Armenian nationalists use two main devices to denigrate their neighbors. One is to suggest that because most of them were "nomads," they were a class lower than the settled village dwellers. Dismissing the claims of the people who used to live in Kelbajar, Samvel told me, "The people who lost their homes are third generation or fourth generation maximum. They were nomads, the tsar forced them to settle in those villages." The other line of attack is that Azerbaijan is a recent twentieth-century creation and that its people therefore have fewer "historical rights." In an interview in February 1988, the writer Zori Balayan haughtily declared: "We can understand the terms *Georgia, Russia, Armenia*—but not *Azerbaijan*. By using such a term we confirm the existence of such a country."[5] One is reminded of Golda Meir's famous alleged remark about the Palestinians that "they never existed."

In response to this, Azerbaijani historians might usefully have focused their research on the rich history of the Safavid period, when Karabakh was part of a Turkic-speaking dynastic empire based in northern Iran. A thoroughly researched study of that epoch would reveal the fascinating and mixed history of Karabakh between the sixteenth and nineteenth centuries.

They did not take this approach. Perhaps because Soviet politicians wanted more literal examples of home-grown statehood to buttress the histories of the new Union Republics, Azerbaijani historians set off down a different route. The role of patriot-historian-in-chief fell to a very controversial figure. Zia Buniatov could at least lay claim to being a real warrior. He was one of those Red Army soldiers who crossed the whole of Europe, entered Germany, and helped plant the Soviet flag on the Reichstag in Berlin in 1945. For this he was subsequently made a Hero of the Soviet Union, a distinction that helped him make a success-ful career as an academic historian of the Caucasus. Buniatov later went into politics. His strange career ended with his mysterious assassina-tion in the doorway of his house in February 1997.

One of Buniatov's earliest historical observations was well made. He was among the first historians to point out that a good proportion of the Armenians in Armenia and Karabakh were descended from nine-teenth-century immigrants. In 1828–1830, shortly after their conquest of the southwestern Caucasus, the Russians resettled 57,000 Armenians from Turkey and Iran in Armenia and Nakhichevan. Smaller numbers also settled in Karabakh, where the villages of Melikjanlu, Tsakuri, and Maragha were founded by Persian Armenians. The historians do not seem to have clarified what proportion of the 19,000 Armenians who lived in Karabakh in the 1830s were settlers (a half, a quarter, a tenth?), but many clearly were.

This interesting historical point makes a dent in the "unbroken lin-eage" of the Karabakh Armenians. Azerbaijani polemicists, however, were not interested in dents but in knockout blows, which is why Rufa, the café owner in Samed Vurgun Park in Baku, told me that Alexander Griboyedov, the Russian poet who was Russia's ambassador to Persia, brought "all the Armenians" into the Caucasus in the 1820s.

In 2001, a joint Azerbaijani-Chechen newspaper published in Baku used the "Griboyedov argument" to express its support for Chechnya's liberation struggle, without having to equate Chechen separatism from Russia with Armenian separatism from Azerbaijan. So to square this particular circle, the editors wrote: "As distinct from the Armenians, who were settled in Karabakh from Turkey and Iran in the nineteenth century, the Chechens live in the land of their ancestors. For this reason no one has the right to deprive the Chechens of the right to live on their own land."[6]

The dispute about the nineteenth century is a relatively light skirmish compared to the main theater of war between Armenian and Azerbai-jani historians: the medieval period and churches and monuments, like Hurekavank, that Samvel Karapetian is investigating. It is about men like Hasan-Jalal, the prince who ruled an autonomous principality in Karabakh, who built the region's finest monasteries, and whose dag-ger—complete with Armenian inscription—is now exhibited in the

Hermitage in Saint Petersburg. One might reasonably assume a consensus that the owner of this dagger was an Armenian—insofar as that makes sense, when talking about the thirteenth century. But nothing is so simple.

This is where Professor Buniatov made his most audacious claims. He chose as his main field of study the "ancient history of Azerbaijan," and in particular "Caucasian Albania." And he devised the theory that the Karabakh Armenian rulers, like the Beglarians and Hasan-Jalal, were not really Armenians but *Armenianized Albanians*.

The "Albanians" Buniatov was referring to have nothing to do with the nation in the Balkans. This was the name the Romans gave to a Caucasian people when they first made incursions into the Caucasus in the first century B.C. When Buniatov began to popularize the subject in the 1960s, the Caucasian Albanians were a long-forgotten ancient people. The scholarly consensus was that they were a Christian people or group of peoples who had mainly inhabited what is now the North of Azerbaijan and that by the time of the Arab invasions in the tenth century, they had begun to assimilate with the peoples around them. So although "Albanian" blood surely flowed through veins all over the Caucasus in the medieval period, "Albania" had vanished as a cultural and political idea by then. However, it also continued as a territorial name in that after the Albanians themselves had been assimilated, the name "Albania" was sometimes used to describe the area in and around Nagorny Karabakh.

Buniatov challenged this orthodoxy and reclaimed a great historical role for the Albanians. In actual fact, he argued, the Albanians were one of three major nations of the Caucasus and the progenitors of most of the population of Azerbaijan; they had survived well into the modern era, but the Armenians had forcibly suppressed their church, and translated their literature and then destroyed the originals. Not only Karabakh but large areas of eastern Armenia, said Buniatov, were in actual fact "Albanian."

Buniatov began a poisonous quarrel for which the Caucasian Albanians themselves should take none of the blame. (Their true history has not become any clearer as a result.)[7] Buniatov's scholarly credentials were dubious. It later transpired that the two articles he published in 1960 and 1965 on Caucasian Albania were direct plagiarisms. Under his own name, he had simply published, unattributed, translations of two articles, originally written in English by the Western scholars C. F. J.

Dowsett and Robert Hewsen.[8] But his main intention was evidently political and here he succeeded brilliantly. The subtext to his theory was
obvious to anyone who lived in the Caucasus: the Karabakh Armenians
had no relation to the Armenians of Armenia. They were either "guests"
of Azerbaijan (nineteenth-century immigrants) or Azerbaijanis under
the skin (descendants of Albanians) and should behave accordingly.

Armenian scholars were outraged. An Armenian historian, A. S.
Mnatsakanian, set out to rebut Buniatov's historical geography and relocated Caucasian Albania well to the northeast, toward the Caspian
Sea. Mnatsakanian said that it had entirely disappeared by the tenth
century; as for the medieval-era "Albania," to the west and in and
around Karabakh, he said this was "New Albania," a region adminis-
tered by Persia, of which the only Albanian component remaining was
the name, but which was entirely populated by Armenians.

In the 1970s, a younger generation of Armenian and Azerbaijani
historians took up the war over Caucasian Albania and wrote articles
full of scornful footnotes. Then a young Azerbaijani student of Buniatov's, Farita Mamedova, opened a new front. Her doctoral thesis, "The
Political History and Historical Geography of Caucasian Albania" was
so provocative that she was not allowed to defend it for five years.
Gorbachev himself reportedly asked what the fuss was about and a
copy of Mamedova's thesis was laid on his desk. When I visited Mamedova in a small poky office in Baku's Western University, it was
hard to believe at first glance that this diminutive, dark-haired pleasant woman could have caused such a destructive row. Then, as she
began to speak quickly and intensely, spelling out the main elements
of her thesis and recounting how "the Armenians passed a death sentence on me," her eyes gleamed; it was obvious that she relished the
fight with the Armenians.

I gathered that Mamedova had taken the Albanian theory and used
it to push the Armenians out of the Caucasus altogether. She had relocated Caucasian Albania into what is now the present-day Republic of
Armenia. All those lands, churches, and monasteries in the Republic of
Armenia—all had been Albanian. No sacred Armenian fact was left un-
attacked. Armenia's conversion to Christianity in the fourth century
A.D.? It had actually taken place thousands of miles to the south of present Armenia, on the River Euphrates. The seat of the Armenian church
at Echmiadzin? It had been Albanian right up until the fifteenth century,
when the Armenians relocated there.

As for the primary written traces of this Albanian civilization, Mamedova said they had all been deliberately destroyed, first by the Armenians and the Arabs in concert, then in a second campaign of systematic destruction in the nineteenth century. Mamedova then told me how in 1975 she had gone to the great monastery of Gandzasar in Karabakh, the seat of Hasan-Jalal, with a group of French scholars. Her companions had been skeptical of her theories, but then, using the fluent medieval Armenian she had learned in Leningrad, she had read off the inscription on the façade. It began: "I, Hasan-Jalal, built this church for my people of Aghvank . . ." "Aghvank" was the ancient name for Albania. And she added another detail that I ought to know. Down below in the village of Vank, she had noted the physiognomy of the locals—none of them looked Armenian, she said, and that was because they were not. They were actually all Albanians.

But how come all those hundreds of "Albanian" inscriptions, I managed to say, in places like Gandzasar and Hurekavank were all written in medieval Armenian? Mamedova explained that although Albanians, such as Hasan-Jalal, had written in Armenian, they had never referred to themselves as Armenians, only as "Aghvank," as Albanians. She had another theory as to the inscriptions, although this had not been substantiated: "There is a theory that the inscriptions were superimposed later, in the nineteenth century, but we don't have any evidence of that yet."

Mamedova had consistently said that she was not political; but in a second meeting her political views did shine through. "It is impossible to solve the Karabakh problem without the Albanians," she said. I must have looked skeptical. "There are only two nations with an identity but no state," she went on. "The Jews and the Armenians. The difference is that the Jews created a state in their historical homeland; the Armenians created one not in their historical homeland."[9]

The urbane Mamedova is the sophisticated end of what, in Azerbaijan, has become a very blunt instrument indeed. The crudest version of the Albanian argument has swept through Azerbaijan. Not once did I hear any pre–nineteenth-century church in the entire country called anything other than "Albanian." The Albanians have even spread to the distant southeastern region of Nakhichevan, all of whose surviving Armenian churches have been declared to be Albanian.

A 1997 pamphlet entitled "The Albanian Monuments of Karabakh," by Igrar Aliev and Kamil Mamedzade, ducks the issue of the medieval Armenian inscriptions altogether. The front cover bears a drawing of the façade of the church of Gandzasar, but the draftsman has carefully left out all the Armenian writing. All the photographs in the church were taken from a safe distance, so the Azerbaijani reader has no idea that there is any Armenian writing there at all. Aliev and Mamedzade finish their historical overview by saying:

> The undisputable conclusion follows from everything said above that the so-called Armenians of Karabakh and the Azerbaijanis as such (who are the descendants of the Albanian population) of northern Azerbaijan share the same mother. Both of them are completely indisputably former Albanians and therefore the Armenians *as such* on the territory of Nagorny Karabakh, into which they surged in huge numbers after the first quarter of the nineteenth century, have no rights.[10]

In Armenia meanwhile, the Albanian dispute helped propel a number of scholars of ancient history into frontline politics. One of the founding members of the Karabakh Committee in 1988 was Aleksan Akopian, a leading Armenian historian of the Albanian period. He now pursues his enthusiasm for history and archaeology as the "governor" of the occupied Azerbaijani province of Lachin, situated between Armenia and Nagorny Karabakh.

I went to see Akopian in his office in the Armenian parliament. An engaging man with a thick moustache, he said he was delighted to hear news of Farita Mamedova. "Ah, my sister!" he exclaimed. The two of them had studied ancient Armenian in Leningrad under the same professor, and Akopian seemed to look back on their bitter academic quarrels, fought in obscure historical journals, with something like tenderness. "I had brothers and sisters in Azerbaijan," he explained. "I was always fighting with them. For ten years I took part in the war between Armenia and Azerbaijani historians. The war had begun earlier and I took part in the last ten years of it."[11] Then Akopian set off at a rattling pace to outline the borders of his own "Albania." It had almost nothing in common with the Azerbaijani version, being an ancient northerly province. It was not to be confused with "New Albania," situated in Nagorny Karabakh, a province that took only its name from the Albanians, when they were fast becoming extinct. The fact that Hasan-Jalal was the prince "of Albania" in the thirteenth century was perhaps equivalent to Queen Elizabeth's youngest son's being the Earl of Wessex, a long-vanished English kingdom.

It would have taken a few years to spare and knowledge of several ancient languages to form an informed judgment on the Albanian question. Fortunately, Professor Robert Hewsen of Rowan College, New Jersey, the foremost expert on this period of Caucasian history, was able to advise. In his elegant, carefully worded reply to my list of questions, I detected the voice of someone who had spent his career negotiating the reefs of Caucasian historical politics.

Hewsen enclosed an article from 1982 in which he had gone back over the original sources; he had strongly reprimanded Buniatov for bad history but also criticized the Armenian Mnatsakanian for being selective with the evidence.[12] In his letter, he stressed that the amount of evidence on Caucasian Albania was really quite small, but he concurred with the idea that by the tenth century the Albanians had pretty much been broken up: "Since, according to Strabo, the Albanians were a federation of twenty-six tribes, the general consensus is that their state began to disintegrate in the Arab period and was gone by the tenth century; an Albanian ethnic group may have survived longer: we don't know."

Hewsen said it was hard to find any traces of the Albanians. Most people assumed that the Udins, a tiny Christian nationality, who used to live in northern Azerbaijan, were descendants of the Albanians. They spoke an indigenous Caucasian language related to Lezghian. Apart from that, the few fragments of their writing in existence had yet to be deciphered. There was almost no supporting evidence for the charge that the Armenians had deliberately destroyed the Albanian literature. If "Albania" had survived, it was as a separate branch of the Armenian church, based in Karabakh. Finally we came to the Karabakhi prince, Hasan-Jalal. Professor Hewsen concluded that "I have found not a shred of evidence that [the *meliks*] ever thought of themselves as anything but Armenians, albeit members of the Albanian branch of the Armenian Church."

Hewsen had also traced Hasan Jalal's genealogy and found it to be almost exclusively Armenian:

[Hasan-Jalal's] descent can be traced back to the fourth century and involves the following houses: In the male line, (1) the princes (who later became kings) of Siunik. Through various princesses, who married his ancestors, Hasan-Jalal was descended from (2) the kings of Armenia or the Bagratuni dynasty, centered at Ani; (3) the Armenian kings of Vaspurakan of the Artsuni dynasty, centered in the region of Van; (4) the princes of Gardman; (5) the Sassanid dynasty of Persia, and (6) the Arsacids, the second royal house of Albania, itself a branch of (7) the kings of ancient Parthia.[13]

All of this confirmed what perhaps no one should have doubted in the first place: that the man whose dagger in the Hermitage bears an Armenian inscription was not in fact a latter-day Caucasian Albanian. Yet it needed a scholar in New Jersey to prove it.

The great thick beech forests of Nagorny Karabakh are one of the red bands that curled down Samvel Karapetian's map of the Caucasus in 1914. Before we parted, Samvel and I were to go on one more expedition deep into these forests, to one of Karabakh's most famous and remote monasteries.

Our two local guides, Boris and Slava from the village of Talish, led the way, carrying double-barreled hunting rifles. We entered a timeless forest wilderness and walked for hours, picking our way over great rotting timbers, beneath the silver shafts of beech trees. Samvel strode in front with the guides, keeping up an eager pace. As he darted along, he sometimes seemed less a human being than some strange marine creature flitting through the green. My feelings toward this tireless historian veered between admiration and alarm. He was, an Armenian friend justly said, "a constructive ultranationalist." Whatever Samvel is seeking to prove, the general effect of his work will be to record for the wider world treasures of medieval Christian art that are little known in the outside world and might otherwise be lost. Yet, if his political views were to predominate, would the Caucasus ever move out of its suspended animation in the medieval period?

After three hours, we spotted our destination. A tiny splash of pale stone stood out in the greenery, with a small square belfry jutting skyward. Yeghishe Arakyal stands on a rocky outcrop above a gorge, the foaming River Terter far below. A thick defensive wall surrounds the seven churches; the medieval princes obviously needed to protect themselves well. As soon as we came through the gate, Samvel and his team got out their tape measures and cameras and immediately set to work.

When darkness had fallen, we were under the spell of the Karabakh forests. All I could hear was the crackle of the bonfire, an owl, and the distant surge of the river. Then there was something else: a faint patter of Armenian voices. I got up, went out into the darkness, and crept around the pale shapes of the monastery chapels, pressed against each other like the hulls of ships. Samvel, Emma, and Narine were standing with their faces pressed against the low stone doorway of one of the churches. Narine held a flashlight whose beam fell onto the inscription above the door, Emma stood with pen poised above a pad of paper. Samvel, his big bald head capped by a navy-blue-and-orange woolly hat, was reading out the Armenian letters, one by one. Samvel was unstoppable. He was even using the hours of darkness to gather more intelligence in his long war.

# I I

# August 1991–May 1992

*War Breaks Out*

## INDEPENDENCE DAYS

Early on the morning of 19 August 1991, the Russian parliamentary deputy Anatoly Shabad woke up in the village of Haterk in the northern hills of Nagorny Karabakh. He was there to try to negotiate the release of forty Soviet Interior Ministry soldiers who had been taken hostage by Armenian partisans. Soviet troops from the 23rd Division, based in Azerbaijan, had surrounded the village and been given orders to free the hostages by force. There were fears that it would end in bloodshed.

Then Shabad switched on the radio and heard shattering news. In Moscow, a newly declared State Committee for Emergencies (or, in its Russian initials, the *GKChP*) was announcing the resignation of the Soviet president, Mikhail Gorbachev. A coup d'état had taken place. This changed everything in the Soviet Union. With the security elite now in charge in Moscow, the Soviet army commanders in Karabakh became more aggressive. Emissaries arrived from Yerevan and secured an agreement for the release of the captured soldiers.

The next day, Shabad went up into the thickly forested hills above Haterk to meet the freed men and escort them down to the village. As they were descending the mountain paths, he noticed that the young well-built soldiers were lagging behind him, a Moscow intellectual of slight build. He was worried:

> I said, "What happened to you? Did they beat you? Perhaps they haven't fed you for two weeks?" They said, "No, no, everything is fine." Later it turned out that they had drunk very heavily the night before with their captors because Gorbachev had been overthrown. Both sides were terribly pleased that Gorbachev had been deposed and so all of them had got dead drunk.[1]

For the leaders of Azerbaijan, Ayaz Mutalibov and Viktor Polyanichko, the takeover by the hard-liners in Moscow looked like a vindication of their loyalty to the Soviet system; they could now expect support for a tougher crackdown on the Karabakh Armenians. On 19 August, Mutalibov was on a visit to Iran. His chief foreign policy adviser, Vafa Guluzade, says that he counseled Mutalibov to wait until he got back to Baku before commenting on the situation in Moscow. However, the Azerbaijani leader did not stick to the advice:

> In Tabriz [Mutalibov] had a telephone call from Polyanichko, the second secretary, who said, "I congratulate you, it's our victory" and Mutalibov was very happy. . . . And in the memorial of Shahriar, the Azeri poet, when he was under the lights of lamps, I was just inside. Journalists asked him what happened there, and Mutalibov began to say that the policy of Gorbachev was wrong, et cetera et cetera.[2]

Yet within three days everything was turned on its head as the coup attempt collapsed. Gorbachev was reinstated, the coup plotters went to jail, and the Russian leader Boris Yeltsin was triumphant. In Azerbaijan, the damage had been done. Polyanichko had reportedly told Baku Radio, "I am ready to give my Karabakh experience to the *GKChP* of the Soviet Union."[3] He left Azerbaijan. Mutalibov's more cautious remarks in Iran allowed him to cling to power, but with much reduced authority.

The events created a power vacuum in Nagorny Karabakh. The last members of Polyanichko's Organizing Committee left the province in September, and the Soviet army, which had been enforcing Azerbaijan's authority, was demoralized and leaderless. No longer facing proper resistance, the Armenian fighters moved back into Shaumian region, recapturing the villages of Erkech, Manashid, and Buzlukh, which they had lost during Operation Ring.

The August events accelerated the breakup of the Soviet Union, and the Union Republics began to make declarations of independence. Mutalibov declared Azerbaijan independent on 30 August 1991, and the Azerbaijani Communist Party dissolved itself on 14 September—although the same leadership stayed in charge. On 8 September, Mutalibov was elected Azerbaijan's first president, but it was a mechanical victory: his was the only name on the ballot after all the opposition contenders either boycotted the polls or withdrew. In the same week, Heidar Aliev began his political comeback, being elected speaker of parliament in the exclave of Nakhichevan and acquiring a new independent power base.

In Armenia, the referendum on independence scheduled for 21 September 1991 became a technicality and 95 percent of the population voted in favor. Three weeks later, on 16 October, Levon Ter-Petrosian was elected president with a large majority. Ten of the original eleven members of the Karabakh Committee were given senior state posts in government or parliament, completing their triumph.

The independence of Azerbaijan and Armenia—recognized internationally early in 1992—raised their conflict to a new interstate level. Azerbaijan immediately felt it possessed an even stronger argument than before. Formally, the new states retained their old borders and so Nagorny Karabakh was—and is—an internationally recognized part of Azerbaijan. The Armenians risked international opprobrium, by laying claim to a part of an independent country. They sidestepped this problem by declaring Nagorny Karabakh "independent"—and thus no longer the responsibility of Yerevan. The regional Soviet in Stepanakert declared the independence of the new "Nagorny Karabakh Republic" on 2 September 1991, three days after Azerbaijan had declared independence. It asserted that under Soviet law autonomous regions had the right to secede from newly independent states.

The declaration of "independence" by Nagorny Karabakh—a region with little more than 100,000 inhabitants—was primarily a sleight of hand that allowed Armenia to say that it was only an interested observer, not a party to the conflict. However, it was also an act of self-assertion by the Karabakh Armenians whose agenda never fully coincided with that in Yerevan. The speaker of Karabakh's newly elected parliament and de facto leader of the region was a young historian named Artur Mkrtchian. He and many of his comrades were members of the nationalist Dashnaktsutiun Party, whose relations with the Ter-Petrosian administration in Yerevan were poor. On 14 April 1992, Mkrtchian died in mysterious circumstances. The official version was that he had accidentally shot himself while cleaning his gun; other accounts said that he had committed suicide or been murdered by political rivals. After his death, relations with Yerevan improved.

The internationalization of the conflict brought a new generation of mediators to Nagorny Karabakh. The first was Boris Yeltsin, who came to Stepanakert in September 1991, fresh from his triumph defeating the coup plotters in Moscow and accompanied by the president of Kazakhstan, Nursultan Nazarbayev. Negotiations followed in the Russian spa town of Zheleznovodsk, and a Russian-brokered "Zheleznovodsk declaration" was signed, which set out a framework peace agreement.

Yeltsin's precarious peace agreement was blown apart on 20 November, when an Azerbaijani helicopter carrying twenty-two passengers and crew crashed over the Martuni region in southern Karabakh, apparently after being shot down by Armenian fighters. Among the senior Azerbaijanis who died were the head of Shusha Region, Vagif Jafarov, and President Mutalibov's press spokesman. The dead also included Russian and Kazakh officials who had come to implement the peace deal. In Azerbaijan, both government and opposition erupted in anger. Bowing to opposition pressure, Mutalibov transferred most of the powers of the 360-member parliament to a smaller (50-seat) *Milli Shura* or National Council, half of whose members were from the opposition. On 26 November, Azerbaijan's new National Council voted to revoke Nagorny Karabakh's autonomous status and declared it to be an ordinary province of Azerbaijan, without any special rights. It also formally renamed Stepanakert "Khankendi." The Karabakh Armenians responded on 10 December by holding a referendum on independence, in which, naturally, no Azerbaijanis took part. According to the returns, 108,615 people had voted in favor of Nagorny Karabakh's independence and 24 had voted against. The "war of laws" had reached its *reductio ad absurdum*, and any compromise was now impossible.


## VOLUNTEER ARMIES

The collapse of the Soviet Union left Armenia and Azerbaijan independent states at war with each other but with no armies. Despite Armenia's denials that it was a party to the conflict, the facts on the ground showed that the so-called Nagorny Karabakh war was also a conflict between the new states of Armenia and Azerbaijan. Ordinary Armenians experienced this as a fact. Their economy had almost collapsed with the closure of the border with Azerbaijan, which now turned into a fighting zone. Hardest to ignore was the fact that Armenian citizens were dying in the conflict in Karabakh.

Armenia was better prepared for war. A core of Soviet army officers had set about creating an Armenian army. Some were Russians, who had served in Armenia, like Lieutenant General Anatoly Zenevich, who began to work with the Karabakh Armenians in 1992. Others were Armenian officers who had demobilized from the Soviet army, such as the deputy head of the Soviet General Staff, Norad Ter-Grigoriants, who became chief of Armenia's new General Staff.

These men were less important than the *fedayin* fighters, who were already hardened from fighting in the hills. Independence brought a new flood of Armenian volunteers for what was still an emotive and popular cause. Samvel Danielian was one of a group of Dashnak students at Yerevan University who volunteered for the front. "The state gave out nothing as such," he recalls. "Every man found himself clothes and weapons and camouflage and boots. There were sometimes cases when the Dashnaks came and handed out things."[4]

The situation was chaotic. Weapons were being handed out to men who had displayed nothing more than a willingness to go and kill. The Karabakh Armenian leader Serzh Sarkisian admits: "At first lads of a rather criminal type were attracted to weapons, to fighting. That was impermissible." There was almost no coordination or training. The cameraman and reporter Vartan Hovanisian covered the whole first phase of the war:

> At the beginning, there were disparate units, created in different ways, either on the idea of Dashnaktsutiun or coming from a certain region. A village formed its own units, or two people met in a courtyard, got in a car and just went. One person found a weapon, another a hunting rifle. The weapons were absolutely extraordinary, people even made their own do-it-yourself weapons and blew themselves up.[5]

Azerbaijan was in a much weaker position. The fundamental issues of power had not been resolved and there were fears of civil war between President Mutalibov and the nationalist opposition. For many politicians, the war effort was less important than the domestic power struggle.

President Mutalibov had created the Ministry of Defense in October 1991. However there were few officers available to staff it. The Soviet army had traditionally discriminated against Muslim soldiers, so while there were thousands of Armenians with high rank and frontline training, Azerbaijanis were more likely to have served as cooks or builders than professional officers. As a basis for the army, there was only the

OMON, which had played only a supporting role to the Soviet army in Nagorny Karabakh. Armenian Interior Minister Ashot Manucharian says: "Because we had been forced to create everything in secret, invisibly, in spite of the Soviet authorities, everything that was created turned into an army. What the Azerbaijanis had was a police force."[6]

As a result, Azerbaijan's new Defense Ministry had a staff of fewer than one hundred and offices in the former KGB club in downtown Baku. Within its first six months, as Azerbaijan went through one crisis after another, it went through no fewer than four ministers. The second defense minister, Tajedin Mekhtiev, a Soviet career officer, who lasted two months, describes the ministry he took over in December 1991:

> There was not a single piece of military equipment. . . . There was no communications equipment at all. Now we have mobile phones. Then there was absolutely nothing. It was impossible to conduct a conversation with anyone. Everything was listened to. At that time all the government lines went through the GRU [Russian military intelligence] and they listened to all our conversations. And there were no other lines. There were no barracks, no training grounds, no weapons, no equipment.[7]

Mekhtiev, a large man with a military bearing and ruddy face, says that for the entire nine weeks that he was minister the Popular Front demonstrated outside his office calling on him to resign. His solution was simple. He told Mutalibov that they had "to shoot a hundred people, five hundred" in order to impose order. Mutalibov's reluctance to carry this out Mekhtiev puts down to "indecisiveness."

The Defense Ministry had almost no control over the real fighting men of Azerbaijan: a plethora of armed groups, many of which were essentially the personal militias of opposition leaders. The Popular Front leader in the southern town of Lenkoran, Aliakram Humbatov, formed his own brigade. So did the opposition veteran Etibar Mamedov, who says that by the middle of 1992, he had about two thousand men, mainly students, under arms. It was obvious that these men had arms not just to fight the Armenians but to take part in the power struggles for Azerbaijan itself. Mamedov says that President Mutalibov first tried to bring his battalions under the control of the new overarching Defense Council and then changed his mind:

There was no subordination, because the Defense Council was created, they held one session and after that we didn't meet. And on 27 [1992] January, [Mutalibov] published a decree dissolving the Defense Council. But by then it was too late. Instead of leading this process himself, [Mutalibov] was afraid that these armed groups could be turned against him and did everything to stop them being formed.[8]

The city of Aghdam, situated in the plains below Stepanakert, was officially the Azerbaijani army's forward post, yet in 1992 it lived by its own rules. Aghdam's problems were symptomatic of the country as a whole. It had always had a reputation for being a haven for outlaws and black marketeers, and now several underworld leaders tried to control the war effort. Kemal Ali, a neurophysiologist, went to fight in Aghdam in the spring of 1992:

When I was in Aghdam in 1992 there wasn't a single army, there were six or seven separate units, fighting the Armenians. These units were organized by local criminals, bandits, who'd spent many years in Soviet jails for murder, for different crimes. . . . But these units were in conflict with each other as well as with the Armenians. For example, they agreed to seize some kind of Russian weapons warehouse. They captured it, one man got five tanks and another didn't get a single one. That's it! They're now enemies! So these six units could never carry out one attack together. One attacked and the next one said, "No I won't, I don't want to attack today."[9]

One of the criminalized commanders was Yaqub Mamed, a man who had formerly made his living inscribing tombstones and who based his paramilitary group at the town cemetery; he was later arrested and charged with drawing the pay of dead soldiers whom he kept frozen in cold storage tanks. Another was Asif Makhamerov, who had recently been released from jail, where he had served time for murder. He went by the sobriquet "Freud" because of his reputation as an intellectual.[10] Kemal Ali comments: "Criminals are often very big patriots. War is a very good place for criminals. You can do whatever you want. You can stab and kill. An educated person never goes to war, criminals go to war. And at that time our army was commanded by criminals."

## THE ARMING OF KARABAKH

At the end of 1991, Nagorny Karabakh was still a mosaic of Azerbaijani and Armenian villages. As Soviet forces pulled out, each side tried to redraw this complex map in its favor. The less numerous Karabakh Azerbaijani villages found themselves in dozens of small traps, at the mercy of Armenian *fedayin*. According to the Armenian leader Robert Kocharian, "When [the Soviet] forces withdrew we were left one on one with Azerbaijan, one on one, but organized and having as a minimum three or four years of experience of underground activity."[11] These Armenian fighters began to intimidate Karabakh Azerbaijanis out of their villages. In the euphemistic explanation of the Armenian military commander Serzh Sarkisian, "We took the decision to try to reduce the line of the front."[12]

Yet while the Azerbaijanis were in a number of traps, the Armenians found themselves in one large trap. Stepanakert, Karabakh's main town and the Armenians' capital, was extremely vulnerable. Situated on an open, gently sloping hillside, it was surrounded by Azerbaijani settlements. Fifteen miles to the east was Aghdam and the plain of Azerbaijan; five miles to the north were the large Azerbaijani village of Khojali and Karabakh's only airport; directly above it, to the south, was the hilltop town of Shusha. Stepanakert's only link to the outside world was by helicopter across the mountains to Armenia.

The Armenians armed themselves by taking over most of the arsenal of the Soviet forces, stationed in Karabakh. "It was a very solid foundation," said Robert Kocharian. "All of the equipment stayed, we did not allow it to be removed."

Some of the weapons came from the four regiments of the Soviet Interior Ministry stationed in Nagorny Karabakh in 1991. On 22 December, armed Armenians broke into the barracks of the police regiment in Stepanakert, seized the ammunition store and armored vehicles, and forced the unit to leave Karabakh without its weapons. One Russian driver was killed in a shoot-out. That at least is the official version of events—it is possible that the raid was a cover for a business deal.[13]

The regular units of the 4th Army of Azerbaijan, manned by conscripts from across the Soviet Union, were in disarray. Soldiers from farflung republics simply left their units and traveled home. Stepanakert had been the base for the 366th Motorized Regiment since August 1988. Officers in the 366th began to help the Armenians, and men in sister units in the 23rd Division in Ganje began to work with the Azerbaijanis. Anatoly Shabad observed what was in effect the privatization of the Soviet army:

> Parts of the same 23rd Division practically fought with each other. Those parts that were stationed in Stepanakert openly supported the Armenian armed forces. That was obvious to me . . . and I saw that the commander of the military unit in Stepanakert was giving military support to the Armenian side at the same time as his commander Budeikin in Ganje was, without any doubt, helping the Azerbaijani side.[14]

Around 50 of the 350 or so remaining soldiers of the 366th Regiment were Armenian, including the commander of its 2nd Battalion, Major Seiran Ohanian. For the Karabakh Armenians, the regiment and its large stores of weaponry were a godsend. Even before the August putsch in Moscow, soldiers had been offering their weapons for sale or for hire. The American human rights activist Scott Horton says that in July 1991, an officer named Yury Nikolayevich, mistaking him for a businessman, offered to sell him a tank for three thousand dollars. Others tell how Armenians simply paid the regimental officers in vodka or rubles to open fire or deploy its weapons.[15]

The most prized assets of the 366th were its ten tanks, the only such heavy armor in Nagorny Karabakh. At the beginning of 1992, the Armenians "borrowed" the tanks on several occasions. The Azerbaijani prosecutor Yusif Agayev says he was in the southern village of Yukhari Veisali in February when the armor of the regiment rolled in, supporting an Armenian offensive to expel the Azerbaijani population.

Most of the regiment's conscripts, however, were caught between both sides. In February 1992, the Moscow weekly newspaper *Argumenty i Fakty* printed a letter sent by a young conscript to his friend Maksim. He described a base in which between two and three hundred soldiers remained under siege. They had no gas or water and had killed or eaten all the dogs; they were unable to go out and face the Armenian fighters, while enduring an Azerbaijani missile bombardment from Shusha. The conscript writes:

> When they release us I don't even know how we will get out of here. The Azerbaijanis won't let us out beyond Stepanakert. Everyone who

leaves either "sells" our regiment or gets taken hostage. Here you only think about getting drunk so as not to go mad. The whole fence around the regiment is mined, so that we are armed to the teeth and they won't disarm us without a fight.[16]

## A NEIGHBORS' WAR

War was never declared in Nagorny Karabakh, and only at the very end was it waged between two armies. In 1991–1992, the irregular soldiers were paid little or nothing and war became business by other means. The two sides actually traded with each other. Samvel Danielian remembers that he and his comrades fighting on the northern front in 1991 were constantly short of food but had plenty of alcohol, so they did business with the enemy: "We traded by night and fought by day." The Armenians exchanged cognac and alcoholic spirit for canned food and bread rusks.[17] A nastier form of commerce was hostage taking, which had been practiced in Karabakh since 1989 but now became universal. Azerbaijani fighters went to Baku, seized some of the remaining Armenians there, and tried to exchange them for their captured comrades; this stopped only when the Karabakh Armenian side refused to accept Baku Armenians as currency. Only in 1993 did both sides form committees to arrange exchanges of prisoners, but freelance hostage taking carried on.[18]

Most of the conflict was irregular, improvised, even intimate. The lack of any rules of engagement made it more brutal. Both sides revived the practice of the early 1900s employed by the Armenian guerrilla commander Andranik: chopping off the ears of enemy dead as war trophies. The British photographer Jon Jones recalls how, in the winter of 1992, a commander in Hadrut pulled a piece of greaseproof paper from his pocket and unwrapped an ear for him. It was the commander's latest souvenir of battle.

The Azerbaijani volunteer Kemal Ali says: "Humanity lasts until the first terrible situation. After you see what they did to your friend, humanity disappears and you want to do even worse. That happened with the Armenians and with us. I could hold myself back. I was thirty-plus, educated, but mostly they were twenty-something boys from villages." He goes on:

I saw cases when we killed their prisoners and they killed our prisoners. You can see that their fingers were cut off, ears were cut off. By education, I am a neurophysiologist. In my last tour in the war, I served in a military hospital in Kubatly and they brought in our captives who had been exchanged to be treated. They died in hospital. A man arrives healthy and a week later he is dead. Then when we did an autopsy, it turned out that he had petrol under his skin. He had been given an injection, which they told him was antibiotics. In fact it was petrol.

Yet both sides in Karabakh knew each other and often this was, literally, a neighbors' war. The widow of the Armenian military commander Seta Melkonian recalls how a fighter from the Martuni region in the south of Karabakh inadvertently captured a friend of his own father: "A hostage is sitting in the room, [the fighter] comes in and they start talking, talking, they start asking about the whole family, 'How's your dad, your mum, your this, your that, your cousins, your brothers?' And they're so happy to see each other, but one of them is the hostage and one of them is the commander there."[19]

The Karabakh Azerbaijanis and Armenians, each knowing the other's language, would tune into each other's radio frequencies and exchange news and abuse across the airwaves. Stories of Karabakh friends coming across each other on the field of battle are legion. A story from the village of Kornidzor has one of the Armenian defenders of the village taking aim with his gun at an Azerbaijani attacker; his friend stopped him, saying, "Wait, don't shoot! It's my neighbor, Ahmed, he owes me 800 rubles!"[20] Seta Melkonian tells of another fighter under her husband's command who kept up an affair with an Azerbaijani woman from Fizuli across the border, even as the fighting escalated; when he was killed, they were unable to tell her the news. This neighborliness could act as a brake on brutality—but it did not always work that way.

## KHOJALI

Beginning in the New Year of 1992, the Armenians began to break out of the Karabakhi capital, Stepanakert. They captured the Azerbaijani villages that surrounded the town, expelling the hundreds of Azerbaijanis who remained there. Their main target was now Khojali, five miles northeast of Stepanakert and the base for the region's airport. Khojali had been the focus of a large Azerbaijani resettlement program. In 1991, it had a population of 6,300.[21]

In October 1991, the Armenians cut the road connecting Khojali and Aghdam, so that the only way to reach the town was in a helicopter: a quick flight from Aghdam followed by a rapid corkscrew descent. In January, when the American reporter Thomas Goltz made this terrifying trip, he found the town cold and poorly defended. "There were no working telephones in Khojali, no working anything—no electricity, no heating oil, and no running water," Goltz wrote. "The only link with the outside world was the helicopter—and these were under threat with each run." By the time the last helicopter flew in to Khojali on 13 February 1992, perhaps fewer than 300 people had been evacuated by air and about 3,000 people remained. The town was defended by the OMON commander of the airport, Alif Hajiev, and 160 or so lightly armed men. The inhabitants waited anxiously for the expected Armenian attack.[22]

The Armenian assault began on the night of 25–26 February, a date probably chosen to mark the anniversary of the Sumgait pogroms four years earlier. Armored vehicles from the Soviet 366th Regiment lent their support. They surrounded Khojali on three sides before Armenian fighters went in and overwhelmed the local defenders.

Only one exit out of Khojali was open. Hajiev reportedly told the civilians to escape and make for Aghdam, and that his OMON militiamen would accompany them for their protection. In the middle of the night, a large crowd fled through the woods, which were ankle-deep in snow, and started to descend the valley of the small Gargar river. In early morning, the crowd of Khojali civilians, interspersed with a few militiamen, emerged onto open ground near the Armenian village of Nakhichevanik. There they were hit by a wall of gunfire from Armenian fighters on the hillside above. The militiamen returned fire, but were heavily outnumbered and killed. More fleeing civilians kept on coming onto a scene of appalling carnage. A Khojali resident, Hijran Alekpera, told Human Rights Watch:

> By the time we got to Nakhichevanik it was 9:00 A.M. There was a field and there were many people who had been killed. There were maybe one hundred. I didn't try to count. I was wounded on th[is] field. Gajiv Aliev was shot and I wanted to help him. A bullet hit me in

the belly. I could see where they were shooting from. I saw other bodies in the field. They were newly killed—they hadn't changed color.[23]

A few days later, a terrible aftermath greeted the reporters and investigators who came to these hillsides. Torn bodies littered the snowy
ground. Anatol Lieven of *The Times* noted that "several of them, including one small girl, had terrible injuries: only her face was left."
The Azerbaijani prosecutor Yusif Agayev saw powder around the gun-
shot wounds and concluded that many of the victims had been shot
at point-blank range: "They were shot at close range. We went to the
place where it happened. It was obvious to me as a specialist."[24] As
well as those shot down, dozens of victims died of cold and frostbite in
the woods. More than a thousand Khojali residents were taken prisoner, among them several dozen Meskhetian Turks, refugees from
Central Asia.

There are varying estimates of how many Azerbaijanis were killed
in or near Khojali. Probably the most reliable figure is that of the official
Azerbaijani parliamentary investigation, which put the death toll at
485. Even taking into account that this number includes combatants
and those who died of cold, it still dwarfs any body count of the Nagorny Karabakh war. The number of Azerbaijanis who returned fire
was small; this could not excuse the clear targeting of hundreds of civilians, including children, in an open space and the shooting of defenseless people on the ground.[25]

Slowly the news got out that a massacre had taken place at Khojali.
At first many in the outside world were reluctant to believe it because
most international media coverage of the conflict had hitherto portrayed the Armenians as the main victims of the conflict, rather than ag-
gressors. A self-justificatory newspaper interview given in April 1992
by the former Azerbaijani president Ayaz Mutalibov did not help. Mutalibov, seeking to minimize his own role in the failure to defend the
town, put the blame for the massacre on the Popular Front. His interview was much quoted in Armenia.[26]

Yet Armenians now do admit that many Azerbaijani civilians were
killed as they fled Khojali. Some blame irregular Armenian fighters,
acting on their own behalf. An Armenian police officer, Major Valery
Babayan, suggested revenge as a motive. He told the American reporter
Paul Quinn-Judge that many of the fighters who had taken part in the
Khojali attack "originally came from Sumgait and places like that."[27]

Asked about the taking of Khojali, the Armenian military leader Serzh Sarkisian said carefully, "We don't speak loudly about these things." "A lot was exaggerated" in the casualties, and the fleeing Azerbaijanis had put up armed resistance, he claimed. Sarkisian's summation of what had happened, however, was more honest and more brutal:

> But I think the main point is something different. Before Khojali, the Azerbaijanis thought that they were joking with us, they thought that the Armenians were people who could not raise their hand against the civilian population. We were able to break that [stereotype]. And that's what happened. And we should also take into account that amongst those boys were people who had fled from Baku and Sumgait.

Sarkisian's account throws a different light on the worst massacre of the Karabakh war, suggesting that the killings may, at least in part, have been a deliberate act of mass killing as intimidation.

## MUTALIBOV FALLS

The Khojali killings triggered a crisis in Baku. Azerbaijanis denounced their government for not protecting the town. Hundreds of men for whom Karabakh had hitherto been a distant dispute volunteered to fight. Accusations flew back and forth as to why a planned operation to break the siege of the town had not been mounted. A Khojali survivor, Salman Abasov, complained later:

> Several days before the events of the tragedy the Armenians told us several times over the radio that they would capture the town and demanded that we leave it. For a long time helicopters flew into Khojali and it wasn't clear if anyone thought about our fate, took an interest in us. We received practically no help. Moreover, when it was possible to take our women, children, and old people out of the town, we were persuaded not to do so.[28]

When the Azerbaijani parliament met on 3 March, opposition deputies demanded that a film shot by the cameraman Jengiz Mustafiev be shown in the chamber. "The first frames of the film started rolling—

and the next ten minutes changed the history of the country," writes Goltz. Mustafiev had flown into the hills above Aghdam in a helicopter. As he landed, his camera scanned dozens of dead bodies strewn along the valley. There were villagers in bright headscarves and winter coats lying in the mud and half-melted snow. A sobbing man picked up a dead child in a red anorak, its face muffled in a scarf, and handed it into the helicopter.

Faced with images like these, the ruling regime crumbled. On 6 March, facing an ultimatum from the opposition, Mutalibov resigned. Officially the new speaker of parliament, Yaqub Mamedov, became Azerbaijan's acting head of state. He was, however, not a professional politician but merely the head of Baku University's Medical Faculty. In practice power was slipping into the hands of the opposition. Mamedov acknowledged this by appointing the Popular Front radical Rahim Gaziev minister of defense. New presidential elections were called for three months hence, which the Popular Front fully expected to win.

## THE SIEGE OF STEPANAKERT

Following the ignominious part it had played in the storming of Khojali, the Soviet 366th Regiment was ordered by Moscow to withdraw from Karabakh. At the beginning of March 1992, a column of troops was sent to Stepanakert to escort the regiment out, but local Armenians blocked the roads to stop its leaving. The soldiers were eventually airlifted out by helicopter, and almost all their equipment stayed behind. Major Ohanian also stayed, as did many of his Armenian comrades and several Slavic officers—including the would-be tank salesman Yury Nikolayevich, who was later spotted training Karabakhi fighters.[29] On 10 March, the 366th Regiment was disbanded in Georgia.

On 3 March, as the regiment was preparing to pull out, a retired Armenian officer and former tank commander, Gagik Avsharian, got a call from his comrade Samvel Babayan:

> [Babayan] meets me. I say, "where are you going?" "To the base."
> So we went there. He said, "can you start this tank?" I started up the
> tank and stole it, as they say, from the unit. Either it was organized or
> how it was organized, I can't say. It's impossible to start up a tank in
> the unit without the commander's knowing [about it]. Either they'd

already taken control or there'd been a coup, I can't say. The thing is that when we arrived, I sat in this tank and started it up, and we towed away another tank.[30]

According to Avsharian, of the regiment's ten tanks, departing troops blew up one; one was without an engine and hence unusable; the remaining eight were left behind and, after some repair work, were fit for battle. The Armenians faced another problem, however. Avsharian had served in a T-64 tank in the Soviet army, not a T-72, while some of his fellow fighters had never driven a tank before at all. They were called upon to learn how to use them, literally in the heat of the battle. On 6 March, they faced an Azerbaijani attack at Askeran, just outside Stepanakert:

When we went into battle the first time we didn't even know how to arm this tank. We could load the shell into the barrel by hand, as in all tanks, but we didn't know how to drive it into the barrel automatically. We went into battle with shells in our hands, on our knees. Our commander was also in a BMP-2 [a type of armored vehicle]. When [the Azerbaijanis] attacked Askeran they wanted us to go and stop them. He didn't know how to load the shell into the barrel of the BMP-2. And we were told that Seiran Ohanian was in Askeran and "he can show you how to do it." They met on the road, Seiran showed him how to plunge the shell into the barrel, and after that they went into battle.

Throughout the spring of 1992, Stepanakert was under siege. Officially, the town had fifty-five thousand inhabitants. Without any access by road to Armenia for almost two years, many of its residents had been virtually trapped there all that time. Then in early February, Azerbaijani Popular Front commander Rahim Gaziev took two Grad multiple-rocket launchers up to the clifftop town of Shusha to fire on to Stepanakert.[31]

The Grad launcher is named after the Russian word for "hail." Highly inaccurate, it is a terrifying weapon, designed for use against soldiers, not civilians. Up to forty rockets are loaded into tubes, generally in a grid raised on the back of a truck, and then launched all at once. They make a hideous whining sound as they rain down over a wide area. The Armenians also acquired two Grad launchers from a Soviet base in Armenia at the time, but they appear to have had many fewer missiles; probably the logistics of bringing in rockets by helicopter from Armenia worked against them. In early 1992, the advantage was on the Azerbaijani side. Stepanakert is spread below Shusha like an open plate and an easy target for artillery. However, there was no coordination in how or when the Grads were fired. The Azerbaijani officer Azai Kerimov said: "Anyone could just get up with a hangover, after drinking the night before, sit behind the Grad and fire, fire, fire at Stepanakert without any aim, without any coordinates."[32]

From mid-February, hundreds of rockets rained down from Shusha onto Stepanakert, causing havoc. Over the course of the spring of 1992, the accumulated casualty figure from the bombardment probably ran into the hundreds. Many of the town's residents lived in high-rise apartment blocks, which presented a sitting target for Azerbaijani artillery. The Azizian family was out collecting water on 12 March when a rocket ripped through their front room. They came back to find half the front wall of their apartment torn away; their curtains had been carried several hundred yards into the kindergarten next door.

Residents spent every night in their basements; first, they lit gas pipes, then, when the gas ran out, they lived by candlelight. In the morning, they emerged to fetch water from springs several kilometers outside the town. Food and medicine supplies ran low. The journalist Vadim Byrkin recalls: "If I have a memory, it is the cold. When you spend the night sleeping in a bomb shelter, in a basement, and when the stove goes out before morning, then it gets terribly cold. In the morning, when you go upstairs, you don't know whether your home will be there or not."[33] In May, when Shusha had been captured and the siege lifted, Stepanakert was a shattered town. This is what the British reporter Vanora Bennett found:

> Stepanakert was in a frenzy of spring-cleaning. In brilliant sunshine, tiny old women were sweeping up rubble and shifting bits of wall. The crunch of broken glass being dragged over broken pavements was the loudest sound. There were ruined buildings on all sides, and almost every house had some trace of war damage, an exposed roof, bullet holes, cracks, staring windows. There were no shops, no gas, no electricity, no phones, no post, and no cash money.[34]

Beyond Stepanakert and Shusha, this was a war fought between villages, many of whose stories have never been recorded. One of the little-reported massacres of the war occurred in the northern Armenian village of Maragha, just across the border from the Azerbaijani town of Terter. On 10 April, Azerbaijanis captured the village and the Armenian defenders retreated. The next day the Armenians retook the village and reported that they had found and buried the bodies of at least forty-three villagers. A group from the organization Christian Solidarity International, headed by the British peer and passionate supporter of the Karabakh Armenians Baroness Caroline Cox, went to Maragha to investigate. They recorded the villagers' accounts and exhumed and photographed "decapitated and charred bodies." At least fifty Maragha villagers were also taken hostage, of whom nineteen never returned.[35]

## THE FALL OF SHUSHA

In the spring of 1992, the course of the war hinged on Shusha, the high citadel in the heart of Karabakh. The Azerbaijanis, driven out of most of the province, were concentrated in the town and a few surrounding villages. They still controlled the road from Karabakh to Armenia and could keep up the siege of Stepanakert. With cliffs on two sides, Shusha had been built as a fortress and was easily defensible. It had famously withstood two long sieges by Persian armies in 1795 and 1826. If the Azerbaijanis could hang on to this mountain stronghold, they could still hope to squeeze the Karabakh Armenians into submission slowly.

However, Shusha itself was besieged. The only access by road to the town was from the west, through the town of Lachin, next-door to Armenia. After a helicopter was shot down over Shusha on 28 January, with the death of all its passengers, this long road became Shusha's lifeline. Water supplies, always a problem in the town, became scarce. Different commanders came and went. Azerbaijan's second defense minister, Tajedin Mekhtiev, arrived in Shusha on 20 January. His stint in the town showed that years of service in the Soviet General Staff were no preparation for warfare in the Caucasus. Mekhtiev led a disastrous sortie out of Shusha to try to capture the Armenian village of Karintak (known as Dashalty by Azerbaijanis). He was ambushed and up to seventy soldiers died, many shot down as they fled. When the photographer Jon Jones arrived on the scene, he saw a snowy hillside scattered with bodies. After this debacle, Mekhtiev left Shusha and was sacked as defense minister.[36]

In early February, Rahim Gaziev arrived to take command of the town. Gaziev was a mathematics lecturer, not a professional soldier, full of passionate rhetoric but few practical ideas. He told a crowd in Shusha that he would leave the town only "on the road to Khankendi [Stepanakert]." Yet he failed to unite the four different armed groups that were nominally under his command. None of the units trusted one another, and there was not even radio contact between them. Azai Kerimov, one of the police commanders says: "Every leader of a party had his own battalion. There was no joint command. We had people who wanted to fight and weapons and food, we had everything. But people did not want to defend the town."[37]

Azerbaijan's domestic political feuds began to tell on the defense of Shusha. Promised reinforcements failed to materialize. In March, Gaziev was made minister of defense and returned to Baku. In April, a new "Shusha Brigade" was formed under the command of Elbrus Orujev, a lieutenant colonel and career army officer. Orujev was given overall command of the towns of Lachin, Kubatly, and Zengelan to the west, as well as Shusha—an absurd amount of responsibility for one man. As he arrived in Shusha, other units were simply abandoning the town. The reporter Mirshahin Agayev remembers seeing a column of troops and armor leaving Shusha by night, their headlights switched off.[38]

For the Armenians, the capture of Shusha was an absolute priority. The man entrusted with the operation to take the town was Arkady Ter-Tatevosian, also known by his nom de guerre "Komandos," or "Commando." A quiet professional soldier from Georgia, Ter-Tatevosian had the advantage of having no political ambitions. When the capture of Khojali reopened Karabakh's main airstrip, he also received new supplies of weaponry from Armenia.

Ter-Tatevosian says his first goal was to encircle Shusha, capture the villages around it and draw some of the Azerbaijani garrison away from the defense of the town: "We had to pretend that we would take those villages in order to distract their units."[39] Some of the heaviest fighting took place outside the town itself. In a bloody battle at the end of April, the Azerbaijanis narrowly failed to dislodge the Armenians from the so-called 26th Heights outside the town. Many men were killed. "If they had made a greater effort to take the 26th Heights, they could have taken them," said Ter-Tatevosian. The assault was ready to begin in early May but was delayed for a few days, supposedly because of bad weather. It thus coincided with a visit by Armenia's President Ter-Petrosian to Iran.

Two days before the assault was due to start, Shusha's communications were cut. Orujev says that he had only a few hundred defenders left inside the town, and he made a radio appeal for reinforcements:

> I said, "Who can hear me? I am in Shusha. I have only seven men with me. Do you hear me?" I was in the television station there. They said, "Aghdam here. I hear you," "Barda here. I hear you," "Kubatly. I hear you." I said, "It's Elbrus Orujev here, the commander of Shusha. We are holding Shusha. I have beaten back the Armenians. I beg of you, as many men as you have, whoever loves his country, take up arms and come and defend the town."[40]

The only Azerbaijani military commander to heed the call was Orujev's own brother, Elkhan Orujev, who launched a diversionary attack from Aghdam but too late to make any impact. As Orujev made his appeal, more troops were abandoning Shusha. One local defender, Yusif Husseinov, recalls that "Even on the seventh of May some troops were withdrawn from the town. And we didn't know. I myself went down [on the eighth] and saw the barracks were empty, the equipment had been withdrawn from the town."[41]

The Armenian assault began at 2:30 A.M. on 8 May. Ter-Tatevosian says he had counted on "three to four days" for the operation. He hoped to spread panic among the defenders and make them leave without a fight. A large contingent of soldiers was ordered to the road open out of Shusha to the west, with instructions not to fire at anyone fleeing the town but to bar the way to any reinforcements. Among these men was Robert Kocharian, now president of Armenia. Another group of commandos was sent with orders to climb the cliff at Karintak, but bad weather stopped them from doing so. That put the main burden on other Armenians soldiers climbing up paths from the north and east. "We went up the paths that they had attacked by and [that] we had noticed," said Ter-Tatevosian.

In the middle of the day, there was intense fighting for Shusha's television tower on the northern edge of the town and for the prison to the east. Gagik Avsharian was told to take his T-72 tank up the road and cover the northern approach to the town. One of the Azerbaijanis' three tanks appeared, and the two tanks opened fire at each other at a distance of 350 meters. "He was an excellent shot," comments Avsharian. Avsharian managed to open the hatch just as a third shell hit his tank. He was thrown clear and, although badly burned, survived; his driver and gun operator were killed.[42]

By evening, the defenders thought they had repulsed the Armenian assault on Shusha. Orujev says that at 8:00 P.M. he heard on his radio a Russian commander who went by the name "Cossack" giving the order to pull back from the town. "If we had stood for another two hours, they would have retreated," says Azai Kerimov. What proved fatal was that in the course of the day, as Ter-Tatevosian had hoped, large numbers of defenders had simply fled Shusha.

Many Azerbaijani civilians stayed almost until the end, but joining the flight as the day wore on. Sona Husseinova, who had worked as a cook in Shusha, said she left "in the last tank" with fourteen others. So loud was the artillery bombardment that "for a long time my ears buzzed and I couldn't hear anything."[43] Yusif Husseinov says he virtually dragged his father out of the town, after all hope of relief had faded. "Psychologically people lost confidence, they didn't expect any help. In the end, all those five years were preparing people to leave the town. And even on the last day when everything was settled they didn't give us any substantial help, almost no help at all." Orujev lacked enough men to carry on fighting and ordered a retreat. One of the last fighters to leave Shusha was the Chechen volunteer Shamil Basayev, later to become the most famous guerrilla commander in Chechnya's war against Russia.

The battle had taken only one day but perhaps three hundred had died.[44] The first Armenians entered Shusha only on the morning of 9 May, fearful that the town that had suddenly gone quiet before them was some kind of trap.

## SHUSHA CAPTURED

On 10 May, hundreds of Armenians converged on the captured town of Shusha. They found the interior of the Gazanchetsots church piled high with hundreds of boxes of Grad rockets that the Azerbaijanis had failed to use. "When I went in and saw the ammunition I almost had a heart attack," says Ter-Tatevosian. Film footage shows lines of Armenian volunteers carefully carrying the wooden boxes, shaped like tiny coffins, out of the church. As they were doing so, looters and arsonists were beginning to set fire to the whole town—despite the protestations of the returning Shusha Armenians and Karabakh Armenian officials. "The Karabakhis have a very bad habit, a superstition, of burning houses, so the enemy cannot return," says Ter-Tatevosian.

The fall of Shusha came as the Armenian president, Levon Ter-Petrosian, was meeting the acting Azerbaijani leader Yaqub Mamedov in Teheran for peace talks. It was Iran's first attempt at mediation and also Ter-Petrosian's first visit to his important southern neighbor. On 9 May, the two delegations signed a communiqué on the general principles of a peace agreement. Mamedov says that Ter-Petrosian tried to persuade him that he was in favor of peace but that he had difficulties with the Karabakhi radicals: "He had an opposition in the same way as we did. I felt that he was interested in having this problem solved positively and politically."[45]

The talks ended. Ter-Petrosian and his delegation flew on to the city of Isfahan, and the Iranian president Hashemi Rafsanjani escorted Mamedov to Teheran airport. At the steps of his plane, Mamedov was handed a message saying that the Armenians had attacked Shusha. The news was a public relations disaster for the Iranians—and this proved to be their first and last attempt at mediation in the conflict. It was also a grave embarrassment for Ter-Petrosian, who had known that an assault was planned on Shusha but not its specific timing. It now looked as though he had either been double-crossing the Azerbaijanis or was not in control of the situation. Some suspected that the delay in starting the attack was not due to bad weather but was a deliberate ploy by the local leaders in Karabakh to wreck the talks in Iran and humiliate Ter-Petrosian.[46]

The loss of Shusha was the greatest blow to Azerbaijan. It removed its last strategic foothold in Karabakh, but its importance went even beyond that. Shusha is also known as a cradle of Azerbaijani culture. Even eight years later, Elbrus Orujev's eyes glistened with tears as he spoke of the last days of the town: the pain of the experience and of his own failure to defend Shusha evidently still lived with him.

The capture of the "impregnable fortress" of Shusha instantly spawned conspiracy theories as to the reason it fell: Shusha had been sold; a deal had been struck with the Armenians; Rahim Gaziev had betrayed the town to the Russians in order to engineer the return of Ayaz Mutalibov to power. Yet, in interviews, the two main opposing commanders in the battle dismissed these conspiracy theories. Both Orujev and Ter-Tatevosian stressed the point that Shusha simply had not been properly defended. "They did not have one commander, whom they obeyed," declared Ter-Tatevosian. He himself was put in sole charge of the operation and had fighters for whom a failure to take Shusha meant the continued bombardment of Stepanakert. The Azerbaijanis had no organized defense at all until the arrival of Orujev, only days before the attack began. By then, many defenders had already left for Baku. Orujev himself blames the politicians in Baku for failing to make the defense of the town a priority, saying, "If there had not been this mess in Baku, no one would ever have taken Shusha." This straightforward explanation for the fall of Shusha is backed up by one of its defenders, no less an authority than the Chechen warrior Shamil Basayev. In 2000, interviewed high in the hills of Chechnya, he told the Azerbaijani television company ANS:

> Shusha was just abandoned. About 700 Armenians launched an offensive and it was just a veneer. With such a strong garrison and so many weapons, especially as Shusha itself is in a strategically significant position, one hundred men can hold it for a year easily. There was no organization. Today we can take one specific general or minister, we can just take them and say you betrayed it, you took it, you sold it. It is all talk. There was no single management. No one was responsible for anything.[47]

## "ONLY CHAOS"

The fall of Shusha deepened the political divisions in Azerbaijan. In Baku, all sides traded accusations of incompetence and betrayal. Heidar Aliev, now speaker of the local parliament of Nakhichevan, continued his subtle campaign to be a "third force" in Azerbaijan. He told a reporter from Reuters news agency that it was impossible to hold the scheduled presidential elections "when war is raging in Azerbaijan"—elections from which he had been barred from standing on the grounds of age. "There's no leadership in Baku at the moment," Aliev stated flatly. "There's only chaos."[48]

On 14 May 1992, parliament reconvened in Baku and the former Communist deputies suddenly staged a constitutional coup d'état to restore Ayaz Mutalibov to office. The deputies announced that because the preliminary findings from the investigation into Khojali had just exonerated Mutalibov from guilt, his resignation was therefore unconstitutional. Mutalibov came back to the parliament chamber and announced that he gladly accepted his restoration to the presidency. Naturally, the 7 June presidential elections were to be canceled, for he was now Azerbaijan's president once again.

This maneuver was effectively a declaration of civil war. Azerbaijan's nationalist opposition had the constitution on their side in that all the mechanisms had already been set up to hold new elections, and the vote to restore Mutalibov had been taken without a proper quorum. Still, Mutalibov had taken physical control of the parliament and the presidential apparatus. Volunteers flocked to the Popular Front headquarters to join a counteroperation being planned by the paramilitary leader and head of the Azerbaijani "Gray Wolves," Iskender Hamidov. On the afternoon of 15 May, Hamidov led a column of armor and soldiers up the hill and stormed the parliament building and the television station. Astonishingly, fewer than a dozen people were killed in the shooting as Mutalibov was ousted again, this time for good.

The opposition consolidated its victory. The opposition veteran Isa Gambar became not only speaker of parliament but Azerbaijan's acting head of state until the reinstated 7 June presidential election. Hamidov, who had spearheaded the countercoup, became interior minister; Gaziev remained defense minister, and another opposition veteran, Tofik Qasimov, became foreign minister. Then the old parliament, under duress, was made to dissolve itself and have its authority replaced by the fifty-member Milli Shura.

The political showdown in Baku had, however, again stripped Karabakh of Azerbaijani forces. The Popular Front "Geranboi Battalion" and many other smaller units had left the front and hastened to Baku to help overthrow Mutalibov. More seriously, no one was bothering to reinforce Lachin, the Azerbaijani town straddling the narrow corridor between Nagorny Karabakh and Armenia. Lachin had perhaps three thousand defenders, but no extra troops were sent to help them. There had been no single commander in control since the "Lachin Regiment" under the command of local military leader Arif Pashayev had been dissolved the previous month. "The regiment had been liquidated by then, but there had been no orders as to whom the members of the regiment should report, what they should do," complains Pashayev, a Popular Front leader who stayed on as an informal commander of his hometown.[49]

By 17 May, the Karabakh Armenians had advanced to the heights above Lachin. Again, it was a defensible town, situated on a hill. Again, most of the defenders simply fled. "I had the impression that they were holding us up, so people could leave," said the Armenian commander Seiran Ohanian, who experienced only light resistance from the enemy.[50] Footage shot by an ANS television crew shows a mass flight from Lachin of horse-drawn carts, civilians on foot, shepherds driving their sheep, and armored vehicles and trucks full of soldiers. Jengiz Mustafiev, the long-haired ANS reporter, pleads with the soldiers to return, accusing them of being cowards and traitors, but they reply that they have no idea where their commanders are. On 16 May, the ANS camera crew films a forlorn command post that has lost almost all its defenders.[51]

On 18 May 1992, the Armenians captured and burned Lachin with minimal losses on either side. They had now linked Nagorny Karabakh with Armenia. A road that had been closed for more than two years was reopened and available to carry supplies and reinforcements from Armenia through to Karabakh. All the Azerbaijanis had been expelled from Karabakh. For the Armenians, it seemed to be the culmination of a triumphant campaign—but in fact, the active phase of the war had only just begun.

# 12

# Shusha

## The Last Citadel

ON A ROCK above the serpentine road that twists up from Stepana-kert to Shusha stands a victory memorial. It is the same T-72 tank from which Gagik Avsharian was thrown headlong in the heat of battle at midday on 8 May 1992. After the Armenians had won the war for Kara-bakh, they had the burned tank rebuilt, resprayed olive green, and placed on the hill with its original number, 442, repainted in white on its hull. It pointed toward Shusha.

Eight years and one day later, on 9 May 2000, Armenian Nagorny Karabakh was celebrating its Victory Day. It was marked in three stages on the way up to the citadel of Shusha, like three stations of a crusader pilgrimage, beginning with the memorial tank and ending with a serv-ice of thanksgiving in the Gazanchetsots church.

The hull of the tank had been strewn with red and white carnations, and a group of relatives were making a personal memorial. Of the three men in tank 442, only Gagik, the commander, had survived. At the rear stood Stella, the widow of Ashot, the driver, and Hovanes, his ten-year-old son. Stella looked pale, forlorn, and still absurdly young. The grand-mother of Shahen, the gun operator, was wearing a black head scarf and holding a handkerchief in her clenched hand. She began to keen with grief for her lost grandson, wailing and beating the back of the tank with her fists.

Suddenly, the grieving relatives were overtaken by brash official celebration. A brass band struck up martial tunes in the road below as a line of dignitaries climbed the steps. The Karabakhi archbishop Parkev under his arched black cowl, military officers in full uniform, and the prime minister in a gray designer suit all filed past and laid more flow-ers. A few minutes later, members of the brass band were running to jump on their bus. A cavalcade of cars roared toward Shusha and every-one reassembled in the lower part of the town for the next ceremony, the unveiling of a monument to a World War II fighter pilot named Nelson Stepanian.

Our final destination, the Gazanchetsots church, was, when completed in 1887, one of the largest Armenian churches in the world and a token of the success of the Shusha Armenian bourgeoisie. Closed by the Communists, it was rebuilt after 1992, clad in shiny white limestone. It now towers, immaculate once more, above the ruined town. Inside, the church was echoing and impersonal. Archbishop Parkev, looking formidable in his steep black cowl, boomed out the Armenian liturgy and the choir's antiphons rebounded from the walls. After the commemoration of the recent war against Azerbaijan and the Great Patriotic War against the Germans, this was the final benediction, before everyone could go down to Stepanakert's football stadium for a pop concert.

Shusha has been called the "Jerusalem of Karabakh." Whoever possesses the town controls not only a strategic fortress in the heart of the enclave but also a place saturated with history. Shusha is called, as well, the cradle of Azerbaijan's music and poetry, the home of poets like Vagif and Natevan. For cultured Azerbaijanis, its loss in 1992 was a stab in the heart. "When we heard the news, I and a lot of my friends simply wept," one Baku intellectual told me.

To the Armenians, Shusha is a more troubling place. The lonely steeple of Gazanchetsots, rising above a still-ruined town, suggests that it is still more a symbol than a real town that people will readily inhabit. A long time ago, before 1920, Shusha was a great Armenian merchant town. More recently, to pursue the crusader image, most Armenians have come here either to loot or to pray—but not to live. I supposed that most of the Armenians I rubbed shoulders with here on Victory Day had come not so much to celebrate Shusha, the Armenian citadel, as to give thanks for the destruction of Shusha, the Azerbaijani gun emplacement. The retention of the mountain fortress is a guarantee of their security—and almost no Armenians will countenance the return of Shusha's Azerbaijani inhabitants in an eventual peace deal.[1]

On the evening of Shusha's Victory Day, I was invited to dinner in Stepanakert. A rich cross section of Karabakh Armenian society had gathered in an old two-story house in the center of the town. The women sat at one half of a long table, nearer the kitchen, the men at the other. The table was strewn with sheaves of tarragon and oregano, and the meat was hare or deer from the hills.

These Armenians were defiantly different from the Armenians of Armenia. The Karabakh Armenians are highlanders, famous for their hospitality and heavy drinking. They have a highlander's distrust of lowland Armenians, who often call them "*ishak*," or "mule," because they are so stubborn. Other Armenians find it hard to understand the thick Karabakh dialect, where the stress falls later in the word and whose vocabulary is strewn with Persian, Turkish, and Russian words. At dinner, many of the guests spoke Russian to one another—a legacy of life in Soviet Azerbaijan but also of traditional ties with Russia. In Stepanakert, someone had told me: "We Karabakhis hate the Armenians. We love the Russians, we love the Persians, but we hate the Armenians." A joke, of course, but with a dose of truth in it.

Among Armenians, Karabakh has the reputation of being a place of refuge and the last line of defense against the Islamic east. This helped create a military tradition among the Karabakhis similar to that of the Scots in the British Empire. Among the Armenian warriors born here were two marshals of the Soviet Union, a clutch of heroes of the Soviet Union like Nelson Stepanian and even—so far from the sea—a Soviet admiral, Hovanes Isakov. Further back, Karabakh produced General Valerian Madatov, a tsarist general who fought Napoleon and, fighting against him, Rustam, the man who served as Napoleon's manservant.

Carried away by this military tradition, the Karabakhis have even appropriated as their own Napoleon's great marshal and king of Naples, Joachim Murat. I was repeatedly told that he was an Armenian, born in the Karabakhi village of Kerkijahan. Yet this is a myth—Murat's biographers say he was in fact the son of a provincial innkeeper from the central French region of Guyenne. Kurban Said, the author of the great novel of the Caucasus, *Ali and Nino*, actually got there before me. His hero visits Shusha in 1914 and observes: "[The native nobles] never tired of sitting on the steps that led up to their doors, smoking their pipes and telling each other how many times the Russian Empire and the Czar himself had been saved by Karabagh generals and what horrible fate would have overtaken them if their defense had been left to anyone else."[2]

The Armenians would be surprised to learn that the Karabakh Azerbaijanis were famous warriors too. After the province was incorporated into the Russian empire in 1805, famous tall steeds from Karabakh carried the Azerbaijani cavalry of the Karabakh Regiment, one of four Muslim regiments serving in the tsar's army. At first glance, it may seem surprising that Azerbaijanis should have fought in the Russian army against the Ottoman Empire, but they were Shiites, fighting against Sunnis, split by the great divide of Islam.[3] In 1829, Alexander Pushkin saw the "Karabakh regiment" in action, outside Kars, as it returned to camp with eight Turkish banners. He dedicated a poem to the young warrior Farhad-Bek, adjutant to the regimental commander:

> Do not be captive to fleeting fame,
> O my young beauty!
> Do not throw yourself into bloody battle
> With the Karabakh horde![4]

The rich character of Karabakh is better illustrated by the dozens of different dishes on my dinner table in Stepanakert than by the smooth surfaces of the reconstructed tank or the Gazanchetsots church. The region has been a crossroads and meeting place between Christianity and Islam, Armenians, Azerbaijanis, Persians, and Russians. Older people do not need reminding of this. In 1924, the Armenian scholar Stepan Lisitsian made a detailed ethnographic study of the newly formed Nagorny Karabakh Autonomous Region. This work, which he submitted for publication in Baku, was never published in his lifetime, presumably because it defied Soviet preconceptions of what Azerbaijani Karabakh ought to be. But Lisitsian's message was not nationalist and he was fascinated by the crossbreeding of cultures in Karabakh:

The continuous vicinity of the Turk-Tartars of the plains (Karabakh and Mughan) and of the mountain plateaux (Mountainous Kurdistan), the centuries-old political subjection to the supreme authority of the Persian shahs, constant relations with the Turkic tribal elders (there were frequent cases of marriage contracts between them and the *melik* houses)—all this brought about a broad penetration of Turkish-Iranian influence not only amongst the local feudal lords, but in other levels of the Karabakh Armenian population, in the form of a universal knowledge, especially by its male section, of the Turkic language, the giving of children Muslim names, the learning of Turkic-Iranian music, an increasingly closed and humble situation for women and in rare cases polygamy (in the family of the Shakhnazarian *meliks*), the holding of a second wife outside marriage if no children were born and so on. Unfortunately, there has been little scholarly elucidation and study of the important question of the interaction of Turkic-Azer-baijani and Armenian cultures.[5]

At the Victory Day dinner table, an old man with a handsome birdlike face framed with gray sideburns sat on my right. He told me he had lived in the town for seventy years, from the time when it was only a small village. He must have seen unimaginable changes in his lifetime, I commented. "Well, of course, the main change is that there used to be a lot of Azerbaijanis," he responded laconically. "And all of them have gone."

Midway through the meal, my neighbor rose to his feet and proposed a toast in *tutovka*, the local stinging but sweet mulberry vodka. He began—for my benefit—in Russian, swerved into the thick Kara-bakh Armenian dialect, and then into a smoother gliding language that I realized with a shock was Azeri. I heard the repeated word "Aghdam" and gathered that he was telling a funny story about a trip he had made in Soviet times to the Party headquarters in the Azerbaijani city of Agh-dam. The older guests at the table, all of whom understood Azeri per-fectly, chuckled and tears came to their eyes, as he told his anecdote; the younger diners looked at one another and me in smiling confusion, un-derstanding nothing.

The history of Shusha contains the best and worst of Nagorny Kara-bakh. It is a story of joint prosperity and dynamism. But it has ended with the gene of nihilism in both communities triumphant, destroying both each other's achievements and their own. In a sense, the ruins of Shusha are a testament to both sides' refusal to accommodate each other's histories.

The town's history begins in the 1740s, when Panakh Khan, leader of the Javanshir dynasty in Azerbaijan, made a bid to be the ruler of Karabakh. The Persians and the Ottomans were in retreat, and the Rus-sians had not yet arrived in the Caucasus. Panakh Khan built a series of fortresses to establish himself as the khan of Karabakh. He cemented his position by a marriage alliance with one of the five Armenian *meliks*, or princes, Shakhnazar of Varanda. In 1750, Panakh Khan built a fortress in Shusha. The cliffs on the southern side provided a natural defense and only two gates were needed in the new city walls.

Under Panakh's successor, Ibrahim Khan, the town flourished. The Azerbaijani poet and politician Vagif settled here in the 1750s and became Ibrahim's court poet and chief *Vezir*. Vagif was killed at the end of a long war with Persia in 1795–1797, during which the Persian shah, Agha Mohammad Khan, was also assassinated at Shusha. In May 1805, Ibrahim Khan negotiated terms of submission to the Russians. He kept most of his local powers but agreed to cut all links with foreign powers and to pay the Russians an annual tribute of eight thousand gold coins. The subsequent treaties of Gulistan and Turkmenchai in 1813 and 1828 entrenched Russia's control over the Karabakh khanate. The last khan, Mehti Kulu, was forced to flee to Iran in 1822.

In the nineteenth century, Shusha was one of the great cities of the Caucasus, larger and more prosperous than either Baku or Yerevan. Standing in the middle of a net of caravan routes, it had ten caravanserais. It was well known for its silk trade, drawing on Karabakh's famous mulberry trees; for its paved streets and big stone houses; its brightly colored carpets; and for its fine-bred horses. In 1824, George Keppel, the earl of Albemarle, on his way back to England from India, arrived here from Iran, crossing into "the black and lofty mountains of the fruitful province of Karabaugh." "Sheesha" made a strong impression on him: "The town is built on a huge mass of sloping rock of great height. The ascent is so precipitous that the houses appear to be hanging on it like bird-cages. I was upward of two hours in reaching the top."[6] Keppel found two thousand houses in the town, with three-quarters of the inhabitants Azerbaijanis and one-quarter Armenian: "The language is a dialect of the Turkish; but the inhabitants, with the exception of the Armenians, generally read and write Persian. The trade is carried on principally by the Armenians, between the towns of Shekhi, Nakhshevan, Khoi and Tabriz."[7]

The town was a crucible of talent. The Armenians were the builders and architects, and two Shusha Armenian sculptors, Stepan Agajanian and Hakop Gurdjian, made careers in Paris. For the Azerbaijanis, Shusha was the "conservatoire of the Caucasus" and the center of their musical tradition. Natevan, Azerbaijan's most famous woman poet, was the daughter of the last khan, Mehti Kulu. Uzeir Hajibekov and one of Azerbaijan's first twentieth-century novelists, Yusif Vezir Chemenzeminli, were born here.

Yet prosperity depended on the Russians' keeping order. In 1905, the town fell victim to the violence of the Armenian-Tartar war. Luigi Villari, the British journalist and writer described how it ended:

On the 2nd [of September], the Moslem chiefs sent a messenger to the Armenians, and finally a peace conference was held at the Russian church. Tartars and Armenians publicly embraced one another and swore eternal friendship—until next time. Prisoners were exchanged, as between properly constituted belligerents. The number of killed and wounded amounted to about 300, of whom about two thirds were Tartars, for the Armenians were better shots and also enjoyed the advantage of position. The damage is estimated at from 4,000,000 to 5,000,000 rubles. The [Russian] troops of whom 350 were available, seem to have done nothing at all while the fighting was going on, but the military band performed to celebrate the conciliation![8]

Two more sackings in the twentieth century ended Shusha's greatness. In March 1920, an Azerbaijani army sacked the town, burning the Armenian quarter and killing some five hundred Armenians. In the Soviet era, the town, which formerly had forty thousand inhabitants, contained only half that number. Then in May 1992, it was the Armenians' turn to destroy the town.

Both Armenians and Azerbaijanis also did their best to destroy the other's cultural legacy. In 1992, the Azerbaijanis stored cases of Grad rockets in Gazantchetsots church. They dismantled the stone statues outside the church and sold off its great bronze bell. In December 1992, an Armenian officer reported that he had found the bell being sold in a market in the Ukrainian city of Donetsk. He bought it for three million rubles and sent it back to Armenia.[9]

In their turn, the conquering Armenians dismantled and sold off dark bronze busts of three Azerbaijani Shusha musicians and poets. Again, these memorials were rescued by chance, this time from a scrap-metal merchant in the Georgian capital, Tbilisi. I saw the three bronze heads, forlorn and pocked with bullets, lying in the courtyard of the headquarters of the Red Cross in the center of Baku: the poet Natevan, an earnest girl in a head scarf reading a book, missing a thumb; the composer Hajibekov, a bullet-ridden gentleman in double-breasted suit and broken spectacles; and Bul Bul, a famous singer with a serious domed bronze forehead.

But for the efforts of a few brave Shusha Armenians, much more might have been destroyed. Mher Gabrielian, an Armenian artist, told me how he came back to his native town on the morning of its capture on 9 May 1992 and saw with horror that marauders and vandals were burning it to the ground. Mher and a couple of his friends stood in front of one of Shusha's two nineteenth-century mosques to stop a group of young men in an armored personnel carrier firing tank shells into its facade. They barricaded themselves inside the town museum for several days, preventing looters from stripping its collection of carpets, pots, and paintings. As one of the Armenian minority in Shusha, a largely Azerbaijani town, Mher had many Azerbaijani friends. He wanted me to understand how the burning of Shusha grieved him as much as it did them: "I know it's very painful for them, and it is for us too. I personally do not consider myself the victor of this town. The town as such is dead."[10]

I do not believe Shusha will ever recover its former grandeur. In 2000, it was virtually a ghost town. Most of its population of two thousand were refugees who had moved here only because they had nowhere else to live. I saw poverty in their faces. By the upper mosque, still intact but eerily deserted, I met beggars for the first time in Nagorny Karabakh: two small children, who pestered me for money. The only prominent Armenian who has made a commitment to Shusha is the local archbishop, Parkev. He moved here only a few days after the town was captured in 1992 and began raising money to rebuild its churches. But few people, it seems, share his vision of rebuilding the old Shusha.

"If only we can find jobs, lots of people will come here," Parkev told me. "We have opened a tea business and a jewelry business. There's a proposal for a jam-making business that would mean thirty or forty people would come here. But we also need money to restore buildings." It was three days after Victory Day and I was sitting in the archbishop's study in Shusha. Parkev has keen intelligent eyes, quick sentences, and the kind of big bushy black beard that small birds could make their nests in. People talked of him as a figure of authority in Karabakh who could intercede with the politicians on behalf of ordinary people. It seemed that, as well as the spiritual leader of the province, he was also Shusha's small-business project planner.[11]

The archbishop said he first came to Karabakh in the spring of 1989 when Arkady Volsky's administration allowed churches to be reopened. Early in the twentieth century there were 118 churches and 12 monasteries in Karabakh, but after 1930 they were all closed and all the priests were banned, imprisoned, or shot. His job was to begin the revival. I wondered if it was possible to be an Armenian and not a

Christian. No, not really, Parkev replied, to be an Armenian and to be a Christian was one and the same.

In the archbishop's stories, Christianity was more a collective badge of identity and defiance than a spiritual creed. He had always been in the thick of events. He told the story of how one night in November 1991 he went into his bedroom in his apartment in Stepanakert. A few minutes later, a rocket fired from Shusha smashed into the room he had just left, burning everything in its path.

When the Armenian offensive to take Shusha was bogged down on the evening 8 May 1992, Parkev said that it was he who had identified the problem and the solution. The trouble was that the statue of the Antichrist—Lenin—was still standing in Stepanakert's central square: "I said, 'Take down Lenin,' and a few hours later we captured Shushi. That's how it was. In two or three hours we were almost in the center."

Archbishop Parkev was careful to say that he had supported the capture of Shusha spiritually and that he had not taken part in the actual attack. Yet I knew that one priest at least had not bothered with that distinction. Four years before, on my first visit to Shusha in 1996, not far from where we were sitting, I had met a real warrior-priest, straight out of medieval Christendom. It was a Sunday morning, and a colleague and I came upon a service being held in the small church of Kanach Zham. The words of the Armenian liturgy sounded clearly off the stone walls. It was led by Father Koryun, a tall, young priest with a thick black beard and bright enthusiastic eyes.

After the service, Father Koryun invited us to his home in a semi-ruined apartment block. He plied us with cognac and introduced us to his wife and son. Yet most of his conversation was that of a fanatic, mixing the recent war with events of more than a thousand years ago. Koryun said he had come to Karabakh "on the summons of the blood of my ancestors." He had not only taken services but fought as well. "I would kiss my cross and put my cross and gospel aside," he related, acting this out with gestures. "I would take off my cassock, put on my uniform, take up my gun and go into battle."

We must have looked surprised. Unabashed, the priest explained that he was not only a priest but a "son of the Armenian people." "All of our territories will be liberated," he said. "Look at the map." He pointed to a map of Greater Armenia on the wall, in which landlocked Armenia had burst its bounds and spread out across Turkey, Georgia, and Azerbaijan to three seas. "I don't know if I'll see it or not, if my son will see it or not. It will be up to my grandson."

When I asked Archbishop Parkev, four years on, about this warrior-priest, he was evasive and said there must have been some mistake. Some priests had baptized soldiers at the front, using helmets to hold the baptismal water, but no more. "A priest should fight with a cross," he declared, suggesting I had mistaken the metaphorical for the real. I did not press him.

The archbishop was more reasoned than his warrior-priest, but his priorities were almost as tough. He saw Shusha/Shushi as a purely Armenian city. When I mentioned the town's neglected mosques, Parkev refused to call them "Azerbaijani" because they dated from the nineteenth century when—Armenians would have you believe—there were no Azerbaijanis" in Karabakh. But why had they done nothing to restore them? "We asked the Persians, we gave them permission to rebuild them," he replied. "So far they're in no hurry to do so." When I brought up the subject of the Azerbaijanis returning to Shusha, the archbishop was grave. He said he came from a village in Lower Karabakh to the north, now purged of its Armenian population. "My village, Chardakhlu, is in Azerbaijani hands," he said. "For a thousand years it's been an Armenian village. Tell me when I can go back there." More thoughtfully, he added: "It has to be a comprehensive question. All problems are soluble, but we need time for such painful questions."

"I would like Shushi to be the capital again," said Parkev. We were standing on the porch of his house, saying our good-byes and looking out at the vast pinnacle of Ganzachetsots and the ruins behind it. But how? And whose capital? It seemed a remote prospect at the beginning of the twenty-first century, when the town was in ruins and had just two thousand inhabitants; a hundred years before, it had had forty thousand residents, six churches, two mosques and twenty newspapers.

The archbishop asked me where I had studied Russian. I said I had a Russian literature degree, and Parkev's bearded face lit up. "I studied Russian literature too. My dissertation was on Bulgakov's *Master and Margarita*." He went on in careful English: "I learned English also." It transpired he had learned his English at home in front of the record player. "My favorites were the Beatles," Parkev said and quickly reeled off a long list of his favorite songs: "'Yesterday,' 'A Hard Day's Night,' 'Eleanor Rigby,' 'Paperback Writer' . . ." And with this unexpectedly endearing glimpse of the Beatles-loving archbishop, I left the ruined town.

# 13

# June 1992–September 1993

## Escalation

### AN ARMENIAN COLLAPSE

In the middle of June 1992, an exodus of thousands of people streamed south through Nagorny Karabakh, fleeing their homes in the face of an enemy attack. Film footage of the human tide shows trucks overloaded with people bouncing over the dirt roads. Others follow on foot. They are country folk: old women in head scarves, younger women with children slung over their shoulders, farmers leading bullocks on ropes or driving them with sticks. Weary villagers try to scrape the mud from the house shoes they are trudging in. A gaunt woman with gray straggly hair appeals to the camera: "Who laid a curse on us? What are we, the orphans of the world that they torment us like this?"[1]

This was an exodus of Armenians, but it could just as well have been Azerbaijanis. Wholesale expulsion of civilians was the most terrible feature of the Armenian-Azerbaijani war—and a much greater number of Azerbaijanis eventually became victims of it. The conflict saw fewer casualties than other comparable wars, such as Bosnia or Chechnya, with perhaps twenty thousand dead on both sides. But the refugee crisis it created, with hundreds of thousands of people displaced, was one of the most terrible in the world.

This flood of Armenians was escaping an unexpected Azerbaijani offensive, which began on 12 June 1992 and quickly overran the whole northern part of Nagorny Karabakh. The Azerbaijanis took the Shaumian region within four days, putting its villagers, who had been deported in "Operation Ring" the year before and then returned home, to flight once again. Over the next three weeks, the Martakert region was conquered.

Most people, both fighters and civilians, simply fled before the advancing Azerbaijani army could overtake them. The volunteer Kemal

Ali was one of the first soldiers to enter Martakert on the evening of 4 July, only a few hours after the Armenians had left. He found that the defenders had left the town in panic. "They had abandoned their weapons and fled," said Ali. "When we came into the town we had the impression that everyone was asleep at night and in the morning they would wake up and go to work. There wasn't a single cartridge there. There was no damage. The furniture, everything, had been left behind."[2] By early July, around forty thousand Armenians were on the move, heading toward Stepanakert.

Azerbaijan's attack was launched just five days after Abulfaz Elchibey was elected the country's president on 7 June 1992, finally bringing the Popular Front to power. Elchibey's victory appeared to have resolved the country's long-running political crisis, and morale at the front was high. Units like Iskender Hamidov's extreme nationalist Gray Wolves division were now fighting for a government they supported. The Armenians, by contrast, had succumbed to a false sense of euphoria after capturing Shusha and Lachin. Many *fedayin* fighters, assuming the war had been won, simply went back to Armenia. The Karabakh Armenian authorities had expected that an attack would come from the east and had left the northern sector poorly defended. When the offensive was launched, the front simply collapsed.

Azerbaijan's attack was spearheaded by a phalanx of armored vehicles and tanks—by some accounts as many as 150 of them—which swept aside the poorly armed Armenian defenders. The use of heavy armor was a dramatic escalation in the conflict. In July, the Russian military journalist Pavel Felgenhauer wrote: "The partisan period of the conflict in Karabakh is over. A 'normal' war is beginning in which the role of the volunteer, defending his own village with a Kalashnikov in his hand from all conceivable enemies, will become smaller and smaller."[3]

The heavy armor was Russian and the drivers were Russians. Azerbaijani commanders had moved quickly to take over the abundant Soviet military equipment in Azerbaijan and had cut deals with the 23rd Division of the 4th Army based in Ganje. Attempts were made to conceal the Russians' presence, although it was obvious that Azerbaijan did not possess this number of trained tank drivers. But the Russian soldiers were sighted, not only by the Armenian villagers but by a Western diplomat and an American journalist.[4]

The attack was led by Russians and—extraordinary to say—it appears to have been stopped by Russians. In early July, the Karabakh

Armenians faced being overwhelmed. According to one Armenian senior official, "This flood [of people] was moving toward Stepanakert like
a herd and it was impossible to stop or to organize a defense. So I have
to say that that flood was stopped by the Russians." The official, who
asked to be anonymous, said the Armenians persuaded the Russian
military to intervene and help them turn the tide. Russian attack helicopters were sent in and carried out air strikes, which halted the offensive in its tracks. So elements of the Russian military ended up fighting
one another. The Armenian official was insistent that this was the only
occasion during the Karabakh war when Russians actively intervened
to help the Armenian side (an assertion that most Azerbaijanis would
strongly dispute).

After the Russian-Armenian counterthrust, "One or two days were
needed to restore the front," said the Armenian official. But the Karabakh Armenians were still close to collapse. Azerbaijani forces had occupied almost half of Karabakh and were only half an hour away from
Stepanakert in the East. In August, the Azerbaijanis, again using mostly
Russian or Ukrainian pilots, began air attacks on the town. The bombers
destroyed dozens of houses that had escaped the artillery battering of
the winter and spring. The local parliament was in disarray. The Ter-
Petrosian administration in Armenia and its allies in Karabakh now decided to take charge. According to Robert Kocharian:

> There was a situation of panic. Forty-eight percent of Karabakh was
> occupied by Azerbaijani forces, there was a huge number of refugees,
> and constant sessions of the presidium of the Supreme Soviet [the
> Karabakhi parliament], which was in a semishocked situation, inca-
> pable of taking decisions. Then I proposed two or three solutions, and
> the condition for them accepting these solutions was that I would be
> ready to take responsibility for further actions. The plan was to intro-
> duce military rule, create a state defense committee . . . it was adopted
> literally in thirty or forty minutes.[5]

Nagorny Karabakh's new State Defense Committee, created on 15
August, was modeled, both in name and purpose, on the decision-mak-
ing body of the same name that Stalin formed in the Soviet Union in
1941. It assumed all executive powers. The entire Karabakh Armenian
male population between the ages of eighteen and forty-five was con-

scripted into a new army that numbered around fifteen thousand men. All local businesses were put at the service of the war effort.

Robert Kocharian, the new head of the committee and of the Karabakh Armenians was thirty-seven. He had been the quietest and most dogged of the Karabakh Armenian activists and was something of an enigma even to those who knew him well. In Soviet times, Kocharian had been head of the Party section in Stepanakert's Silk Factory and came across as a good Communist, albeit with reforming tendencies. (Arkady Volsky remembers that he used to love to quote the Marxist philosopher Georgy Plekhanov.) He was a poor public speaker and more comfortable in Russian than Armenian. His Azerbaijani friend and colleague, Zahid Abasov, remembers that he was always calm and never drank or smoked. A better clue to the aggressive inner drive is that he is a fan of active sports such as parasailing and hang-gliding, and among which he has reportedly listed "war."

At the same time, Kocharian's old comrade, Serzh Sarkisian, was put in charge of the logistics of the Karabakh military campaign. Sarkisian, had been senior to Kocharian when the two were the leaders of the Stepanakert Young Communist organization, the Komsomol, and, in Sarkisian's words, "There wasn't a week that we didn't go hunting or fishing."[6] Abasov remembers that "Serzhik" Sarkisian was more gregarious, drank heavily, and on the surface seemed more of a natural leader. In the new Defense Committee, the two men resumed a tandem, which would eventually bring them jointly to power in Armenia.

## THE GREAT CARVE-UP

On 15 May 1992, at a meeting in Tashkent, both Armenia and Azerbaijan formally inherited vast amounts of Soviet weaponry as their due from the dividing up of the Soviet army. On paper, the two new states were allowed to acquire 220 tanks, 220 other armored vehicles, 285 artillery pieces, and 100 combat aircraft. For two combatants who had been relying a year before on meteorological rockets and hand-held weapons, it was a great lurch forward in their destructive capabilities.[7]

In practice, both sides acquired many more weapons than were allowed. In the spring of 1992, a series of mysterious explosions were reported at army bases in both Armenia and Azerbaijan, which permitted military equipment to be written off. A likely explanation was that arms were changing hands—in the words of one Armenian military specialist, because of "money, personal contacts and lots of vodka."[8]

The free-for-all gave an initial advantage to Azerbaijan. In Soviet times Armenia, next door to NATO-member Turkey, was envisaged as a combat zone in the event of war and therefore had only three divisions and no airfields on its soil. Azerbaijan was a rear zone and the base for a much greater concentration of forces, with five divisions and five military airfields. It also had far more ammunition than Armenia on its territory. According to one estimate, Armenia had only five hundred railroad cars of ammunition on its territory; Azerbaijan had ten thousand cars.[9]

Leila Yunusova, who was now Azerbaijan's deputy defense minister, says that by spending money in the right places, her republic was able to acquire a large part of this arsenal, giving it a military advantage. "So that [the Russians] would give us more than was in the agreement, we simply paid the commanders of the divisions. It was more difficult for the Armenians, because they didn't have such a number of divisions there." Everyone, from factory directors to housewives, took part in a great patriotic money-raising exercise to buy the weapons. "We all paid," recalls Yunusova. "Every shop paid out some money, factories gave money. . . . Women brought in gold and diamonds for weapons. Everyone brought something."[10]

Two prominent Azerbaijanis were able to get weapons from the Russians easily and on favorable terms. The defense minister, Rahim Gaziev, unusually for a Popular Front radical, was a strong supporter of Russia. After the experience of being imprisoned in Moscow after the January 1990 events, "Something turned in his head," said his old acquaintance Hikmet Hajizade. "After [the Moscow prison] Lefortovo, he had the idea that you have to be friends with Russia, you have to bribe Russia."[11] Another Russophile Azerbaijani was Suret Husseinov, the sleek young director of a textile plant in the town of Yevlakh. Husseinov, who had no military background, set up his own armed brigade for the Karabakh front and was so successful that he was made a Hero of Azerbaijan and the president's "special representative" for Karabakh. Husseinov was extremely rich. One of Azerbaijan's black market kings, he outspent all his rivals on the war effort, paid his soldiers high wages, and—most important—became a close friend of the commander

of the 23rd Division in Ganje, General Alexander Shcherbak. The net result was that by the summer of 1992, Azerbaijan had acquired a vast arsenal of weapons. The Azerbaijani Foreign Ministry admitted in November 1993 that it had taken over 286 tanks and 842 armored vehicles
and 386 artillery pieces in May 1992, well in excess of the limits set by
the Tashkent agreement.[12]

The Armenians now began to call on Russia to close the gap. Armenia's traditional close relations with Moscow and personal ties
formed between Boris Yeltsin and Levon Ter-Petrosian proved vital.
Ter-Petrosian now confirms that President Boris Yeltsin personally authorized arms shipments for Armenia. He says that he would put a request for weapons in writing to Yeltsin, who would ask Russia's Ministry of Defense to supply the corresponding amount of equipment.
According to Ter-Petrosian, because Azerbaijan had inherited far more
Soviet weaponry than Armenia had, Yeltsin wanted to preserve a military balance in the Karabakh conflict:

> It turned out that there were three times more weapons in Azerbaijan
> than in Armenia. And when we talked to the Russian side, we came to
> the conclusion—and I managed to get them to agree to this—that we
> should be compensated for this. And Yeltsin agreed to this and agreed
> that the balance had to be preserved. No more than a balance. In the
> following years—1992, '3, '4—we were almost completely compen-
> sated for the gap between us and Azerbaijan. And in 1994, we were on
> the same level. That means equipment, tanks, artillery, APCs, hand-
> held weapons.[13]

The extent of the arms shipments to Armenia came to light only in 1997,
in a report made to the Russian parliament, the State Duma, by the
Russian general Lev Rokhlin. Rokhlin, who estimated the total cost of
the deals at one billion dollars, said he was reporting on them because
they were in contravention of a commitment by Russia not to arm either
of the combatants in the conflict. According to Rokhlin, most of the
heavier weaponry in the operation had been sent to Armenia only when
the fighting had ended, in 1995–1996. These included eighty-four T-72
tanks and fifty BMP-2 armored personnel carriers. However, some of
the supplies had arrived as early as the summer of 1992. From August
1992 to June 1994, according to Rokhlin, there had been mass deliveries

of ammunition from warehouses in the Russian military base at Moz-
dok to Armenia. In the same period, Russia had also supplied Armenia
with spare parts and fuel. He gave no dates as to when other items, such
as 350,000 hand grenades, had been transported to Armenia.[14]

The transport of all these weapons to Armenia was a vast and com-
plicated operation. Pavel Felgenhauer says: "It was authorized by the
Kremlin and signed by Kolesnikov. I enquired, 'Was it authorized?' Yes,
of course, it was authorized. These things don't happen in Russia without authority—like flying in tanks by air. The biggest transport aircraft
there is, the Antonov-124 or Ruslan, flew them in."[15]


## THE RUSSIAN FACTOR

Moscow's arms supplies to Armenia are just one piece in the biggest
puzzle of the Karabakh war, the Russian factor. The issue is complex.
Toward the end of 1992, as Russia began supplying the Armenians with
arms and fuel, the Russian defense minister, Pavel Grachev, also appears to have forged a close relationship with his colleagues in the Armenian military. Yet it is not entirely clear how this support for the Armenians was translated on to the battlefield; to complicate things further, the Russians also gave some assistance to Azerbaijan. So, although
obviously Russian help was clearly essential for the Armenians to close
the military gap with Azerbaijan in 1992–1993, it is debatable if it was
the primary cause of the Armenian victory in 1993–1994.

Another complicating element in this story is that much of the
"Russian support" to both combatants did not come from Russia itself.
Early on in the conflict, in the chaos immediately following the end of
the Soviet Union, there were dozens, if not hundreds, of "Russian" free-
lancers and mercenaries fighting on both sides. Many of these were not
actually "Russian" in the strictest sense. They were former Soviet soldiers—mainly Russians, but also Ukrainians or Belarussians—who,
when their units were withdrawn, had stayed behind in Ganje or Stepanakert to earn a living. They were generally military specialists in
short supply locally, such as the Ukrainian pilot Yury Belichenko, who
was shot down over Stepanakert in August 1992. A month later, six
Russian soldiers were captured by the Azerbaijanis in the Kelbajar region. They said they had been part of a group of twelve Russian "special forces" mercenaries from the 7th Army, who had been fighting on

the Armenian side. They were reprieved from a death sentence after a personal plea from Russian Defense Minister Pavel Grachev.

Russians also fought as tank drivers. They led Azerbaijan's June 1992 offensive, and several witnesses said that they saw Russian tank drivers serving later on the Armenian side. As one Karabakh Armenian farmer in the village of Talish put it: "The Russians helped the Azerbaijanis, then they turned round and fought for us." The Azerbaijani officer Zahid Neftaliev said that in February 1993, he and his comrades were cut off by an Armenian attack at the "Globe" cliff outside Martakert. They had run out of ammunition and were facing annihilation:

> We didn't have anything left to fight with. We had either to die or to surrender. A Russian tank came up with a Russian crew. He came out of the hatch and said, "Go, I won't kill you." The Russians let us go and said, "We don't want to kill you. Leave the territory and go." They conquered the territory and gave it to the Armenians.[16]

Most or all of these soldiers appear to have been acting as mercenaries, independently of Moscow. Leila Yunusova says of this period:

> You know how many officers came from the Soviet army? Clever, educated officers, rocket specialists, signalers—they were left completely without salaries. They had nothing. There were pilots. They had their families, lived in garrisons, their children and families were here, they had no salary, nothing. They literally didn't have money for food. Do you think they listened to Moscow? What Moscow! Money alone decided everything.

Kemal Ali remembers Russians who did not even ask the *mafioso* commander "Freud" in Aghdam for money:

> [Freud] had some equipment, which he'd bought from the Russians somewhere. No one knew how to mend Russian military equipment. They could fire it, but it broke down quickly. Then they brought in three colonels from Ganje to mend the equipment. They worked well from morning until lunchtime, then they started drinking wine and they were drunk all night. In the morning [Freud's men] beat them up to sober them up and wake them up. Then they would start working again and mend the equipment.

The Azerbaijanis gradually lost their advantage. From late 1992, the Russian military began to pull out of Azerbaijan and close down its bases. As a result, the Azerbaijanis received only one crop of Russian soldiers in 1992, when they "privatized" hundreds of former Soviet officers of the 4th Army. In Armenia, however, the Soviet 7th Army, based in Gyumri, stayed behind and turned into a Russian force. That ensured that a large number of friendly Russian officers stayed on Armenian soil. This new army's assets were also subtly "nationalized" in that the majority of its serving soldiers were actually Armenians. In the words of one Russian military observer: "An army whose soldiers are 60 to 80 percent Armenian and whose officers are 20 to 30 percent Armenian can hardly be called 'Russian.'"[17] It came as no surprise, therefore, when in January 1994 the Azerbaijanis captured eight trucks and five Armenian officers belonging to the Russian 7th Army on the battlefield.

The two sides dispute whether Moscow made a political decision to help Armenia win the war. With regard to Russia's arms deliveries, Ter-Petrosian says that Yeltsin wanted only to achieve a "balance" between Armenia and Azerbaijan: in effect, they did not so much want an Armenian victory as not want to see an Armenian defeat. "All the stories that the Russians helped the Armenians more is a legend, it's nonsense. The Russians behaved very honestly and preserved a balance. How do I know this? Because I know that when we asked for a bit more, they didn't give it. I knew that. They never gave more than the balance."

For their part, Azerbaijani officials are categorical that at least from the autumn of 1992, Moscow was working against them. They say that Russian officials consistently used veiled threats that Azerbaijan might be defeated on the battlefield to try to dictate their own peace settlement. This became more marked in the spring and summer of 1993, when the pro-Western government of Yegor Gaidar had left office in Moscow and the nationalist Elchibey regime was still in power in Azerbaijan. Elchibey pressed for the withdrawal of Russian bases and insisted that Azerbaijan would not join the new Moscow-led organization of post-Soviet republics, the Commonwealth of Independent States (CIS). Elchibey's ambassador in Moscow, Hikmet Hajizade, said that he was constantly being coerced into giving his agreement to a peace plan, which involved Russian military monitors.

> During my term as ambassador, I received three [draft] agreements like this. It began at the end of 1992. So, for example, they said, "Here

is an agreement, sign it. The Russians will stand here. The war will stop for a while, negotiations will begin." And we said, "This could turn into Cyprus." They said, "Fine, and then Armenian forces will take Kelbajar. . . ."[18]

If Russia's intentions, especially in 1992, seem opaque, that is probably because one arm of the Russian government was not bothering to inform the others about what it was doing. In the Caucasus, the most active Russian player was the Defense Ministry, which did not bother to keep other branches of the Yeltsin administration informed of what it was up to.

Three senior Russian military men took an active interest in the Caucasus and progressively gave more support to the Armenians. Colonel-General Fyodor Reut had been former commander of the Soviet 7th Army in Armenia; now in charge of Russian forces in the Transcaucasian Military District based in Tbilisi, he helped landlocked Armenia get supplies to and from the Black Sea ports in Georgia. Mikhail Kolesnikov, another former 7th Army commander, had risen to become chief of the Russian General Staff and could be expected to take a pro-Armenian stance. Most important, the new Russian defense minister, Pavel Grachev, began to adopt a more pro-Armenian line.

Grachev chose Armenia as the destination for his first foreign trip in May 1992, only a few days after being appointed Russia's new defense minister. There had just been armed clashes on the border between the Azerbaijani exclave of Nakhichevan and Armenia, and tension was high because Turkey, a NATO member, had announced that it might act to uphold its obligations to protect Nakhichevan by the 1920 Treaty of Kars. Grachev, together with Yeltsin's right-hand man, Gennady Burbulis, came to Yerevan to pledge Moscow's continuing commitment to guard Armenia's frontier with Turkey and to face down the "Turkish threat."

Grachev was an unsophisticated man, and his views on the Caucasus appear to have been formed from a mixture of commercial and personal motives and a crude vision of Russia's strategic interest there. Put simply, this meant maximizing the number of Russian troops on the ground. It was a strategy that went beyond support for one particular regime or country. As Felgenhauer puts it: "The Defense Ministry had good relations with Armenia, but did not fully break with Azerbaijan." Grachev personalized his policy making and struck up close relationships with fellow defense ministers. In Georgia, he even chose the then Georgian defense minister as his godfather when he unexpectedly chose to be baptized—and yet he had given support to the Abkhazian rebels in their war to break away from Georgia. In 1992, shortly after visiting Yerevan, Grachev befriended the Azerbaijani defense minister Rahim Gaziev and spent several days as his guest in Gaziev's home region of Sheki in the mountains of northern Azerbaijan. Gaziev even went to the funeral of Grachev's mother.

Grachev's strongest friendship, however, was with the Armenian defense minister and military leader Vazgen Sarkisian. After Sarkisian's death, in December 1999, Grachev attended a reunion of the "Yerkrapah" veterans' union and was made a freeman of Yerevan. He returned in March 2001 to commemorate Sarkisian's birthday and told his hosts, "Vazgen Sarkisian was my friend and a good student. I was happy to teach him military arts."[19]

In September 1992, Grachev convened a meeting in the Black Sea town of Sochi with the ministers of defense of all three Caucasian states, Gaziev, Sarkisian, and Georgia's Tengiz Kitovani. Gaziev and Sarkisian reportedly signed a brief agreement, which called for a ceasefire and the deployment of "observers" in Nagorny Karabakh from CIS countries. However, Grachev failed to inform a long list of interested parties about the meeting. These included not only the governments of Ukraine, Belarus, and Kazakhstan, who were supposed to be sending observers, but also the Russian Foreign Ministry's recently appointed mediator for the conflict, Vladimir Kazimirov, who was in Baku at the time. Kazimirov says: "I had brought a message from Yeltsin to Elchibey for the settlement of the conflict, but I knew nothing about the fact that on 19 September, the next day, Grachev was organizing that meeting in Sochi."[20] Kazimirov learned about the meeting only when a fellow diplomat pointed out to him a report on it in the *International Herald Tribune*. By the time he tried to join the meeting, it was too late for him to take part.

A week later, Grachev sent fifty-six Russian observers to the combat zone but had to withdraw them when the fighting carried on. Gaziev had failed to consult most of his colleagues in the Azerbaijani leadership and, as a result, faced a row when he got back to Baku. The details of what he had agreed to are not clear, but according to Tofik Zulfugarov, then a senior Azerbaijani Foreign Ministry official, the Russians had identified the "Lachin corridor" between Armenia and

Karabakh as their strategic prize. "[Gaziev] gave his agreement to temporary use of the so-called Lachin corridor" by the Russians, said Zulfugarov. Whatever the truth of this, Gaziev had certainly not received President Elchibey's approval for the document he signed and this drew wrath on his head. The Azerbaijani interior minister Iskender Hamidov declared on 28 September, "It is perfectly clear that [the] bringing of the Russian peacekeeping forces into Azerbaijan is nothing less but a veiled form of aggression."[21] This strong anti-Russian stand isolated Gaziev and pushed the Russian Defense Ministry further toward the Armenians.

## ARMENIA BESIEGED

Independent Armenia barely survived 1992. Politically, the country was stable. The taking of power by the nationalist opposition had been bloodless, and many old Communists served the new Ter-Petrosian administration. Ter-Petrosian's main critics were in the nationalist opposition, especially the Dashnaktsutiun Party, which organized the first hostile demonstrations to his government in the summer of 1992. Overall, however, he commanded broad support.

Armenia's problem was sheer economic survival. One of the Soviet Union's most prosperous republics only a few years before, Armenia was now destitute. Azerbaijan's economic blockade deprived it of electricity, goods, and railway connections. Russia was far away and the country's other three neighbors were all unreliable. Turkey expressed solidarity with Azerbaijan and, after a tentative thaw in relations, completely closed its borders with Armenia in 1993. The northern neighbor, Georgia, was in permanent crisis and its gas pipelines, roads, and railways were all frequently shut down. Iran thus became Armenia's friendliest neighbor, but it was remote and could be reached only by winding mountainous roads. Nonetheless, without Iranian trade, Armenia might not have survived the two miserable winters of 1991–1992 and 1992–1993.

Over these winters, Armenian citizens were forced back into premodern living conditions. City dwellers collected their water from wells, cut down trees to feed wood-burning stoves, and lived by candlelight. One ingenious method of heating hot water was to suspend a wire with a razor blade attached to it from a trolleybus cable, whose low voltage would eventually transmit enough electricity to boil a saucepan of water. Armenia recovered a decent power supply only in 1996 with the—extremely controversial—reopening of the Metsamor atomic power station.

The shortages did have a perverse psychological effect in that they induced a spirit of wartime solidarity. In that respect, hardship mobilized Armenian support for the war in Karabakh. Yet the reality behind the economic misery was more complex. When the war was over, there were allegations that Armenia had actually produced plenty of electricity, which had been sold to Georgia for large profits, and that political leaders had used the wartime situation to take over sectors of the economy.

Armenia's "mafia" was also a powerful behind-the-scenes actor. It suddenly became visible in January 1993, when an Armenian gangster named Rafik Bagdasarian, known as Svo, was murdered in his Moscow prison cell. Svo's body was flown home to be buried in the most prestigious section of Yerevan's Toghmagh cemetery. The Soviet criminal fraternity paid no heed to ethnic conflict, and so Svo's old comrades from Azerbaijan decided to fly in to Yerevan to pay their last respects. For the first and only time in the 1990s, planes traveled between Baku and Yerevan and the gangsters arranged for gas and electricity supplies to be switched on for the three days around the funeral. Only when all the *mafiosi* guests had left did the blockade resume, and darkness descended once again.

## IMPROVISED ARMIES

Behind the Armenians' victory and Azerbaijan's defeat in 1994 lay three factors: Azerbaijan's political and military chaos, greater Russian support for the Armenians, and the Armenians' superior fighting skills.

The last factor had historical roots. Like the other highland rebels in the Caucasus, the Chechens, the Karabakh Armenians had a strong warrior tradition. In 1993, Karabakhi fighters were offered cash rewards if they could immobilize a tank by hitting it in the treads, so that it could be repaired; if they hit it in the turret, destroying the tank, they would not be paid. The Armenian journalist Vartan Hovanisian remembers being in the Martakert region when three Azerbaijani tanks suddenly attacked. The group of fighters he was with had only one grenade launcher. As Hovanisian pleaded with them to open fire, they began to argue as to who would shoot at the first tank and claim the reward; they had already come with some old grudge from their village past. The tanks were almost two hundred meters away when one of the fighters finally seized the weapon and opened fire. He hit one tank in the treads, stopping it dead—and incidentally thereby not killing the crew inside. The other two tanks fled.

At first, the Armenian volunteer army was chaotic. "No one was in charge," says Samvel Danielian. "A unit would stop fighting and go off *en masse* to Armenia to bury one of their dead." The *fedayin* movement was only gradually overhauled as fighters were assigned special tasks within the more regular armed forces. Vartan Hovanisian uses the Russian word *shturmovik*, or "assault-man," to describe their role. They were the ones who had the courage and fanaticism to be able to attack an enemy trench by night or in fog, causing panic among the defenders. "We had to succeed in quality, not quantity," says Hovanisian.[22]

A handful of Armenian volunteers from the Diaspora arrived to fight in Karabakh. The most famous was Monte Melkonian, a California-born archaeologist who had been a member of the ASALA terrorist organization, which assassinated Turkish diplomats in the 1970s and 1980s. Melkonian had been on the run for several years before ending up in Armenia in 1990. When war broke out in Karabakh, Melkonian was given command of the southeastern Martuni region. Melkonian, who went by the nom de guerre of Avo, was a professional warrior and an extreme Armenian nationalist who saw Karabakh as a sacred cause. He forbade his soldiers to drink alcohol and tried to stop their looting. This, says his widow Seta, caused him problems as he took command of an irregular post-Soviet fighting force:

> People would come and offer [Monte] bribes. He wouldn't even understand what they were talking about. "What? What?" It wouldn't enter his mind that this was a bribe being offered, for example, to take his family out. Someone wants to take his family out, and Monte says, "No." If the civilians are not here, the soldiers will not fight well. And they bring a bottle of drink, for example, and he wouldn't understand. He was against looting, which a lot of people didn't like because that was something that made them feel better and good for their families, they thought. He was against torturing anybody, including Azeri soldiers, when they are wounded. Several times he

would punish Armenians for harassing or hitting or doing something to wounded Azerbaijanis.[23]

Melkonian was killed in June 1993. Around this time, as the Karabakh Armenians broke out of their own territory and began rampaging their way through Azerbaijani towns and villages, even loyal Armenians noticed a shift in attitude. "When we were fighting for Karabakh, people put up pictures of [Armenian guerrilla heroes] Andranik or Njdeh in our barracks," said the military adviser Gurgen Boyajian. "When we were in Aghdam, people put up pictures of naked girls. The psychology was completely different."[24]

Azerbaijan's commanders had to build a fighting force from very disparate elements. The experience of the professional officer Isa Sadyqov was typical. Sadyqov, an Azerbaijani, moved to Azerbaijan from Georgia in the summer of 1992 and was given command of the Kazakh district in the Northwest of the republic. He inherited an undisciplined ragged group of soldiers: "The first problem at that time was drunkenness." Then "there were volunteers, who were already quite old, people with beards. It was difficult for me to shave their beards, but I had them shaved off." Sadyqov says he imposed strict penalties for desertion and refused to let soldiers evacuate their families from the region. He explains: "The war basically had a psychological character. The Armenians shot at large population points, created panic, people fled and after them went the army. I saw the main thing was to stop this flood of refugees. I managed to do that."[25]

When they had the upper hand in the summer of 1992, the Azerbaijanis lacked the men and expertise to exploit their advantage. In October 1992, the army was bogged down in the northern hills of Nagorny Karabakh. Some film shot by the Azerbaijani Ministry of Defense shows a passionate argument between officers as to the reasons for their lack of success. The Azerbaijani commander Najmedtin Sadyqov complains that Grad missiles are being launched indiscriminately and squandered. Leila Yunusova, deputy defense minister, adds: "We hear that we have a huge quantity of rockets and that we fire them and simply destroy the forests." Worse than that, the attempts by inexperienced soldiers to use powerful weapons led to some horrific cases of "friendly-fire" casualties. On one occasion Azerbaijani planes bombed the Azerbaijani town of Fizuli. Kemal Ali remembers: "It often happened that I shot for a whole day at some mountain. Then it turned out that our men were sitting there. They'd spent the whole day firing at us. The same happened to the Armenians."

The Armenians performed perhaps the most spectacular act of self-destruction in the war. They had only two SU-25 attack aircraft, but one was shot down by Karabakh Armenians, who mistook it for an Azerbaijani airplane. The pilot parachuted to safety and was surrounded and beaten up by local villagers, who realized only belatedly that he was an Armenian. After this, Karabakhis joked that they had "destroyed fifty percent of the Armenian air force."[26]

In the longer run, the Armenians proved better at husbanding their resources. To defend themselves against Azerbaijani air attacks, the Armenians set up an antiaircraft system in the fall of 1992, a move that Leila Yunusova believes was done with Russian help: "We had airplanes, in Stepanakert there were open skies. Then within a matter of weeks they had created a fine antiaircraft defense system." From that point on, an air force was an expensive luxury in the war.

The Armenians also recycled captured equipment. An Armenian military expert estimates that after every battle 15 to 20 percent of the equipment was put out of order and that the life expectancy of a Soviet tank in battle is only one and a half days.[27] To deal with this problem, the Karabakh authorities converted a tractor-repair plant into a workshop for the repair of tanks. The American reporter Lee Hockstader visited the workshop in September 1993 and saw thirty T-72 tanks and at least a dozen APCs under repair. "We can fix 90 percent of the tanks that come in here, depending on the extent of the damage," said Andrei Musayelian, the thirty-seven-year-old engineer in charge of the tank yard. He told Hockstader that 80 percent of the tanks in the warehouse had been captured from the Azerbaijanis. Many of them still had the Islamic crescent painted on their barrels. The remainder, he said, were "ours."[28]

## THE TIDE TURNS

The fall of 1992 was the high-water mark of Azerbaijan's military success in the war. At one point, the Azerbaijanis possessed the village of Srkhavend to the north of Stepanakert and the road to the east of the town, and were poised to recapture the Lachin corridor. The Ministry of Defense in Baku was making plans to bring in buses to ship the

Armenian civilian population out of the territory Azerbaijan planned to conquer. By October 1992, however, the advance had halted and the offensive had run out of steam.

In both Karabakh and Armenia, an irregular fighting force became more organized. In Karabakh, the creation of the Defense Committee began to have an effect. The twenty-seven-year-old former garage mechanic Samvel Babayan employed ruthless tactics to form a Karabakh Armenian "army" of at least ten thousand men. Other commanders, such as Arkady Ter-Tatevosian, the conqueror of Shusha, went back to Armenia because they were unable to work with Babayan.

In Armenia itself, Ter-Petrosian appointed his old comrade and rival Vazgen Manukian to be defense minister in October 1992. Manukian, who was not a military professional, worked with Norad Ter-Grigoriants, the chief of the General Staff, to create a new army. He admits that public declarations that the Armenian army took no part in the war was purely for foreign consumption: "You can be sure that whatever we said politically, the Karabakh Armenian and Armenian army were united in military actions. It was not important for me if someone was a Karabakhi or an Armenian." Manukian says that on several occasions he deliberately ordered the Armenian military into action without properly informing the more politically cautious Ter-Petrosian.[29]

Meanwhile in Azerbaijan, support for Elchibey's grip on his country was weakening. Heidar Aliev, who ran Nakhichevan as a semi-independent principality, was one source of worry. Aliev's relations with the Baku regime cooled after local Popular Front activists tried to remove him from power in October 1992. Aliev was a master of the long game and the building of alliances. He used the opening of a land bridge with Turkey in May 1992 to build a separate relationship with Ankara while also keeping up contacts in Russia.

Aliev also decided to do everything to prevent fighting between Nakhichevan and Armenia. After one bout of serious cross-border fighting in May 1992, both sides decided they did not want to open a second front in the war. Aliev was in daily touch by telephone with Ashot Manucharian, the Armenian presidential security adviser, as they sought to defuse cross-border tensions, and Manucharian regularly gave clearance for Aliev to fly from Nakhichevan to Baku across Armenian territory. In April 1993, the story goes that Aliev needed to fly back home from Turgut Özal's funeral in Ankara over Armenian airspace. He called Manucharian at home, seeking clearance to fly but found only his mother, with whom he had spoken before. She promised to pass on the message to her son but was unable to locate him. An Armenian aircraft tried to intercept Aliev's plane and the pilot asked Aliev who had given him permission to fly across Armenian airspace. The message came back: "Ashot's mother!"

In Baku, President Elchibey began to face open insubordination from his defense minister, Rahim Gaziev, and his main commander, Suret Husseinov. It increasingly looked as though both men were working with the Russian military.

In February 1993, the commander Zahid Neftaliev saw direct evidence of the two top Azerbaijanis' treachery. The Armenians were beginning to win back territory in the North of Nagorny Karabakh, and an Azerbaijani unit had been surrounded in the village of Haterk. Neftaliev says that when he arrived at the nearby staff headquarters, a telephone operator he knew ran to him in tears. She said she had overheard Gaziev telling Husseinov by telephone that he was deliberately abandoning the soldiers encircled in Haterk to their fate. Neftaliev immediately called in the interior minister, Iskender Hamidov, to investigate this apparent treachery. "Iskender Hamidov came to Rahim Gaziev's office," said Neftaliev, "and they began to quarrel loudly. And he forced Gaziev to give a command for our brigade to leave Haterk. After that, our men left Haterk and got out of there with heavy casualties."[30] After this incident, Husseinov moved two brigades away from the front line. Elchibey sacked him from all his posts, but Husseinov simply moved his 709th Brigade back to base in Ganje and refused to disband it. Soon afterward, on 20 February, Gaziev was forced to resign as defense minister.

## KELBAJAR

Suret Husseinov's departure from the front left a gaping hole in one of the most sensitive parts of Azerbaijan's defenses, the mountains of its largest region, Kelbajar. The Kelbajar region is a sliver of land running between the Northwest of Nagorny Karabakh and Armenia. A place of great strategic importance for both sides, it is also the source of most of the rivers in the region.

The Armenian offensive began on 27 March 1993. Kelbajar had only a small group of defenders protecting it and no reinforcements came to assist them. "We got no help from our side," says Shamil Askerov, the leader of Kelbajar's large Kurdish community.[31] The main thrust of the Armenian attack came from the west, from the Vardenis region of Armenia—although this was denied at the time for political reasons. A supporting offensive came from Karabakh.

The operation sharpened the divisions in the Armenian leadership between President Ter-Petrosian, those who were interested in a diplomatic settlement to the war, and those, like Defense Minister Vazgen Manukian and the Karabakh Armenians, who wanted to press their military advantage. Manukian says that he had deliberately omitted to inform Ter-Petrosian of the full extent of Armenia's involvement in the Kelbajar operation because he knew that the president would have misgivings about it. "I presented a small part of this operation," Manukian said. "Receiving permission for this small part, we did more." Ter-Petrosian sent a letter to the Karabakhi leader, Robert Kocharian, calling on him to stop the assault.[32]

On 3 April, the Armenians captured the town of Kelbajar itself. Military losses were minimal, and most of the soldiers had left with the civilian refugees. A new desperate tide of refugees set off in flight, this time along the only route the Armenians had left open: the fifty miles of snowy road north across the Murov Mountains. Askerov's house—and also his unique library of thirty thousand books—had been destroyed by a Grad missile. He was among the fifty thousand refugees on the roads. "On 2 April we climbed to the top of the Murov Pass," Askerov said. "One villager wanted to drive eighty lambs. They surrounded me. They all died. There was snow and wind. I took one lamb under my coat. My tears froze." The vast majority of the several hundred civilians who died in the capture of Kelbajar perished from cold. The Armenians occupied the whole region, having suffered almost no casualties.

The loss of Kelbajar shook the Popular Front regime. President Elchibey declared a sixty-day State of Emergency to cope with his first big military defeat. Press gangs began to conscript young men into the army.[33] At the same time Elchibey's administration came under new pressure from Moscow to accept a peace agreement involving a Russian peacekeeping force. Even if the Russians had not directly taken part in the capture of Kelbajar, it evidently suited their purposes as a lever against Azerbaijan.

For the Armenians, the success of the Kelbajar operation threw another land bridge from Karabakh to Armenia, but it came with a heavy diplomatic cost. For the first time, strong evidence was produced that troops from the Republic of Armenia had fought inside Azerbaijan and outside Karabakh. Allegations were also made that soldiers from the Russian 7th Army had taken part in the operation.[34]

The capture of a region of Azerbaijan outside Nagorny Karabakh, together with the allegations of outside involvement, brought international condemnation on Armenia. On 30 April 1993, the United Nations Security Council passed its first resolution on the Nagorny Karabakh conflict. While calling on both sides to cease hostilities, the resolution singled out the Armenian side and demanded an "immediate withdrawal of all occupying forces" from Kelbajar. Armenia's fragile relationship with Turkey was also wrecked. In 1992, Turkey had not opened diplomatic relations with Armenia but neither did it sever all ties; it had for instance agreed to allow 100,000 tons of wheat from the European Union to pass through its territory en route to Armenia. After Kelbajar, Ter-Petrosian tried to keep up the contacts and even went to the funeral of Turgut Özal in Ankara, but Turkey decided to curtail the relationship and the second half of the EU wheat shipment was halted.

Responding to this pressure, Ter-Petrosian threw his support behind a new peace plan sponsored by Russia, the United States, and Turkey. It stipulated that the Armenians would withdraw from Kelbajar in return for security guarantees for Nagorny Karabakh. On 14 June, the Armenian leader traveled to Stepanakert to try to persuade the Karabakh Armenians to accept the plan. There were heated discussions, and the local parliament accepted the plan only after its speaker, Georgy Petrosian, resigned. However, the Karabakhis asked for a month's delay for the plan to be implemented. They had incentives to play for time because they could see that Azerbaijan was falling victim to civil strife.

## AN AZERBAIJANI COLLAPSE

Abulfaz Elchibey's presidency collapsed with astonishing speed. On 4 June 1993, he sent in government troops to try to disarm the garrison of the dissident army commander Suret Husseinov. When that operation failed, the governing regime did almost nothing to defend itself. Within two weeks, as Husseinov was moving his men toward Baku, Elchibey had surrendered power and fled the capital.

Colonel Isa Sadyqov was one of those sent to disarm Husseinov. He says that when he arrived in Ganje on 4 June, Husseinov had already been tipped off that troops were being sent against him. The rebel commander had collected a group of women and children in front of his headquarters to serve as a "human shield" against the threat of armed attack. When Sadyqov and a colleague went to see Husseinov in his office, they were set upon, beaten up, and thrown into a basement. They barely escaped with their lives.

Husseinov acted with a supreme self-confidence that suggested he was already looking forward to taking power. The government delegations that arrived to negotiate with him behaved more like supplicants than superiors. Thomas Goltz, who traveled to Ganje, saw the reason for Husseinov's arrogance in the courtyard of the base: he had inherited all the weapons of the 104th Airborne Division, which had pulled out of Ganje only ten days before. Facing no resistance from a confused government Husseinov began a "march" on Baku.[35]

The desperate Popular Front government then invited Heidar Aliev to come from Nakhichevan to Baku to its aid, the equivalent, as Goltz puts it, of "inviting a crocodile into the goat-pen." A rapid train of events was set in motion, which saw Elchibey lose power and Aliev become president in his stead. First, on 15 June, Aliev succeeded Isa Gambar as speaker of parliament. Three days later, with Husseinov's men still advancing on Baku, Elchibey fled to his native region of Nakhichevan. On 24 June, Aliev was voted extraordinary presidential powers by parliament in a motion sponsored by the eternal opposition figure Etibar Mamedov. On 30 June, Aliev appointed Husseinov—a rebel no longer—Azerbaijan's new prime minister. He also canceled a series of oil contracts that Elchibey had signed earlier in the month with Western oil companies. Less than two months later, on 28 August, Aliev used the device of a nationwide referendum to allow the Azerbaijani public to vote no confidence in Elchibey. That left the way clear for him to be elected president in elections on 3 October.

The transition was rapid and brutal. Most onlookers assumed that Aliev had been working in concert with Husseinov to overthrow the Popular Front administration and take power. However, subsequent evidence suggested that Husseinov and Aliev may actually have been thrown together by events. Another revolt in a different part of the country suggests another scenario was being plotted. Shortly after Husseinov's uprising, the military commander Aliakram Humbatov staged another rebellion in the Lenkoran region and proclaimed a new separatist "Talysh-Mugham Republic" in the South of Azerbaijan. Humbatov received the support of former defense minister Rahim Gaziev and swore loyalty to former president Ayaz Mutalibov. This revolt, which collapsed in August with almost no bloodshed, appeared to be part of the same larger design as Husseinov's rebellion in Ganje. It suggested that Husseinov, supported by his friends in the Russian military, may actually have been planning to return Mutalibov to power, but his plan was derailed by the improvised alliance between Aliev and the parliament.

The Armenians ruthlessly exploited the crisis, which had left the Karabakh front almost undefended. Shortly after Husseinov's rebellion, they began an offensive against Aghdam. On 27 June, they recaptured the town of Martakert and most of the northern part of Karabakh, now the most ravaged and plundered part of the whole war zone. On 23 July, facing almost no resistance, they took the large strategically vital city of Aghdam. A month later, they advanced south and captured Fizuli and Jebrail. The end result was that in four months, as power changed hands in Baku, the Azerbaijanis lost a staggering five regions of their country as well as the North of Nagorny Karabakh itself. They gave up an area of almost five thousand square kilometers, or nineteen hundred square miles.

The Armenians preceded all their offensives with a crude propaganda campaign, insisting that they were acting in self-defense against heavily defended positions. In fact, on most occasions, they walked into empty towns and villages after the Azerbaijanis had fled. One jaundiced observer called it "military tourism." Gabil Akhmedov, a villager from the Fizuli region said:

> Our men didn't defend our lands. The Armenians just took their positions. On 18 August, the Armenians captured twenty kilometers in three or four hours. The Lenkoran Brigade did nothing. They just took their weapons, their grenade launchers, and left. It's a flat region, it's easy to fight there, but in our village the soldiers had gone long before. It was the civilians who left last.[36]

The offensive caused one of the biggest refugee exoduses in Europe since the end of World War II. Around 350,000 people were expelled from their homes. Thomas Goltz saw this human tragedy in motion:

From a distance, they looked like a caravan of Gypsies on the move to a rural flea market or county fair. Beat-up cars, piled high with rugs, pots and pans, clanking down the road on wheels with no rubber on the rims. Smoke-belching crowds overloaded with mattresses and steel bed frames, trying to pass tractors pulling wagons designed to contain tons of cotton but filled with clothes, dirty children and squawking ducks. The rear was usually brought up by men riding donkeys or leading mule-drawn carts, while on the shoulder of the road, barefoot shepherds were to be seen, dodging in and out of the traffic to keep sheep and cows and oxen out of harm's way.[37]

After them came the Karabakh Armenian forces, systematically burning, looting, and taking hostage those who had not fled in time. Thousands were driven across the River Araxes into Iran. Many of them drowned as they tried to swim for safety.

# 14

# Sabirabad

## The Children's Republic

MUSIC WAS COMING out of the big hall with the corrugated iron roof. There was the rasping gut of a stringed instrument, the beat of stamping feet, an accordion, and a banging drum. Inside a line of young girls, hand in hand and dressed in pinks and greens, glided in a line, urged on by a clutch of musicians sitting in the corner. The dancing master clapped his hands, the music stopped, and the girls laughed and went back to their positions.

The hall teeming with *joie de vivre* was in a refugee camp outside the town of Sabirabad in the arid plains of central Azerbaijan. Every weekend this courtyard becomes the headquarters of an exceptional project. In the next-door room to the dancing class, another group of children was studying a text of an operetta by the composer Uzeir Hajibekov. On a square of baked mud and grass outside, a game of soccer was in progress. Animated children, bustling between activities, came up to chat to me. Despite the circumstances, I found it the most inspiring and hopeful place I had seen in the Caucasus.

The six or seven hundred children of Camp C-1 are willing guinea pigs. A few years ago a group of Azerbaijani educational psychologists found that several years after the war over Karabakh had ended, many refugee children were still frightened and disturbed. The elder ones still remembered the traumatic scenes, when they had been driven from their homes in the summer and fall of 1993. The younger ones had different problems; not remembering their original homes, they were growing up without any motivation in the listless environment of the camps.

The psychologists decided they had to catch these children before they slipped further into depression. Azad Isazade was one of the founding psychologists and my guide to C-1 camp. He told me, "The children don't know it's happening of course, but the teachers are trained to observe them and identify what they need." They had devised four sets of activities—folk dancing, theatre, art, and sports—that were also forms of therapy. "It's a process," said Azad, a slight man with an endlessly inventive and inquiring mind. "So with music, for example, they first of all needed to hear depressive melodies, then neutral ones, then cheerful ones. Or drawing. We gave them one page and asked them to draw the saddest day of their life—then later on lots of pages to draw the happiest day of their life."

The program has had remarkable effects on the children, as I saw. Yet its depressing corollary is that far more refugee children—not to mention their parents—in Azerbaijan are moldering without this kind of care or attention.

Azerbaijan may have the largest proportions of displaced people per capita of any country in the world. The total numbers may be greater in Afghanistan or Congo, but in Azerbaijan every tenth person is a refugee from the conflict with Armenia. First, approximately 200,000 Azerbaijanis fled Armenia in 1988 and 1989. Then, between 1992 and 1994, came all the Azerbaijanis of Nagorny Karabakh and the inhabitants of seven regions around Karabakh—more than half a million people in all. Six years after the cease-fire agreement was signed, in the year 2000, around eighty or ninety thousand of them were still in refugee camps. Hundreds of thousands more were living in a vast archipelago of sanatoria, student hostels, and makeshift accommodations. All remained in a terrible limbo while the conflict was unresolved.[1]

The basic ingredients the psychologists needed to get the program going in the camp, a surplus of time and unused energy, were already there: refugee schoolteachers, musicians, and sportsmen worked for free and gradually took on most of the teaching. Then, in the summer of 1999, the psychologists set up what they called The Children's Republic, a minigovernment run entirely for and by children. The children elected a "parliament" with twelve MPs, which took collective decisions. The Ministry of Ecology planted a garden, the Ministry of Information put out a newspaper. Children from the two camps the psychologists were working in played competitive games with one another and traveled to music and dance festivals, where their trainers were heartened to see that their children were the most self-assured and confident of all the competing teams.

Out on the soccer field, a boy in yellow track-suit trousers was shouting to his team. "We had him elected to parliament," Azad explained, as a way of channeling his aggression in a creative direction. He pointed out the sports shoes that the boys were wearing; they were the fruits of a policy of "tough love" that Tony Blair or Bill Clinton could be proud of. "We don't buy them presents," Azad said. "They have to achieve something. So the sports children get new shoes only if they play in the competitions." This policy caused problems when the trainers were handing out the shoes. All the parents, who had become used to humanitarian aid handouts, came out, expecting to get free gifts, but those whose children had not signed up for the weekend activities were turned away.

The experience had changed the lives of the trainers as well. Azad had been press officer in Azerbaijan's Defense Ministry during the war but turned back to his former profession, clinical psychology, after the 1994 cease-fire. I wondered what had kept him coming here to Sabirabad, four hours' drive from Baku, every weekend for the past few years. His reply, coming from a citizen of a deeply cynical society, was affecting: "I feel responsible for these people. I wasn't able to defend them."

More than twenty thousand people live in the camps of this region. They are mostly from the southern regions of Fizuli, Jebrail, and Zengelan, which were conquered by the Armenians in the summer and fall of 1993. "It was good that it was summer," Nagir Tadirov, an official in charge of the refugees told me. "Winter would have been much worse. There were some people who even forgot their documents. The ones from Jebrail and Zengelan crossed the Araxes into Iran."

Life in Camp C-1 is hard and tedious. The camp is in a former cotton field, near the confluence of two gray, flat rivers, the Araxes and the Kura; it is a sea of mud in winter and baking hot in summer. We had come in the most benign season, early spring. It looked as though a great biblical exodus had been washed up here. Mud-and-straw bricks were drying in the sun. Improvised houses had been put together from whatever came to hand: straw, clay, and cellophane. Azad pointed to a tractor drunkenly parked on a hump of clay, facing downward. "The battery's gone flat and so no one can use it," he said. "There's just no money here even for simple things like that."

We came to a low hut with a corrugated-iron roof, in front of which Zahra and her husband were sitting on a bench and invited us to join them. Zahra was wearing a green housedress, worn shoes, and flowery headscarf. They had done their best to domesticate their home. The door panels were made out of vegetable-oil cans labeled "FINAL." One or two spindly roses were growing in the yard. Nowadays they had nothing to do. They were kept from starvation by aid handouts but had no work. Everyone received a flat-rate pension or salary of 25,000 *manats* a month, or about five dollars. On top of that, they got humanitarian food aid: five kilos of flour, one kilo of seed, one of peas, and one of vegetable oil.

Zahra said they had had a two-story house with a garden full of mulberry trees in the Zengelan region. The Armenians had come in October 1993. "We fled across the Araxes. We managed to take thirty neighbors with us." She pointed to an open truck still parked in the far end of the yard. "We took only mattresses. Our forces held out for three days, then they fled too."

My arrival had caused some interest. Some of Zahra's neighbors leaned over the fence to take a look and offer me their worldview. The Armenians had "behaved worse than the fascists," they related, burning everything they had laid their hands on, chopping off noses and ears. The whole problem had started with Peter the Great and Russia's imperialist designs on the Caucasus, explained one man in a gray, flat "aerodrome" cap (so-called because you could land an airplane on it). Gorbachev had been an Armenian spy, who merely picked up where the tsars had left off. "How do you live here now?" I asked him. "How? Like sheep!" he laughed bitterly.

These people had all the time in the world to talk but very little idea of what fate the politicians and international peace negotiators were deciding for them. They complained about *satkinliq*, an Azeri word meaning "sell-out-ness." It seemed that no one had defended them against the Armenians in 1993 and no one was really bothered about their fate now. "The rich men in Baku drive around in Mercedes," said one man. "They don't think about the war. All the burden of the war has fallen on us." I asked Zahra, if there were anyone she trusted to improve her situation. "Only Allah," she answered.

The paradox is that the Azerbaijani leadership mentions the refugees at almost every opportunity. President Aliev (exaggerating somewhat) constantly repeats that there are "one million refugees" in his country. Yet, several years on, all government measures are still short-term; there is no state program that aims to give the refugees jobs or give them skills. As a result, many have turned to crime or smuggling—or else retreated into complete dependency on their meager handouts. One former Azerbaijani aid worker told me that government officials gave him angry stares when he had suggested ways of integrating the refugees into the local economy. The implication is that would mean losing them as refugees and objects of pity: they may be more useful to the government as a symbol of Azerbaijan's suffering than as people with real problems.

In the meantime, the focus of the international aid community has moved on. "A few years ago I would get a flood of journalists," Vugar Abdusalimov, press officer in Baku for the United Nations High Commission on Refugees, told me. "Now I am lucky when one or two come along. And then it always gets harder for us, when another refugee crisis happens—like in Congo or Kosovo." In 2001, just as they were planning to expand the Children's Republic to other camps, the Baku psychologists' funding dried up and they began to wind down their program.

"I left all my books behind," said Gabil Akhmedov. "There are some things it's impossible to find, like Fenimore Cooper. I used to love his *Last of the Mohicans*."

Force of character is needed to survive the demeaning process of losing your home. In Camp S-3 outside the town of Saatly, I found one man who possesses it. I was looking for someone who would give me something different from the stock answers and recycled opinions I heard from others. Gabil, a teacher of Azeri language and literature, had formed his own opinions. Tall, with thick coal-black eyebrows and an unshaven chin, he was too large for the two-room hut made of cane and pebbles he now inhabited with his wife.

Gabil had insulated the walls of the hut on the inside with a web of old newspapers, blankets, and flour sacks. The space was taken up by a kerosene stove, a carpet, a television set with a wreath of artificial roses on it, and a shelf of books. Gabil's wife, Agiyat, delighted to have a guest, insisted on cooking us an omelet and brought a plate of dried fruit. The couple came from the village of Yukhari Abdurahmanly in the Fizuli region in the foothills south of Nagorny Karabakh. Gabil said that the view from their two-story house, sitting on a hill, stretched for twenty kilometers. "Here you feel you like you live in a well or a pit. You can't see anything around you." He missed his orchard, which had had pomegranates, quince, walnuts, cherries, apples, and mulberries. "When my eldest son got married, he shot a film with the house and garden in it," Gabil said. "My family has seen the film three or four times. But I can't watch it because with my own hands I built that house and grew that garden."

Gabil's life had been blighted by two wars. In the "Great Patriotic War" of 1941–1945, his father had been sent to the front in Crimea, was reported missing in action, and never came back. That left his mother to bring up four sons on her own and a life of crushing poverty. There had never been enough bread, and they had stolen wheat from the fields. They did not have shoes and went barefoot to school. He remembered how people wore clothes made out of bandages. "It was even worse then," Gabil said.

In the postwar years, Gabil and his brothers all studied hard and got good jobs. He qualified as a teacher and was on the verge of retirement when the war over Nagorny Karabakh began. Everything they had worked for went very quickly. In mid-August 1993, during the chaotic period when Azerbaijan's second president, Abulfaz Elchibey, had been ousted but Heidar Aliev had not yet taken over as president, Armenian soldiers stormed into the Fizuli region in a lightning offensive. The Azerbaijani army simply abandoned Yukhari Abdurahmanly, and many of the villagers did not have time to flee. The invading Armenians killed twelve innocent villagers in cold blood, Gabil said, and then burned the village. "A month later one of our villagers came back in a prisoner exchange," he went on. "He said that the whole village had been burned. Only three buildings were left."

I wondered about the future. "I am 66. How can I not be sad, when I don't know what the future will be?" he declared in his deep gruff voice, more with stoicism than bitterness. But he was adamant that he did not feel hatred for the Armenians—merely the deepest possible regret. As a teacher, he had had many Armenian colleagues. "We were great friends with the Armenians for many years," he explained. He had gone back and forth to Nagorny Karabakh and had friends in Stepanakert, then, reflectively, "It's a shame, such a great shame. I feel sorry—for them and for us."

Every shift of a kilometer on the map of the Nagorny Karabakh war altered people's lives forever. In the late summer of 1993, the Armenians captured the Fizuli region. In January 1994, the Azerbaijanis launched a counterattack and recaptured two-thirds of the region. Unfortunately for Gabil, their offensive ran out of steam a few miles short of his village and his home remained just on the Armenian side of the front line.

A few days after meeting Gabil, I traveled to the recaptured parts of Fizuli. They are a tiny example of the vast problem that faces Azerbaijan if it ever recovers all of the "occupied territories." In three months of occupation, the Armenians had laid waste to the whole area. With lonely ruins scattered over a flat plain, it still looked like a World War I battlefield. Here and there, dotted across the landscape, were incongruous splashes of Mediterranean color; reconstructed houses had been painted pink, like Italian villas. Using money from the World Bank and the United Nations, the Azerbaijanis had done reconstruction work, but it looked as though the work of rehabilitating the area had only just begun.

The railway junction at Horadiz was a wreck. An idle good train had nowhere to go along the railway tracks that used to run west to Nakhichevan and Armenia. The local Azerbaijani administration had set up its officers in a former Irrigation Department building. "Everything was a problem," said Magiram Nazarov, one of the officials who came back here in 1994. "Everything had been burned. There were no doors, no roofs. There was no food." He admitted that people had flooded back here too soon. There was no work to come back to and several returnees had been blown up by mines—so most of them were forced to go back to camps again. "It was a lesson of life," Nazarov said. "If more territory is liberated, we will try to stop the population [from] going back until there are proper conditions."

In Baku, I was told that altogether around fifteen hundred houses had been rebuilt and about six million dollars had been spent here since 1996—and also that the corruption was such that a lot of the money had bypassed Fizuli altogether. Yet this was only a fraction of the enormous area of seven thousand square kilometers that the Armenians occupy. It was a bad omen for Gabil and his fellow refugees. Even if they get their homes back in a future peace settlement, it will be far from being the end of the story.

A couple of miles from the front line an elderly couple sat in front of their patched-up house, surrounded by more of the debris of international aid. Yellow and white sacks that had held rice and flour from Dubai, Thailand, and the United States covered the walls of their recently repaired house. The garden was a cacophony of dogs, turkeys, and hens.

Kurban and Sayat Abilov had lived for two years in the camps of Saatly before coming back here. They said all of their eight children were now in Baku. These two had almost nothing to live on—but they were much better conversation than most of the people in the camps. The wife jumped up to shoo a bullock away from one of the trees and prod a chicken off the porch; the husband joked and talked expansively. It seemed at least that the couple had one precious resource, which they shared with the children of the Children's Republic at Sabirabad: a sense of their own future. For hundreds of thousands of homeless Azerbaijanis, it is more a matter of what the gods decide for them.

# 15

# September 1993–May 1994

*Exhaustion*

## THE MOMENTUM OF WAR

On 3 October 1993, Heidar Aliev was elected president of Azerbaijan. The result was preordained and he was awarded an improbable 98.8 percent of the vote. What was in doubt was whether Azerbaijan was a functioning state at all. By the time Aliev was elected, Armenian forces had conquered a vast crescent of land to the east, west, and south of Nagorny Karabakh. It constituted the entire southwestern part of Azerbaijan, save only the thirty thousand people of the Zengelan region, who were trapped in a pocket of territory with the Iranian border to the south. In late October, a joint offensive from Armenia and Nagorny Karabakh overran Zengelan as well.

In a string of speeches, Aliev lambasted the army commanders and the leaders of the captured regions for betraying their country. Announcing to parliament the fall of the towns of Fizuli and Jebrail, he accused the commanders who were supposed to be defending the front of being in Baku instead, doing up their *dachas*. On 11 December, at a meeting with the heads of administration of the lost regions, which lasted for several hours and was shown on national television, Aliev rounded on each leader in turn, demanding to know why they had fled ahead of the mass of the population. The president asserted scornfully that the whole of the Zengelan province had been surrendered for the loss of just twenty-seven soldiers.[1]

Aliev's indignation carried a strong political charge. He was undercutting the authority of military commanders, who might be plotting to depose him—including his own ally in the ousting of the previous regime, Suret Husseinov. Up to a point, he may even have welcomed the reverses at the front. The new president used his new powers to disband thirty-three battalions loyal to the Popular Front, consisting

225

of about ten thousand men in all, and vowed to create a new national army instead.[2] Tens of thousands of teenagers without fighting experience were conscripted. As press gangs rounded up young men, restrictions were put on bars and restaurants and military censorship was introduced.

At the same time, Aliev, a master at keeping his options open, began to talk peace with the Armenians. In September 1993, he authorized the first public meeting between an Azerbaijani politician and an official from Stepanakert, thereby conceding for the first time that the Karabakh Armenians were a "party to the conflict." This was a confirmation of realities: the speaker of the Karabakh Armenian parliament, Karen Baburian, said that they got "dozens of telephone messages from Heidar Aliev, a mass of telephone calls" during this period.[3] In Moscow on 13 September, the deputy speaker of the Azerbaijani parliament and trusted Aliev supporter Afiyettin Jalilov met Arkady Gukasian, the "foreign minister" of Karabakh. They agreed to prolong a cease-fire, which later did not hold; the fact of the meeting had more significance.

On 24 September, Aliev himself, not yet president of Azerbaijan but already acting as one, traveled to Moscow to sign the accession documents for Azerbaijan to join the Russia-led club of post-Soviet nations, the CIS. The next day, in the Russian Foreign Ministry's *art nouveau* mansion on Spiridonovka Street, Aliev held confidential talks with the Karabakhi Armenian leader Robert Kocharian. The Russian envoy had tried to organize a meeting between the two men on seven previous occasions. On 9 October, the day before Aliev was inaugurated as president of Azerbaijan, he met Kocharian again in Moscow, this time in another Foreign Ministry residence in the Sparrow Hills. The meeting had no results but did lay the basis for a working relationship, which the two men picked up again six years later, when Kocharian became president of Armenia.[4]

The autumn of 1993 seemed a good time to negotiate an end to the Nagorny Karabakh war. President Aliev had the opportunity to make compromises by laying responsibility for past defeats on the previous regime. The Armenian president, Levon Ter-Petrosian, who was suffering the cost of economic isolation, as well as the heat of four critical United Nations resolutions, evidently wanted a peace deal. Ter-Petrosian had reportedly had strong misgivings about all the Armenian offensives outside the borders of Karabakh since the attack on Kelbajar in the spring of 1993. "After Kelbajar Ter-Petrosian was almost frightened to death," said Ashot Manucharian. "After that he was categorically against any other military actions."[5] However, the conflict had acquired its own momentum, and Ter-Petrosian was not in full control of the Armenian war effort. Riding their string of successes, the Karabakh Armenians had become more aggressively independent. The enclave itself had turned into a little Sparta, with all adult men serving in the army.

The main Karabakh army commander, Samvel Babayan, had become, at the age of twenty-eight, the most powerful man in the region and had ambitions to be reckoned with. Small in build, this "little Napoleon" was a creature of the war. He was uneducated and had previously made his living washing cars and working in a café. In 1991, he had been arrested and jailed by the Azerbaijanis, becoming a local hero on his release (although according to the Azerbaijani prosecutor Yusif Agayev, his offense had been criminal, not political).[6] In 1992, Babayan acquired the reputation of being a ruthless military commander and an excellent military organizer. Later on, he and many of his comrades in arms treated the seized Azerbaijani territories as an endless source of plunder.

The machine of war could not be stopped. In Azerbaijan, Aliev was also evidently tempted by the appeal of another push to retake Azerbaijan's lost territories. On 10 October, the day after his second meeting with Kocharian and of his inauguration as president of Azerbaijan, he made a bellicose speech, threatening the Armenians with many years more of conflict. On the same day, each side accused the other of breaking the cease-fire. Within ten days, heavy fighting had resumed. The Armenians began their last big offensive to the south, capturing the railway junction at Horadiz and the Zengelan region. They thereby shortened their southern front from 130 to 22 kilometers—and by doing so drove tens of thousands more civilians from their homes and across the Araxes River into Iran. The Iranians disarmed the soldiers and housed the fleeing civilians in makeshift refugee camps before repatriating them to Azerbaijan.

## THE MEDIATORS

The interlocking human geography in and around Nagorny Karabakh was so complex that from early on it promised three possible endings to the Armenian-Azerbaijani conflict.

One possible ending was that Azerbaijan would be able fully to encircle Nagorny Karabakh, so that it could either expel all the Karabakh Armenians or dictate the terms of their submission. This is what they almost achieved in June 1991 and again in June–July 1992. Arkady Gukasian says of negotiations he took part in in the summer of 1992: "We were interested in a cease-fire at that point and negotiations were going on at that time. But they behaved provocatively, they basically laid down terms for our capitulation. . . . They did everything to prevent a cease-fire. And then, when the situation changed, they began to ask for peace."[7]

Another possible outcome was that the Armenians could redraw the old borders in blood, expel all the Azerbaijanis in and around Nagorny Karabakh from their homes, and carve out a zone of conquered territory with defensible borders. They would then be able to call for a permanent cease-fire on their terms. This is what eventually happened. As early as the winter of 1991, the first Karabakh Armenian leader, Artur Mkrtchian, had sketched out a map of what he thought of as "defensible frontiers," which was remarkably similar to the one eventually drawn on the battlefield.[8]

The third possible conclusion to the conflict was a mediated agreement that would carry such weight that it could force both sides to stop fighting. Achieving that was the goal of the international mediators, but for most of the conflict all they could achieve was temporary cease-fires. Gukasian says:

> Agreements were possible, but unfortunately neither side thought seriously about cease-fires; they were tactical ruses. There was no trust. We agree to a cease-fire, let's say, and then some local conflict springs up somewhere. In principle, I think [an earlier agreement] was possible, although it's hard for me to say at what actual stage. But if the world powers had taken [the conflict] more seriously, then it would have been possible to stop it earlier.

In 1991–1992, a galaxy of negotiators offered to mediate. There was the joint mission by Presidents Yeltsin and Nazarbayev; a trip by the former U.S. Secretary of State Cyrus Vance on behalf of the United Nations secretary general; the short-lived mediation by Iran. The result was confusion as the two sides were being encouraged to "shop around" for whichever mediation effort suited them best.

In 1992, one organization, the forty-nine-member Conference for Security and Cooperation in Europe, the CSCE, began to take a more sustained interest. It began, in the words of one of those present, "almost as an afterthought" at the end of a meeting in Prague on 31 January 1992 at which most of the former Soviet republics were admitted to the organization. As the meeting was winding up, the British delegate pointed out that the organization had just admitted two members, Armenia and Azerbaijan, who were at war with each other and that the CSCE was obliged to do something about it. A CSCE fact-finding mission was dispatched to the region.[9]

At the organization's next major meeting, in Helsinki on 24 March, CSCE foreign ministers resolved to hold a peace conference on Nagorny Karabakh—for which another new delegate, from Belarus, suddenly volunteered his capital, Minsk, as a venue. When no one objected, the idea of a "Minsk Conference" was born. Armenia, Azerbaijan, and nine other CSCE nations agreed to take part, as well as "elected" and "other" representatives of Nagorny Karabakh, a formula that included both Karabakh Armenians and Azerbaijanis. The conference was canceled because of the escalation in the fighting, so the Minsk Conference became instead the Minsk Group, with the former Italian deputy foreign minister Mario Raffaelli as its first chairman. As a result, the first negotiations were actually held in Rome rather than Minsk.[10]

Through the creation of the Minsk Group of the CSCE (later the OSCE) in 1992, western European countries, the United States, and Turkey all had a stake in the resolution of the conflict. Both combatants welcomed the broad international involvement, but it also carried dangers. It tied the Karabakh peace process to the wider issue of the West's engagement with Russia. The risk grew that competition between Washington and Moscow for influence in the Caucasus would hinder, rather than help, the search for a solution to the conflict.

Both Armenians and Azerbaijanis are scathing about the early work of the OSCE and the Minsk Group. The Azerbaijani presidential foreign policy aide Vafa Guluzade recalls "completely incompetent ambassadors from France, from other countries. They were taking part there without any knowledge of the region, the core of the conflict, without any tools of pressure on the parties."[11] The former Armenian president Levon Ter-Petrosian comments: "The OSCE began to take this question seriously only in 1996. Before that, it was simply a bluff, there was absolutely no peace process. The opposite was true. They competed among themselves more than they thought about the Karabakh issue."[12]

Some of the mediators themselves do not dispute this. "It was clear, especially to the negotiators who represented the parties to the conflict, that the Western countries were not very interested in the Karabakh war," says the former U.S. representative to the Minsk Group, John Maresca.[13] The CSCE meeting in Stockholm in December 1992 almost succeeded in brokering an agreement, but the Azerbaijanis rejected it at the last moment. That the two sides even got close was a tribute to those who actually managed to show up. The Italian chairman, Mario Raffaelli, did not attend, pleading family obligations. There was virtually no Russian representation. And apart from Maresca, almost no other State Department officials were on hand to discuss what Washington evidently deemed to be a low-priority issue. Moreover, the way the group was set up made it virtually unworkable. Maresca writes:

> In addition the fact that the Italian chairman had to have translation into Italian meant that the French and German representatives also insisted on the equal use of their own languages. This made the Minsk Group into an unwieldy and absurdly heavy piece of negotiating machinery, including eleven countries, two non-countries, a Chairmanship plus a secretariat, and five interpreting booths. Concessions involving war and peace, life and death, are not made in such a setting.[14]

The peace process was bedeviled by the peculiar nature of a dispute that was both an international and internal conflict. The Azerbaijanis took the position that the conflict was an irredentist war waged by Armenia on Azerbaijan and therefore refused to accept the Karabakh Armenians as a party to the conflict. The Armenians countered that the Karabakh Armenians were waging a separatist conflict against Baku in which Armenia was only a concerned neighbor. Both these stances were clearly false and adopted only as tactical positions, but they bogged the talks down.

It was evident that some kind of dialogue between the Azerbaijani government and the Karabakh Armenians would have to take place for any peace agreement to work. Yet the two sides circled round each other, with Azerbaijan afraid to lend political legitimacy to Stepanakert by talking publicly to the Karabakh Armenians, who were constantly seeking to maximize their status at the talks. Arguably, the bright glare

of international diplomatic gatherings only made things worse. Encouraged to negotiate, using UN resolutions and the vocabulary of international law, both sides turned the discussion of status into a rhetorical battleground. Vartan Oskanian, now Armenian Foreign Minister,
has this to say:

> As I now recall the situation in [19]92, [19]93, we used to fight over
> very childish things—what would be the shape of the table, where the
> Karabakh people would sit, how they should be treated, were they an
> equal party or not. I remember we used to fight on commas, on where
> the commas in the text would be put. I remember during the Buda-
> pest summit we were fighting whether we should use the words
> "among" or "between"—the argument was "between," between two,
> but "among" can mean more than two and that could also include
> Karabakh. So we were fighting on symbolism. But after six or seven
> years of this kind of bickering, you really get tired, you begin to think
> more in terms of results.[15]

The problem of an unrecognized state entity, such as Nagorny
Karabakh, was perhaps easier for the CSCE to deal with than it was for
the United Nations, with its stronger institutional bias toward the na-
tion-state. Yet the CSCE had a strong disadvantage vis-à-vis the UN in
that it had no experience of running peacekeeping operations. This was
a major reason why the CSCE's most serious peace plan stalled in the
summer of 1993. Everyone knew that only one country was prepared
instantly to send troops or monitors to the mountains of the Caucasus—
and that was Russia.

## ENTER MR. KAZIMIROV

The Russians had many advantages in Armenia and Azerbaijan. In
1992, the Caucasus and Russia were still part of the same economic
space; everyone spoke Russian; even the old official telephone lines still
went directly through to Moscow. From May 1992, Russia also had, by
general consensus, the most talented and experienced diplomat working on the Nagorny Karabakh issue, Vladimir Kazimirov.

Kazimirov was a seasoned Soviet diplomat who had served as ambassador in Angola at the height of the war there. Hikmet Hajizade

called him "the conductor" of the Armenian-Azerbaijani talks, the man in the middle who always knew better than anyone else what was going on. Kazimirov, very jovial and avuncular in conversation, was later demonized by Azerbaijanis for allegedly trying to impose a Russian neo-colonialist peace settlement on them. Yet it would be a misrepresentation to think of him as merely an agent of Russian imperial power: he put in far more time and effort than any other one individual into ending the conflict and made dozens of trips to the region over four years; in retirement he was still passionately interested in the Karabakh issue and even wrote poetry about it.

The problem for the Russian Foreign Ministry was that, for obvious reasons, it had no experience in the republics of the former Soviet Union. It had plenty of specialists on France or Vietnam, but none in a region, which had only just ceased to be part of the same state. This was one reason that the Defense Ministry, with thousands of men on the ground in the Caucasus, was able to play a leading role. Grachev deliberately underlined this primacy when he excluded Kazimirov from his negotiations in Sochi in September 1992.

In 1993, Russian policy became more coordinated. On 28 February, President Yeltsin announced that the moment had come "when responsible international organizations, including the United Nations, should grant Russia special powers as a guarantor of peace and stability in the region of the former union." It was a bid for Russia to have special rights in, and to guard the borders of, what it still insisted on calling the "near abroad."[16]

The Russian Defense Ministry wanted to enforce the desired policy in the Caucasus. Grachev's idea was that if Russian troops could monitor a cease-fire agreement, they would maintain Russian leverage in the region. This is what had happened in the Georgia-Abkhazia conflict, in which a Russian military force was eventually stationed between the two sides. Nagorny Karabakh was much more problematic. Although the Armenians saw a Russian military presence as the best guarantor of their security, Azerbaijan had made the withdrawal of Russian troops from its territory an absolute priority and was opposed to their return in any form.

A pattern established itself. The Russians would cajole Azerbaijan, sometimes threateningly, to sign on to an agreement that included a Russian military contingent. Hikmet Hajizade recalls:

They would show us an agreement. They said, "Sign this agreement on a cease-fire with Armenia." And how does a cease-fire take place? It is a technical process. First point: stop firing from 22:00 hours on this day. Second point: in three days withdraw your artillery five kilometers. Third: establish contact with the observers who are in the middle. And finally, the peacekeeping forces arrive. And who are these peacekeepers? The UN doesn't have money; they told us so. America does not plan to pay; they are a bit too far away. Of course, it's the Russians. "Do you have any other suggestions?" "No." "Here's the piece of paper." I was given five or six pieces of paper like this.[17]

For the presidential foreign policy aide Vafa Guluzade, Azerbaijan's leading critic of Russian policy, the problem was Russia per se. After the fall of Kelbajar in April 1993, Guluzade was invited to Moscow for a meeting with First Deputy Foreign Minister Anatoly Adamishin. He says that in Moscow he was met by a big Foreign Ministry delegation at the airport and given a grand lunch in one of the ministry's official residences, at which they tried to convince him of the benefits of a plan under which Russian troops would be stationed in Kelbajar: "Mr Adamishin asked me to persuade President Elchibey that it will be to our advantage if we allow Russian forces to come to Kelbajar. Even one Russian battalion. And here we had very sharp discussions. I asked them what they meant: 'Why should the Russian military come to Kelbajar?'"[18] Guluzade says that he urged his masters to reject any peace plan involving Russian troops.

The Armenians dismiss the charge that they were the stooges of Moscow, declaring that they also experienced pressure from the Russians. Gukasian says that in the spring of 1993, Russia leaned heavily on them to give up Kelbajar. A year later, Kocharian wrote a letter to the Russian foreign minister in which he turned aside their advice to give up one of the occupied regions as a "goodwill gesture."[19] The crux of the problem was that Russia was both involved in the conflict and also its only serious mediator. The Russian monopoly increased after the Minsk Group plan failed in the summer of 1993 and lost authority. After this, Moscow began to push the idea of an even more ambitious Russian-led military "separation force" stationed between the Armenians and Azerbaijanis.[20]

## THE U.S. POSITION

The United States was a newcomer to the Caucasus, a region in which it never before played a role. It found it had conflicting interests. On the one hand, Washington supported the ambitions of Georgia and Azerbaijan to be more independent from Russia and saw Azerbaijan as a potential locus of investment for U.S. oil companies. On the other hand were the claims of the one-million-strong Armenian American community, one of the most vocal ethnic lobbies in the United States. In 1992, Armenia had a U.S.-born foreign minister, Raffi Hovannisian. The Armenian lobby in Congress, supported by eminent figures like Senator Bob Dole, was extremely powerful and consistently voted through large aid grants to independent Armenia. U.S. government aid to Armenia, still worth $102.4 million in 2000, was the second highest per capita after Israel.

On 24 October 1992, in the midst of an election campaign in the United States, the Armenian lobby helped push Section 907a of the Freedom Support Act through Congress. The act punished Azerbaijan by prohibiting the allocation of almost all American governmental aid "until the President determines, and so reports to the Congress, that the Government of Azerbaijan is taking demonstrable steps to cease all blockades and other offensive uses of force against Armenia and Nagorno-Karabakh." Section 907, which was finally lifted only in 2002, stood for years as one of the most striking examples of how domestic politics could shape the foreign agenda of the United States.

In 1992, relations between Washington and Moscow were at an all-time high on most issues, but not on the Caucasus. The United States was suspicious of Russia's interference in Georgia and Azerbaijan, and Russia accused the Americans of meddling in its backyard. This rivalry fed through into the CSCE Minsk Group. In 1994, shortly after departing as U.S. negotiator, John Maresca made this charge against the Russians:

> Russia wished to reestablish its dominance in the region and to exclude outsiders, namely the US and Turkey. Russia wants to dominate Armenia and Azerbaijan for a number of reasons. Most obviously, Moscow would like to reestablish control of the former Soviet frontier with Turkey and Iran, and to share in Azerbaijan's oil riches. To ac-

complish these aims, Russia has been pressuring Azerbaijan to accept the reentry of Russian troops as a separation force and as border guards, as to give Russia a share of the oil concessions being developed by Western companies. For leverage the Russians have used an implicit but dramatic threat: if Azerbaijan does not comply, Russia will step up its backing for Armenia (Russian troops are already stationed there), with disastrous military results for the Azerbaijanis.[21]

To which Kazimirov retorted that Washington seemed so intent on keeping the Russians out of the region that it seemed to regard peace in Nagorny Karabakh as a secondary priority:

> The former representative of the USA in the Minsk Group, who played "first violin" in it at one time, writes fairly openly in his notes and articles that it was necessary to "restrain" Russia in its "neoimperial ambitions" and even makes no exceptions for the cease-fire. The publications of the American envoy show that—to all appearances—in Washington's view the cease-fire did not have value in and of itself but was only one element in a large geostrategic game, aimed at reducing the role of Russia in the Transcaucasus.[22]

The period 1993–1994 saw the low point of American involvement on the Karabakh issue. On 30 November 1993, the Swede Jan Eliasson, who replaced Mario Raffaelli as chairman of the Minsk Group, decided to rely less on the group as a whole and make more visits to the region to talk directly to the parties. This reduced the U.S. role in the Minsk Group and gave correspondingly more influence to the Russians. John Maresca gave up his job as U.S. representative to the Minsk Group. It was a period when mediation was needed more than ever because in December 1993 the war entered a final phase of new ferocity.

## 1993–1994: A WINTER OFFENSIVE

The last phase of the Karabakh war was also the bloodiest. "Real war began on 17 December 1993 and lasted until 12 May 1994," says Ter-Petrosian. "That was a war, when both sides had real armies." He estimates that the Azerbaijanis had a hundred thousand men at its disposal and the Armenians had thirty-five thousand. For the first time both sides relied heavily on young and inexperienced conscripts, thousands of whom died in pitched battles.

Most of the soldiers on the Armenian side came from Armenia itself, whose denials that it was fighting a war with Azerbaijan were now generally disbelieved. In any case, the Karabakh Armenian Serzh Sarkisian had become Armenia's minister of defense in August 1993, blurring completely the distinction between the fighting forces of Nagorny Karabakh and Armenia. In 1994, Human Rights Watch researchers estimated that 30 percent of the soldiers to whom they talked at random on the streets of Yerevan were regular recruits from the Armenian army fighting in Karabakh.[23] The Azerbaijanis also recruited between fifteen and twenty-five hundred Afghan *mujahadin* fighters. Officials denied that they were there, but sightings of the long-haired and bearded fighters in Baku, some wearing traditional Afghan dress, became so frequent that their involvement was an open secret.[24]

Fierce fighting resumed in December 1993. The Armenians attempted to push east of Fizuli but met with unprecedented resistance and fell back. Azerbaijan then attacked on three fronts. An offensive in the Northeast of Nagorny Karabakh made gains in the Martakert region. In the Southeast, Azerbaijan recaptured the Horadiz rail junction on the Araxes River on 6 January and pushed north toward Fizuli.

The biggest Azerbaijani offensive came in the new year, 1994, in the Northwest. This campaign, the bloodiest of the whole war, was also among the least reported.[25] It took place in bitter winter conditions in an almost empty territory that had lost its civilian population. It began when a large force crossed the high Murov Mountains and the Omar Pass and headed into the Kelbajar region. At first, the Azerbaijanis made quick progress against unprepared conscripts from Armenia's Vanadzor Division. On 24 January, they announced they had encircled and destroyed almost an entire Armenian battalion of 240 men near the village of Charply.

By the first week of February, the Azerbaijanis were close to the town of Kelbajar itself. However, they had already moved a long way from their rear positions on the other side of the Murov Mountains, and the Armenians sent in more experienced soldiers from Karabakh to bolster their positions. On 12 February, the Armenians counterattacked, just as heavy snow started falling. The Azerbaijanis began to retreat in panic, and hundreds of young soldiers were reported missing or frozen to death. By 18 February, the Azerbaijanis were in full retreat over the Omar Pass.

Two Azerbaijani brigades had now been completely cut off and tried to fight their way back north through the narrow pass. The Armenians fired a barrage of Grad missiles into the encircled brigades, with appalling results. In this single attack, they may have killed as many as fifteen hundred men. Several years later travelers to Kelbajar still came across frozen corpses there. Soon afterward the Armenians recovered hundreds of "military tickets"—or military ID cards—from the young Azerbaijani dead in the Omar Pass. In some of the most poignant images of the war, an Armenian television crew filmed a long heap of the red cardboard "military tickets" strewn along a wooden table—all that remained to identify dozens of the young Azerbaijanis who had died.

The 1994 winter campaign moved the front line far less than previous offensives had, with Azerbaijan recovering only small pieces of territory in the North and South. Casualty figures however, were dramatically higher, with perhaps four thousand Azerbaijanis and two thousand Armenians killed.[26]

## TOWARD A CEASE-FIRE

In February 1994, when the fighting was at its height, both the Swedish chairman of the Minsk Group, Jan Eliasson, and the Russian envoy, Vladimir Kazimirov, made trips to the region. They were now acting virtually in competition. Kazimirov later returned with the Russian deputy defense minister, Georgy Kondratyev, who was tipped to be head of a Russian-led peacekeeping force.

Again there are suggestions that the Russian military was playing both sides in order to shape a peace deal to its own advantage. The Armenians allege that Azerbaijan received Russian military aid in the winter of 1993–1994. "Russia wanted to help Aliev, to tie him to the Russian chariot," said one Armenian official. In the last week of January 1994, Levon Ter-Petrosian traveled to Saint Petersburg for the fiftieth anniversary of the lifting of the siege of Leningrad. According to two Armenian sources—although Ter-Petrosian himself refused to confirm this story—the Armenian president was desperate to secure a new supply of weapons for the front and went to the Kirov Ballet to try to meet President Yeltsin one-on-one. He finally secured a private meeting with

Yeltsin and a deal to receive more weapons, which helped prop up the battered Armenian front.

On the Azerbaijani side, the presidential official Eldar Namazov said that in early 1994 he was present in Aliev's office in Baku when Kazimirov delivered a warning from the Russians that if the Azerbaijanis did not cooperate, they risked losing more territory: "Kazimirov came to Baku and threatened that if you don't allow in Russian peacekeeping battalions between the Armenian and Azerbaijani forces, in a month's time the Armenians will take Ganje, Terter, Barda, and the railway leading to Georgia."[27] The Armenians did indeed launch a new offensive in the Northwest in the direction of Terter and Barda. Every new attack was now bringing heavy losses on both sides among the inexperienced conscripts, a fact that began to persuade both sides that it was time for a proper cease-fire.

On 4–5 May, parliamentary delegations from CIS countries gathered for a meeting in Bishkek, the capital of Kyrgyzstan. Karen Baburian, the speaker of the Karabakh parliament, also attended the meeting. A document, the "Bishkek Protocol," was drawn up, which "called on all conflicting sides [in Nagorny Karabakh] to heed again the voice of reason: to cease fire at midnight on 8 to 9 May." Six men signed the protocol, including Kazimirov and the two Armenian officials.

The spotlight turned on the leader of the Azerbaijani delegation, the deputy speaker of parliament Afiyettin Jalilov. He did not sign the document, saying he needed the approval of President Aliev first. The Azerbaijani leadership faced a stark choice. If they signed the protocol, they would embrace the best chance yet of peace but also have to give up military ambitions and confront a domestic backlash. In Bishkek, it was agreed that a space on the document would be left vacant for Jalilov's signature while he consulted with Aliev.

At the time of the Bishkek meeting, Aliev was in Brussels. After he had returned home on 8 May, Kazimirov also flew to Baku and met with the entire Azerbaijani leadership. In a stormy meeting in Aliev's office, the speaker of parliament, Rasul Guliev, led those in favor of signing the Bishkek document. In the end, there was consensus that the Azerbaijanis should sign, if they could make two minor alterations to the document and add the signature of the Karabakh Azerbaijani leader, Nizami Bakhmanov. A search was made for Bakhmanov, but he could not be found in Baku and therefore could not sign the document. So Guliev alone signed the "Bishkek Protocol."[28]

Guliev later quarreled with Aliev and left Azerbaijan to live in New York. Unsurprisingly therefore, he tells the story of how he signed the cease-fire document in a light unflattering to Aliev. Guliev says he had just returned from the front line near Terter, where he had seen that Azerbaijani positions were at a breaking point. That persuaded him that Azerbaijan needed a cease-fire. Guliev asserts that Aliev was deliberately equivocal: "[Aliev] didn't say 'Yes' or 'No' to me. I thought that we had to sign it."[29] The device of an appeal for a cease-fire signed by parliamentary speakers was certainly useful for the president, who had to withstand a storm of protest from the opposition. Aliev waited for a few days for the storm to pass before he spoke up in public in favor of the cease-fire agreement.

With the principle of a cease-fire agreed to by both sides, it now had to be put into effect on the ground. This was done by a round of what Kazimirov called "fax diplomacy" conducted through his office in Moscow. The Azerbaijani defense minister, Mamedrafi Mamedov, signed his commitment to a cease-fire in Baku on 9 May. The next day the Armenian defense minister, Serzh Sarkisian, signed the same document in Yerevan. Samvel Babayan, the Karabakh Armenian commander, signed on 11 May in Stepanakert. At midnight on 11–12 May 1994, the cease-fire took effect and—despite a shaky start—it held.

Pavel Grachev then moved to implement his part of the plan, the introduction of an eighteen-hundred-strong Russian peacekeeping force. He invited three military leaders, Azerbaijan's Mamedov, Armenia's Sarkisian, and Bako Saakian representing Nagorny Karabakh (who was seated to one side of the other delegations) to Moscow. Grachev began the meeting by insisting that the three men should all sign a cease-fire agreement, apparently overlooking the fact that Kazimirov's truce had already held for four days. His blunt and aggressive language angered Mamedov, who refused to agree to Grachev's plan. The defense minister "did not always reckon with what the diplomats were doing," says Kazimirov. "He was his own peacemaker." The Azerbaijani leadership upheld its commitment to the cease-fire but refused to accept a Russian peacekeeping force to enforce it.

The 12 May 1994 cease-fire reflected a number of realities. Both the Armenians and Azerbaijanis were exhausted. Azerbaijan, which had lost thousands of men to achieve only small advances in the front line, accepted the need for a cessation of violence but could not tolerate a Russian military force. This gave birth to the unusual situation of a cease-fire line, which had no neutral troop contingent to patrol it and was, in effect, self-regulated. The Armenians were less interested in a peacekeeping force per se than in a defensible front line. According to Robert Kocharian: "We seriously began to think about [a cease-fire], when we came to borders, where we could seriously organize the defense of Karabakh."[30] They had achieved this basically by conquering the entire southwest corner of Azerbaijan, an area that—including Nagorny Karabakh—comprises almost 14 percent of Azerbaijan's officially recognized territory. With a cease-fire in place but no political agreement signed, the dispute now entered a strange phase of "no war, no peace." The battles were over, but the fundamental issues of the conflict were still unresolved.

# 16

# Stepanakert

## A State Apart

THE SMALL AUSTERE room was lined with wooden benches and illuminated by a bank of strip lights. But for the floor-to-ceiling metal cage on the left side, it could have been a school classroom. Inside, two rows of young men sat together under guard; seated at a short distance from them was Samvel Babayan, a small man with a wispy moustache and an inscrutable expression. The former commander of the Karabakh Armenian armed forces was on trial for attempted murder and high treason.

Babayan had a swift fall from power. For five years after the 1994 cease-fire agreement with Azerbaijan, still not yet thirty years old, he was acclaimed as the all-Armenian hero. Combining the posts of minister of defense and commander of the army in the self-proclaimed statelet of Nagorny Karabakh, Babayan had been the de facto overlord and master of the territory. Then at the end of 1999, a power struggle with the rest of the leadership broke into the open and he was sacked from his posts. Three months later, in March 2000, the region's elected leader, Arkady Gukasian, was riding home late one night through Stepanakert when his Mercedes sustained a fusillade of bullets fired by two gunmen. Gukasian was hit in the legs, and his bodyguard and driver were wounded. Babayan and his associates were arrested and accused of plotting to assassinate Gukasian and seize power.

Now, in October 2000, seats were hard to come by in Stepanakert's courtroom for the daily drama of the trial. Three of the former commander's fellow accused had rejected their former boss and pleaded guilty, but he himself denied all the charges against him. His lawyer, Zhudeks Shagarian, said that an early confession had been beaten out of him.

The trial was a small-town affair that was forcing open a clammed-up and secretive society. The lawyers, defendants, and witnesses all knew one another. The prosecutor asked one witness, a doctor, to define her exact relationship to the main defendant. "Yes, I am Babayan's second cousin," she conceded. She was then asked for her address. "Who gave you the apartment?" the prosecutor asked, seeking to establish whether it was a gift from Babayan. Distributing apartments had been one of his ways of securing loyalty.

Outside the courtroom other facts about Babayan were emerging into the daylight. The list of assets held by him and his family and confiscated when he was arrested included eight foreign cars, among them a Mercedes, a BMW, and a Landrover; two farms; two houses; five apartments; around forty thousand dollars' worth of jewelry and sixty thousand dollars' worth of cash.[1] By world standards, that may not have been excessive; in Nagorny Karabakh, that made him unimaginably wealthy.

Babayan and his family had made money out of both war and peace. In wartime, the wealth came from the "occupied territories," when everything they contained was stripped, taken away, and sold, generally to Iran. The marauders missed nothing, whether it was scrap metal, factory equipment, copper wire, or roof beams. An Armenian friend described to me how he went to the ravaged city of Aghdam one June day after the war and saw the Felliniesque sight of men filling a line of flattop Iranian trucks to the brim with rose petals. The petals came from the thousands of rosebushes scrambling over the ruins of the deserted town, and the Iranians bought them to make jam.

In peacetime, Babayan and his family exploited the economic isolation of Nagorny Karabakh. He founded a company called Jupiter, registered in his wife's name, which earned vast sums by acquiring the monopoly on cigarette and fuel imports to the enclave. Economic power was only half of it. "You couldn't open a kiosk or be appointed as a schoolteacher without Babayan's say-so," said one disgruntled local. All political rivals were neutralized. A feud between Babayan and one military commander named "Vacho" ended in an armed showdown and Vacho's fleeing Karabakh. Anyone who got in Babayan's way risked ending up in Shusha jail and being ordered to pay a large bribe to secure his or her release. One father was asked to pay a much higher price: the delivery of either of his teenage daughters to Babayan. He told his daughters to stay at home while he frantically raised a ransom of five thousand dollars.

This part of the Babayan story was the most disgusting and also the hardest to report on because no Stepanakert girl would go on the record about Babayan's rapist propensities. But several people told me how young women were afraid to go out in the evenings because Babayan and his friends would crawl the streets in their Mercedes at five miles an hour, in the manner of Stalin's henchman Lavrenty Beria, looking for female prey. Some parents sent their daughters to Yerevan to escape his rapacity; other young women bore children who were nicknamed "little Samo."

A repellent man certainly—but was Babayan plotting to seize power in March 2000? Some said that if Babayan, a proven military professional, had organized the assassination attempt on Gukasian, it would not have failed. The Bulgarian journalist Cvetana Paskaleva, a keen Babayan supporter, said that when she visited him just before his arrest, he was entirely focused on rebuilding his career peacefully, as a politician. Most of Stepanakert, however, seemed to believe him guilty. "If not him, then who?" people said. The veteran activist Zhanna Galstian declared that the trial was the logical culmination of the commander's ambitions: "Samvel Babayan took away our initiative, he made people slaves. If this trial wasn't happening, it would all have been in vain."

The Babayan phenomenon was the most lurid example of a wider postwar phenomenon. As in Azerbaijan, many ordinary Karabakh Armenians felt betrayed by their leaders. There was cruel disappointment for those who had fought out of genuine conviction or lost sons and husbands. Seta Melkonian, the widow of the Armenian volunteer warrior Monte Melkonian, told me that she found it disheartening nowadays to go back to his old region of Martuni where he had been commander:

> I know a family that lost their three boys, three young men. This was a refugee family from Baku. They came to Martuni, and one day they lost their three sons. One was married with two kids, one diabetic. One was engaged. The other one wasn't married. And every time I see that mother, I feel bad. What do you tell that kind of a mother? These are the people that I'm in contact with, and there are a lot I don't know. They feel "Was it worth to give all the sacrifice that they gave for this?" ... I know this other lady, a cleaning lady from the [army] headquarters. From her face, you could see how she feels. She lost her house; a

244 STEPANAKERT: A STATE APART

Grad hit her house. She lost her two sons. She lost her son-in-law. What do you tell that woman? Six grandkids—and a guy just passes by with a hundred-thousand-dollar car![2]

The costs have been different for each side in the Armenia-Azerbaijan war. For Azerbaijan, there was the immense trauma of losing land and of the refugees; yet defeat did have one healthy side effect of cutting the ambitions of the country's warlords out from under them. Would-be Bonapartes like Suret Husseinov and Rahim Gaziev met their political and military graveyards in Karabakh.

The Karabakh Armenians emerged into the cease-fire of May 1994 victorious, yet victory allowed the Armenian military commanders to control the peace. In Armenia, the veterans' group Yerkrapah—its leader was Vazgen Sarkisian—became the most powerful organization in the country. In Karabakh, everyone remained subordinate to the whim of the military leaders.

Postwar Armenian Karabakh faced a fundamental problem: What kind of future was there for an economically isolated statelet, unrecognized by the outside world, while the dispute with Azerbaijan was unresolved? What was the price of lasting peace? When I met Babayan for the first and only time, a few weeks after he had been sacked as army commander and a few weeks before he was arrested, he showed he had started thinking about these issues. Physically, the commander looked more like Marcel Proust than a fearsome warlord. He was small, dapper, and neat, and had a shiny black moustache. Yet I was also struck by his uncanny resemblance—in short stature, soft voice, and the almost identical name and age—to another famous Caucasian loose cannon, the Chechen warrior leader Shamil Basayev. As with Basayev, the hard black eyes gave a clue to the breaker of human lives underneath.

Babayan talked about war and peace in the same breath. He mused that what he called a "fourth round" of the war might finally bring Azerbaijan to its knees. "If there is this fourth round, it will be decisive and then we won't have to stop the war and sit down at the negotiating table. If we stop again, as we did in 1994, then we will forget again that this problem existed."[3]

Yet he also wanted to cut a deal with Azerbaijan. Perhaps as a result of several years in charge of Nagorny Karabakh's feeble and isolated economy, Babayan recognized that economic development could come only through trade with the eastern neighbor. "We are very interested in the Azerbaijani market." He added that as a man who had won territory on the battlefield, he was the best man to give it up at the negotiating table. Then, in an offhand manner but evidently wanting to gauge my reaction, he threw out one sensational tidbit. "Ilham Aliev keeps wanting to meet me in Paris," he said, referring to the son and heir of the Azerbaijani president. "So far I haven't said yes."

Babayan was never able to keep his rendezvous with Ilham Aliev—if indeed it was a real proposal, not just a fantasy. He was arrested three weeks later, and in February 2001 he was sentenced to fourteen years in jail for organizing the assassination plot against Gukasian.

"We kept this myth [of Babayan] for the outside world. Unfortunately it didn't work." Nagorny Karabakh's elected "president" Arkady Gukasian was propped up on a divan in his residence. More than six months after the attack, one of his feet was still bare and bound with bandages. Gukasian is a former journalist, but with his round balding head, neat moustache, and cheerful countenance he looks more like a bank manager. In 1997, he took over as Nagorny Karabakh's elected leader when Robert Kocharian moved to Yerevan to become prime minister of Armenia. I wanted his explanation for why he had promoted the cult of Samvel Babayan the hero, who had then become his enemy. "Many people are guilty for the way he became what he is," Gukasian conceded.[4]

Being the leader of an unrecognized state is an unenviable job. No country—not even Armenia—has recognized Nagorny Karabakh's declaration of independence. That means that no one invites you to international meetings. The United Nations does not answer your letters. When you visit a foreign embassy, you are received by the first secretary, not the ambassador.

The Karabakhi leaders insist that statehood is conferred by history, not by international resolutions. The statelet's sleek prime minister, Anushavan Danielian, who came to Karabakh from another semi-independent post-Soviet province, Crimea, demanded to know when history started and stopped. "Is there something in world legislation that says that seventy years ago isn't history and ten years ago is history?" he asked rhetorically.[5] In other words, why was Nagorny Karabakh's status as part of Azerbaijan until 1988 more valid than its status over the past ten years? Gukasian argued that Babayan's trial was an "exam" that proved how "Karabakh is developing as a society." He insisted that

Nagorny Karabakh was making itself into a state, regardless of what the outside world thought.

Shunned by the outside world, the Nagorny Karabakh Republic luxuriates in the form if not the content of statehood. A large crest is embossed on the façade of the president's office in former Lenin Square, and from the flagpole flies the Nagorny Karabakh flag, a red-blue-and-orange Armenian tricolor with what looks like a flight of jagged white steps descending through it on the right side. Government desks carry Nagorny Karabakh inkwells and the headed notepaper of the "Nagorny Karabakh Republic." "Independence Day" is celebrated each year with great pomp on 2 September.

This rhetoric of self-promotion puts Nagorny Karabakh in the company of four other unrecognized statelets in the former Soviet Union. It is a strange club of five would-be states, consisting entirely of former Soviet autonomous regions, which in 1991 refused to accept the terms of the breakup of the USSR into fifteen states that formerly were its Union republics. All five managed a de facto breakaway from their metropolitan parent but then slipped into a twilit state of anarchy or war. In the year 2000, none of them was in a happy condition. Chechnya had been plunged into a second war with Moscow. Abkhazia and South Ossetia had politically seceded from Georgia but were desperately poor and isolated, as was Transdniestria, the breakaway province of Moldova.[6]

If Nagorny Karabakh was the least miserable of the five breakaway regions, that was mainly because its declaration of independence was basically a smoke screen. On an everyday level, Karabakh had become a province of Armenia. Karabakh Armenians were entitled to carry Armenian passports. Its currency was the Armenian dram. The budget was supported by free credits from the Armenian Finance Ministry. Yet internationally, Nagorny Karabakh remained as much an outlaw as Chechnya. None of its laws or institutions were valid outside its own borders, and no foreign diplomats, apart from peace negotiators, set foot there. That was virtually an incitement to become a rogue state. There were plenty of rumors, hard to verify but easy to credit, that Karabakh was exploiting its status as an international black hole. Military attachés speculated whether extra Russian weaponry, which exceeded its quota limits in the Conventional Forces in Europe treaty was being stored there. The Azerbaijanis asserted that the province was a transit route for drug smuggling. When the Kurdish leader Abdullah Öcalan was on the run, there were rumors that he was heading for Karabakh. The rumors were not true, but logically it was one place where he could have sheltered from the long reach of international law.

Whose fault is all this? The Karabakhis', naturally, but perhaps ours as well. International isolation only helps create a siege mentality and leaves the field clear to those, especially in the Armenian Diaspora, who want to invest in the myth of Nagorny Karabakh rather than the reality.

"Excuse me for saying this, Tom," said Valery. "But I think that we are fools and the Azerbaijanis are fools."

Valery drove me around Karabakh in his coffee-brown Lada taxi. He was generous and stoical and went at speeds of such sedative slowness that we had plenty of time to admire the beauty of the forests and talk over many topics. Valery had worked in Baku, had Azerbaijani friends, and had only the warmest memories of communal life in Soviet times. We had a running joke that if we just nipped across the front line, we could be in Baku in four hours' time, ready for an evening out by the Caspian Sea. He had a favorite cassette in his car of Azerbaijani music that was so ancient and overused that the singer was reduced to a strangled moan.

Valery did not want to return to rule by Azerbaijan, but he would gladly have put the clock back and returned to Soviet days, when everybody belonged to the larger state and rubbed along fine. As far as he was concerned, the present situation was a big mess that was beyond the scope of little people like him to see a way out of. We were on our way to the town of Martakert with a couple of Armenian friends. The person we had come to see was thirty years younger than Valery but shared his fatalistic lack of enmity toward the Azerbaijanis.

At the guard post of the army base in Martakert, Ruben, a long, lanky young conscript, aged about nineteen, emerged and walked over to us. He came from Yerevan and was doing his military service here on the Karabakh front line. The fact that Armenian conscripts serve in Nagorny Karabakh underscores how completely the two territories are united. We gave Ruben a meal in a little café just outside the base. We had brought him some letters and money from his family in Armenia, as well as a large carton of cigarettes to help ease slightly the almost lethal boredom of guard duty. The soldiers were paid between one and two thousand drams (approximately two to four dollars) a month; they had no holidays and had almost nothing to eat. They mainly used their weapons for shooting snakes or stray dogs, which they barbecued and ate.

Ruben told us that at the front line there was a spot where the trenches on either side were only thirty or forty meters apart. When the officers were not around, the Armenian conscripts would contact their Azerbaijani counterparts. They would fire in the air or shout "Mullah!" or the Azerbaijanis would shout out "Vazgen!" Then, just as on the Western Front at Christmas 1914, they would meet in the middle, in no-man's-land. What did they talk about? "We just meet, exchange cigarettes, and tell each other, 'We are not enemies, we are all the same, we are friends.'" Valery approved.

As we were waiting for Ruben, the conscript at the guard post, a stocky woman with short-cropped hair and wearing combat fatigues looked us up and down and said, "Hello!" in a West-Coast American accent. Later on we called on Ani, Martakert's only American resident. Ani talked nonstop, evidently glad of some English-speaking company. She lived in a one-story house with simple wooden floors and a metal bedstead. Water came from a well and heat from a wood-burning stove. She said she had been burgled so many times she had lost count.

The Armenian Diaspora has developed a passionate interest in Nagorny Karabakh. The more reports have reached them of corruption and bad government in Armenia, the more foreign Armenians have projected their hopes and ideals onto Karabakh. They have been instrumental in persuading the U.S. Congress to vote twenty million dollars of aid to the province. There are schools, clinics, and water pumps funded by patrons in Watertown or Beirut. The tarmac road from Armenia to Karabakh, complete with signs, barriers, and white lines, is by far the best road in the Caucasus; it cost ten million dollars, raised entirely by the Diaspora-funded "Hayastan Fund." Karabakh has also been the major recipient of aid and propaganda support from Christian Solidarity Worldwide and its president, a British peer, Baroness Cox of Queensbury.

All of these friends of Karabakh have done good work pulling people out of poverty, helping children, and tending the sick. But their notions of Nagorny Karabakh as a beleaguered outpost of brave besieged Christians were hard to take. After all, they encouraged the Karabakhis to take a hard line in the dispute with Azerbaijan, without having to face the consequences of that. Perhaps they saw in Nagorny Karabakh somewhere they could begin again in Year Zero, a Turk-free zone. Valery and his Azerbaijani music tape and friends in Baku didn't quite fit the picture. Nor did Ruben swapping cigarettes with Azerbaijani soldiers on the front line.

Nor, as it turned out, did many of Ani's neighbors in Martakert. It was to Ani's credit that she was one of only about a half dozen Armenian Americans who actually had the courage to follow through on their convictions and come to live in Karabakh. The reality had made her an Armenian Don Quixote. Hers was a story of a quest to bring her notions of Armenian solidarity to an idealized place, only for them to collide against the reality of a post-Soviet Armenian province with a resounding crash.

Why had Ani come to Karabakh? we asked. "I saw this as a continuation of the Genocide" she replied. She had come to Martakert eight years before as a volunteer, invited by Monte Melkonian, a fellow student in Berkeley. "Never seen a war, never seen a funeral, never seen a dead body," she rattled out. She proudly showed us her cross, made out of two bullets and given to her by the family of a dead comrade. "One of my friends was very angry and told me to cut it off," she said, "but I told her, 'God is also a freedom fighter.'"

Ani's cottage was a picture gallery of her endeavors for the Armenian cause. She pulled out photographs of demonstrations she had helped organize to get the world to recognize the Armenian Genocide. And there she was, going round Kenyan villages with her traveling exhibition of the Genocide. She had tried, without much success, to get Armenians to reach out to Native Americans and other oppressed peoples. "I said in New York on 24 April [Genocide Day], we should invite Native Americans to join the ceremony with us. Because they lost their ancestral homelands, so did the Armenians."

Ani was a feminist and the only woman who drove in Martakert. She tried to teach girls painting and photography, but many parents would not allow it. The police, the priest, and the local authorities all disapproved of her. She was having a serious running battle with the army base. She worked there as a private individual after having been dismissed from the army and was engaged in a sexual harassment court case against one commander. According to Ani, there were a lot of problems with rape and attempted rape. The other running battle was to stop the aid from abroad from being stolen. Much of the aid received from the Diaspora was being siphoned off or going to the families of those who handled it. "I am helping hand out aid," Ani said. "Americans send me clothes and shoes and they know I have no relatives here."

I wondered if Ani would stick it out in Martakert, trying to realize her dream of Nagorny Karabakh, which only persisted in defying her and living by its own rules. I guessed she would probably give up eventually and head home. "If they don't like you, decide you're not on their side, they close doors and they want to get rid of you," she said wearily. "I can live here all my life and I still won't be accepted." This strange place, by turns attractive and unwelcoming, has embarked on a strange future all its own.

# 17

# 1994–2001

## No War, No Peace

### ALIEV'S STABILITY

In May 1994, both Armenia and Azerbaijan entered a state of frozen conflict, in which mass violence had ended but the political dispute was unresolved. Armenia spent the next few years in continuous political turbulence; Azerbaijan, unable to develop peacefully, was condemned to the suffocating order imposed by Heidar Aliev.

President Aliev used the end of fighting to begin stamping his control on Azerbaijan. He gradually cleared the field of actual or would-be opponents, beginning with the army. In August 1994, a group of army commanders, including the former defense minister Rahim Gaziev and the Popular Front commander Arif Pashayev, were put on trial for allegedly having surrendered Shusha to the Armenians two years before.

In October 1994, the president was in New York when he heard that assassins had killed the deputy speaker of parliament, Afiyettin Jalilov, and that elements of the paramilitary police force, the OPON (successor to the OMON), were in revolt. Aliev hurried back to Baku, where, with theatrical suddenness, he turned on Prime Minister Suret Husseinov and accused him of plotting to seize power. Husseinov fled to Russia to join Gaziev, who had mysteriously escaped from prison. In Moscow, the two men revealed where their deep loyalties lay by declaring support for the former president Mutalibov. Later both men were extradited to Azerbaijan and given long prison sentences.

Having dealt with the pro-Russian opposition, Aliev turned on a different set of enemies. In March 1995, the OPON leader, Rovshan Javadov, who had been cleared of involvement in the previous coup attempt, seized a barracks in Baku and refused calls to disarm. Aliev sent in government troops to quell the rebellion. Dozens of men were killed, including Javadov, who died of blood loss on his way to hospital. The shadowy backers of this uprising were never identified but appear to have included rogue elements of the Turkish security establishment and members of the "Gray Wolves" Bozkurt movement. Among those arrested and jailed this time was the local Bozkurt leader and former interior minister, Iskender Hamidov.

By now Aliev had acquired a priceless strategic card to play in his drive to stabilize his country in Azerbaijan's oil resources. In 1994, some experts began to predict another Baku oil boom. Some initial predictions that the Caspian Sea could be a new Persian Gulf were wildly optimistic, but more sober assessments suggested that it could at least become a second North Sea and eventually provide as much as 5 percent of world oil output.

In 1993, shortly before he was overthrown, Azerbaijan's then president, Abulfaz Elchibey, had been negotiating contracts with Western companies to develop Caspian oil fields. The talks resumed under Aliev but were hampered by demands for bribes by Azerbaijani officials (one reportedly asked BP [British Petroleum] for a 360-million-dollar down payment in return for a signature on the contract). In the autumn of 1994, the government eventually signed a contract to develop three oil fields with a consortium of companies that had joined together to form the Azerbaijan International Operating Company (AIOC). The deal was estimated to be worth eight billion dollars and was dubbed the "contract of the century."

The Azerbaijani president worked on building a broad international coalition of support for the new oil projects. Initially, Russia was central to his plans. He assumed that the oil would flow through Russian pipelines and the Russian oil company Lukoil was given a 10 percent stake in the AIOC consortium. However the lion's share of the consortium belonged to Western companies, especially BP and Amoco, who began to change Aliev's political agenda. At American insistence, Aliev had to withdraw an offer of a 5 percent stake in the AIOC to the Iranians.

The AIOC was a success. Perhaps the high point of Aliev's presidency came in November 1997, when, observed by guests from all over the world, the first "early oil" began to flow from the Chiraq field to the Georgian Black Sea port of Supsa. The ceremony, sending oil to Georgia rather than Russia, also marked Aliev's full embrace of the West. Three months before, he had made a highly successful visit to Washington, where the Brezhnev-era veteran was feted by such former Cold Warriors as Zbigniew Brzezinski and Henry Kissinger. A new goal had been identified to cement this relationship: a main export pipeline running from Baku to the Turkish Mediterranean port of Ceyhan, to be completed in 2004. From 1997, the U.S. government began to give the Baku-Ceyhan project strong political support, despite the misgivings of some oil companies that its commercial viability was not proven. The pipeline project became a symbol of Washington's desire to link Azerbaijan and Georgia to the West via Turkey and to contain both Russia and Iran. By doing so, it polarized Armenia and Azerbaijan in a new way, pulling Azerbaijan closer into Washington's orbit and pushing Armenia further into alliance with Russia and Iran.

## MEDIATING RIVALS

Although the May 1994 cease-fire agreement in Nagorny Karabakh held, no international force was deployed to monitor the front line and no political agreement followed. The most the mediators could achieve was a renewed agreement by the military leaders of Armenia, Azerbaijan, and Karabakh on 26 July—putting their signatures to the same piece of paper for the first time—to uphold the cease-fire indefinitely.

Both sides slowly fortified their defenses, turning the front line into one of the most inpregnable borders in the world. For the whole length of the front outside Nagorny Karabakh, there was not even a telephone line between the opposing commanders, mainly because the Azerbaijanis feared that even this level of contact would give legitimacy to a force occupying its lands. Several dozen soldiers a year continued to die on both sides, although they were as much the victims of mines or accidents as of enemy fire. A gradual easing of tension was reported over time, however. In 2000, the Armenian defense minister Serzh Sarkisian reported that the number of Armenians killed by sniping across the line had fallen to eight that year, down from thirty-three in 1998. The figures were doubtless similar on the other side.[1]

Speaking six years after the cease-fire agreement, one of the veteran negotiators, Armenian Foreign Minister Vartan Oskanian, regretted that chances were missed in 1994:

That momentum was not utilized. So once that was not utilized, with the passing of time, some of the realities on the ground suddenly

began to be liabilities. It was much easier to return the occupied territories two months after the cease-fire than it is today. It was much easier to lift the blockade for Azerbaijan right after the cease-fire than certainly it is today. And the same applies for all the other elements.[2]

A central reason for the lack of progress was the fact that Azerbaijan feared the intentions of the leading negotiator, Russia. After the
cease-fire, Azerbaijan rejected Grachev's proposed Russian-led peacekeeping force. With Azerbaijan's support, the Western diplomats of the
Minsk Group, none of whom were invited to Grachev's May 1994 meeting in Moscow, argued that any peacekeeping force had to be multinational. The trouble was that the CSCE lacked the mechanisms to set up
such a force. Moreover, the West was heavily preoccupied with Bosnia,
and it was unlikely that Western countries would wish to commit
troops to police an even more remote conflict zone.

As a result, in 1994 relations between Russia and the Westerners
in the Minsk Group, hit a new low. The Russians accused the Minsk
Group of trying to sabotage the only serious peace initiative on offer;
the Westerners accused the Russians of trying to wreck the formation of
a broader-based alternative plan.

Each side worked against the other. The Russian mediator, Vladimir Kazimirov, says that before the cease-fire the Swedes twice scheduled meetings of the Minsk Group, in Paris and Prague, that clashed
with CIS meetings in Moscow at which the Russians were intending to
hold peace talks. He saw this as a direct attempt to undermine the Russian mediation track. The quarrel worsened. The Minsk Group mediators complained that the Russians had convened talks in Moscow for 8
September without informing them. For their part, the Russians objected that the CSCE had deliberately put forward a Minsk Group meeting in Vienna to 12 September, when they were planning more negotiations in Moscow. The Russians did not send a representative to the Vienna meeting.[3] These disputes led the Armenian president, Levon
Ter-Petrosian, to grumble that "the impression is created that the mediating countries and international organizations are not interested so
much in settling the conflict, as in settling their own accounts and relationships, which are unconnected with it."[4]

The two sides struggled toward a compromise arrangement to be
approved at the CSCE summit in Budapest in December 1994. The plan
was to give the organization a mandate to create its first-ever interna-

tional peacekeeping force, specifically for Nagorny Karabakh, in which the Russians would play a major, but not an exclusive, part.

Azerbaijan seized this opportunity. The Russians had invited both presidents to come to Moscow before the Budapest meeting. The Azerbaijanis sent their deputy foreign minister, Tofik Zulfugarov, ahead to elucidate what the agenda of the Moscow talks was to be. Zulfugarov says that he concluded the Russians were trying to undermine the coming agreement in Budapest. Aliev therefore pleaded illness and did not come to Moscow, causing Ter-Petrosian to stay away as well. According to Zulfugarov: "If they had flown to Budapest from [Moscow], no decision on deploying an international force would have been worked out."[5]

At the Budapest summit on 5–6 December 1994, the CSCE turned itself into the Organization for Security and Cooperation in Europe, the OSCE. Aside from Nagorny Karabakh, relations between Russia and the West were good, and Western leaders reaffirmed their support for President Yeltsin just as he was fatefully preparing to send his army into Chechnya. Over Karabakh, the OSCE acknowledged Russia's special role in the dispute by promoting it to become one of two cochairs of the Minsk Group, alongside Sweden. The OSCE then secured a mandate for its new peacekeeping force. There would be three thousand men, with no single country providing more than 30 percent of the total, but the force would be deployed only with the UN's approval and when a political settlement was reached.[6]

In fact, a political settlement looked as remote as ever. The two sides had fundamental disagreements on several key issues. The Armenians were ready in principle to see the return of six regions they occupied outside Nagorny Karabakh—Aghdam, Fizuli, Jebrail, Kelbajar, Kubatly, and Zengelan—if they had satisfaction on other issues. But they said that their continued possession of Shusha, inside Nagorny Karabakh, and Lachin, giving them a land bridge to Armenia, was non-negotiable. For Azerbaijan, the loss of both regions was unacceptable. Azerbaijan also still refused to hold direct talks with the Karabakh Armenians.

The most vexing problem remained the future status of Nagorny Karabakh itself. A resolution of the issue had to reconcile the competing claims of Azerbaijan's territorial integrity and Karabakh's self-determination (or, in blunter language, de facto secession). In 1995, a second channel of negotiations was set up between the special advisers of the

Armenian and Azerbaijani presidents, Gerard Libaridian and Vafa Guluzade. They began to meet informally every month to work on the status question in particular and made substantial progress.

In December 1996, the OSCE held another summit, in Lisbon,
which strengthened the Azerbaijani position. The OSCE decided to set
out three broad principles for the resolution of the dispute. One of them
was an affirmation of the territorial integrity of Azerbaijan, including
Nagorny Karabakh. Armenia objected that this predetermined the status of Nagorny Karabakh. The Armenians ended up isolated and veto-
ing the inclusion of the principles in the summit's final communiqué.
The Lisbon summit effectively ended the Guluzade-Libaridian negotiating track.

## A KARABAKHI TAKEOVER

After the 1994 cease-fire agreement, Armenia proper and the de facto
separatist statelet of Nagorny Karabakh began to knit themselves together. Construction work started on a sixty-four-kilometer road linking the Armenian town of Goris with Stepanakert, replacing the old
road, whose appalling condition had made travel between Nagorny
Karabakh and Armenia almost impossible in Soviet times. The new
highway, which took five years to build, cost ten million dollars, which
was raised by the Armenian Diaspora. When the finished product—
broad and asphalted, with white lines, road signs, and crash barriers—
was completed in 1999, it was a defiant symbol of the marriage of Armenia and Karabakh. The Diaspora also helped rebuild Karabakh's
shattered infrastructure and the semidestroyed town of Stepanakert.
The reconstructed Armenian towns and villages were a striking contrast to what were known as Karabakh's "green villages," once inhabited by Azerbaijanis but now pillaged and sliding into ruin.

Nagorny Karabakh's military success was hailed by Armenians as
a rare and historic victory. This gave Karabakh and its leaders a heroic
reputation and great influence in Armenia. Robert Kocharian, the head
of the State Defense Committee, became Nagorny Karabakh's first
"president" in December 1994 after a vote in the local parliament. He
was reelected, by popular vote, in November 1996. In May 1994, the
Karabakhi military leader, Samvel Babayan, was made a major-general
in the Armenian army and began to gather economic and political

power beyond Karabakh itself. He helped form a parliamentary party named "Right and Accord" to fight the 1999 parliamentary elections in Armenia. Babayan was heard to joke that if he did not like what the Armenian government was up to, he would move his tanks on Yerevan.

The army was now the most powerful institution in Armenia. Officially, it consumed 8 to 9 percent of the GDP; unofficially, it probably received much more than that. It formed the backbone of the "Karabakh Party," which contained not only Karabakhis. The chief generalissimo was Vazgen Sarkisian, Armenia's charismatic first defense minister, most prominent military leader, and emerging feudal baron. In 1993, he founded the Yerkrapah veterans movement, which took over large areas of the economy.

The "Karabakh Party" was one wing of the Armenian ruling elite. The other comprised Levon Ter-Petrosian's Armenian National Movement (ANM), which had become a ruling party that monopolized political life in the country. In 1994–1995 Ter-Petrosian moved to suppress the only other party with strong grassroots support in the country, the nationalist Dashnaktsutiun. He alleged that it was harboring a secret terrorist organization named Dro. The Dashnaktsutiun was suspended and the ban was lifted only after the 1995 parliamentary elections.

In September 1996, Ter-Petrosian stood for reelection. His public support had ebbed. Tens of thousands of professionals were emigrating, and the country was desperately poor. Disillusionment with the ruling elite was strong. Ter-Petrosian's former comrade, now turned bitter political rival, Vazgen Manukian, capitalized on the popular mood and his support surged after three other presidential candidates stood down in his favor. At public rallies, Manukian outshone Ter-Petrosian, who came across as remote.

On polling day, 22 September, most international observers concluded that Ter-Petrosian had failed to win the first round of the election outright. However, the Central Electoral Commission declared him the winner, with 52 percent of the vote. Manukian's supporters protested and took the parliament building by storm, beating up the speaker and deputy speaker. Ter-Petrosian moved tanks on to the streets of Yerevan and had several opposition figures detained. The observers declared that the polls had been marred by serious irregularities—saying in effect, that Ter-Petrosian's election was illegitimate.

The shabby manner in which Ter-Petrosian was reelected tarnished his reputation and put him in the debt of his security ministers, who had helped him fend off Vazgen Manukian. At the height of the crisis, Defense Minister Vazgen Sarkisian famously blurted out: "Even if they [the opposition] win 100 percent of the votes, neither the army nor the National Security Service, nor the Ministry of the Interior would recognize such political leaders."[7]

The president tried to bolster his authority by appointing as his new prime minister Armen Sarkisian, Armenia's ambassador in London and a man with an honest reputation. But in March 1998, Sarkisian fell ill and was forced to step down. Considering possible successors for Sarkisian, Ter-Petrosian hit on the candidature of another popular figure, Robert Kocharian. Ter-Petrosian commented: "I thought that by being here, as prime minister of Armenia, Robert would understand Armenia, would understand what Karabakh represents from the point of view of Armenia."[8] In other words, if Kocharian was put in charge of the Armenian economy, he would get firsthand experience of how Armenia was suffering from the nonresolution of the Karabakh dispute.

## THE FALL OF TER-PETROSIAN

In 1997, the Minsk Group mediators were more coordinated and preparing for a new push to solve the Karabakh dispute. At the Lisbon summit in December 1996, France had been nominated to join Russia as cochair of the Minsk Group. Azerbaijan objected on the grounds that France, with its large Armenian community, was biased toward Armenia. In February 1997, a compromise was reached whereby the United States became a third cochair of the Minsk Group, alongside Russia and France.

The presence of three heavyweights in the Minsk Group gave the peace process new impetus, and in May 1997 the cochairs presented a new comprehensive plan. The Karabakh Armenians had reservations, but the leaders of both Armenia and Azerbaijan were positive. Speaking in Washington, President Aliev made an important public concession when he declared that Azerbaijan should not expect the immediate return of Lachin and Shusha. In September 1997, the Minsk Group mediators presented a modified "step-by-step" version of the plan, in which security issues for Nagorny Karabakh were included in a first phase. It was stated that following Armenian withdrawal from the occupied territories and the demilitarization of Karabakh, the parties would agree to continue negotiating in order "to speedily attain an all-encompassing regulation of all other aspects of the conflict, including the political aspect, which includes defining the status of Na-gorno-Karabakh and resolving the problem of Lachin, Shusha and Shaumian."[9]

Ter-Petrosian was enthusiastic about the plan he was shown. He says that earlier that year he had received a gloomy prognosis from the Armenian Transport Ministry and the World Bank on how the Armenian economy was coping with the Azerbaijani and Turkish "blockade." He concluded that transport costs were prohibitively high and that sustained economic growth was unattainable. He also doubted the ability of the Armenian Diaspora to rescue the economy—a view that brought him into conflict with his prime minister and defense minister. Ter-Petrosian says:

> We were getting ten million dollars from the Diaspora every year. That's all. Robert [Kocharian] and Vazgen Sarkisian said that if we worked well, we could get 450 million dollars a year. I showed them that that was impossible. On those grounds, analyzing all this, I concluded that if we didn't solve the Karabakh question, it would be bad for both Armenia and Karabakh. Time was playing against us.

On 26 September 1997, Ter-Petrosian used his first major press conference in five years to set out his arguments in favor of compromise on Nagorny Karabakh. He said the international community would never recognize Karabakh's independence or its unification with Armenia, and the current situation was also unacceptable. "I do not consider a maintenance of the status quo realistic," he said. "I concede that we could insist on holding out for six months or a year, but in the end the international community's cup of patience will overflow." The president offered the example of the Bosnian Serbs, who had to settle for less in the Dayton agreement, after holding out for more. The only answer, he concluded, was to agree to a step-by-step solution to the dispute, which did not betray the Karabakh Armenians' fundamental interests.[10]

Ter-Petrosian's remarks raised a storm of allegations that he was betraying Karabakh. The president responded on 1 November with a newspaper article entitled "War or Peace? Time to be Thoughtful." His tone was dry and sarcastic as he rebutted his critics point by point. Ter-Petrosian wrote that only six people in Armenia and Nagorny

Karabakh understood the complexities of the dispute and accused his opponents of being enslaved to myths.

Public dismay in Armenia was to be anticipated. More worrying for Ter-Petrosian was that the Karabakh Armenian authorities were also indignant. On 6 November, the Nagorny Karabakh "Foreign Ministry" issued an unprecedented statement in which it disputed several of Ter-Petrosian's points. Arkady Gukasian, who had just been elected "president" of Karabakh in succession to Kocharian, spelled out his dissent in an interview on 7 October. He rejected the Minsk Group's latest proposals and said that "however badly the people live, there are holy things, there are positions that they will never surrender under any circumstances." And Gukasian also had words of warning for Ter-Petrosian:

> It has been said that Armenia will agree to any decision taken by Nagorny Karabakh. So in that sense our disagreements [with Yerevan] are disturbing, they are bad. But if these disagreements worsen, I think Armenia should keep its word and leave the decision to Karabakh. We ourselves ought to take the decision that we think necessary.[11]

The quarrel came to a head in the new year of 1998. Gukasian attended a meeting of Armenia's Security Council on 7–8 January, when Kocharian and the interior and defense ministers, Serzh and Vazgen Sarkisian, all spoke out against the Minsk Group plan. The ruling party began to crumble around Ter-Petrosian. His foreign minister was forced to resign. Facing a "palace coup" from his closest ministers, Ter-Petrosian decided to bow to the inevitable. On 3 February 1998, he announced his resignation.

Ter-Petrosian was the third president to lose office, wholly or partly as a result of the Nagorny Karabakh conflict, following in the steps of Azerbaijan's Ayaz Mutalibov and Abulfaz Elchibey. In his case, his popular legitimacy had already been undermined, perhaps fatally, by his falsification of the 1996 presidential election results. He appeared distant and had lost the popular authority needed to mobilize Armenian popular opinion behind a peace plan. Most important, Ter-Petrosian had underestimated the determination and strength of feeling of the "Karabakh Party" inside his administration, which now had a leader in Robert Kocharian, the man he himself had brought to Yerevan. A gulf in attitudes had opened between the president, a Yerevan intellectual, whose political career had been devoted to Armenia's independence and economic development, and those who had physically fought a war for Nagorny Karabakh. Serzh Sarkisian puts the position of his rejectionist camp in stark terms:

> Do you think we weren't fed up with war? That we didn't want to live and develop peacefully? . . . But we couldn't in actual fact make these compromises. I understand that Levon was in charge of all this. I understand that he was president. But we had directly led these lads into battle. I lost almost all my friends. Almost all. I lost my nephew. He came with his father at the age of eighteen to help me.[12]

## A COLD PEACE

In 1998, following Ter-Petrosian's downfall, a new chilly phase of cold peace settled between Armenia and Azerbaijan. Their lack of dialogue reflected an increased polarity between Russia and the West. Azerbaijan had strengthened its ties with the United States and signed a military cooperation treaty with Turkey, while the Russian-Armenian alliance remained strong. The Russian military maintained a strong presence in Armenia, and there seemed to be little incentive for the parties to want a peace settlement in Karabakh. In 1995, the Armenians had agreed to keep the Russian base at Gyumri for a further twenty-five years. This was followed by the comprehensive "Treaty on Friendship, Cooperation and Mutual Assistance" in 1997 between the two countries.

Yet Russia's outlook was also changing, and the Russian military no longer had a monopoly on policy related to the Caucasus. Yeltsin began his chaotic second term as president in the summer of 1996 by sacking his longtime defense minister, Pavel Grachev, putting an end to the career of the Russian military's chief interventionist in the Caucasus. A month later, the new Russian foreign minister, Yevgeny Primakov, relieved Russia's longtime envoy for Karabakh, Vladimir Kazimirov, of his job and sent him to be Moscow's ambassador to Costa Rica. Primakov took a greater interest in the Caucasus than his predecessor, Andrei Kozyrev. He clearly hoped to counter Western influence in the region, but by diplomatic rather than military means. A third group of Russian actors, oil companies such as Lukoil, were developing their own agenda, which was to get as big a stake as possible in Caspian Sea oil projects.

On 30 March 1998, Robert Kocharian completed the takeover of the "Karabakh Party" and was elected president of Armenia. His accession to power was bumpier than anticipated. He won a runoff vote against an unexpectedly strong candidate, the former first secretary of the Communist Party, Karen Demirchian. Demirchian had kept a low profile for ten years since having been sacked in 1988 and when he reemerged to run for president, Armenians recalled his years in office in the 1970s with fondness. On the campaign trail the former Party boss showed a talent for saying very little with great charm worthy of Ronald Reagan. It was also indicative that he barely mentioned Nagorny Karabakh and concentrated on domestic issues. Nonetheless, Kocharian's advantages—his incumbency, continuing popularity, the support of the state media, as well as alleged voting fraud—ensured his victory.

Kocharian had been elected with the support of the nationalist Dashnak Party, which he had unbanned. Its influence was palpable in a new tougher tone in the public language on Karabakh. In June 1998, the new foreign minister, Vartan Oskanian, accused Azerbaijan of intransigence and stated that if nothing changed in the next few years, Armenia might take steps to annex Nagorny Karabakh. Facing strong condemnation abroad, Oskanian retreated and said that his words had been misunderstood.

In Azerbaijan, Aliev had now achieved strong—his opponents would say deadening—stability. He felt sufficiently secure to tolerate the return of the deposed president, Abulfaz Elchibey, from internal exile to Baku at the end of 1997. Elchibey failed to rally a broad-based opposition around himself and died of cancer in August 2000.

In October 1998, Aliev was reelected president with a predictably vast majority, defeating the veteran nationalist Etibar Mamedov. Aliev's second term was quieter than the first, but gradually his firm grip on power appeared to loosen. One reason was economic. In 1999, predictions for the promised oil boom were being scaled back. The oil price fell, and prospectors were disappointed with their drilling in the Caspian. Several foreign companies and consortia pulled out of Azerbaijan, many citing systematic corruption as a major problem. No palpable benefits of the oil economy appeared to have fed through to the wider population. The United Nations Development Program reported that

"the country's progress in translating economic growth into human development has been very limited" and that the non-oil sectors of the
economy were stagnating.[13]

In January 1999, the seventy-five-year-old Aliev abruptly flew to
Ankara for a health checkup and three months later underwent heart
bypass surgery in Cleveland, Ohio. This reminder of the president's
mortality reminded everyone that he did not have an impressive heir
apparent. One previous candidate, the former parliamentary speaker
Rasul Guliev, had gone into exile in the United States in 1996 and joined
the list of Aliev's enemies. The most obvious heir, the president's son
Ilham Aliev, who was deputy head of the state oil company SOCAR,
lacked gravitas and political experience.


## NEW MEDIATION . . .

In April 1999, both Aliev and Kocharian attended the summit in Washington marking the fiftieth anniversary of the founding of NATO. With
the Georgian president, Eduard Shevardnadze, they had an informal
meeting with U.S. Secretary of State Madeleine Albright in her office.
Albright left Kocharian and Aliev together to talk one-on-one. Thus, almost by accident, a new kind of dialogue began. The two men had virtually not seen each other since their secret wartime discussions in
Moscow in 1993. They found there was a common base of understanding between them. Both were hard, lonely leaders who were more comfortable with the format of confidential top-level talks. As a former
Komsomol official from Stepanakert, Kocharian had an almost filial respect for Aliev, who was more than thirty years older. Over the next two
years they met fifteen times or so.

The fact that Kocharian came from Karabakh reduced the problem
of Nagorny Karabakh's representation in the talks: in practice, he represented the Karabakh Armenians as well. It was clear that for Kocharian, Karabakh's de facto independence was paramount. This was one
reason that at one of their early meetings the two men appear to have
revived what had been called the "Goble Plan." The project was
named after a former U.S. State Department specialist on the Caucasus, Paul Goble, who had written a briefing paper in 1992 in which
he proposed the idea of a territorial exchange to resolve the Karabakh
dispute. Basically, in return for Armenia's being given the "Lachin

corridor" linking it to Nagorny Karabakh, Azerbaijan would receive a land corridor across Armenia's southern Meghri region connecting it with Nakhichevan.[14]

The idea had the virtue of simplicity and would also give Aliev a substantial prize to brandish before the Azerbaijani public when he announced other painful and unpopular concessions. Yet it did not escape notice that a plan that suited both Nakhichevan and Karabakh was being discussed by men who were natives of the two regions involved. Many in the Azerbaijani elite rejected the plan on offer in 1999 as meaning a surrender of Karabakh. In October 1999, three of Aliev's top aides all resigned, apparently over this issue, depriving him of his most experienced advisers. They were his long-term foreign affairs aide, Vafa Guluzade; the head of his secretariat, Eldar Namazov; and his foreign minister, Tofik Zulfugarov.

In Armenia, the "Goble Plan" was even more controversial because giving up Meghri would mean the loss of Armenia's southern border with its friendliest neighbor, Iran. Kocharian, a Karabakhi, would be vulnerable to the charge that he was selling land of the Republic of Armenia to secure the future of Nagorny Karabakh. That was why, to have any hope of selling the plan, Kocharian badly needed the support of Defense Minister Vazgen Sarkisian, who in the summer of 1999 had become the most powerful man in Armenia.

In May 1999, Vazgen Sarkisian's Republican Party, based on the Yerkrapah movement, won a resounding victory in Armenia's parliamentary elections. It had formed a strong alliance with Karen Demirchian's People's Party, and together they supplanted the former ruling party, the ANM, which failed to win any seats at all. After the elections, Kocharian made Sarkisian Armenia's prime minister, and Karen Demirchian became speaker of parliament.

It seems that over the next few months, Sarkisian, who had led the palace coup to oust Ter-Petrosian, was gradually persuaded of the advantages of a peace deal on Karabakh. The new prime minister made a trip to the United States, during which he was told that financial support from the Diaspora was decreasing and could not be relied on to sustain Armenia. On 11 October, Aliev and Kocharian met for two hours on the border between Nakhichevan and Armenia—their fifth meeting in six months. The Azerbaijanis barbecued a sheep and the mood was friendly. There were hopes that some kind of framework declaration on

Nagorny Karabakh could be made at the coming OSCE summit in Istanbul in November.

## . . . AND MASSACRES

On 27 October 1999, U.S. Deputy Secretary of State Strobe Talbott visited Yerevan en route to Istanbul. He held talks with Kocharian and Vazgen Sarkisian before heading to the airport. Sarkisian then crossed to the Armenian parliament to answer government questions. Shortly after 5:00 P.M., as the session was winding up, a man wearing a long raincoat and carrying a machine gun burst into the chamber through one of the side doors. He immediately opened fire on the front row of seats, where Vazgen Sarkisian was sitting. Bullets flew across the chamber and people threw themselves to the floor. Another assailant, the leader of the gang, entered and fired at the podium, where speaker Karen Demirchian lay. Three more of the gang followed their comrades. Within a few minutes eight men, including Sarkisian and Demirchian, were dead and eight others were wounded.

The leader of the gang, a former journalist named Nairi Hunanian, announced that he was taking power from the "blood-suckers" who were ruling Armenia. The assailants barricaded themselves in the chamber; they seemed, witnesses said, to be waiting for something to happen. Troops surrounded the parliament building and President Kocharian arrived. Ever the hands-on leader and contrary to advice, Kocharian negotiated personally with the attackers. By morning, they appeared to be satisfied with an offer to speak on television and to be guaranteed a fair trial. Around 10:30 A.M. the five men were driven to jail.[15]

The shootings devastated the Armenian political landscape, depriving the country of its two biggest political heavyweights. The immediate cause of the attack was the inadequate security in the Armenian parliament. Its deeper causes were highly controversial. Nairi Hunanian was a prominent extremist who had been expelled from the Dashnaktsutiun Party in 1992. He was known to have a grudge against Vazgen Sarkisian—although it later transpired that his brother Karen may have killed Sarkisian against Nairi's orders. Most observers assumed that the gang was not acting on its own but as a weapon in the hands of others. Yet it was far from clear who might have planned the killings.

One line of speculation was that the attackers had been instructed to prevent an imminent breakthrough on Nagorny Karabakh by getting rid of Sarkisian, who was now prepared to support a peace deal. The timing of the killings, just after Strobe Talbott had met Sarkisian, was certainly very striking. Talbott was later quoted as saying that the two sides were "very, very close" to agreement and called the massacre "a human, political, and geopolitical catastrophe."[16] Yet several other clues suggest that the timing was a coincidence and that the killings probably had a domestic political motive: throughout the all-night vigil in parliament, the Hunanian brothers did not mention Karabakh; if someone had planned to derail the Karabakh peace process, then Sarkisian was not the obvious first target; it was not yet manifest that he had actually signed on to a peace agreement; finally, Sarkisian was a close ally of the Russian security establishment, the most likely suspect for wanting to sabotage a United States–led peace deal.

### KEY WEST AND AFTER

In 1999, the peace process was put on hold while Armenia sorted out its domestic politics. Kocharian faced the anger of the Yerkrapah movement; its accusation was that he had failed to cede the power it had demanded of him as recompense for the loss of Vazgen Sarkisian. It was more than a year before Kocharian had reestablished his authority. The Aliev-Kocharian dialogue resumed in earnest at the end of 2000. By then, the idea of a wholesale territorial exchange had disappeared from the agenda, chiefly because it was deemed unsellable to the public in Armenia. In May 2000, Kocharian said of the plan: "It is not realizable today for reasons that are entirely well known."[17]

Russia's position had also changed. The new Russian president, Vladimir Putin, initiated a more coordinated policy for the Caucasus. While launching a new war in Chechnya and toughening his stance on Georgia, Putin continued the thaw in relations with Azerbaijan. On an official visit to Baku in January 2001, Putin made a symbolic gesture of support for Aliev by presenting him with his 1949 graduation certificate from the KGB academy in Leningrad. It was the first-ever public confirmation that Aliev had even studied in Leningrad.

In 2001 for the first time, the three countries in the Minsk Group, France, Russia, and the United States, appeared to be working in close harmony. The peace process moved up a gear. Aliev and Kocharian had two successful meetings in Paris, chaired by President Jacques Chirac. In what looked like a coordinated move, newspapers in both Armenia and Azerbaijan printed leaked copies of the three Minsk Group peace plans of 1997 and 1998. The leaks were intended to test public opinion on Karabakh and pave the way for a fourth, entirely different, plan. The reaction to the three old plans, especially in Azerbaijan, was overwhelmingly hostile. Almost no one in Baku spoke up in public in support of compromise.

In April 2001, the Armenia-Azerbaijani conflict briefly became a world issue once again, when the U.S. State Department organized five days, in Key West, Florida, of the most high-profile and intensive negotiations ever on the dispute. The new format combined the confidential dialogue of the two presidents with the specialist advice of the Minsk Group negotiators. After the meeting, one of the mediators said they had reached agreement on "80 or 90 percent" of issues.

A follow-up meeting was planned for Switzerland in June, and there was even talk of a peace agreement's being signed by the end of 2001. The two presidents were given time to broaden their consultations at home. In Armenia, the response was low key but hardly encouraging. The Armenian parliament repeated that Karabakh's status was non-negotiable and rejected compromise.

But it was in Azerbaijan that the deal really came unstuck as those to whom Aliev talked firmly opposed some of the concessions Aliev had considered at Key West.

The almost-breakthrough had come, as it had to, in dramatic fashion, with Aliev offering dramatic concessions on the most sensitive issue of all, the status of Nagorny Karabakh. "He was basically offering for it to become part of Armenia," said one official close to the talks. This astonishing offer of surrender of what was to many a sacred truth in Azerbaijan was to be met by a string of concessions from the Armenian side, including a road link across Armenia from Azerbaijan to Nakhichevan, to be policed by international troops, and the right of return of refugees to Shusha. Why this dramatic move on the part of the Azerbaijani president? As one Western diplomat explained it, Aliev was basically a control freak: "He either wants Karabakh back properly or not at all." The last thing the president wanted was a troublesome

Armenian-dominated province, a serpent in the Azerbaijani garden he had spent years tending; better not to have it at all and win concessions from the Armenians on other issues.

But Aliev's attempt to cut the knot was too bold and too cynical for the rest of the Azerbaijani elite. After all, this was from the same leader who talked every year of "celebrating Novruz next year in Khankendi," of a full restoration of Karabakh to Azerbaijani control. The gap between what Aliev was saying in private and saying in public was too wide, and even his limitless guile could not bridge it. Of course, Aliev would never admit that that was what he was thinking—nothing was ever written down on paper.

The trap snapped shut again. When the international mediators visited the region and crossed the Nagorny Karabakh front line on 19 May 2001, the barrier it symbolized seemed as forbidding and unbreachable as ever.

# Conclusion

## Sadakhlo: The Future

"THEY FIGHT, WE don't," said Mukhta, a trader from Azerbaijan, giving his view of war in the Caucasus and locking his Armenian colleague, Ashot, in a tight embrace.

The two black-moustachioed men were standing in front of a sea of ancient box-shaped Soviet-era cars and a heaving crowd of commerce. We were in Sadakhlo, a village on the Georgian-Armenian border—close to the hinge on the map where the three Caucasian republics meet—the site of the largest wholesale market in the southern Caucasus. At the edge of the village stood a line of white and dirty-yellow buses, from Baku, Yerevan, and Nagorny Karabakh. At Sadakhlo, the Azerbaijanis sell food, clothes, and flour from Turkey and Russia and the Armenians sell Iranian products, like the improbably named Barf washing powder. The fact that fruit and vegetables ripen in Armenia later in the year helps both sides. "Soon there will be new carrots from Azerbaijan, then later they will buy ours," explained Ashot. "In summer we sell our tomatoes," added Mukhta. "In autumn, when ours are over, they bring in lots of theirs." Both men said they preferred trading with each other than with the Georgians.

In March 2001, the Armenian finance minister Vartan Khachaturian called for the Sadakhlo market to be closed, declaring that it was the "main point of import of contraband [to Armenia] and a center of corruption." The minister said that three to four hundred million dollars' worth of customs-free goods passed through the market every year, equivalent to the entire budget revenues of Armenia.[1] Ordinary people would retort that Sadakhlo enables them to clothe and feed themselves, where governments have failed in that duty. Perhaps half of the population of Yerevan dresses in Turkish clothes bought at Sadakhlo. The Armenians of Nagorny Karabakh use the market to import Azerchai, their favorite brand of Azerbaijani tea from Soviet times. Another large quantity of the goods traded here ends up in the shops and market stalls of Ganje and northern Azerbaijan.

There is another reason why the market should be kept going: it is a vivid illustration that there is no innate hostility between Armenians and Azerbaijanis. As soon as you enter the territory of neutral Georgia, all "ethnic hatreds" die away. In the old center of the Georgian capital Tbilisi, I visited a carpet shop jointly owned by an Armenian and Azerbaijani, old friends fluent in half a dozen languages, who thought the Karabakh conflict was nonsense. Similar scenes of harmony can be found in Moscow or Tabriz. The cultural divide between the two peoples is far narrower than that between, say, Israelis and Palestinians. Certainly, Mukhta and Ashot had a hundred times more in common with each other than they did with me.

Unfortunately, the closure of the borders makes the kind of friendship enjoyed by Mukhta and Ashot all too rare. Most Armenians and Azerbaijanis have no contact at all with the other country and, since 1994, this mutual alienation has been built into the status quo. Azerbaijan's only lever of pressure is Armenia's isolation, and therefore most Azerbaijani officials reject overtures for dialogue and "normalization" with Armenia as an attempt to tip the situation in Armenia's favor. The Azerbaijani foreign minister Vilayat Guliev said: "Regional cooperation cannot be a means for reaching peace. What cooperation can there be between the aggressor and the state whose territory is occupied?"[2]

The outlook in 2002 is bleak. The Armenian-Azerbaijani conflict may not have been the worst of modern wars, but it has produced one of the worst peaces. In the post-cease-fire situation, misery blankets the region. The most miserable people are surely the half million or so Azerbaijanis expelled from the regions in and around Nagorny Karabakh in 1992–1994. Since then their situation has barely improved. But, in lesser ways, the vast majority of Armenians and Azerbaijani also suffer the results of the conflict. In Armenia, perhaps 80 percent of the population lives in poverty, on less than twenty-five dollars a month.[3] Emigration rates are catastrophic and deprive Armenia of the young, able-bodied, and well-educated citizens it needs most.

Nakhichevan, the isolated province of Azerbaijan, squeezed between Armenia, Iran, and Turkey, is an emblem of everything that is wrong with this situation. Separated from the rest of Azerbaijan, it has been almost entirely cut off from the outside world since 1991, when the

Armenians closed their border—putting Nakhichevan in a double blockade.

Nakhichevan used to be a major junction on the Moscow-Teheran railway line; theoretically, its geographic location, situated between Russia and Iran, Turkey, and Central Asia, could make it a major junction in the greater Middle East. Instead, with its border with Armenia closed, it is the ultimate dead end, as remote as Patagonia. Great rusting trains stand idle in the sidings of the town station. The factories are full of useless Soviet machinery that never found its way to markets.

It is hard to get to Nakhichevan. You must go either by airplane from Baku, from the very far east of Turkey, or via Iran, where the customs authorities levy expensive charges on any vehicle crossing the border. When I flew in at the end of October, the first winter chill was already in the air. In his office, the mayor of Nakhichevan city, Veli Shakhverdiev, flicked the trigger on a heater lit by a gas bottle, demonstrating how people would heat themselves through the next six months. The mayor said he was about to impose tighter electricity rationing on the town because of new energy shortages. All street lamps would go off and shops would lose their electricity supply. Before, the Nakhichevanis used to receive their gas—and most other products— via Armenia, and Yerevan, not Baku, was the nearest metropolis. "I can tell you that our relations with the Armenians were very close, they were excellent," Shakhverdiev said. "I went to university in Moscow and I didn't travel to Moscow once via Baku. I took a bus, it was one hour to Yerevan, then went by plane to Moscow and the same thing on the way back."[4] Unusually for an Azerbaijani official, he spoke up warmly in favor of a peace deal on Karabakh.

Nakhichevan's politics are as dark as its streets. Three courageous locals wanted to talk about harassment, oppression, and censorship. They were worried about being overheard, so we sat outside a café in an unlit square, our conversation dimly illuminated by a flashlight planted on the table. The three told how the thuggish local leader, Vasif Talibov, a relative by marriage of the Azerbaijani president, Heidar Aliev, intimidates anyone who stands in his way. Mysterious assailants had beaten up several opposition candidates running in the parliamentary election campaign. On election day, it came as no surprise to hear that the official poll results, obtained by comprehensive fraud, had delivered a landslide victory to the governing party, New Azerbaijan.

■

At first sight, it may seem extraordinary that such a small dispute has done so much damage. Nagorny Karabakh seemed like a freak cyclone: from its tiny center in 1988, it began to cause destruction over a wide area, throwing up barriers, blocking roads, and turning former neighbors against one another. Yet what happened there stemmed from real structural weaknesses in the politics of the region and has a lot to tell us about how conflicts start.

It is worth restating what the dispute is *not*. Three misconceptions should be rejected. The good news is that as has been shown, this is not a conflict born of "ancient hatreds." Before the end of the nineteenth century, Armenians and Azerbaijanis fought no more often than any other two nationalities in this region. Even after the intercommunal violence of the early twentieth century, the two nationalities have generally gotten along well—and can do so again, as the Sadakhlo market shows.

But another wrong assumption is that like the wars in Abkhazia and Chechnya, for example, the conflict was basically triggered by top-down politics. The evidence shows that, contrary to the consensus in the region, from 1988 the Soviet political leaders were running to keep pace with the dispute, rather than leading it; the fire began below them, spread around them, and helped to incinerate most of them from power—including, arguably, Mikhail Gorbachev. Almost no voices were heard calling for dialogue or compromise. That means that many ordinary people must take their share of responsibility for the bloodshed and Armenian and Azerbaijani grassroots public opinion remains a major force.

Finally, the Armenian-Azerbaijani conflict cannot usefully be reduced to its socioeconomic components. In 1988, both sides began by flouting their own economic interests. They went out on strike, disrupted transport, severed ties with the other community, all in the name of political goals. Moscow's attempts to use socioeconomic incentives to solve the problem, through its viceroy Arkady Volsky, failed. Later on, certainly, weapons traders, profiteers, and warlords began to enrich themselves from the conflict, but they cannot be said to have started it—and socioeconomic palliatives will not be enough to end it.

Uncomfortable as it is for many Western observers to acknowledge, the Nagorny Karabakh conflict makes sense only if we acknowledge that hundreds of thousands of Armenians and Azerbaijanis were driven to act by passionately held ideas about history, identity, and rights. That the vast mass of these ideas was dangerous and delusory does not make them any less sincerely felt. From 1990 and 1991, there were plenty of volunteers prepared to risk their lives for them. The ideas expanded inside the ideological vacuum created by the end of the Soviet Union and were given fresh oxygen by warfare. The darkest of these convictions, the "hate narratives," have taken such deep root that unless they are addressed, nothing can change in Armenia and Azerbaijan.

If I formed one overriding impression from my travels around the south Caucasus, it is that the lines of division run straight through the middle of people. Hateful impulses coexist with conciliatory feelings in the same person. Armenians and Azerbaijanis can be simultaneously enemies and friends. They are torn between aggression and conciliation, personal friendships, and the power of national myths.

The contradictions are there in the topmost figures. The Karabakh-born Armenian Serzh Sarkisian is a hard man, defense minister of Armenia and one of the two most powerful figures in his country, yet he spoke with real affection of former Azerbaijani colleagues with whom he had worked in Soviet times in the Stepanakert Komsomol. "I knew Azeri, I had a lot of Azerbaijani friends," Sarkisian told me, but he did not translate these memories into any expression of regret for the war with Azerbaijan. As the minister was seeing me out at the end of our interview, he said, unprompted: "The most important thing is not the territory. It's that one ethnic group is left in Armenia. In Vardenis and other regions, the Azerbaijanis used to be 70 percent of the population. Our cultures are not compatible. We can live side by side but not within each other. . . . There are very few of us."[5] Evidently for Sarkisian, the march of history, as he understood it, sounded louder than the voices of his old friends.

Another military man, the former Azerbaijani defense minister Tajedin Mekhtiev, delivered his bellicose speech first, before showing an unexpected ray of tenderness. Mekhtiev is one of the founders of an Organization for the Liberation of Karabakh, which advocates Azerbaijan's reconquest of Karabakh by force. "We will drive the Armenians from Karabakh," Mekhtiev boomed at me. "And then we will go on and drive them from our ancient territory of Zangezur." After the interview, the general gave me a lift into the center of Baku in his Mercedes. Hearing that I was about to go to Armenia, the would-be conqueror of Karabakh and Zangezur told me: "If you are in Yerevan, you must look up Mikhail Harutiunian and give him my best regards.

He is the chief of the General Staff now. We studied in Staff College together."⁶

I was struck that often the people who had lost most could be the most generous hearted. Nailia Mustafieva, for example, was an Azerbaijani teacher in the "Children's Republic" outside Sabirabad. Like everyone else there, she was a refugee who had lost her home to the Armenians. Yet she talked fondly about two Armenian girls with whom she had been friends in teacher-training college in Baku, how they had shared their meals together and taught one another songs. Nailia said she was worried about her daughter, who was forming different views: "When they showed pictures of [the] Khojali [massacre] on television, my daughter asked me, 'Are Armenians people?' She didn't believe people could do things like that, kill. I told her, 'Yes, they are people.' Then on Russian television there was a program with an Armenian presenter. I said, 'That's an Armenian. She has a family, children.'"

In bringing up her daughter like this, Nailia is working against a daily onslaught of official propaganda. In Azerbaijan, the losing side in the war, the official hate narrative is especially strong. On 9 May 2001, only a month after serious discussions of a peace deal at the Key West talks, President Aliev laid a wreath at the monument for the World War II dead and made a comparison between the Nazi invasion of the Soviet Union and Armenian occupation of Azerbaijani lands. He told the crowd that "an aggressor must always be punished."⁷

Telling the story of the past fourteen years, both Armenia and Azerbaijan compulsively portray themselves as victims of the other's aggression and their own violence as necessary acts of self-defense. The Armenian narrative begins with the Sumgait pogroms, carries on to Baku in January 1990, Operation Ring, the shelling of Stepanakert and the conquest of Shaumian region. The Azerbaijanis begin the story with the forcible expulsion of Azerbaijanis from Armenia in 1988, move on via their own sufferings in Baku in January 1990 to the killings at Khojali and end with the conquest of the regions east of Nagorny Karabakh. These one-sided versions of recent history have now started to enter school textbooks.

These stories are also tales of decolonization and independence. Hearing them endlessly repeated, I began to detect two larger enemies, Russia and Turkey, lurking in the background. The sense that the Russians and the Turks are the real threat is so pervasive in both countries that here are two commentaries, picked from my interviews almost at random. Aram Sarkisian, former first party secretary of Armenia, told me: "Today Armenia is simply a small barrier on the road of Turkey's hopes for unification of the Turkish-speaking states because we do not allow them to unite with Azerbaijan."[8] In other words Azerbaijan is an accomplice in Turkey's historic ambition to destroy Armenia. This Armenian narrative, springing from the experience of the 1915 Genocide, overlooks the fact that Azerbaijanis are not the same as Turks; that Azerbaijan was never part of the Ottoman Empire; that twentieth-century history has as many pages of atrocities committed by Armenians against Azerbaijanis as the other way round; and that the Armenians treated the Azerbaijanis on their territory with great brutality.

The words many Azerbaijanis use to describe Russia are a mirror image of the Armenian story. I heard that the Karabakh Armenian demands for secession are part of Russia's bigger plans to subjugate and break up Azerbaijan. The former Azerbaijani presidential aide Vafa Guluzade has written:

> [W]hen we say that the conflict, into which we have been drawn, is "Armenian-Azerbaijani," we mislead both others and ourselves. In reality this is the latest action in the old Russian-Turkish confrontation, in which Armenia is only an executor of its master, but Azerbaijan is a little obstacle on this path to the main goal. It is known that even at the beginning of the century during the First World War, Russia used the Armenians against Turkey. History, apparently, is repeating itself.[9]

So, instead of Armenia the "small barrier" standing in the way of Greater Turkey, we have Azerbaijan the "little obstacle" blocking the onward march of Russian imperialism. In this Azerbaijani story, the Azerbaijanis are the passive victims of Russian/Armenian aggression. Yet it ignores the fact that Moscow has sometimes identified Azerbaijan as a strategic ally, not a threat, and it reduces the Armenians to mere automata carrying out Russian instructions, rather than actors with their own legitimate aspirations. In both cases a small country is excusing its aggression against its small neighbor by invoking the threat of a much larger "Great Power."

No one emerges with much credit from the sorry story of the Karabakh conflict, including the "Great Powers." American, Russian, and Turkish politicians probably have little idea how closely any comments they make about the south Caucasus are studied and interpreted. The small-est comments they make about the region are magnified in importance on the small local canvases.

In and of itself this region is still strategically insignificant. The combined GDP of its three states is perhaps ten billion dollars (compare that with the turnover for the year 2000 of one big Western company working in the region, BP: 148 billion dollars). The south Caucasus is chiefly important to the wider world because it is where the interests of the "Great Powers" collide, and where a transport route for Caspian Sea oil is being built.

The disproportion between the small states in the middle and the big neighbors makes the responsibilities of the "Great Powers" all the greater. Their input is essential to making a solution to the Armenia-Azerbaijan conflict work. And in 2002, this is one area, where the news was at last modestly encouraging.

Russian policy in the south Caucasus has been skewed by its im-perial legacy and the traditional ambitions of the Russian military. Russian generals still have a close relationship with Armenia, and many of them would rather not see the Armenia-Azerbaijan conflict resolved and their influence in the region diminished. Yet their role in the region has been slowly declining since the departure of Pavel Gra-chev as Russian defense minister in 1996. It is likely to continue to do so under President Putin. In 2002, although Russian policy toward Georgia remains aggressive, a thaw was well under way in Russia's re-lations with Azerbaijan. Moreover, Russia was working much more harmoniously with France and the United States in the Minsk Group negotiations.

U.S. policy in the region has been distorted by narrow domestic in-terest groups who have all but privatized U.S. policy toward Armenia and Azerbaijan. The Armenian lobby in Congress was responsible for one of that body's most anomalous pieces of foreign policy legislation: Section 907 of the Freedom Support Act, which prohibited U.S. govern-ment aid to Azerbaijan. Other pro-Azerbaijani players have peddled an opposite message, pledging support for Azerbaijan so long as it stands up to Russia and Iran—and therefore also isolates Armenia. These pos-tures have made the job of the State Department negotiators on Kara-bakh much more difficult. Yet there were signs in January 2002 that that was beginning to change, when the U.S. Congress agreed to waive Section 907.

Turkey's role in the Caucasus has been dogged by the shadow of the Genocide debate with Armenia. In 2000, the Armenian-Turkish relationship got worse, not better, as European parliaments passed resolutions on the Genocide. Yet even here the news was not all discouraging. A group of defiant Armenians and Turks set up an Armenian-Turkish Reconciliation Committee; the governors of Kars and Gyumri keep up a dialogue about potential business and trade. In many ways—and somewhat paradoxically, given the relative historical importance of 1915 and 1988—Armenia's future relationship with Turkey is far more promising than its relations with Azerbaijan.

The 11 September attacks resharpened priorities. In their aftermath, the United States, Russia, Turkey, Armenia, and Azerbaijan—and even, to a certain extent, Iran—found themselves in the same coalition facing a common enemy. But in early 2002, it is far too early to tell what long-term effects this reorientation would have.

The tragedy of the aftermath of the Armenia-Azerbaijan conflict is that even if the dispute were to be solved tomorrow, it has ensured that the immediate future for the region will be grim. The opening of Armenia's borders with Turkey and Azerbaijan is a necessary, but no longer sufficient, condition for economic recovery. In a study published in 1999, Richard Beilock, an economist at the University of Florida, estimated that if the closed borders were reopened, transport costs between Armenia and Turkey would fall by between a third and a half and Armenia's GDP would rise by 180 million dollars.[10] Several foreign companies would also be able to use Armenia as a base to reach the large eastern Turkish market. That would boost Armenia, but it would still take years for it to catch up with a relatively modest economy like Russia. In the meantime, it would be too late for Armenia to have any Caspian Sea export pipelines on its territory. This is Armenia's modest future, if peace is reached. If it is not, Armenia's future is bleak indeed. It is unlikely to collapse—its friends in Russia and the United States are too powerful to let that happen. But it risks turning ever more in on itself, slowly becoming, in the caustic phrase of one Western diplomat, into "a theme park for the Diaspora."

Clearly, Azerbaijan's economic prospects are brighter. In 2002, the Baku-Ceyhan pipeline project finally got underway, and from 2006 onward its exports could bring Azerbaijan steady oil revenues of around 500 million dollars a year. Sudden oil wealth carries the risk of what has been called the "Dutch Disease." Much of it will go to a small elite, it will feed the country's already rampant corruption, and it could destroy what is left of the non-oil sector in the economy. Yet some of the prosperity will be shared around and a new oil boom will further open up Azerbaijan to the outside world.

What is less clear is how prosperity could help Azerbaijan cut the Karabakh knot. The country's medium-term socioeconomic outlook is still dreadful. Its refugee population is vast and will not disappear overnight, even if a peace deal is signed. The slowness of reconstruction work in the recaptured areas of Fizuli suggests that it could be five or ten years from the day when a town like Aghdam or Zengelan is handed back to the day when it is habitable again. In the meantime, Azerbaijan's sharpening disparities of wealth could aggravate social tensions and political instability. The country already faces great uncertainty on what Azerbaijanis call "Day X," the day when President Aliev is incapacitated or dies. Under Aliev, all decisions, large and small, have been taken by one man. When he goes, a power vacuum and a dirty struggle for the succession are almost inevitable.

A wealthier and more confident Azerbaijan will inevitably begin to consider the option of going to war again to recapture its lost lands. Tajedin Mekhtiev's Organization for the Liberation of Karabakh has attracted plenty of public support. Yet the rhetoric about "liberating" Karabakh may not go as deep in society as public debate suggests. On a practical level, in 2002 all the evidence suggests that Azerbaijan will be entirely unready for war for at least five to ten years and possibly longer. President Aliev has deliberately run down the army in his efforts to prevent any military coups against him. A Western military specialist who visited the Azerbaijani front line outside Karabakh in 2000 told me that the troops he had seen were dismally unprepared for battle. He saw four divisions on the border, manned at only 40 percent capacity, whose morale was undermined by low pay, inedible rations, and indiscipline. The specialist said that to prevail in that kind of terrain, the attacking side would need an advantage in numbers and equipment of between three and six to one. The twenty thousand or so Armenian troops they face on the opposite side of the Kara-bakh front line are perhaps not as formidable as they claim to be, but they are well equipped with Russian weaponry and extremely well dug in. Even if Azerbaijan begins to spend large amounts of money on sophisticated military hardware, there is no guarantee of victory. As an Azerbaijani friend put it, "Azerbaijan is not ready for peace or for war."

An Azerbaijani rearmament would increase the risk of hostilities starting from the other side. This could be something on the lines of the "fourth round" of conflict that Samvel Babayan predicted, in which the Karabakh Armenians' forces would launch a lightning attack, seize more territory, and try to force a complete Azerbaijani capitulation. In this scenario they would perhaps aim to disrupt the Baku-Ceyhan pipeline running thirty kilometers to the north. Yet this is also fantastic. It is no accident that the front line is where it is now. To extend it would mean to take heavy casualties in the name of a cause with dubious objectives. That campaign would have to be fought mainly by conscripts in the Armenian armed forces who have never seen proper combat. Here too failure is more likely than success.

War would be catastrophic—and no wars ever end as the men who launch them intend. But that does not mean that we should rule out what the Russian scholar Valery Tishkov calls in talking about Chechnya, the "factor of stupidity." What renewed fighting *would* guarantee we can be more certain of: much heavier loss of life than in 1991–1994 as both sides use more destructive weapons to attack well-defended positions; angry international and diplomatic reaction; disintegration of the already limping economies. Another more nightmarish scenario also could not be ruled out: the open intervention of the Russian armed forces, stationed in Armenia on the Armenian side and that of Turkey, a NATO member, on Azerbaijan's. Even the remotest prospect of a third world war fought in the Caucasus should be actively avoided.

If not war, then peace. For a moment in 2001, peace seemed more possible than it had for many years. But by the end of the year the Key West initiative appeared to have foundered. The paradox of the Armenia-Azerbaijan peace process is that, in private, the leaders of both regimes had traveled a long way toward mutual compromise, yet in public they keep up aggressive rhetoric toward one another. In October 2001, Aliev was quoted as warning the negotiators, "Either the OSCE Minsk Group takes a principled position in this question or we will have to liberate our land by military means."[11] Asked why they do nothing to move their discussion of peace into the public domain, both presidents give the impression that they think of their populations as material to be molded rather than as citizens to be engaged in dialogue. Queried in

280 CONCLUSION: SADAKHLO: THE FUTURE

May 2001, for example, why he was not preparing Armenians for the possibility of compromise with Azerbaijan, Kocharian replied that "disappointment and extra expectations in this situation would in fact be worse than a certain caution in providing information."[12] Basically he was saying that it was better if ordinary people were kept in the dark.

There are several reasons for the presidents' strange reserve. Neither Aliev nor Kocharian is by nature a democrat, and each tried to win a military victory against the other in 1993–1994. Dialogue does not come naturally to either. For both men, staying in power is almost certainly a greater priority than a peace deal—however desirable one may be. Moreover their hard-line instincts reinforce each other: both men probably worry that a public espousal of compromise will come across as weakness and cause the other side to harden its negotiating position.

Yet the public intransigence of the leaders clearly alienates opinion abroad and boxes them in at home. For example, the Karabakh Armenians still watch Azerbaijani television; as they see themselves depicted as "fascists" and "terrorists" on the evening news, they have no incentive to want to become citizens of Azerbaijan once again. As one democratically minded Azerbaijani said candidly to me: "If I were a Karabakh Armenian, I wouldn't want to be united with Azerbaijan!" At home meanwhile, the lack of a public constituency for peace restricts the presidents' capacity to make the kind of compromises essential for a peace agreement.

Any just solution to the Nagorny Karabakh dispute will entail painful compromises on both sides, and it will have to balance radically opposing principles. The international community is very reluctant to endorse a deal that is seen to set a precedent—and it has good reasons to do so, fearing that to legitimize the secession of a region like Nagorny Karabakh might help destabilize other conflict zones. That is the main reason that under most solutions discussed before Key West, Nagorny Karabakh, if only de facto, became part of the sovereign territory of Azerbaijan again.

Yet if the integrity of states is a powerful force in international affairs, the fact of history on the ground is an immoveable object. The reality is that Nagorny Karabakh has seceded from Azerbaijan and for more than ten years the Karabakh Armenians have had nothing to do with Baku. It would be dangerous to give any successful armed secessionists the right to possess their territory—that would legitimize the deportation of hundreds of thousand of people and would also legitimize Azerbaijan's right to retake Karabakh by force, releasing an endless cycle of violence. But a peaceful resolution of the conflict has to respect the force of will—if not the force of arms—that led to that secession. A peaceful solution will not be possible unless it gives the Karabakh Armenians the de facto self-rule they have now and strong security guarantees.

There is precious little mutual understanding on these points. Many Azerbaijanis assume that territorial integrity is somehow their "sacred right" and they have no responsibility to share sovereignty, even over a province as long-disputed as Karabakh. Since 1994, there has been precious little understanding in Azerbaijan of the implications of the Karabakh Armenians' secession. One evening in Baku, a senior Azerbaijani journalist said to me in all seriousness, "I don't understand why we cannot simply be given our lands back. If the Karabakh Armenians don't want to live with us, they can go and live in Armenia." For their part, many Armenians fail to understand why they should give up what they have achieved on the battlefield—and entirely overlook the rights of the Karabakh Azerbaijanis. "We don't need Azerbaijan, we don't want any relationship with Azerbaijan," said the Karabakh Armenian leader Arkady Gukasian in 1997, as if they could live in permanent isolation from their nearest neighbor. "It's Azerbaijan that wants a relationship with us."

The issues of principle to be resolved are serious, but their overall importance may be overstated. The biggest problem remains the lack of any reasoned conversation about them. For Azerbaijan not to be talking directly to the Karabakh Armenians—people whom it claims to be Azerbaijani citizens—is extraordinary and counterproductive. For their part, many Armenians talk implausibly as though Azerbaijan is somehow not a real country and its claims will simply fade away with the passing of time. In that sense, the biggest problem is not so much lack of a readiness to compromise as lack of a readiness to contemplate any future with the other side at all. Gukasian tells a story that illustrates this well. In 1995, he was one of the Armenian delegation invited by Finland to talks on the Aaland Islands. These Swedish-speaking islands are part of Finland but have generous powers of self-government. At one point, says Gukasian, his Finnish hosts took him aside and pointed out that this was a good model for Nagorny Karabakh: "They said, 'Here is a good model,' and I said, 'I am ready—right now if you want—to become part of Finland! But we are talking about Azerbaijan."[13]

Gukasian's story suggests that the format of the peace negotiations between the Armenian and Azerbaijani presidents may be badly flawed. Both presidents have been concentrating on finding a comprehensive or "package" agreement under which all issues can be resolved at once. They have adopted this approach partly because of the sense of urgency they feel about President Aliev's failing health. But it also stems from the controlling authoritarian instincts of two leaders, who are unwilling to let the process out of their grip.

Having failed to find a comprehensive plan, the only logical way out is to pursue a "step-by-step" agreement in which some smaller steps—the opening of the Armenia-Nakhichevan border, the return of small areas of occupied land—get the peace process under way on the ground. Such symbolic, incremental steps carry their own risks, but they could begin to give society a stake in peaceful cooperation, rather than defiance and cynicism. They could begin to thaw the frozen landscape.

Even without the war, Armenia and Azerbaijan leaders have cooperated very little over the past hundred years. In Soviet times, they would conduct most of their business in and through Moscow. Since then, the south Caucasus has been a tangle of front lines, closed borders, dead ends, and isolated enclaves. In any real political or economic sense, it is not a proper region at all.

This was not always the case. The eighteenth-century Armenian troubadour Sayat-Nova wrote in Armenian, Georgian, and the *lingua franca* of the Caucasus of the time, Azeri (some of his Azeri poems were even written in Armenian script) and moved happily between the different nations and regions of the Caucasus. He thought of himself as a bridge builder. In one of his Azeri poems he elegizes on his posthumous fate:

> Mercy on the old master building a bridge,
> The passer-by may lay a stone to his foundation.
> I have sacrificed my soul, worn out my life, for the nation.
> A brother may arrange a rock upon my grave.[14]

Sayat-Nova's biographer, Charles Dowsett, speculates on the use of the word "nation" in the poem:

What nation? If the Armenian nation, or the Georgian, why is the poem in Azeri? It would seem his horizons are broader, and that he is thinking in terms such as a Caucasian unity, in which Armenian, Georgian and Azeri might live together in harmony, under the beneficent rule of a wise leader like Irakli II, and Azeri, as the common language, was the best vehicle for the message.[15]

In a few lines Sayat-Nova spells out a different kind of future for Armenians and Azerbaijanis, locked in their self-destructive states of fear and defiance: a gentler future based on a much more harmonious past.

But sadly the poet's message is not being heard.

# Appendix I

*Statistics*

Proper understanding of the Armenia-Azerbaijan conflict has been confused by the dissemination and repetition of false statistics.

This is, of course, a phenomenon common to all wars and their accompanying propaganda campaigns—and also to human disasters, where initial casualty estimates are often much higher than the final body counts. In this case, the problem has been compounded by the traditions of a region where the authorities have never been held accountable for the information they give and that until 1991 was part of the Soviet Union, which regularly suppressed information. That is one reason that wild claims were made about cover-ups on both sides. Some Armenians alleged, for example, that hundreds of bodies had been hidden after the Sumgait pogroms in 1988. In January 1990, Azerbaijanis alleged that helicopters had dumped the bodies of victims from the Soviet army intervention in the sea. Fortunately, when final casualty lists were compiled, they showed that both claims were false.

What follows is principally the work of the most thorough and objective statistician of the period, Dr. Arif Yunusov, with a few of my own additions, mainly regarding the question of the amount of Azerbaijan under Armenian control.[1]

The population of Azerbaijan was estimated in July 1999 at 7.9 million, although up to a fifth of its people, chiefly young men, may have emigrated to Russia and Turkey in search of work.[2] The population of both Armenia and Nagorny Karabakh in 2001 was unknown. Armenia held a much-postponed census in late 2001. Experts estimate that the decline in Armenia's population from 3.7 million in 1991, as a result of emigration, has been dramatic, some putting it as low as two million. In Nagorny Karabakh, the prime minister Anushavan Danielian told me on 16 May 2000 that the population of the region is a "state secret." The last reliable census for the region was in 1979, which estimated the population to be 162,000, including 123,000 Armenians and 37,000 Azerbaijanis. Since the conflict began, all the Azerbaijanis and many of the Armenians have left. Foreign aid workers estimated the number of Armenians in Karabakh in 2000–2001 at between 60,000 and 80,000, but nobody knew for sure.

The number of casualties in the war is hard to verify. The U.S. State Department uses the figure of 25,000 dead. Politicians on both sides have named much higher figures. On 14 May 1994, for example, after the cease-fire, the speaker of the Azerbaijani parliament, Rasul Guliev, said that 20,000 Azerbaijanis had been killed and 50,000 had been wounded in the conflict.[3] Arif Yunusov has done his own calculations; he estimates the number of dead as 17,000 (11,000 Azerbaijanis and 6,000 Armenians) and the number of wounded as 50,000.

Refugees are a little easier to account for, and again I refer to the work of Yunusov.[4] On the Armenian side, he has counted 353,000 Armenian refugees from Azerbaijan to Armenia and Russia as a result of the conflict. They include about 40,000 Armenians from the Shaumian and Khanlar regions of Nagorny Karabakh. Up to 80,000 people also left their homes in border regions of Armenia, as a result of the conflict, although most probably have returned since the 1994 cease-fire.

On the Azerbaijani side, the total number of displaced people comes to about 750,000—considerably less than the figure of "one million" regularly used by President Aliev, but still a very large number. The number includes 186,000 Azerbaijanis, 18,000 Muslim Kurds, and 3,500 Russians who left Armenia for Azerbaijan in 1988–1989 (around 10,000 more Kurds and Russians left Armenia for Russia at the same time). In 1991–1994 approximately 500,000 Azerbaijanis from Nagorny Karabakh and the bordering regions were expelled from their homes, and around 30,000 Azerbaijani residents fled their homes in border areas. Azerbaijan's refugee numbers have also been swelled by around 50,000 Meskhetian Turks fleeing Central Asia.

Finally, it is possible to count the amount of what is officially recognized as Azerbaijan but that is under Armenian control. On 27 October 1993, Aliev said that "20 percent" of his country was occupied by the Armenians. Perhaps because Azerbaijanis did not want to contradict their president or because it was a powerful round number, this figure has been repeated by Azerbaijanis ever since. That is understandable. Less forgivably, it has also been used extensively in the Western media, including Reuters, the *New York Times*, and the BBC. The calculations that follow are still approximate, but I believe they are accurate to within one-tenth of one percentage point.

The Armenians hold all but approximately 300 square kilometers ($km^2$) of the 4,388 $km^2$ of the former Nagorny Karabakh Autonomous Region. (The Azerbaijanis hold the easternmost fingers of Martakert and Martuni regions. The governor of Martakert told visiting journalists on 19 May 2001 that the Azerbaijanis held 108.5 $km^2$ of his region. On the map, the area of Martuni under Azerbaijani control is approximately twice that). This means that the Armenians occupy 4,088 $km^2$ of Nagorny Karabakh, about 4.7 percent of the territory of Azerbaijan.

The Armenians fully occupy five of the seven "occupied territories" outside Nagorny Karabakh. They are Kelbajar (1,936 $km^2$), Lachin (1,835 $km^2$), Kubatly (802 $km^2$), Jebrail (1,050 $km^2$), and Zengelan (707 $km^2$). They also occupy 77 percent or 842 $km^2$ of the 1,094 $km^2$ of Aghdam region (this figure was given by the head of Aghdam region, Gara Sariev, at the front line on 19 May 2001) and approximately one-third (judging by maps) or 462 $km^2$ of the 1,386 $km^2$ of Fizuli region. The Armenians also occupy two former village enclaves of approximately 75 $km^2$ in the Nakhichevan and Kazakh regions. (For their part, the Azerbaijanis occupy one former Armenian enclave of about 50 $km^2$).

This means that the combined area of Azerbaijan under Armenian control is approximately 11,797 $km^2$ or 4,555 square miles. Azerbaijan's total area is 86,600 $km^2$. So the occupied zone is in fact 13.62 percent of Azerbaijan—still a large figure, but a long way short of President Aliev's repeated claim.

# Appendix 2

*Chronology*

1214–1261  Reign of Hasan Jalal, prince of Khachen.

1501–1525  Shah Ismail I founds Safavid Dynasty in Tabriz, makes Shiite branch of Islam his official religion.

1722  End of Safavid Dynasty.

1747  Death of Nadir Shah ends direct Iranian sovereignty over Karabakh.

1752  Panakh Khan builds a fortress at Shusha.

14 MAY 1805  Panakh Khan's successor, Ibrahim Khan, surrenders to Russians.

12 OCTOBER 1813  Treaty of Gulistan formally incorporates Karabakh within Russian Empire.

NOVEMBER 1822  Mekhti Kuli Khan flees to Persia. End of Karabakh khanate and *melik*s.

1827  Russian capture of Yerevan.

10 FEBRUARY 1828  Treaty of Turkmenchai between Russia and Iran.

1868  Karabakh becomes part of Elizavetpol (Ganje) Province.

AUGUST–SEPTEMBER 1905  Fighting in Shusha.

31 MARCH 1918  Beginning of "March Days" in Baku, massacre of Azerbaijanis.

28 MAY 1918  Armenia and Azerbaijan declare independence.

15 SEPTEMBER 1918  Turks enter Baku, massacre of Armenians.

AUGUST 1919   British mission withdraws from Karabakh.

20 MARCH 1920   Azerbaijani army sacks Shusha.

28 APRIL 1920   Bolshevik takeover in Azerbaijan.

MAY 1920   Bolshevik takeover in Karabakh.

29 NOVEMBER 1920   Bolshevik takeover in Armenia.

1 DECEMBER 1920   Azerbaijani leader Narimanov declares Karabakh part of Armenia.

5 JULY 1921   "Kavburo" declares Nagorny Karabakh part of Soviet Azerbaijan.

13 OCTOBER 1921   Treaty of Kars between Bolshevik Russia and Turkey.

30 DECEMBER 1922   Establishment of the Soviet Union.

7 JULY 1923   Nagorny Karabakh Autonomous Region created.

1948–1950   Deportation of Azerbaijanis from Armenia, immigration of Armenians.

1965–1967   Demonstrations in Yerevan lead to construction of Genocide Memorial.

1969   Heidar Aliev becomes first secretary of Azerbaijani Communist Party.

1974   Karen Demirchian becomes first secretary of Armenian Communist Party.

7 OCTOBER 1977   New "Brezhnev Constitution."

NOVEMBER 1982   Aliev promoted to Politburo, Kamran Bagirov becomes first secretary in Azerbaijan.

MARCH 1985   Gorbachev becomes general secretary of Soviet Communist Party.

## 1987

AUGUST   Karabakh Armenians send petition with tens of thousands of signatures to Moscow.

18 OCTOBER   Demonstration in Yerevan to protest incidents in Armenian village of Chardakhlu, north of Karabakh.

21 OCTOBER   Aliev removed from Politburo.

NOVEMBER   Intercommunal violence in Kafan.

16 NOVEMBER   Gorbachev's adviser Aganbekian, speaking in Paris, advocates Karabakh's joining Armenia.

## 1988

25 JANUARY   Azerbaijanis flee Kafan.

13 FEBRUARY   First demonstration in Stepanakert.

19 FEBRUARY   First demonstration in Baku.

20 FEBRUARY   Regional Soviet in Stepanakert votes to request transfer of Nagorny Karabakh to Armenia.

21 FEBRUARY   Mass demonstrations begin in Yerevan.

22 FEBRUARY   Two Azerbaijanis killed in violence at Askeran.

24 FEBRUARY   Boris Kevorkov removed as Party boss of Nagorny Karabakh.

26 FEBRUARY   Gorbachev receives Armenian writers Zori Balayan and Silva Kaputikian.

27–29 FEBRUARY   Anti-Armenian pogroms in Sumgait.

21 MAY   Bagirov and Demirchian removed as Party leaders of Azerbaijan and Armenia.

15 JUNE   Armenian Supreme Soviet votes to accept Nagorny Karabakh into Armenia.

17 JUNE   Azerbaijan Supreme Soviet reaffirms that Nagorny Karabakh is part of Azerbaijan.

18 JULY   Presidium of Supreme Soviet of USSR resolves that Karabakh remains part of Azerbaijan.

26 JULY   Arkady Volsky sent to Nagorny Karabakh as Politburo's representative.

18–20 SEPTEMBER   Armenians driven out of Shusha, Azerbaijanis out of Stepanakert.

21 SEPTEMBER   "Special rule" introduced in Karabakh.

NOVEMBER   Mass expulsions of Azerbaijanis from Armenia.

17 NOVEMBER–5 DECEMBER   Mass demonstrations in Baku.

7 DECEMBER   Armenian earthquake.

10–11 DECEMBER   Gorbachev visits Armenia. Karabakh Committee arrested.


## 1989

12 JANUARY   Special Administration Committee, headed by Volsky, set up in Nagorny Karabakh.

31 MAY   Release of Karabakh Committee from prison.

11 SEPTEMBER   Azerbaijani Popular Front registered.

25 SEPTEMBER   Azerbaijan's Supreme Soviet passes declaration of sovereignty.

NOVEMBER   Rail blockade of Armenia and Nakhichevan.

28 NOVEMBER   Special Administration Committee dissolved.

1 DECEMBER   Supreme Soviet of Armenia and Karabakh Armenians' National Council declare unification.


## 1990

13–15 JANUARY   Anti-Armenian pogroms in Baku.

15 JANUARY   State of Emergency imposed in Nagorny Karabakh.

19–20 JANUARY   Soviet troops enter Baku, killing protestors.

20 JANUARY   Ayaz Mutalibov becomes Azerbaijani Party leader.

26 JANUARY   Azerbaijan's second secretary Viktor Polyanichko arrives in Nagorny Karabakh to try to set up new Organizational Committee.

MAY   Armenian National Movement wins parliamentary elections in Armenia.

MAY   Nagorny Karabakh returned to budget of Azerbaijan.

25 JULY   Central Committee in Moscow passes decree on disarming illegal formations.

4 AUGUST   Levon Ter-Petrosian elected speaker of new Armenian parliament.

23 AUGUST   Armenian parliament passes resolution on sovereignty.

## 1991

17 MARCH   Referendum on preservation of the Soviet Union. Azerbaijan takes part, Armenia does not.

30 APRIL   Troops and Azerbaijani OMON attack Armenian village of Getashen (Chaikend), begin to deport villagers. Beginning of Operation Ring.

12 JUNE   Boris Yeltsin elected president of Russian Federation.

4 JULY   Operation begins against Armenian villages in Shaumian region.

10 AUGUST   Valery Grigorian assassinated in Stepanakert.

19–21 AUGUST   Attempted coup against Mikhail Gorbachev in Moscow fails

30 AUGUST   Azerbaijan declares independence from Soviet Union.

SEPTEMBER   Armenians recapture Shaumian region.

2 SEPTEMBER   Nagorny Karabakh announces its secession from independent Azerbaijan.

3 SEPTEMBER   Heidar Aliev elected speaker of Nakhichevan parliament.

8 SEPTEMBER   Mutalibov elected president of Azerbaijan.

23 SEPTEMBER   Armenia declares independence. Russian-Kazakhstani peace plan signed in Zheleznovodsk.

16 OCTOBER    Ter-Petrosian elected president of Armenia.

20 NOVEMBER    Helicopter crash over Karabakh kills twenty-two, wrecks peace plan.

26 NOVEMBER    Azerbaijani parliament declares abolition of autonomy of Nagorny Karabakh, renames Stepanakert Khankendi.

10 DECEMBER    Nagorny Karabakh Armenians vote in referendum in favor of independence.

25 DECEMBER    Mikhail Gorbachev resigns as president of the Soviet Union.

31 DECEMBER    End of the Soviet Union.


### 1992

26 JANUARY    Dozens of Azerbaijani soldiers killed in attack on village of Karintak.

30 JANUARY    CSCE admits Armenia and Azerbaijan, takes up mediating role for Nagorny Karabakh.

25–26 FEBRUARY    Hundreds of Azerbaijanis killed after Armenians storm Khojali.

6 MARCH    Mutalibov resigns as president of Azerbaijan.

10 MARCH    366th Regiment of 4th Army disbanded in Georgia, after being withdrawn from Karabakh.

24 MARCH    CSCE Minsk Conference for Nagorny Karabakh proposed, Minsk Group formed.

10 APRIL    Dozens of Armenians killed as Azerbaijanis storm village of Maragha.

14 APRIL    Death of Karabakh Armenian leader Artur Mkrtchian.

8–9 MAY    Armenians capture Shusha.

14–15 MAY    Mutalibov briefly returned to power in Baku, then removed again.

18 MAY    Armenians capture Lachin.

15 MAY    Tashkent agreement divides Soviet weaponry among CIS countries.

1 JUNE–5 AUGUST    Minsk Group negotiations in Rome.

7 JUNE    Abulfaz Elchibey elected president of Azerbaijan.

12 JUNE    Azerbaijani offensive begins, capturing Shaumian region.

4 JULY    Azerbaijanis take Martakert (and rename it Agdere).

14 AUGUST    Georgian forces attack Abkhazia, war breaks out.

15 AUGUST    Karabakh Armenian State Defense Committee created, headed by Robert Kocharian.

1 SEPTEMBER    Azerbaijanis take village of Srkhavend, control almost half of Nagorny Karabakh.

19 SEPTEMBER    Russian defense minister Pavel Grachev convenes meeting of Caucasus defense ministers in Sochi.

24 OCTOBER    U.S. Congress passes Section 907 of Freedom Support Act, barring U.S. government aid to Azerbaijan.

14–15 DECEMBER    CSCE meeting in Stockholm.

## 1993

10 FEBRUARY    Suret Husseinov sacked as Azerbaijan's "special representative" for Karabakh.

20 FEBRUARY    Rahim Gaziev sacked as Azerbaijani defense minister.

27 MARCH–5 APRIL    Armenians capture Kelbajar Region.

30 APRIL    UN Resolution 822 calls on Armenians to withdraw from Kelbajar.

4 JUNE    Husseinov begins uprising against Elchibey government in Ganje.

14 JUNE    Ter-Petrosian travels to Stepanakert to promote CSCE peace agreement.

15 JUNE    Aliev elected speaker of Azerbaijani parliament.

17–18 JUNE    Elchibey flees to Nakhichevan.

24 JUNE    Aliev given extraordinary powers by parliament.

27 JUNE    Armenians recapture Martakert.

30 JUNE    Aliev makes Husseinov prime minister.

23 JULY    Armenians capture Aghdam.

23 AUGUST    Armenians capture Fizuli.

25 AUGUST    Armenians capture Jebrail.

28 AUGUST    Nationwide referendum in Azerbaijan votes no confidence in Elchibey.

31 AUGUST    Armenians capture Kubatly.

24 SEPTEMBER    Azerbaijan joins CIS.

25 SEPTEMBER    Aliev and Kocharian meet in secret in Moscow.

3 OCTOBER    Aliev elected president of Azerbaijan.

24 OCTOBER    Armenians capture Horadiz, cutting off Zengelan region.

29 OCTOBER    Armenians capture Zengelan.

30 NOVEMBER    Italy's Mario Raffaelli resigns as chairman of Minsk Group. Replaced by Jan Elliason of Sweden.

11 DECEMBER    Aliev publicly criticizes Azerbaijani army.

22 DECEMBER    New Azerbaijani offensive.

## 1994

20–24 JANUARY    Azerbaijanis push into Kelbajar Region, Armenians retreat with heavy losses.

12–18 FEBRUARY    Armenians counterattack, thousands of Azerbaijanis killed.

APRIL    Armenians begin offensive against Terter.

4–5 MAY   Talks in Bishkek lead to drawing up of Bishkek Protocol, calling for cease-fire.

MAY   Russian-led peacekeeping force deployed in Abkhazia.

12 MAY   Cease-fire agreement comes into force.

16 MAY   Grachev calls meeting of military leaders in Moscow.

20 SEPTEMBER   Azerbaijan and foreign oil companies sign contract to develop Caspian Sea oil fields.

3–4 OCTOBER   Husseinov flees Azerbaijan after failed coup attempt.

22 DECEMBER   Kocharian elected "president" of Nagorny Karabakh by parliament.

5–6 DECEMBER   CSCE becomes OSCE at summit in Budapest. Peacekeeping mandate for Karabakh approved.

11 DECEMBER   Russian invasion of Chechnya.

## 1995

6 JANUARY   Russia becomes cochair of the Minsk Group with Sweden.

13–17 MARCH   "Turkish" coup attempt in Baku.

21 APRIL   Finland replaces Sweden as cochair of Minsk Group.

12 NOVEMBER   Parliamentary elections in Azerbaijan.

## 1996

3 JULY   Yeltsin reelected president of Russia

16 AUGUST   Khasavyurt agreement ends fighting in Chechnya.

23 SEPTEMBER   Ter-Petrosian reelected in disputed election.

24 NOVEMBER   Kocharian elected president of Nagorny Karabakh in popular vote.

2–3 DECEMBER   Lisbon summit of OSCE.

## 1997

I JANUARY   France replaces Finland as cochair of Minsk Group.

14 FEBRUARY   United States admitted as third cochair of Minsk Group.

20 MARCH   Kocharian made prime minister of Armenia.

29 AUGUST   Russian-Armenian Friendship Treaty signed.

I SEPTEMBER   Arkady Gukasian elected "president" of Nagorny Karabakh.

20–24 SEPTEMBER   Minsk Group mediators present a new peace plan in the region.

26 SEPTEMBER   Ter-Petrosian argues for compromise on Karabakh at press conference.

I NOVEMBER   Ter-Petrosian's newspaper article "War or Peace?" published.

12 NOVEMBER   "Early oil" starts flowing from Azerbaijan's Chiraq oil field to Supsa.

## 1998

3 FEBRUARY   Ter-Petrosian resigns.

30 MARCH   Kocharian elected president of Armenia.

11 OCTOBER   Aliev reelected president of Azerbaijan.

## 1999

25 APRIL   Kocharian and Aliev hold first bilateral meeting in Washington.

29 APRIL   Aliev has heart surgery in Cleveland, Ohio.

30 MAY   Parliamentary elections in Armenia won by Vazgen Sarkisian's Republican Party.

11 JUNE   Vazgen Sarkisian made prime minister of Armenia.

I OCTOBER   Russian ground troops reinvade Chechnya.

II OCTOBER   Aliev and Kocharian meet on Nakhichevan-Armenia border.

27 OCTOBER   Sarkisian and Demirchian shot dead in Armenian parliament.

I7 DECEMBER   Babayan sacked as commander of Nagorny Karabakh armed forces.

31 DECEMBER   Yeltsin resigns as president of Russia.

## 2000

22 MARCH   Assassination attempt on Gukasian in Stepanakert. Babayan arrested.

25 MARCH   Putin elected president of Russia.

5 NOVEMBER   Parliamentary elections in Azerbaijan.

## 2001

26 JANUARY   Aliev and Kocharian meet in Paris.

FEBRUARY   Former OSCE peace plans leaked to media in Armenia and Azerbaijan.

26 FEBRUARY   Babayan sentenced to fourteen years in jail for attack on Gukasian.

4–5 MARCH   Aliev and Kocharian again meet in Paris.

3–7 APRIL   Peace talks in Key West, Florida.

I9 MAY   Minsk Group cochairs cross front line into Nagorny Karabakh.

# Notes

NOTE TO INTRODUCTION

1. Ker Porter, *Travels in Georgia, Persia, Armenia, Ancient Babylon*, 513–514.


NOTES TO CHAPTER I

Unless specified otherwise, all interviews were carried out by the author in Russian. Any subsequent quotations from the same source in a chapter that do not have a note reference number derive from the same interviews. Information that does not have a note reference number comes either from general English-language literature on the period in the Bibliography or from conversations with sources who had not agreed to be quoted directly.

1. *Sovetsky Karabakh*, 21 February 1988.

2. Interview with Galstian, 10 October 2000.

3. Interviews with Vyacheslav Mikhailov, 5 December 2000, and Zahid Abasov, 10 November 2000.

4. A Petrov, "Dlya politikov Karabakh—urok, dlya soldat—vtoroi Afgan-istan" [For politicians Karabakh is a lesson, for soldiers it is a second Afghanistan], *Krasnaya Zvezda*, 19 February 1992.

5. Interview with Iskandarian, 1 December 2000.

6. Several published accounts say that seventeen of the thirty Azerbaijani deputies voted against the resolution. *Sovetsky Karabakh* says that the decision was unanimous, and other interviewees confirmed that Azerbaijani deputies refused to vote.

7. TASS, 23 February 1988, quoted in *The Karabagh File*, 98–99.

8. Interview with Kharchenko, 4 December 2000.

9. Interview with Rustamkhanli, 8 November 2000.

10. Interview with Yunusov, 27 November 2000. Yunusov, the most scrupulous chronicler of the Karabakh conflict on either side, did not succeed in finding out any more details. The authorities were keen to hush up evidence of a conflict that they hoped would die down. Another factor, which also came into play when Armenian girls were raped a week later in Sumgait, was the

shame associated with rape in the Caucasus, which made it hard for its victims to find husbands.

11. The Russian writer Alexander Vasilevsky, who visited Nagorny Karabakh at the end of April 1988, writes that he talked to the brother of Ali Hajiev, Arif Hajiev, who said that his brother had quarreled with an Azerbaijani policeman and been shot by him at point-blank range. The policeman was then spirited away by a colleague. Vasilevsky, "Tucha v Gorakh" [Storm cloud in the mountains], *Avrora*, Leningrad, no date given; reprinted in *Glazami nezavisimykh Nablyudatelei* [Through the eyes of independent observers], 45–46. Grigory Kharchenko said that the policeman fired his gun after slipping against a car door. The deputy head of the KGB, Filip Bobkov, says that Hajiev worked in the Agdam vineyards; Vasilievsky says he worked in a machine-tool plant. Bobkov blames the death of Bakhtiar Uliev on a shot fired by an Armenian. Filip Bobkov, *KGB i Vlast'* [The KGB and power] (Moscow: Veteran MP, 1995), 295–296.

12. Rost, *Armenian Tragedy*, 16–18; Bobkov, op. cit., 296. The Russian poet Yevgeny Yevtushenko wrote a poem in praise of Abasova.

13. From a transcript of the all-day Politburo session devoted to Nagorny Karabakh on 3 March 1988, published in *Soyuz Mozhno Bylo Sokhranit'* [It was possible to preserve the union], 22.

14. Interview with Muradian, 5 May 2000. Muradian's high-up connections have stimulated speculation that he was working for the KGB. He of course denies it, although he does concede that one of his contacts was the Armenian KGB chief Yuzbashian. It does seem unlikely that the KGB would have recruited someone who did such sustained damage to the Party, the Soviet Union—and ultimately to the KGB as well.

15. Interview with Pashayeva, 14 December 2000. This is not her real name. She asked to be referred to by a pseudonym.

16. Interview with Babayan, 29 September 2000.

17. The letter at the head of the petition, written by the geologist Suren Aivazian, called on Gorbachev to attach not only Nagorny Karabakh but also the Azerbaijani region of Nakhichevan to Soviet Armenia.

18. *The Caucasian Knot*, 148, quoting the Armenian newspaper *Haratch*, 19 November 1987.

19. A commonly repeated story in the region has it that Zhanna Galstian received a message of encouragement in Moscow by the Central Committee expert Vyacheslav Mikhailov. In interviews, Galstian and Mikhailov confirmed that they did meet, but neither said that any positive message was given.

20. Interview with Balayan, 23 May 2000. Ironically, in 2000, both the Nairit plant and the nuclear power station were working again in Armenia, for environmental concerns had been entirely supplanted by economic ones.

21. *Forgotten February*, Yerevan Film Studios, 2000.

22. Interview with Manucharian, 4 May 2000.

23. Interview with Shugarian, 14 October 2000.

24. Interview with Gazarian, 22 October 2000.

25. Interview with Voskanian, 28 September 2000.

26. Quoted in *The Karabagh File*, 98.

27. The transcript of the Politburo session of 29 February 1988 is in the Russian Archives Project, State Archive Service of Russia/Hoover Institution (hereafter Russian Archives Project), Fond 89, Reel 1.003, 89/42/18.

28. Shakhnazarov, *Tsena Svobody* [The price of freedom], 206. Shakhnazarov died in May 2001, aged seventy-six.

29. Interview with Kaputikian, 26 September 2000.

30. Kaputikian told the American reporter Robert Cullen that Gorbachev had mentioned a poem she had written in the 1950s called "Secret Ballot." She said that she had written the poem during the Khrushchev thaw, "when there was a little renaissance." Later in the meeting, Gorbachev had repeated the phrase when he promised reforms for Karabakh. Cullen, "Roots," 65.

### NOTES TO CHAPTER 2

1. Russian Archives Project, Fond 89, Reel 1.003, 89/42/18. Bagirov died in October 2000 at the age of sixty-eight.

2. The English translation is by Audrey Alstadt, from the *Journal of the Institute of Muslim Minority Affairs* 9, 2 (July 1988): 429–434.

3. The official was Grigory Kharchenko.

4. Interview with Musayev, 14 November 2000.

5. In July and December 1988, according to Musayev and Zardusht Alizade. Two interviewees in Moscow, Vyacheslav Mikhailov and Grigory Kharchenko, also gave credit to Musayev.

6. The first two statistics were cited by the Soviet interior minister Viktor Vlasov in the Politburo session of 29 February 1988; the third comes from Gasan Sadykhov and Ramazan Mamedov, *Armyane v Sumgaite* [Armenians in Sumgait] (Baku: Shur, 1994), 31–32

7. This story was compiled from three conversations with past and present Sumgait residents: Eldar Zeynalov in Baku on 9 November 2000; Eiruz Mamedov in Sumgait on 24 November 2000; and Rafik Khacharian in Armenia on 15 December 2000.

8. Unless specified otherwise, the account that follows is based on three sources: conversations in Sumgait itself on 24 November 2000; conversations in Kasakh, Armenia, with Sumgait Armenians on 15 December 2000; and *The Sumgait Tragedy*, ed. Shakhmuradian.

9. Two of the rioters put on trial later for murder, Zakir Rzaev and Azer Turabiev, both came from the Gukark region in northwest Armenia, according to V. Sarkisian, "Nastal li chas rasplaty?" [Has the hour of reckoning arrived?],

*Kommunist* 30 October 1988, reprinted in *Glazami nezavisimykh nablyudatelei:* [Through the eyes of independent observers], 68.

10. Konstantin Pkhakadze in *The Sumgait Tragedy*, 77.

11. This information comes from Grigory Kharchenko.

12. "USSR Deputy Prosecutor General: Two Inhabitants of Azerbaijan 'Fell Victim to Murder,'" Baku Radio 1545GMT (1845 GMT in Baku), 27 February 1988, as transcribed by BBC Monitoring. There has been much speculation as to why Katusev made a point of mentioning the two dead men. Possibly he was trying to intimidate the Armenians into curtailing their protests. Katusev committed suicide on 21 August 2000. According to the Interfax news agency, he was depressed after the death of his wife and son.

13. Zinaida Akopian in *The Sumgait Tragedy*, 191.

14. Konstantin Pkhakazde in *The Sumgait Tragedy*, 77.

15. Interview with Tagieva, 24 November 2000.

16. The book, edited by Samvel Shakhmuradian, was published in Russian (the language of the initial interviews) as *Sumgaitskaya Tragediya* in Yerevan in 1989, and in English as *The Sumgait Tragedy* in 1990.

17. Samvel Shakhmuradian and his researchers were preparing a second volume of eyewitness accounts telling tales of resistance, but it was never published.

18. One explanation for the decision not to touch the television sets was that they were valuable and therefore good looting material. Another is that Soviet sets had a reputation for exploding.

19. *The Sumgait Tragedy*, 127.

20. This information comes from Famil Ismailov, who was a member of the Sumgait Komsomol at the time. He noted that the head of the Komsomol, Eldar Mamedov, was nonetheless expelled from the Party along with other officials.

21. Ignatieff, *Blood and Belonging*, 14.

22. Interview with Kharchenko, 4 December 2000.

23. From the Politburo session of 29 February 1988, as cited.

24. The leading Politburo conservative, Yegor Ligachev, says that the fact that restraint had led to mass bloodshed in Sumgait was used to justify the use of force during the crisis in the Georgian capital Tbilisi in April 1989. On that occasion, troops were used earlier and killed twenty unarmed demonstrators. "The leitmotif of all the speeches [in the Politburo], which were received with approval, was to prevent ethnic conflict and more victims," wrote Ligachev. "We had to learn a lesson from Sumgait—not to be late again." Ligachev, *Inside Gorbachev's Kremlin*, 154.

25. Angus Roxburgh, "Gorbachev in Desperate Dash to Resolve Armenian Crisis," *The Sunday Times*, 6 March 1988.

26. *The Caucasian Knot*, 150.

27. "Teper' ya znayu chto chuvstvovali evrei Germanii v 1938 godu"

[Now I know what the Jews of Germany felt in 1938], *Krug*, Tel Aviv, 23 July 1989, reprinted in *Glazami Nezavisimikh Nablyudatelei* [Through the eyes of independent observers], 93–96. An Armenian source quotes Baku Radio from 27 February 1993 as saying that a commission on the Sumgait events had posthumously exonerated Akhmedov and called him a "hero"; Harutiunian, *Sobytiya* [Events], V, 30.

28. These versions come from, in order, Lyudmila Harutiunian, Isa Gambar, and Alexander Yakovlev. Yakovlev, who as a member of the Politburo could be expected to be well informed, said he had no firm evidence and proceeded to talk about how the KGB had organized the Vilnius events of 1991. It seemed as though he was telescoping the two events and retrospectively interpreting the events of 1988 in the light of what happened in 1991.

29. From *Elm*, the weekly of Azerbaijani Academy of Sciences, 13 May 1989, reprinted in *The Caucasian Knot*, 188–189. It should be pointed out that this article was so odious that the Armenians have reprinted it for their own purposes.

30. I visited Imanov and saw his films in Baku in June 2000, in the mistaken belief that they were objective documentaries. Imanov virtually accused me of being a spy. I therefore decided not to use any material from his films.

31. The figures come from a report by the Secretariat of the Central Committee on 11 June 1988. Russian Archives Project, Fond 89, Reel 1.003, 89/33/11.

32. Muslimzade is now a successful businessman. He declined to give an interview, saying he did not want to "return to the past."

33. On 10 May 1988, the Sumgait Town Party Committee condemned the leadership and employees of the Azerbaijan Pipe-Rolling Plant for the fact that "during the days of the complex situation, production of axes, knives and other objects which could be used by hooligan elements took place in the shops of the plant." As reported in the local newspaper, *Kommunist Sumgaita*, 13 May 1988. *The Sumgait Tragedy*, 7.

34. See Anatol Lieven, *The Baltic Revolution* (New Haven: Yale University Press, 1994), 188–201.

35. Canetti, *Crowds and Power*, 55–56.

36. The suffragette Sylvia Pankhurst saw the violence. "There was a fierce clamor for reprisals," she wrote. "The meanest elements among the jingoes worked up the first of the anti-German riots. These were deliberately organized, in no sense a spontaneous popular outburst; but the prospect of looting without fear of punishment made its appeal to certain sections of the poor and ignorant. Many a home was wrecked; many a peaceable working family lost its all. Stones were flung, children injured." E. Sylvia Pankhurst, *The Home Front, A Mirror to Life in England During the World War* (London: Hutchinson, 1932), 170.

37. Interview with Gukasian, 7 October 2000.

NOTES TO CHAPTER 3

1. In this chapter, I have changed the names of most of the former Shusha inhabitants to spare them any awkwardness.

2. Interview with Shugarian, 13 December 2000.

3. Interview with Galstian, 10 October 2000.

4. Interview with Abasov, 10 November 2000.

5. Interview with Sarkisian, 15 December 2000.

6. Interview with Kocharian, 25 May 2000.

NOTES TO CHAPTER 4

1. Interview with Kharchenko, 4 December 2000.

2. An additional explanation for the name Krunk is that in Russian its initials spell out the words "Committee for the Revolutionary Administration of Nagorny Karabakh."

3. Babken Araktsian, Ashot Manucharian, Vazgen Manukian, and Levon Ter-Petrosian.

4. Interview with Manukian, 5 May 2000.

5. Interview with Ter-Petrosian, 24 May 2000.

6. Russian Archives Project, Fond 89, Reel 1.003, 89/42/19.

7. Interview with Girenko, 2 June 2000.

8. Russian Archives Project, Fond 89, Reel 1.003, 89/42/18.

9. Interview with Yakovlev, 8 December 2000. In his memoirs, Ligachev says that he agreed with what he said in Baku with Gorbachev; Ligachev, *Inside Gorbachev's Kremlin*, 173.

10. Interview with Mikhailov, 5 December 2000.

11. Georgy Shakhnazarov, *Tsena Svobody* [The price of freedom], 212.

12. Quoted in Vladimir Grigorian, *Armenia 1988–1989*, (Yerevan, 1999), 118.

13. Malkasian, *Gha-ra-bagh!*, 116–117.

14. The ANM was known in Armenia by the initials HHK, and in Russia by the initials AOD.

15. According to the statistical calculations of Arif Yunusov, 186,000 Azerbaijanis and 18,000 Muslim Kurds fled Armenia for Azerbaijan, and 7,000 Muslim Kurds later left for Russia. Arif Yunusov, "Migratsionnye potoki—oborotnaya storona nezavisimosti" [Migration flows—the reverse side of independence], in *Rossiya i Zavkaz'ye: realii nezavisimosti i novoye partnyorstvo* [Russia and the Transcaucasus: The realities of independence and new parnership] (Moscow: Finstatinform, 2000), 108.

16. Interview with Stepanian, 28 April 2000.

17. As related by Gurgen Boyajian in an interview on 26 September 2000. This story could not be confirmed.

18. Bakatin, *Doroga v Proshedshem Vremeni* [Road in the past tense], 146.

19. Arif Yunusov, "Pogromy v Armenii v 1988–1989 Godakh" [Pogroms in Armenia in 1988–1989], *Ekspress-Khronika* 9 (186), 26 February 1991.

20. Ibid.

21. Rost, *Armenian Tragedy*, 192.

22. On scenes of celebrations in Baku, see Alexander Lebed, *Za derzhavu obidno* [Ashamed for the fatherland] (Moscow: Moskovskaya Pravda, 1995), 255–256.

23. Interview with Loshak, 6 December 2000.

24. Interview with Gazarian, 22 May 2000.

25. Shakhnazarov, *Tsena Svobody* [The price of freedom], 216.

26. On 11 December 1988. Roxburgh, *Second Russian Revolution*, 123.

27. Relative to the conditions of other Soviet prisoners, the Karabakh Committee lived relatively well. Levon Ter-Petrosian, for example, shared a large cell in the Matrosskaya Tishina (Sailors' rest) Prison with one other inmate, a dissident party leader from Bukhara in Central Asia. In August 1991, the same cell was given to the coup plotter and head of the KGB, Vladimir Kryuchkov.

28. Interview with Bonner by telephone, 17 September 2000.

29. Interview with Alizade, 9 June 2000.

30. Interview with Volsky, 1 June 2000.

31. Interview with Nefyodov, 7 December 2000. Andrei Pralnikov, "NKAO: Budni osobogo upravleniya" *Moskovskiye Novosti*, no. 45, 5 November 1989, reprinted in *Glazami nezavisimykh Nablyudatelei* [Through the eyes of independent observers], 123–124.

32. Interview with Byrkin, 1 June 2000.

33. Interview with Yesayan, 5 October 2000.

34. This summary of the Khojali events comes from the accounts of it in Malkasian, *Gha-ra-bagh!*; Rost, *Armenian Tragedy*; and *Khronika NKAO*.

35. Russian Archives Project, Fond 89, Reel 1.991, 89/10/42.

36. Interview with Manucharian, 4 May 2000.

37. *Le Figaro*, 26 July 1989.

38. Interview with Ter-Petrosian, 24 May 2000.

## NOTES TO CHAPTER 5

1. Villari, *Fire and Sword in the Caucasus*, 223–224.

2. Curtis, *Around the Black Sea*, 148.

3. The Russian civil servant I. Shopen did a detailed survey of the new "Armyanskaya Oblast," or "Armenian Region," between 1829 and 1832. He counted a population of 164,000, which was almost exactly half Armenian and half Shiite Muslim. Of the Armenians, 25,000 were indigenous and 57,000 were

immigrants. I. Shopen, *Istorichesky Pamyatnik Sostoyaniya Armyanksoi Oblasti v Epokhu eya Priosoedinenia k Rossiiskoi-Imperii* [A historical record of the condition of the Armenian region in the era of its joining the russian empire] (St. Petersburg: Typography of the Academy of Sciences, 1852), 639–642.

4. Lourie, "Yerevan's Phenomenon," 177–178.

5. According to different estimates, between 600,000 and 1.5 million Armenians were killed between 1915 and 1923. I use the term "Genocide" without wishing to enter the historical debate as to whether it is the appropriate term for the mass slaughter of the Armenians.

6. Koestler, *The Invisible Writing*, 109.

7. Ibid., 107.

8. Libaridian, "Reimagining the Past, Rethinking the Present," 143.

9. Interview with Harutiunian, 2 October 2000.

10. Quoted on *Russia Today*, 17 October 2000.

11. The story of the destruction of the mosque comes from Robert Cullen's article "Roots" in *The New Yorker*, 15 April 1991. Cullen saw its rubble in 1991.

12. Interview with Namazov, 14 November 2000.

NOTES TO CHAPTER 6

1. Interview with Alizade, 9 June 2000.

2. Interview with Mikhailov, 5 December 2000.

3. Audrey Alstadt, *The Azerbaijani Turks*, 202, quoting *Komsomolskaya Pravda* from 27 November 1988.

4. This story was heavily distorted by the time it got back to Baku. Many believed that there were plans to build an actual factory, not a guest house. Andrei Sakharov, who visited the site, described a bare hillside, with no sign of a "grove." Sakharov, *Moscow and Beyond*, 88.

5. Corley, "Dogging Dashnaks," 30–31.

6. Interview with Namazov, 14 November 2000.

7. Some maintain that Heidar Aliev was actually born in Armenia in 1921, not in Nakhichevan in 1923. His younger brother, Jalal Aliev, interviewed on 4 November 2000, said that the Aliev family came from the village of Jomartly in Zangezur but had moved to Nakhichevan by the time Heidar was born.

8. Interview with Mutalibov, 30 May 2000.

9. Interview with Panakhov, interpreted from Azeri, 8 November 2000.

10. Yunusova, "Mera Otvetsvennosti Politika" [The degree of responsibility of a politician], 11.

11. Avet Demurian and Andrei Pralnikov, "Blokada Armenii v eti dni" [The blockade of Armenia in these days], *Moskovskiye Novosti* 40: 1 October 1989, reprinted in *Glazami Nezavisimikh Nablyudatelei* [Through the eyes of independent witnesses], 125–127.

12. Swietochowski, *Russia and Azerbaijan*, 201.

13. Interview with Saakova, 14 December 2000.

14. Bill Keller, "Did Moscow incite Azerbaijanis? Some see a plot," *New York Times*, 19 February 1990.

15. Interview with Mutalibov, 30 May 2000.

16. Bakatin, *Doroga v Proshedshem Vremeni* [Road in the past tense], 174.

17. Z. Japparov. "Trevozhny Yanvar' v Lenkorani" [Alarming January in Lenkoran], *Bakinsky Rabochy*, 17 January 1990, reprinted in *Chyorny Yanvar'* [Black January], 70–74.

18. Neimet Panakhov, Etibar Mamedov, Rahim Gaziev, and Abulfaz Elchibey.

19. Dr. Arif Yunusov estimates a death toll of eighty-six, of whom sixty-six died in Baku and twenty afterward.

20. Interview with Abdullayeva, 11 April 2000.

21. As related by Arzu Abdullayev and Zardusht Alizade.

22. Interview with Girenko, 2 June 2000.

23. Interview with Mamedov, 22 November 2000.

24. This is according to Vyacheslav Mikhailov, who was present when Primakov spoke to Gorbachev by telephone.

25. From the report by the military investigation group Shchit, published in Melikov, *Ya Obvinyayu* [I accuse], 176–179. Many of the details here are taken from Melikov's collection of documents and articles, which is the fullest account of the 20 January crackdown.

26. The story of Aliev and January 1990 is fertile territory for students of his career. If he had a plan, it may have been to have his old protégé, Hasan Hasanov, become the new Party leader in Azerbaijan. Hasanov, although a top Party official, made an outspokenly anti-Moscow speech in Baku on 8 January, as the trouble was beginning. This was the cue for several members of the Popular Front to propose that he should replace Vezirov—perhaps at Aliev's instigation, if this supposition is correct. In the event, Hasanov was defeated in a straight vote against Mutalibov, although he later became Aliev's foreign minister. After the bloodshed, Aliev also welcomed Etibar Mamedov at the Azerbaijani representative's office in Moscow, shortly before Mamedov was arrested. For some who have plotted Aliev and Mamedov's strange history of opposition and collaboration, this marked the beginning of an alliance between them.

27. Interview with Hajizade, 15 November 2000.

## NOTES TO CHAPTER 7

1. Turan News Agency, 31 March 2000, as reported by BBC Monitoring.

2. Henry, *Baku, An Eventful History*, 173.

3. Hopkirk, *On Secret Service East of Constantinople*, 357.

4. Richards, *Epics of Everyday Life*, 144–145.

5. All of these conversations are from 14 December 2000.

6. Interview with Orujev, 24 November 2000.

7. Sharg News Agency 1 February 2000, as reported by BBC Monitoring.

8. Interview with Asadov, 29 March 2000.

9. Bechhofer, *In Denikin's Russia*, 309–310.

NOTES TO CHAPTER 8

1. Interview with Mirzoyev, 12 April 2000.

2. Interview with Horton, 2 January 2001.

3. Zulfugarov, *NKAO*, 38. Interview with Gukasian, 7 October 2000.

4. The acronym OMOR stands for the Russian name Otryady Militsii Operativnogo Reagirovaniia, or "Operative Response Police Units." OMON stands for Otryady Militsii Osobogo Naznacheniia, or "Special Designation Police Units." I am very grateful to Robin Bhatty for his insights on this and the whole issue of paramilitaries and the formation of armed forces.

5. Report of the Delegation of the First International Andrei D. Sakharov Congress, which visited Azerbaijan and Armenia 13–16 July 1991.

6. Interview with Byrkin, 1 June 2000.

7. Interview with Manukian, 5 May 2000.

8. Interview with Eiramjiants, 28 September 2000. Vladimir Kiselyov, "Doroga v Nikuda" [The road to nowhere], *Moskovskiye Novosti* 35, 2 September 1990.

9. Interview with Avsharian, 18 May 2000.

10. Balayan, *Between Heaven and Hell*, 270.

11. Russian Archives Project, Fond 89, Reel 1.989 89/4/17.

12. Interview with Mutalibov, 30 May 2000.

13. Interview with Manucharian, 4 May 2000.

14. As reported by the Sakharov Congress in July 1991.

15. Shaumian region was renamed Geranboi Region by Azerbaijan in January 1991.

16. Details on the Getashen operation are taken from the reports by Memorial and the Sakharov Congress, and Murphy, "Operation 'Ring,'" 86.

17. According to Major General A. Zaitsev, commander of Soviet Internal Forces in Nagorny Karabakh,

It became clear that the Internal Forces would not retreat one step from the law and a firm barrier would be placed against the looting carried out by the OMONites. Then the 23rd Motorized Division of the Soviet Ministry of Defense, consisting 80 percent of Azerbajianis, was called in to carry out acts of forced deportation of Armenians. After that the situation radically changed: the Azerbaijani leadership resorted to a new tactic. Before the beginning of a deportation the state of emergency was canceled in the given region. We were forced to withdraw our units, after which the Azerbaijani side carried out 'special operations' about which we were not even informed.

"Voennye v Karabakhe—Posredniki ili zalozhniki?" [The military in Karabakh —mediators or hostages?], *Argumenty i Fakty*, 7 February 1992.

18. Interview with Shabad, 7 December 2000.

19. Shakhnazarov, *Tsena Svobody* [The price of freedom], 220–221; interview with Mirzoyev.

20. Interview with Shabad.

21. Cvetana Paskaleva, *Vysoty Nadezhdy* [The heights of hope], 1991. Reissued on *Rany Karabakha* [Wounds of Karabakh], TS Film, Yerevan, 1996.

22. Melander, "The Nagorno-Karabakh Conflict Revisited," 70.

23. Ibid., 71.

24. Report of the Delegation of the First International Andrei D. Sakharov Congress on Events in Nagorny Karabakh, 13–16 July 1991, 3.

25. Interview with Sarkisian, 4 May 2000.

26. Interview with Sarkisian.

27. Interview with Miller, 9 January 2001.

NOTES TO CHAPTER 9

1. Interview with Gambar, 7 April 2000.

2. Interview with Kocharian, 25 May 2000.

3. Laitin and Suny, "Karabakh: Thinking a Way out," 145.

4. Thomson has been rather demonized by Armenian historians for imposing a de facto Azerbaijani rule over Karabakh, which then carried over into the Communist era. The archives suggest that he was acting more out of an instinct for stability than any Armenophobia: while believing that it was best to keep Azerbaijan's control over Karabakh, Thomson also cabled London, arguing that the Armenians should be given territory in eastern Turkey.

5. For Britain's role the Caucasus in 1919–1920, see Artin H. Arslanian, "Britain and the Transcaucasian Nationalities during the Russian Civil War," in *Transcaucasia, Nationalism and Social Change*, ed. Ronald Grigor Suny (Ann Arbor: University of Michigan Press, 1983).

6. Hovannisian, *The Republic of Armenia*, III, 133.

7. Bechhofer, *In Denikin's Russia*, 283.

8. Mutafian, *The Caucasian Knot*, 134.

9. *Istoricheskaya Spravka*, 33.

10. Swietochowski, *Russia and Azerbaijan*, 104–105; Pipes, *The USSR*, 46; *Istoricheskaya Spravka*, 33.

11. On the economic issues and especially the nomads, see Yamskov, *Ethnic Conflict in the Transcaucasus*.

12. Interview with Yakovlev, 8 December 2000.

13. The population figures are taken from Brian D. Silver, "Population Redistribution and the Ethnic Balance in Transcaucasia," in *Transcaucasia, Nationalism and Social Change*, ed. Suny, 373–395.

14. Interview with Shamil Askerov, 20 November 2000.

15. Interview with Tiskhov, 5 December 2000.

16. Vaksberg, *The Soviet Mafia*, 192.

17. *Moskovksy Komsomolets*, 18 October 1995.

18. Interview with Muradian, 5 May 2000.

19. Interview with Rustamkhanli, 8 November 2000.

20. Interview with Kaputikian, 26 September 2000.

21. Interview with Ohanjenian, 5 October 2000.

22. In 1989, the average wage in the Soviet Union was 182 rubles; in Azerbaijan, 135 rubles. Arif Yunusov, "Azerbaijan v Postsovetsky Period: Problemy i Vozmozhnye Puti Razvitiya" [Azerbaijan in the post-Soviet period: Problems and possible paths of development], in *Severny Kavkaz-Zakavkaz'ye: Problemy Stabil'nosti i Perspektivy Razvitiya* [The North Caucasus and Transcaucasus: Problems of stability and perspectives for development] (Moscow, 1997), 130.

23. Sakharov, *Moscow and Beyond*, 88.

24. Vaksberg, *The Soviet Mafia*, 254.

25. Kocharian, interview on Ostankino Russian Television with Andrei Karaulov on the *Moment Istiny* [Moment of truth] program, 10 January 1994, republished in Harutiunian, *Sobytiya* [Events], Part V, 271.

26. Interview with Shugarian, 13 December 2000.

27. Interview with Alekperov, 7 June 2000.

28. Velichko, *Kavkaz* [The Caucasus], 155.

29. Balayan, *Ochag* [The hearth], 21.

30. Slezkine, "The USSR as a Communal Apartment," 229. The image of the mansion is an adaptation of Slezkine's brilliantly employed metaphor of the Soviet Union as a communal apartment.

31. Gellner, *Nationalism in the Vacuum*, 250.

NOTES TO CHAPTER 10

1. On the *meliks*, see Hewsen, "The Meliks of Eastern Armenia," 1972, and Dudwick, "Armenian-Azerbaijani Relations and Karabagh." Yermolov's letter is reprinted in *Armyano-russkiye otnosheniya* [Armenian-Russian relations], vol. II, 178–181.

2. *The Bondage and Travels of Johann Schiltberger*, 86.

3. Haxthausen, *Transcaucasia*, 438.

4. S. A. Mamedov, *Istoricheskiye Svyazi Azerbaidzhanskogo i Armyanskogo naroda* [Historical ties between the Azerbaijani and Armenian peoples] (Baku: Elm, 1977), 172–180.

5. Zori Balayan, interviewed by *The Armenian Mirror-Spectator*, Boston, 20 February 1988, republished in Libaridian, *The Karabagh File*, 76.

6. *Salam* No. 1. (Published as a supplement of *Eliler* 12 (97), 19–30 March 2000).

7. I am grateful to Professor Robert Hewsen for guiding me through this bewildering historical thicket. Any misinterpretations made in what follows are purely my own. There is an excellent account of the whole Caucasian controversy in Karny, *Highlanders*, 371–404.

8. Buniatov's *Mxitar Gosh, Albanskaya Khronika, predislovie, perevod i kommentarii Z. M. Buniatova* [Mxitar Gosh, the Albanian Chronicle, forward, translation, and commentary by Z. M. Buniatov], published in 1960, is an unattributed translation of C. F. J. Dowsett's "The Albanian Chronicle of Mxitar Gosh," published in *Bulletin of the School of Oriental and African Studies* XXI, Part 3 (1958). Buniatov's "O Khronoligicheskom nesootvetsvii glav 'Istorii Agvan' Moiseya Kagankatvatsi" [On the chronological noncorrespondence of chapters of Movses Dasxuranc'i], published in Baku in 1965, is an unattributed translation of Robert Hewsen's "On the Chronology of Movses Dasxuranc'i," published in *Bulletin of the School of Oriental and African Studies* XXVII, Part 1 (1954). Buniatov also selectively quoted and mistranslated European sources and travelers on Karabakh, including Johann Schiltberger; see George A. Bournoutian, "Rewriting History: Recent Azeri Alterations of Primary Sources Dealing with Karabakh," *Journal of the Society for Armenian Studies* 6 (1992–1993): 185–190.

9. Interviews with Mamedova, 8 June and 28 November 2000.

10. Igrar Aliev and Kamil Mamedzade, *Albanskiye Pamyatniki Karabakha* [The Albanian monuments of Karabakh] (Baku: Azerbaijan Devlet Neshriyaty, 1997), 19.

11. Interview with Akopian, 13 October 2000.

12. Robert Hewsen, "Ethno-History and the Armenian Influence upon the Caucasian Albanians."

13. Letter from Robert Hewsen, 10 January, 2001.

NOTES TO CHAPTER II

1. Interview with Shabad, 7 December 2000.

2. Interview with Guluzade in English, 28 November 2000.

3. 20 August 1991. As reported in Harutiunian, *Sobytiya*, IV.

4. Interview with Danielian, 14 October 2000.

5. Interview with Hovanisian, 15 December 2000.

6. Interview with Manucharian, 15 October 2000.

7. Interview with Mekhtiev, 31 March 2000.

8. Interview with Mamedov, 22 November 2000.

9. Interview with Ali, 4 April 2000.

10. On "Mamed the Mule," see Goltz, *Azerbaijan Diary*, 149–153.

11. Interview with Kocharian, 25 May 2000.

12. Interview with Sarkisian, 15 December 2000.

13. The official account of the Interior Ministry's withdrawal is in A. Petrov, "Dlya politikov Karabakh—urok, dlya soldat—vtoroi Afganistan" [For politicians, Karabakh is a lesson; for soldiers, it is a second Afghanistan], *Krasnaya Zvezda*, 19 February 1992.

14. Interview with Shabad.

15. Interview with Horton, 2 January 2001. Ashot Manucharian said that "we often paid the Stepanakert Regiment and they fired at Shusha" (from his interview of 15 October 2000). Arif Yunusov even gives prices, although without sources. He says that twenty liters of alcohol were paid for firing at Shusha; five thousand rubles for the use of an APC in an operation; one thousand for it firing a shot. Arif Yunusov, "Tragediya Khodjaly" [The tragedy of Khodjaly], *Zerkalo* No. 26, 20–26 June 1992. Alexander Kasatov (in "Sama ne Svoya" [Not its own]) estimates that of an original number of 1,200 soldiers in the 366th Regiment, 350 remained when it was withdrawn.

16. "Voennye v Karabakhe—Posredniki ili zalozhniki?" [Soldiers in Karabakh—mediators or hostages?], *Argumenty i Fakty* No. 7, February 1992.

17. Interview with Danielian, 14 October 2000.

18. Goltz, *Azerbaijan Diary*, 150; interview with Ali; Human Rights Watch, *Azerbaijan, Seven Years of Conflict*, 51–57.

19. Interview with Melkonian, 7 May 2000.

20. Agajanov, *Svetlaya Storona Voiny* [The bright side of the war], 57.

21. Arif Yunusov, "Tragediya Khodjaly" [The tragedy of Khodjaly], *Zerkalo* No. 25, 13–19 June 1992.

22. Goltz, *Azerbaijan Diary*, 119; Elman Mamedov, head of the Khojali town administration, interviewed in Aghdam by ANS television, February 1992; Yunusov, "Tragediya Khodjaly" [The tragedy of Khodjaly], *Zerkalo* No. 25, 13–19 June 1992. Goltz says that Hajiev had 60 OMON policemen under his command; Yunusov puts the total number of defenders at 160.

23. Human Rights Watch, *Bloodshed in the Caucasus*, 22.

24. Anatol Lieven, "Bodies Mark Site of Karabakh Massacre," *The Times*, 3 March 1992; interview with Agayev, 25 November 2000.

25. Many different statistics have emerged from the Khojali tragedy. This is not surprising, considering the circumstances. Access to the killing grounds near Nakhichevanik was difficult; hundreds of people were taken prisoner and

for many days were unaccounted for. A general phenomenon of these tragedies—true also of the pogroms in Sumgait and Baku—also has to be taken into
account: lists of dead are compiled that include people who are missing and
later turn up alive, or who were seen lying motionless but were in fact wounded
rather than dead. In ascending order of magnitude, the following figures have
variously been given: Namig Aliev, one of the parliamentary investigators, told
Helsinki Watch in April 1992 that 213 victims had been buried in Aghdam. Another Azerbaijani official, Aiden Rasulov, told the same team of researchers that
more than 300 bodies showing evidence of a violent death—and presumably not
including those who had died of cold—had been submitted for forensic exami-
nation. (The two foregoing figures come from Human Rights Watch, *Bloodshed
in the Caucasus*, 23.) The newspaper *Karabakh* reported that the Commission for
Aid to Refugees from Khojaly had distributed benefits to 476 families of those
who had been killed (letter to the author from Arif Yunusov, April 2001.) The
imam in Aghdam showed Thomas Goltz an incomplete list of 477 reported dead
by their families (Goltz, *Azerbaijan Diary*, 122–123). The Azerbaijani newspaper
*Ordu* (issues 9, 16, and 20, 1992) printed a list of 636 victims (Yunusov letter).

26. Reporting from Aghdam, Thomas Goltz had considerable problems
persuading editors to take his story seriously. The Mutalibov interview was on
2 April 1991 in the Russian newspaper *Nezavisimaya Gazeta*.

27. Paul Quinn-Judge, "Armenians, Azerbaijanis tell of terror; Behind an
alleged massacre, a long trail of personal revenge," *Boston Globe*, 15 March 1992.

28. *Khodjaly, Khronika Genotsida* [Khojali, a chronicle of genocide] (Baku
1992), 32.

29. Quinn-Judge, op. cit.

30. Interview with Avsharian, 18 May 2000.

31. The former Azerbaijani president Ayaz Mutalibov says that he learned
that Gaziev had acquired Grads only when the bombardment of Stepanakert
began: "One day someone reports to me that this Rahim Gaziev is attacking
Stepanakert with Grads. I rang and said, 'Have you gone mad?' He says, 'What
else can I do?' I say, 'What do you think, the Armenians won't get Grads, do you
understand what you're doing?'" Interview with Mutalibov, 30 May 2000.

32. Interview with Kerimov, 13 November 2000.

33. Interview with Byrkin, 1 June 2000.

34. Bennett, *Crying Wolf*, 65.

35. On Maraga, see Human Rights Watch, *Bloodshed in the Caucasus*, 29;
Caroline Cox and John Eibner, *Ethnic Cleansing in Progress: War in Nagorno-
Karabakh* (London: Institute for Religious Minorities in the Islamic World, 1993);
"Tragediya Maragi: Chetyre Goda Spustya" [The tragedy of Maraga: Four years
later], *Golos Armenii*, 9 April 1996.

36. Mekhtiev himself says that only seventeen men died in the Karintak/
Dashalty operation.

37. Many of the details on Shusha come from *Sügüt* [The fall], a film shown by ANS in Baku in 1997.

38. Interview with Agayev, 13 April 2000.

39. Interview with Ter-Tatevosian, 28 September 2000.

40. Interview with Orujev, 29 November 2000.

41. Interview with Husseinov, 12 April 2000.

42. The commander of the Shusha tank was Albert Agarunov, a Baku Jew, who was killed a few days later on the Shusha-Lachin road. Thomas Goltz observed his funeral at Alley of the Martyrs in Baku.

43. Interview with Husseinova, 12 April 2000.

44. Ter-Tatevosian estimates Armenian losses at 58 men and Azerbaijani losses at 200. Orujev says that more Armenians died and that he lost 159 men killed and 22 missing.

45. Interview with Mamedov, 14 November 2000.

46. This is the view of Ashot Manucharian, then Ter-Petrosian's national security adviser.

47. ANS television interview with Basayev, 17 July 2000, as reported by BBC Monitoring.

48. Goltz, *Azerbaijan Diary*, 185–186; David Ljunggren, "Azerbaijanis Say Armenians Attack Town near Karabakh," Reuters, Baku, 12 May 1992; Elif Kaban, "Azeri Strongman Says War Makes Elections Futile," Reuters, Ankara, 11 May 1992.

49. Interview with Pashayev, interpreted from Azeri, 13 November 2000.

50. Interview with Ohanian, 16 May 2000.

51. *Heç Kim va Heç na Unudulmayacag* [No one and nothing will be forgotten], ANS, 1992. Jengiz Mustafiev was killed less than a month later, on 15 June 1992, near Aghdam.

NOTES TO CHAPTER 12

1. The Karabakh Armenian leader Arkady Gukasian says that under a just peace agreement, he would have no objections to Azerbaijanis returning to Shusha, but in the same breath he suggests that in practice it is unlikely to happen. In an interview on 30 March 2001, he said: "We believe that refugees have the right to return to their homes, irrespective of nationality. That concerns both Armenian and Azerbaijan refugees. Another matter is 'Will the refugees want that, when there is no stable peace, there is a risk of a resumption of war?'"

2. Kurban Said, *Ali and Nino*, 44. None of Murat's biographers even mention an Armenian connection. A 1905 biography of Murat relates, for example, that he was born in La Bastide-Fortuniere, a small village in Guyenne, and that "his family's roots there went back several centuries." Jules Chavanon and Georges Saint-Yves, *Joachim Murat* (Paris: Librairie Hachette, 1905), 3.

3. Shushinsky, *Shusha*, 134–135; Swietochowski, *Russia and Azerbaijan*, 10. Swietochowski notes that Shiite volunteers also fought with the Russians against Sunnis in the Russo-Turkish war of 1853–1855.

4. Shushinsky, *Shusha*, 135. Pushkin's description of the Karabakh regiment is in his *Journey to Erzerum*.

5. Lisitsian, *Armyane Nagornogo Karabakha* [The Armenians of Nagorny Karabakh], 44.

6. Keppel, *Personal Narrative of a Journey*, 188.

7. Ibid., 194.

8. Villari, *Fire and Sword in the Caucasus*, 199.

9. Snark news agency, 25 December 1992, quoted in Harutiunian, *Sobytiya* [Events], IV, 301.

10. Interview with Gabrielian, 15 December 2000.

11. Interview with Archbishop Parkev, 12 May 2000.

## NOTES TO CHAPTER 13

1. From the film by Cvetana Paskaleva, *Dorogiye Moi, Zhivye ili Myortviye* [My dears, alive or dead], 1993, re-released by TS Films, Yerevan, 1996.

2. Interview with Ali, 4 April 2000.

3. Pavel Felgenhauer, "Nakanune 'Reshayushchikh' Srazhenii" [On the eve of "decisive" battles], *Nezavisimaya Gazeta*, 18 July 1992.

4. Interview with Western diplomat; Goltz, *The Hidden Russian Hand*, 112.

5. Interview with Kocharian, 25 May 2000.

6. Interview with Sarkisian, 15 December 2000.

7. Human Rights Watch, *Azerbaijan, Seven Years of Conflict*, 87.

8. Interview with Levon Eiramjiants, 28 September, 2000.

9. In part, this discrepancy was the Armenians' own fault. Armenian politicians had objected strongly to the opening of a large new ammunition depot next to Lake Sevan in 1989, and the depot was therefore placed instead near Aghdam in Azerbaijan. For a detailed background on the weapons inherited by both sides, see Petrosian, "What Are the Reasons for Armenians' Success?"

10. Interview with Yunusova, 20 November 2000.

11. Interview with Hajizade, 28 March 2000.

12. Dmitry Danilov, "Russia's search for an international mandate in Transcaucasia," in Coppieters, *Contested Borders in the Caucasus*, note 161.

13. Interview with Ter-Petrosian, 24 May 2000.

14. Rokhlin estimated the cost of the weapons alone at $720 million. The figure of one billion dollars includes transportation costs, spare parts, and fuel. Pavel Felgenhauer says he believes the Armenians paid for some of the costs. In July 1992, Felgenhauer also wrote that the Armenians were handed the weapons of the Yerevan Division of the 4th Army; op. cit. For the most detailed

breakdown of the weaponry, see Lev Rokhlin, "Spetsoperatsia ili komerche-skaya afera?" [A special operation or a commercial deal?], *Nezavisimoye Voen-noye Obozreniye*, 13 (1997). Rokhlin was murdered in July 1998, but there was no suggestion that the crime was connected to his revelations.

15. Interview with Felgenhauer, 6 December 2000.

16. Interview with Neftaliev, 28 November, 2000.

17. Kasatov, "Sama ne Svoya" [Not its own], 1.

18. Interview with Hajizade, 15 November, 2000.

19. Armenian TV Channel 1, Yerevan, in Armenian, 5 March 2001, as reported by BBC monitoring.

20. Interview with Kazimirov, 1 December 2000.

21. Interview with Zulfugarov, 9 November 2000; Turan News Agency, 28 September, 1992. My thanks to Laura Le Cornu for information on the Sochi meeting.

22. Interview with Hovanisian, 15 December 2000.

23. Interview with Melkonian, 7 May 2000.

24. Interview with Boyajian, 26 September 2000.

25. Interview with Sadyqov, 6 April 2000.

26. Agajanov, *Svetlaya Storona Voiny* [The bright side of the war], 33.

27. Interview with Azad Isazade, former press secretary, Ministry of Defense, 21 November 2000; interview with David Petrosian, 25 May 2000.

28. Lee Hockstader, "Armenians Winning with Creativity, Aid," *The Washington Post*, 12 September 1993. Serzh Sarkisian claims that the Karabakh Armenians captured 156 tanks in the course of the war.

29. Interview with Manukian, 3 October, 2000.

30. A Western diplomat who went to visit Elchibey not long after he fled Baku in June 1993 said that he asked Elchibey why he tolerated the dissent of Gaziev and Husseinov for so long. Elchibey said they were the only two men who could easily obtain arms from the Russians.

31. Interview with Askerov, 20 November 2000.

32. Sergei Bablumian, "Kelbadzhar v Ogne" [Kelbajar on fire], *Izvestia*, 6 April 1993.

33. Human Rights Watch, *Azerbaijan, Seven Years of Conflict*, 16.

34. For example, a military map captured by the Azerbaijanis and dated 1 April 1993, had belonged to a Major S. O. Barsegian. The dates on the map showed that Barsegian had been on the shores of Lake Sevan on 2 March, crossed the Armenia-Azerbaijan border at 4:30 P.M. on 27 March, and headed toward Kelbajar. Azad Isazade, formerly of Azerbaijan's Defense Ministry, has a copy of the map. Regarding the alleged Russian involvement, Shamil Askerov says that he saw six airplanes above Kelbajar, which could only have been Russian. The Azerbaijani Security Ministry later released an audiocassette of an intercepted radio conversation between an officer speaking very pure Russian

and a heavily accented Armenian. All Armenian officials strongly deny Russian involvement.

35. The most vivid and authoritative account of the Husseinov coup is in Thomas Goltz's *Azerbaijan Diary*, 356–392.

36. Interview with Akhmedov, 19 November 2000.

37. Goltz, *Azerbaijan Diary*, 399.

## NOTE TO CHAPTER 14

1. For statistics on displaced persons, see Appendix 1. In this chapter I use the general word "refugee" to cover people who are technically "Internally Displaced Persons" because they were driven from their homes inside their own country.

## NOTES TO CHAPTER 15

1. Goltz, Azerbaijan Diary, 413–414; Harutiunian, *Sobytiya* [Events], V, 252–253.

2. Information on the thirty-three battalions was supplied by Arif Yunusov.

3. Interview with Baburian, 7 October 2000.

4. Interview with Kocharian, 25 May 2000; interview with Kazimirov, 1 December 2000; interview with Tofik Zulfugarov, 9 November 2000.

5. Interview with Manucharian, 15 October 2000.

6. Interview with Agayev, 25 November 2000. Agayev says Babayan was arrested after a criminal "settling of scores" in which he shot dead two Armenian brothers in a café in Askeran.

7. Interview with Gukasian, 7 October 2000.

8. As reported by Vazgen Manukian in the interview of 15 October 2000.

9. Maresca, "Lost Opportunities," 475.

10. The composition of the Minsk Group has changed over the years. Its initial eleven members in 1992 were Belarus, Czechoslovakia, France, Germany, Italy, Russia, Sweden, Turkey, and the United States, as well as Armenia and Azerbaijan. By 2000, the former Czechoslovakia had been replaced by Austria, Finland, and Norway.

11. Interview with Guluzade in English, 28 November 2000.

12. Interview with Ter-Petrosian, 24 May 2000.

13. Maresca, "Lost Opportunities," 482.

14. Ibid. After leaving the Minsk Group, Raffaelli was one of the politicians subpoenaed in Italy's Tangentopoli corruption investigations.

15. Interview with Oskanian, 13 December 2000.

16. Quoted in Hannes Adomeit, "Russian National Security Interests," in

*Security Dilemmas in Russia and Eurasia*, ed. Roy Allision and Christoph Bluth (London: Royal Institute of International Affairs, 1998), 38.

17. Interview with Hajizade, 15 November 2000.

18. Interview with Guluzade, 28 November 2000.

19. Harutiunian, *Sobytiya* [Events], V, 317.

20. Kazimirov, "Rossiya i 'Minskaya Gruppa'" [Russia and "The Minsk Group"].

21. Maresca, "Agony of Indifference in Nagorno-Karabakh," 83.

22. Kazimirov, "Karabakh. Kak eto bylo" [Karabakh. How it was], 49.

23. Human Rights Watch, *Azerbaijan, Seven Years of Conflict*, 67–73.

24. Ibid., 46.

25. The following account of the Kelbajar campaign comes from information supplied by Azad Isazade, former press secretary in Azerbaijan's Defense Ministry, and Tigran Kzmalian, who was correspondent for the Russian television news program *Vesti* on the Armenian side at the time.

26. The figures come from Arif Yunusov.

27. Interview with Namazov, 14 November 2000. Kazimirov himself denies ever having threatened the Azerbaijanis.

28. Interview with Kazimirov, 1 December 2000.

29. Interview with Guliev, 13 September 2000.

30. Interview with Kocharian, 25 May 2000.

NOTES TO CHAPTER 16

1. Radio Free Europe/Radio Liberty, Armenian Service, 25 September 2000.

2. Interview with Melkonian, 7 May 2000.

3. Interview with Babayan, 27 February 2000.

4. Interview with Gukasian, 10 October 2000.

5. Interview with Danielian, 16 May 2000.

6. For a stimulating discussion of the issues surrounding the unrecognized states, see Dov Lynch, "End States in Post-Soviet Conflicts: Engaging Separatist States," *WEU Institute for Security Studies*, July 2001.

NOTES TO CHAPTER 17

1. Armenian news agency Snark, 26 March 2001, as reported by BBC Monitoring.

2. Interview with Oskanian in English, 13 December 2000.

3. Interview with Kazimirov, 1 December 2000; Human Rights Watch, *Azerbaijan, Seven Years of Conflict*, 84.

4. From *Respublika Armenia*, 23 September 1994, reprinted in Harutiunian, *Sobytiya* [Events], V, 399.

5. Interview with Zulfugarov, 9 November 2000.

6. Carol Migdalovitz, "The Armenia-Azerbaijan Conflict," CRS Issue Brief for Congress, updated 3 December 1996.

7. There are many versions of this quotation. This one, from the 1997 Annual Report of the International Helsinki Federation for Human Rights, appears to be one of the more reliable.

8. Interview with Ter-Petrosian, 24 May 2000.

9. The details of the two peace plans come from copies leaked to the Azerbaijani press in 2001. The translation is from "OSCE Karabakh Peace Proposals Leaked," RFE/RL *Caucasus Report* 4, no. 8, 23 February 2001.

10. From the Russian translation of Ter-Petrosian's press conference in *Respublika Armenia*, 30 September 1997.

11. Interview with Gukasian, 7 October 1997.

12. Interview with Sarkisian, 15 December 2000.

13. *UNDP in Azerbaijan, Country Review Report, 1999*, 15–16, 17.

14. See Paul Goble, "How The 'Goble Plan' Was Born," RFE/RL *Caucasus Report* 3, no. 23, 8 June 2000.

15. A very detailed account of the massacres and their aftermath was published in *Nouvelles d'Arménie*, no. 48, December 1999. Some clarifications of what happened emerged at Hunanian's trial; see "Chief defendant in Armenian shootings case says plans went awry from start," *Noyan Tapan* in Russian, 15 May 2001, as reported by BBC Monitoring.

16. Turan news agency, 19 June 2001, as reported by BBC Monitoring.

17. Interview with Kocharian, 25 May 2000.

## NOTES TO CONCLUSION

1. *Golos Armenii*, Yerevan, 27 March 2001.

2. Guliev interview in *Ekho* (Baku), 20 June 2001, as reported by BBC Monitoring.

3. The figures are from the sociologist Gevork Pogosian, quoted in John Daniszewski, "A Desperate, Destitute Nation Deserts Itself," *Los Angeles Times*, 30 April 2001.

4. Interview with Shakhverdiev, 31 October 2000.

5. Interview with Sarkisian, 15 December 2000.

6. Interview with Mekhtiev, 31 March 2000.

7. ANS television, Baku, 9 May 2001, as reported by BBC Monitoring.

8. Interview with Sarkisian, 4 May 2000.

9. *Zerkalo*, Baku, 26 December 1998.

10. Beilock, "What Is Wrong with Armenia."

11. *Turkish Daily News*, 25 October, 2001.

12. Interview with Kocharian, 21 May 2001.

13. Interview with Gukasian, 7 October 1997.
14. Dowsett, *Sayat-Nova*, 427.
15. Ibid., 434.

NOTES TO APPENDIX I

1. Yunusov kindly gave me a copy of his unpublished article "Statistics of the Karabakh War."
2. *CIA World Factbook 1999*.
3. Quoted in Harutiunian, *Sobytiya* [Events], V, 348.
4. As well as his unpublished article, Yunusov has written "Armyano-Azerbaidzhansky Konflikt: Migratsionnye Aspekty" [The Armenian-Azerbaijani conflict: Aspects of migration] in Zh Zaionchovskaya (ed.), *Migratsionnaya Situatsiya v Stranakh SNG* [The migration situation in CIS countries] (Moscow, 1999); and "Migratsionnye potoki—oborotnaya storona nezavisimosti" [Migration flows—the reverse side of independence], in *Rossiya i Zavkaz'ye: realii nezavisimosti i novoye partnyorstvo* [Russia and the Transcaucasus: the realities of independence and new parnership] (Moscow, Finstatinform, 2000).

# Bibliography

For sources of news on the Caucasus I have drawn mainly on Radio Free Europe/Radio Liberty (especially the Caucasus Report), which can be found at www.rferl.org; the Armenian Groong news service (http://groong.usc.edu/news/); the Azerbaijani news service Habarlar-L; the Caucasus Reporting Service of the Institute for War and Peace Reporting (www.iwpr.net).

Adams, Terry. *Caspian Hydrocarbons, the Politicisation of Regional Pipelines, and the Destabilisation of the Caucasus*. Brussels: The Centre for European Policy Studies (CEPS), 1998.

Agajanov, L. E. *Svetlaya Storona Voiny* [The bright side of the war]. Yerevan: Noyan Tapan, 1999.

Alstadt, Audrey. *The Azerbaijani Turks: Power and Identity under Russian Rule*. Stanford: Hoover Institution Press, 1992.

*Armyano-russkiye otnosheniya: Sbornik Dokumentov* [Armenian-Russian relations: A collection of documents]. Vols. I–III. Yerevan: Academy of Sciences, 1953.

Bakatin, Vadim. *Doroga v Proshedshem Vremeni* [Road in the past tense]. Moscow: Dom, 1999.

Balayan, Zori. *Ochag* [The hearth]. Yerevan: Sovetakhan Grokh, 1984.

Balayan, Zori. *Between Hell and Heaven: The Struggle for Karabakh*. Yerevan: Amaras, 1997.

Bechhofer, C. E. *In Denikin's Russia and the Caucasus, 1919–1920*. London: Collins, 1921. Reprinted by Arno Press, 1971.

Beilock, Richard. "What Is Wrong with Armenia." *Caucasian Regional Studies* 4 Issue 1 (1999).

Bennett, Vanora. *Crying Wolf: The Return of War to Chechnya*. London: Picador, 1998.

Bournoutian, George (ed.). *A History of Qarabagh. An Annotated Translation of Mirza Jamal Javanshir Qarabaghi's* Tarikh-e Qarabagh. Costa Mesa, Calif.: Mazda Publishers, 1994.

Brook, Stephen. *Claws of the Crab: Georgia and Armenia in Crisis*. London: Picador, 1992.

Canetti, Elias. *Crowds and Power*. London: Penguin, 1973.

Chorbajian, Levon, Patrick Donabédian, and Claude Mutafian. *The Caucasian*

*Knot, The History and Geo-Politics of Nagorno-Karabagh.* London and Atlantic Highlands, N.J.: Zed Books, 1994.

*Chyorny Yanvar'. Baku 1990* [Black January. Baku 1990]. Baku: Azerneshr, 1990.

Coppieters, Bruno (ed.). *Contested Borders in the Caucasus.* Brussels: VUB Press, 1996.

Corley, Felix. "Dogging Dashnaks, Dissidents and Dodgy Dealers. Armenians and the KGB." *Armenian Forum* 2 No. 3 (2001): 1–32.

Croissant, Michael. *The Armenia-Azerbaijan Conflict, Causes and Implications.* Westport, Conn., and London: Praeger, 1998.

Cullen, Robert. "Roots." *The New Yorker* (15 April 1991): 55–76.

Curtis, William Eleroy. *Around the Black Sea.* London: Hodder and Stoughton, 1911.

Dowsett, Charles. *Sayat-Nova, An 18th Century Troubador.* Leuven: Peeters, 1997.

Dubois de Montpereux, Frederic. *Voyage au Caucase chez les Tcherkesses et les Abkhases.* [A voyage to the Caucasus among the Cherkess and the Abkhaz]. Vol. IV. Paris, 1840.

Dudwick, Nora. "The Case of the Caucasian Albanians: Ethnohistory and Ethnic Politics." *Cahiers du Monde Russe et Soviètique* 31, No. 2–3 (April–September 1990): 377–383.

Dudwick, Nora. "The Karabagh Movement: An Old Scenario Gets Rewritten." *Armenian Review* 42, No. 3/167 (Autumn 1989): 63–70.

Dudwick, Nora. "Armenian-Azerbaijani Relations and Karabagh: History, Memory and Politics." *Armenian Review* 46, No. 1–4/181–184 (Spring–Winter 1993): 79–92.

Gellner, Ernest. "Nationalism in the Vacuum." In Alexander Motyl (ed.). *Thinking Theoretically about Soviet Nationalities.* New York: Columbia University Press, 1994: 243–254.

*Glazami nezavisimykh Nablyudatelei: Nagorny Karabakh i vokrug nego . . . Sbornik Dokumentov* [Through the eyes of independent observers: Nagorny Karabakh and around it . . . A collection of documents]. Yerevan: Yerevansky Gosudarstvenny Universitet, 1990.

Goldenberg, Suzanne. *Pride of Small Nations. The Caucasus and Post-Soviet Disorder.* London and Atlantic Higlands, N.J.: Zed Books, 1994.

Goltz, Thomas. "Letter from Eurasia: The Hidden Russian Hand." *Foreign Policy* 92 (Fall 1993): 92–116.

Goltz, Thomas. *Azerbaijan Diary. A Rogue Reporter's Adventures in an Oil-Rich, War-Torn, Post-Soviet Republic.* Armonk, N.Y., and London: M. E. Sharpe, 1998.

Gorbachev, Mikhail. *Memoirs.* London: Doubleday, 1996.

Harutiunian, V. B. *Sobytiya v Nagorno Karabakhe. Khronika* [Events in Nagorny Karabakh. A chronicle]. Parts I–VI. Yerevan: Izdatel'stvo AN ASSR, 1990–1997.

Haxthausen, Baron von. *Transcaucasia, Sketches of the Nations and Races between the Black Sea and the Caspian.* London, 1854.

Henry, J. D. *Baku: An Eventful History.* London: Archibald Constable and Co., 1905.

Herzig, Edmund. *The New Caucasus. Armenia, Azerbaijan and Georgia.* London: Royal Institute of International Affairs, 1999.

Hewsen, Robert. "The Meliks of Eastern Armenia, A Preliminary Study." *Revue des Etudes Armeniennes* IX (1972): 286–329.

Hewsen, Robert. "Ethno-History and the Armenian Influence upon the Caucasian Albanians." In Thomas J. Samuelian (ed.). *Classical Armenian Culture, Influences and Creativity.* Philadelphia: Scholars Press, 1982, 27–40.

Hopkirk, Peter. *On Secret Service East Of Constantinople.* Oxford: Oxford University Press, 1994.

Hovannisian, Richard G. *The Republic of Armenia.* Vols. I–IV. Berkeley, Los Angeles, London: University of California Press, 1971–1996.

Human Rights Watch. *Bloodshed in the Caucasus. Escalation of the Armed Conflict in Nagorno-Karabakh.* September 1992.

Human Rights Watch. *Bloodshed in the Caucasus. Indiscriminate Bombing and Shelling by Azerbaijani Forces in Nagorno Karabakh.* July 1993.

Human Rights Watch. *Azerbaijan. Seven Years of Conflict in Nagorno-Karabakh.* New York, Washington, London, and Brussels: Human Rights Watch, 1994.

Ignatieff, Michael. *Blood and Belonging.* London: Vintage, 1994.

Karny, Yoav. *Highlanders: A Journey to the Caucasus in Quest of Memory.* New York: Farrar, Straus and Giroux, 2000.

Kasatov, Alexander. "Sama ne Svoya" [Not its own]. *Stolitsa* 48 (1992): 1–4.

Kazemzadeh, Firuz. *The Struggle for Transcaucasia (1917–1921).* New York: Philosophical Library, and Oxford: George Ronald, 1951.

Kazimirov, Vladimir. "Karabakh. Kak eto Bylo" [Karabakh. How it was]. *Mezhdunarodnya Zhizn'* No. 5 (1996): 41–52.

Kazimirov, Vladimir. "Proverka Vremenem (k Pyatiletiyu Prekrashcheniya Ognya v Karabakhskom Konflikte)" [The test of time (on the fifth anniversary of the cease-fire in the Karabakh conflict)]. *Mezhdunarodnya Zhizn'* No. 5 (1999): 8–20.

Keppel, George (Captain the Hon). *Personal Narrative of a Journey from India to England in the Year 1824.* London, 1827.

Ker-Porter, Sir Robert. *Travels in Georgia, Persia, Armenia, Ancient Babylon &c. &c. During the Years 1817, 1818, 1819 and 1820.* Vol. II. London, 1820.

Koestler, Arthur. *The Invisible Writing.* London: Hutchinson, 1969.

Laitin, David D., and Ronald Grigor Suny. "Karabakh: Thinking a Way out." *Middle East Policy* 7, No. 1 (October 1999): 145–176.

Libaridian, Gerard (ed.). *The Karabagh File. Documents and Facts on the Question of Mountainous Karabagh 1918–1988*. Cambridge and Toronto: Zoryan Institute, 1988.

Libaridian, Gerard. "Reimagining the Past, Rethinking the Present: the Future of Turkish, Armenian Relations." *Insight Turkey* 2 No. 4 (October–December 2000): 125–143.

Ligachev, Yegor. *Inside Gorbachev's Kremlin: The Memoirs of Yegor Ligachev*. Boulder and Oxford: Westview Press, 1996.

Lisitsian, Stepan. *Armyane Nagornogo Karabakha, Etnografichesky Ocherk* [The Armenians of Nagorny Karabakh, An ethnographic sketch]. Yerevan: Academy of Sciences, 1992.

Lourie, Svetlana V. "Yerevan's Phenomenon: The Formation of a Traditional Social Community in a Modern Capital City." In Vitaly Naumkin (ed.). *State, Religion and Society in Central Asia*. Ithaca: Reading, 1993, 176–198.

MacFarlane, S. Neil, and Larry Minear. *Humanitarian Action and Politics: The Case of Nagorno-Karabakh*. Providence, R.I.: Thomas J. Watson Jr. Institute for International Studies, 1997.

Malkasian, Mark. *Gha-ra-bagh! The Emergence of the National Democratic Movement in Armenia*. Detroit: Wayne State University Press, Detroit, 1996.

Maresca, John. "Lost Opportunities in Negotiating the Conflict over Nagorno-Karabakh." *International Negotiation* 1, No. 3 (December 1996): 471–499.

Melander, Erik. "The Nagorno-Karabakh Conflict Revisited. Was the War Inevitable?" *Journal of Cold War Studies* 3, No. 2 (Spring 2001): 48–75.

Melikov, Arif. *Ya Obvinyayu* [I accuse]. Baku: Gyanjlik, 1994.

Mkrtchian, Shahen. *Istoriko-Arkhitekturnye Pamyatniki Nagornogo Karabakha* [The historico-architectural monuments of Nagorny Karabakh]. Yerevan: Aiastan, 1988.

Murphy, David. "Operation 'Ring': The Black Berets in Azerbaijan." *Soviet Military Studies* 5, No. 1 (March 1992): 487–498.

*Nagorny Karabakh. Istoricheskaya Spravka* [Nagorny Karabakh. A historical reference guide]. Yerevan: Academy of Sciences, 1988.

Petrosian, David. "What Are the Reasons for Armenians' Success in the Military Phase of the Karabakh Conflict (1991–mid 1994)?" *The Noyan Tapan Highlights* 19, 20, 21 (18 May, 25 May, 1 June 2000).

Pipes, Richard. "The Establishment of the Union of Soviet Socialist Republics." In Rachel Denber (ed.). *The Soviet Nationality Reader*. Boulder and Oxford: Westview Press, 1992, 35–86.

Richards, Susan. *Epics of Everyday Life*. London: Viking, 1990.

Rost, Yuri. *Armenian Tragedy*. London: Weidenfeld and Nicholson, 1990.

Roxburgh, Angus. *The Second Russian Revolution*. London: BBC Books, 1991.

Ruseckas, Laurent. "State of the Field Report: Energy and Politics in Central Asia and the Caucasus." *Access Asia Review* 1, No. 2 (July 1998).

Said, Kurban. *Ali and Nino*. London: Hutchinson, 1970. Reprinted London: Chatto and Windus, 2000.

Sakharov, Andrei. *Moscow and Beyond, 1986 to 1989*. New York: Vintage Books, 1990.

Schiltberger, Johann. *The Bondage and Travels of Johann Schiltberger, A Native of Bavaria, In Europe, Asia and Africa 1396–1427*. London, 1879.

Shaffer, Brenda. *Borders and Brethren: Iran and the Challenge of Azerbaijani Identity*. Cambridge: MIT Press, 2002.

Shahmuratian, Samvel (ed.). *The Sumgait Tragedy, Pogroms against Armenians in Soviet Azerbaijan*. Vol. 1. New Rochelle, N.Y.: Aristide D. Caratzas, 1990.

Shakhnazarov, Georgy. *Tsena Svobody, Reformatsiya Gorbacheva glazami ego pomoshchnika* [The price of freedom, The reforms of Gorbachev through the eyes of his aide]. Moscow: Rossika Zevs, 1993.

Shushinsky, Firudin. *Shusha*. Baku: Azerbaidzhanskoye Gosudarstvennoye Izadatel'stvo, 1968.

Slezkine, Yuri. "The USSR as a Communal Apartment, or How a Socialist State Promoted Ethnic Particularism." In Geoff Eley and Ronald Grigor Suny (eds.). *Becoming National: A Reader*. Oxford: Oxford University Press, 1996: 202–238.

Smith, Jeremy. *The Bolsheviks and the National Question, 1917–23*. London: Macmillan, 1999.

*Soyuz Mozhno Bylo Sokhranit': Belaya Kniga. Dokumenty i Fakty o Politike M.S.Gorbacheva po Reformirovaniyu i Sokhraneniyu Mnogonatsional'nogo Gosudarstva* [It was possible to preserve the Union: A white book. Documents and facts on the policies of M. S. Gorbachev for reforming and preserving a multinational state]. Moscow: Aprel'-85, 1995.

Suny, Ronald Grigor. *Looking Towards Ararat: Armenia in Modern History*. Bloomington and Indianapolis: Indiana University Press, 1993.

Suny, Ronald Grigor (ed.). *Transcaucasia, Nationalism and Social Change*, rev. ed. Ann Arbor: University of Michigan Press, 1996.

Suny, Ronald Grigor. "Living with the Other: Conflict and Cooperation among the Transcaucasian Peoples." *Caucasian Regional Studies* 2, Issue 1 (1997).

Swietochowski, Tadeusz. *Russia and Azerbaijan. A Borderland in Transition*. New York: Columbia University Press, 1995.

Tchilingirian, Hratch. "Religious Discourse and the Church in Mountainous Karabagh 1988–1995." *Revue du monde arménien moderne et contemporain* 3 (1997): 67–83.

Vaksberg, Arkady. *The Soviet Mafia*. London: Weidenfeld and Nicholson, 1991.

Valentin, Jean. *Bericht über meine Reise nach Tiflis und die Theilnahme an der Raddeschen Expedition in den Karabagh-Gau. Sommer 1890* [Report on my journey to Tiflis and participation in Dr. Radde's expedition to the region of Karabakh. The summer of 1890]. Frankfurt, 1891.

Velichko, Vasil. *Kavkaz. Russkoye Delo i Mezhduplemmenye Voprosy* [The Caucasus. Russia's work and intertribal questions]. Saint Petersburg, 1904. Reprinted Baku: Elm, 1990.

Vereshchagin, V. V. *Dukhobortsy i Molokane v Zakavkazye, Shiity v Karabakhe* [Dukhobors and Moluccans in the Transcaucasus, Shiites in Karabakh]. Moscow, 1900.

Villari, Luigi. *Fire and Sword in the Caucasus*. London: T. Fisher Unwin, 1906.

Walker, Christopher. *Armenia. The Survival of a Nation*. London: Routledge, 1990.

Walker, Christopher. *Armenia and Karabagh: The Struggle for Unity*. London: Minority Rights Publications, 1991.

Walker, Edward. *No Peace, No War in the Caucasus: Secessionist Conflict in Chechnya, Abkhazia and Nagorno-Karabakh*. Cambridge: Harvard University, John F. Kennedy School of Government, Strengthening Democratic Institutions Project, 1998.

Wright, J., S. Goldenberg, and R. Schofield (eds.). *Transcaucasian Boundaries*. London: UCL Press, 1996.

Yamskov, A. N. "Ethnic Conflict in the Transcaucasus: The Case of Nagorno-Karabakh." *Theory and Society* 20, No. 5 (October 1991): 631–661.

Yunusov, Arif. "Armyano-Azerbaidzhansky Konflikt: Migratsionnye Aspekty" [The Armenian-Azerbaijani conflict: Aspects of migration]. In Zh. Zaionchovskaya (ed.). *Migratsionnaya Situatsiya v Stranakh SNG* [The migration situation in CIS countries]. Moscow, 1999.

Yunusova, Leila. "Mera Otvetsvennosti Politika" [The degree of responsibility of a politician]. *Istiqlal* 4 (1990): 5–23.

# Index

Aaland Islands, 281
Abasov, Rovshan, 107
Abasov, Zahid, 45, 53–54, 197
Abasova, Khuraman, 15, 300
Abdullayeva, Arzu, 90
Abdusalimov, Vugar, 221
Abkhazia, 204, 232, 246, 272
Adamishin, Anatoly, 233
Afghanistan, 88, 124, 218
Agajanian, Stepan, 189
Aganbekian, Abel, 17, 20, 21
Agarunov, Albert, 314
Agayev, Mirshahin, 177
Agayev, Yusif, 167, 171, 227, 317
Agha Mohammed Khan, 189
Aghdam, 6, 15, 107, 165, 166, 170, 171, 173,
    178, 188, 201, 255, 286; fall of, 215; ruins
    of, 6, 242, 278
Agjebedi, 5–6
AIOC (Azerbaijan International Operat-
    ing Company), 252
Aivazian, Suren, 300
Akhmedov, Akhmed, 41, 302
Akhmedov, Gabil, 215, 221–23
Akopian, Aleksan, 155–56
Albanians, Caucasian, 152–57
Albright, Madeleine, 263
Ali, Kemal, 165, 168, 195, 201, 208
*Ali and Nino*, 99, 186
Aliev, Allahverdi, 6
Aliev, Elkhan, 1–2
Aliev, Heidar, 29, 51, 104, 271; and Armen-
    ian Genocide debate, 79; asserts control
    after war, 251–53; and Azerbaijan Geno-
    cide Day, 97, 98; background and career,
    84–85, 306; and "Black January" in
    Baku, 94–95, 307; claims on amount of
    Azerbaijani territory occupied, 285–86;
    feud with Demirchian, 17, 135–136; as
    First Party Secretary of Azerbaijan,

134–36, 138; health problems of, 262,
    282; after Key West talks, 4–5; negoti-
    ates with Kocharian, 263–65, 266–68;
    and 1994 ceasefire, 238–39; 1996–97
    peace negotiations, 255, 258; as parlia-
    mentary speaker of Nakhichevan,
    160–61, 181, 210–11; reelected president
    (1998), 262; and refugees, 220–21, 285;
    resigns from Politburo, 17; secret nego-
    tiations with Kocharian (1993), 226–27;
    succession to 263, 278; suspicion of mili-
    tary, 106, 278; takes power (1993),
    214–15, 225–26
Aliev, Igrar, 155
Aliev, Ilham, 245, 263
Aliev, Jalal, 306
Alizade, Zardusht, 67, 82, 88, 89, 91
Allahverdiev, Rafael, 85
Andranik (Armenian guerrilla leader),
    128, 168, 208
Andropov, Yury, 17
Ani (Armenian American woman in
    Nagorky Karabakh), 248–50
Anoush (Armenian living in Shusha),
    49–50
Ararat, Mount, 76–77
Araxes River, 96, 143, 216, 219, 220, 227,
    236
*Argumenty i Fakty*, 167
Armenia: acquires weapons, 197–200;
    army formation in, 206–9, 210, 257;
    Azerbaijani railway blockade of (1989),
    87; Azerbaijanis deported from, 62–63,
    97, 105; becomes independent state
    (1991), 160–61; claims on NK, 125–26,
    129–31; demographics of, 133, 284,
    305–6; demonstrations in (1988), 22–25,
    28; earthquake in, 7, 63, 64; economic
    hardships of, 205–6, 270, 277; fear of
    Turkey, 274–75; First Republic, 60–61,

Lenin, Vladimir, 57, 131, 192
Leninakan, 64, 216. *See also* Gyumri
Lenkoran, 89, 215
*L'Humanité*, 20
Libaridian, Gerard, 78, 256
Lieven, Anatol, 43, 171
Ligachev, Yegor, 59–60, 302, 304
Lisbon Summit of OSCE (1996), 256, 258
Lisitsian, Stepan, 187
*Literaturnaya Gazeta*, 27
Loshak, Viktor, 64, 66
Lukoil, 252, 261
Lukyanov, Anatoly, 25, 61
*Lusitania*, 44

M., Lyudmila, 35
Madatov, Valerian, 186
Makhamerov, Asif ("Freud"), 165, 201
Mamed, Yaqub, 165
Mamedov, Etibar, 83, 86, 91–92, 94, 214, 262, 307
Mamedov, Mamedrafi, 239
Mamedov, Yaqub, 173, 180
Mamedova, Farita, 153–55
Mamedzade, Kamil, 155
Mamikonian, Vartan, 137
Manashid, 119, 160
Mandelstam, Osip, 52
Manucharian, Ashot, 23, 72, 111, 115, 210–11, 227, 312, 314
Manucharov, Arkady, 109
Manukian, Vazgen, 56–57, 111, 210, 212, 257–58
Maragha, 176
Maresca, John, 230, 234–35
Martakert, 48, 194, 195, 201, 206, 215, 247–50, 286
Martunashen, 116
Martuni, 169, 207, 243, 286
Meghri, 18, 135–36, 264
Mehti Kulu, 189
Meir, Golda, 150
Mekhtiev, Tajedin, 164, 176, 273, 278, 313
Melander, Erik, 120
*Meliks*, 146, 149, 156, 187, 188
Melkonian, Monte, 207–8, 243, 249
Melkonian, Seta, 169, 207, 243–44
Melkumian, Gurgen, 138
Memorial (human rights group), 116
Meskhetian Turks, 110, 171, 185

Metsamor nuclear power station, 22, 206, 300
Miasnikian, Alexander, 130
Mikhailov, Vyacheslav, 13, 59–60, 83, 113–14, 300
Mikoyan, Anastas, 20
Mikoyan, Sergei, 20
Miller, William Green, 124
Minsk Group of CSCE (later OSCE), 237, 256, 267–68, 276, 279, 317; formation of, 229–30; France, USA, become co-chairs of, 258; and 1997 peace plan, 258–61; splits in, 234–35, 254–55. *See also* Key West peace talks; OSCE (Organization for Security and Cooperation in Europe)
Mirzoyan, Seiran, 109–10, 119, 120–21
Mkrtchian, Artur, 161, 228
Mkrtchian, Shagen, 141
Moldova, 246
Moscow, Treaty of (1921), 129
Movsesian, Nelli, 53
*Mujahadin*, 236
Muradian, Igor, 16–18, 20–21, 22, 56, 57, 136, 300
Murat, Joachim, 186, 314
Murov Mountains, 212, 236–37
Musavat, 127
Musayev, Fuad, 31
Muslimzade, Jehangir, 32, 33–34, 43
Mustafiev, Jengiz, 172–73, 183, 314
Mustafieva, Nailia, 274
Mutalibov, Ayaz, 85, 88, 181; and Aliev, 94, 307; alliance with Gaziev and Husseinov, 215, 251, 313; and August 1991 coup attempt, 160; brief return to power, 182; elected president of Azerbaijan, 160; fall from power, 172–73, 260; and Khojali, 171; made First Party Secretary of Azerbaijan, 94, 108; in NK (1990), 109–11; and Operation Ring, 113–14, 120, 121–23; as president of Azerbaijan, 162–65, 313

Nagorny Karabakh dispute: Aliev-Kocharian negotiations, 4–5; Armenians declare independence, 161, 162; Armenian delegation seeks compromise with Baku, 118–20; Armenian partisan units form, 112; Armenian State Defense

# About the Author

THOMAS DE WAAL has reported on Russia and the Caucasus since 1993 for the *Moscow Times, The Times of London, The Economist,* and the *BBC World Service.* He is currently Caucasus Editor with the Institute for War and Peace Reporting in London. He is the coauthor, most recently, with Carlotta Gall, of *Chechnya: Calamity in the Caucasus* (NYU Press, 1998), for which they won a James Cameron Award for Outstanding Reporting in 1998.